Challenging Inequality

Challenging Inequality

Challenging Inequality

Variation across Postindustrial Societies

EVELYNE HUBER AND
JOHN D. STEPHENS

THE UNIVERSITY OF CHICAGO PRESS   CHICAGO AND LONDON

The University of Chicago Press, Chicago 60637
The University of Chicago Press, Ltd., London
© 2024 by The University of Chicago
All rights reserved. No part of this book may be used or reproduced in any manner whatsoever without written permission, except in the case of brief quotations in critical articles and reviews. For more information, contact the University of Chicago Press, 1427 E. 60th St., Chicago, IL 60637.
Published 2024
Printed in the United States of America

33 32 31 30 29 28 27 26 25 24   1 2 3 4 5

ISBN-13: 978-0-226-83463-4 (cloth)
ISBN-13: 978-0-226-83465-8 (paper)
ISBN-13: 978-0-226-83464-1 (e-book)
DOI: https://doi.org/10.7208/chicago/9780226834641.001.0001

Library of Congress Cataloging-in-Publication Data

Names: Huber, Evelyne, 1950– author. | Stephens, John D., 1947– author.
Title: Challenging inequality : variation across postindustrial societies / Evelyne Huber, John D. Stephens.
Description: Chicago : The University of Chicago Press, 2024. | Includes bibliographical references and index.
Identifiers: LCCN 2023055121 | ISBN 9780226834634 (cloth) | ISBN 9780226834658 (paperback) | ISBN 9780226834641 (ebook)
Subjects: LCSH: Equality—Germany. | Equality—Spain. | Equality—Sweden. | Equality—United States.
Classification: LCC HM821 .H833 2024 | DDC 305—dc23/eng/20231204
LC record available at https://lccn.loc.gov/2023055121

♾ This paper meets the requirements of ANSI/NISO Z39.48-1992 (Permanence of Paper).

TO OUR GRANDCHILDREN

Contents

Acknowledgments ix

CHAPTER 1. Introduction 1

PART I. **The Shapes and Determinants of Inequality: Broad Trends**

CHAPTER 2. Wage Dispersion 29

CHAPTER 3. Household Income Inequality 46

CHAPTER 4. Top Income Shares of National Income 72

CHAPTER 5. Poverty 93

CHAPTER 6. Social Policy 113

CHAPTER 7. Social Investment versus Social Consumption? 129

PART II. **A Closer Look at Four Trajectories: Germany, Spain, Sweden, and the United States**

CHAPTER 8. Germany 143

CHAPTER 9. Spain 168

CHAPTER 10. Sweden 193

CHAPTER 11. United States 213

CHAPTER 12. The Cases Compared 230

CHAPTER 13. Conclusion 244

Appendix A.   Figures and Tables, All Countries   275
Appendix B.   Figures and Tables, Case Studies   293
Appendix C.   Operationalization of Variables   303
Appendix D.   Statistical Estimations   313
Appendix E.   Alternative Statistical Estimators   317
Notes   325
References   329
Index   359

Acknowledgments

No academic work is produced in the isolation of an ivory tower, the enduring cliché notwithstanding. Some of the inspirations and collaborations can be clearly identified, others are more subtle and diffuse. We shall do our best here to name those we can clearly identify in connection with this book, but we want to begin by thanking all of our current and former students and colleagues who have influenced our thinking in myriad ways and have inspired us to continue to address the big questions facing our societies.

Four chapters of this book are based on published articles coauthored with (then) current or former graduate students. In all cases, we redid the analyses to make the variables used consistent throughout this book. The only tables that are identical to those published previously are tables 7.5 and 7.6, which were put together by Jacob Gunderson. We also rewrote much of the text, but we did not touch the sections in chapter 4 that discuss "Conceptualizing Union Effects on Top Income Shares" and "Conceptualizing Partisan Effects on Pre-Tax and Transfer Income," which were written by Jingjing Huo. We greatly enjoyed working with all our coauthors and want to thank them and acknowledge the following sources:

Kaitlin Alper, Evelyne Huber, and John D. Stephens. 2021. "Poverty and Social Rights Among the Working Age Population in Post-industrial Democracies." *Social Forces* 99 (4): 1710–44. Oxford: Oxford University Press. [August 2020. https://doi.org/10.1093/sf/soaa073.]

Evelyne Huber, Jacob Gunderson, and John D. Stephens. 2020. "Private Education and Inequality in the Knowledge Economy." *Policy and Society* 39 (2): 171–88.

Evelyne Huber, Jingjing Huo, and John D. Stephens. 2019. "Power, Policy, and Top Income Shares." *Socio-Economic Review* 17 (2): 231–53. Oxford: Oxford University Press.

Evelyne Huber, John D. Stephens, and Kaitlin Alper. 2019. "The Varied Sources of Increasing Wage Dispersion." In *The European Social Model under Pressure*, edited by Ramona Careja, Patrick Emmenegger, and Nathalie Giger, 231–52. Berlin: Springer Nature.

We have also drawn on ideas developed while working on related articles on inequality with Itay Machtei and with Bilyana Petrova. Among our colleagues, we want to thank David Brady in particular. Our collaboration started with work on our Comparative Welfare States Data Set, which has been publicly available and much used for years. He has continued to offer highly insightful and much appreciated feedback on our work, specifically on this book.

We have benefited from feedback offered by participants in a large number of workshops, panels at conferences, and invited lectures over the past decade: the Meetings of the Society for the Advancement of Socio-Economics, Milan, Italy, June 2013; the Meetings of the Council for European Studies, Washington, DC, March 2014; the Meetings of the Council for European Studies, Philadelphia, PA, April 2016; the Meetings of Research Committee 19 of the International Sociological Association, at the University of North Carolina at Chapel Hill, June 2017; the Meetings of the Council for European Studies, Glasgow, UK, July 2017; the Meetings of the Council for European Studies, Chicago, March 2018; the East Asian Social Policy Research Network Annual Conference, Bristol, UK, July 2018; the International Conference on Global Dynamics of Social Policy, University of Bremen, October 2018; the University of Geneva, March 2019; the Pontificia Universidad Católica, Santiago, Chile, April 2019; the Meetings of the Council for European Studies, Madrid, Spain, June 2019; the Meetings of Research Committee 19 of the International Sociological Association, Mannheim, Germany, August 2019; the London School of Economics, March 2021; the DYNAMICS Lecture Series and Social Research Colloquium, Humboldt University and Hertie School, Berlin, December 2021; and two workshops on inequality at the University of North Carolina at Chapel Hill, in April 2018 and October 2022.

For organizing these lectures, workshops, and panels and/or for attending and offering helpful comments, we want to thank Klaus Armingeon, Daniel Béland, Pablo Beramendi, Tomas Berglund, Timo Fleckenstein, Anke Hassel, Liesbet Hooghe, Arne Kalleberg, Nathan Kelly, Herbert Kitschelt, Hanna Kleider, Michaela Kreyenfeld, Juan Pablo Luna, Gary Marks, Stephanie Moller, Jana Morgan, Herbert Obinger, Bruno Palier,

Joakim Palme, Bilyana Petrova, Jonas Pontusson, David Rueda, Hanna Schwander, Christine Trampusch, and David Weisstanner.

For research assistance on this book, we thank—in addition to our coauthors Kaitlin Alper, Jacob Gunderson, Itay Machtei, and Bilyana Petrova—Ayelén Vanegas and Ranko Vranic. Jacob Gunderson read the entire manuscript, made suggestions to improve clarity, and pointed us toward new literature on parties and voting behavior.

We are thankful for financial support from the National Science Foundation in the form of NSF Grant # 9108716 for work on the Comparative Welfare States Data Set and for funding from the Morehead Alumni Distinguished Professorship and the Margaret and Paul A. Johnston Professorships (funding the Gerhard E. Lenski Jr. Distinguished Professorship) in the College of Arts and Sciences at the University of North Carolina at Chapel Hill. For leaves from our teaching and administrative responsibilities that allowed us to focus on this book we thank the Provost's Office and the College of Arts and Sciences at the University of North Carolina at Chapel Hill. Last but by no means least, we want to thank our colleagues in the Department of Political Science at UNC Chapel Hill for making this such a supportive and collegial environment.

We dedicate this book to our grandchildren. May they live in a world where governments protect the rights of labor, invest in human capital, provide access to quality health care and care services, and sustain a strong social safety net.

CHAPTER ONE

Introduction

Rising Economic Inequality in the Transition from Industrial to Knowledge Economies

Rising inequality has become a major cause for concern, even in affluent postindustrial societies. Rising inequality contributes to rising poverty; at any level of affluence in a society, the more unequal the distribution of resources, the higher the levels of poverty. Poverty has lasting effects on children's chances to develop to their full capacity, and thus on the human capital in their generation and ultimately on the productive capacity of the society. Where in the income distribution someone is born profoundly shapes their options in life. If the benefits from economic growth are captured by a small share of the population at the top of the income distribution, even those in the middle may be held back. A case in point is the United States, where real median household incomes remained stagnant for some three decades while the top 1 percent greatly increased their share of national income. Rising inequality generates higher levels of relative deprivation, which is associated with feelings of social exclusion and susceptibility to populist appeals. High levels of income inequality are accompanied by high levels of political inequality—e.g., in campaign financing and paying lobbyists—which violates democratic principles. The list goes on, and the problems have received official attention in OECD Reports (Cingano 2014; OECD 2021).

A wide variety of interrelated factors have been shown to create various kinds of inequality in income. Technological change and globalization have changed labor markets, increasing demand for more highly skilled labor (skill-biased technological change) on the one hand and expanding the low-skill service sector on the other. The mismatch between the skills of the labor force and the skill demands of the knowledge society have widened the earnings gap between high-skilled and low-skilled workers. Technological change and deregulation or privatization of public services and changes in labor legislation have generated more part-time and temporary employment and—together with third world imports and outsourcing—higher levels of unemployment. Various events in different countries (e.g., German unification, and financial crises in the Nordic countries in the early 1990s and everywhere after 2007, with their extended effects in southern Europe) have aggravated the pressures resulting from technological change and globalization and have further contributed to increasing unemployment. Changes in labor markets have weakened the position of organized labor and created dualized labor markets with divisions between those who have stable jobs and access to benefits and those who do not. Dualized labor markets, rising levels of unemployment, and aging populations have increased the risk of poverty. Some of the same developments put financial pressures on generous welfare states that had been developed to reduce poverty and inequality. Globalization has made it more difficult for governments to tax capital and top income earners, and has thus reduced sources of revenue. In Europe, the process of economic integration has limited individual governments' latitude for action. Political changes have also weakened welfare states. Fragmentation of party systems has made it more difficult for left parties, the traditional defenders of generous welfare states, to form stable governments and implement policies that strengthen these welfare states.

We have excellent studies of the various factors contributing to the rise in inequality. Most of these studies are statistical analyses that tell us about the average effect of the specific variables of interest across time and space, everything else held constant or contingent on one or two other factors. For instance, Baccaro and Howell (2017) and Oesch (2013) focus on labor markets, Brady (2009) on welfare states, Goldin and Katz (2008) on technological change and education, and Thelen (2014) on a comparative historical analysis of three countries. There are also excellent edited volumes that offer short pieces of research on a variety of topics related to rising inequality (Gornick and Jäntti 2013b; Dølvik and Martin 2015; Blanchard and Rodrik 2021). We shall focus on average effects of variables here as well in our quantitative analyses, but our aim is to paint a more comprehensive picture—to look at inequality from multiple angles and put the pieces of the puzzle together to show different patterns. We shall look at wage dispersion, top incomes, household market income, and household disposable income in our quantitative analyses, and we shall provide an in-depth comparative historical analysis of four cases with different patterns of inequality: Germany, Spain, Sweden, and the United States. Rising inequality does not look the same in all postindustrial knowledge economies. In some countries, the top 1 percent have run away, in some the bottom sector of low-wage work has grown, in some both things have happened, and in some these trends have been much more muted; also, the welfare state has retained greater capacity in some than in others to reduce poverty and inequality. The common pressures of technological change and globalization meet with different institutional configurations and different political and policy legacies that mediate the effects on inequality and poverty. As Kitschelt et al. (1999, 445) argued long ago, "the political institutions and processes, like those of the political economy, have undergone a refractive process in which similar exogenous developments lead to different outcomes depending on the differing preexisting institutional political configurations of the countries."

We explain these differences within the framework of an updated version of power resources theory. The organizational and legal-institutional strength of labor and of left parties and the generosity of the welfare state are the key factors that shape the effects of technological change and globalization on inequality and poverty. Union density, centralization of bargaining, contract extension, works council rights, and union participation in setting the minimum wage shape the distribution of market income. Investment in human capital through public education at all age levels over the long haul increases skill levels and thus helps to keep market income inequality in check. Generosity of welfare state benefits, particularly unemployment and sickness insurance and social assistance, shapes redistribution and thus disposable income poverty and inequality. Indeed, we shall show that generosity of these benefits remains the single most important factor for reducing poverty and inequality. Incumbency of left parties and strength of organized labor are the crucial driving forces behind welfare state generosity and investment in human capital. Thus, the decline in the organizational strength of labor and the increasingly intermittent incumbency of left parties have significantly contributed to the increase in market and disposable income inequality. At the same time, persistent important differences in the strength of labor and of left parties across countries explain much of the wide variation in inequality and poverty that we observe.

Trends in Inequality

After the Gilded Age in the United States and the Belle Époque in Europe, economic inequality began to decline, and it continued to do so for the first three-quarters of the twentieth century (Piketty 2014, 272–73, 292, 299). Then, in the mid-1970s or the mid-1980s (depending on the country), it began to increase in almost all postindustrial democracies. There were few exceptions, as one can see from the tables and graphs in appendix A charting the development of various measures of economic inequality. As the tables and graphs demonstrate, though inequality increased in most countries by most measures, the degree of increase and the final levels were highly variable across countries and across measures. The countries are grouped by type of political economy, as is conventional in the literature on varieties of capitalism (Hall and Soskice 2001) and welfare state regimes (Esping-Andersen 1990; Huber and Stephens 2001). One can see a clear tendency for the increases to be greatest in liberal political economies.

Let us cite a few examples of the diversity of trends. The trends differ depending on the measure used, such as Ginis or income ratios, and on the unit of analysis, whether we are looking at individuals or households. They further differ according to whether they are measured pre- or post-tax and transfers. In some countries, the top 1 percent pulled away and managed to claim an ever larger share of total national income. In other countries, the bottom — in the form of a low-wage sector — sank deeper and grew larger. In some countries, taxes and transfers greatly reduced poverty and inequality; in others, they did not change the market income distribution much.

As Soskice (2014, 661) noted, the rise of the top 1 percent share is above all an Anglo-American phenomenon (figure A.1). By contrast, the top 1 percent share declined in Denmark and the Netherlands and rose modestly in the other three Nordic countries.[1] Figure A.2 displays the ratio of the 50th percentile to the 10th percentile of the wage and salary distribution, and one sees declines in inequality in the bottom half in Austria, Spain, Portugal, and Canada; stability in the other liberal political economies and in Denmark, Sweden, and Finland (albeit at a much lower level); but increases in inequality in Norway and Germany (ignoring the reunification spike in 1991). There is a strong trend toward more inequality in the upper half of the wage and salary distribution, measured by the 90:50 ratio, as shown in figure A.3. Nevertheless, one still sees diversity, with stability in Norway, Sweden, Finland, and France, and modest increases in most of the rest of the Nordic and Continental political economies.

Tables A.2–A.7 display changes in pre- and post-tax and transfer household income of the working-age population in our series combining LIS, SILC, and OECD data. We include only the working-age population in our analyses because including the elderly would inflate market income inequality and poverty and redistribution in countries with generous public pension systems. Moreover, technological change and globalization are theoretically central factors in the debate about rising inequality, and they affect the labor market and thus the working-age population. While our combined series contains 483 country-year observations, far more than previously available series, we do have a dearth of data prior to 1990 and many gaps in the series, which is why we display the data in tabular form and for a truncated time range, in contrast to our graphs of annual data for wage dispersion and top income shares.[2] We will discuss these data and tables at greater length in later chapters. It suffices here to point out the diversity in trends and outcomes in the disposable household income inequality series in table A.4. The United States, Germany, and Finland experienced large increases in inequality, while the Netherlands and Austria experienced small increases and France and Switzerland saw actual decreases in disposable household income inequality. Most of the rest of the countries experienced modest increases in inequality.

Our aim in this book is to explain both common trends and divergent patterns in the development of income inequality and poverty in the postindustrial world. We analyze market income inequality and poverty and redistribution through the tax and transfer system. We review the extant explanations in the literature and build our case for the importance of both institutional strength of labor and policy and partisan politics, the key components of power resources theory. We are particularly interested in policy, from taxes to social transfers and social investment, because we want to identify political choices with different consequences for inequality and poverty. With regard to the strength of labor, previous literature has recognized the importance of declining union density for increasing inequality (Autor 2014; Goldin and Katz 2008), but did not consider other aspects of the institutional strength of labor, such as contract coverage and the power of works councils. The main focus in the literature has been on skill-biased technological change and globalization as drivers of increasing inequality. Previous literature has also focused mainly on market income inequality and poverty or on disposable income inequality and poverty,

Few studies have analyzed reduction of inequality and poverty through the tax and transfer system (Alper, Huber, and Stephens 2021; Huber, Machtei, and Stephens 2022). We show that generosity regarding social rights remains a key driver of poverty and inequality reduction. Generosity regarding social rights is in turn heavily shaped by partisan politics. Put simply, all countries have been exposed to the inegalitarian pressures on labor markets that result from technological change and globalization, but differences in the strength of labor and in social policies have moderated the effects of these pressures on labor markets and have resulted in widely varying degrees of inequality and poverty reduction.

Explanations for the Rise in Market Income Inequality

The literature associates five major categories of variables with increasing pre-tax and transfer inequality: economic transformations, globalization, changes in labor markets associated with economic transformations and globalization, changes in labor market institutions, and changing demographics. The changes in labor market institutions result in part from economic transformations and globalization, and in part from government policies.

Arguably the most fundamental economic transformation is the transition from an industrial to a service and knowledge economy. This transition entailed deindustrialization and skill-biased technological change, which destroyed relatively well-paying jobs for unskilled workers and raised the demand for highly skilled people. Where investment in education failed to keep pace with technological change, as in the United States, returns to education increased, and therefore so did income inequality (Goldin and Katz 2008). Routine white-collar jobs have increasingly been automated as well, thus eroding employment for the middle-income and middle-education ranks as well (Oesch 2013). Low-skilled and even some middle-skilled people were pushed into low-productivity (and therefore low-paying) service-sector jobs.

Another economic transformation, experienced to different degrees by different countries, is the shift toward financial transactions as an engine of wealth accumulation, which created opportunities for the appropriation of rents by the top 1 percent (Krippner 2005). Accordingly, in some countries the income share of the top 1 percent rose dramatically. Finally, all postindustrial countries deregulated their communication and transportation sectors. This process gave rise to the emergence of private firms competing with state-provided services in these sectors, and ultimately led to significant privatization of public enterprises. The move toward privatization contributed to the replacement of relatively well-paying and secure public-sector jobs with more precarious and low-paying private-sector jobs, and to the creation highly paid chief executive jobs.

The concept of globalization denotes increasing international flows of goods, services, capital, and labor. Increasing imports from low-cost producers contributed to deindustrialization, and increasing outsourcing of services to third world countries introduced direct competition with routine white-collar workers and depressed their wages (Wood 1994). Both of these trends raised the levels of unemployment and precarious employment. Ease of international capital movements made it harder for governments to tax capital and use the revenue to support the losers in globalization. Ease of capital movements and the threat of outsourcing also weakened the bargaining position of labor vis-à-vis employers. Finally, growing movements of labor from the Global South to the North intensified competition at the lowest skill and compensation levels of the labor market. In addition, immigration brought detrimental political consequences by weakening coalitions that favored the protection of low-income groups.

Technological transformations and globalization have worked together to create wide-ranging changes in labor markets. They have resulted in higher levels of unemployment, particularly long-term unemployment. They have led to a decline in stable full-time employment opportunities, instead generating more precarious employment with temporary and part-time arrangements—a process labeled dualization of labor markets. These labor market trends have evolved in interaction with changing labor market institutions. Employment protection laws were weakened, as governments hoped to stimulate employment by making labor markets more flexible. Collective bargaining institutions were decentralized to allow for more flexibility in different sectors or even enterprises. Union membership declined with the shrinking of industrial and public-sector employment and the resistance to unionization by many employers in the service sectors. All of these developments worked toward increasing inequality and poverty in market incomes. While these are trends common to all postindustrial societies, the extent of their advance has differed markedly across countries, as have the patterns of inequality.

A final set of factors contributing to an increase in market income inequality is demographics. Increases in the share of the population age sixty-five and older meant increases in the share of retired people with very low or no market income. Increasing numbers of single-parent (mostly single-mother) households meant increasing numbers of households with few hours worked in paid employment. Again, the pattern across countries varies widely; where public pensions are universal and generous, increases in the elderly population do not necessarily mean increases in low-income households and inequality. Similarly, where free or subsidized childcare is widely available, single mothers are more likely to work and to stay out of poverty.

What needs to be kept in mind is that increases in wage dispersion and in low-wage work and precarious employment do not translate directly and uniformly into increases in household income inequality and poverty. What is relevant is the overall volume of work performed by households, and the remuneration of that work. Where low-wage workers are second earners, they play a potentially vital role in keeping households out of poverty. Societies where the overall levels of employment are high are in a better position to reduce the effects of skill-biased technological change on household poverty because of a greater proportion of dual-earner households. Overall levels of employment are significantly shaped by the integration of women into the labor force. Higher levels of female employment are unambiguously positive for lowering household poverty because they increase the share of dual-earner households. The effects of employment levels on household income inequality, though, are mediated by the degree of assortative mating (that is, the degree to which spouses' educational levels are correlated).

Explanations for the Rise in Disposable Income Inequality

In all postindustrial societies, governments significantly shape the disposable income distribution through the system of taxes, transfers, and social services. The effects of changing labor markets and rising market income inequality and poverty increased the problem load at the same time that governments faced fiscal constraints due to the internationalization of capital markets and, in the European context, European integration (Brady and Lee 2014). Moreover, recurring economic crises, such as the Scandinavian crisis of the early 1990s, the burst of the dot-com bubble, and the 2007 crisis added to both the problem load and the fiscal constraints. In all countries, this situation stimulated a variety of adaptations in government policy. Partisan politics, along with policy legacies, the weight of the problem load, and the severity of external constraints, shaped these adaptations.

Different societies, with different welfare state regimes, were differentially prepared to confront this increased problem load. The one constant in policy response in all postindustrial societies was an attempt to promote activation—that is, labor market integration of the unemployed. What varied was the balance between incentives and coercion, and the availability of support payments and services. Retraining opportunities tied to the receipt of decent unemployment benefits in the context of availability of public childcare and transportation were at the opposite end of the spectrum from requirements to accept any job under threat of loss of unemployment benefits and in the context of lack of public childcare and transportation. The former scenario was characteristic of the Nordic countries, the latter of "ending welfare as we know it" in the United States.

The Nordic countries, with their more service-oriented welfare state regimes and their strong commitments to investment in public education, were best positioned to support training and retraining of their labor force to adapt to changing skill requirements. Moreover, the Nordics—followed by the northern continental European welfare states—had the most generous and redistributive social transfer systems, which enabled them to protect people's income levels during labor market transitions. They were also leaders in facilitating greater women's labor force participation through work/family conciliation policies. Traditionally, work/family conciliation policies were promoted by social democratic parties as part of their gender equality agenda, whereas Christian democratic parties continued to protect the traditional male breadwinner model. After the transition to the twenty-first century, though, as it became increasingly clear that labor markets were no longer able to sustain that model and as women increasingly wanted to enter the labor force, even Christian democratic parties came to promote policies like paid parental leave and public childcare.

An innovative approach to the dual problem of rising market inequality and fiscal constraints led to an emphasis on pre-distribution rather than redistribution, or the attempt to shift from a consumption-oriented to an investment-oriented welfare state (Chwalisz and Diamond 2015). Advocates of this approach argued that social policy should be seen not as a drag on competitiveness and economic growth, as neoliberal economists argued, but as a productive factor. Social investment would make individuals and thus society as a whole more productive in the knowledge economy (Morel, Palier, and Palme 2013). Social investment extended from early childhood education and care through investments in health, education, and training in each stage of life. At some level, these arguments were compelling. Indeed, they became official EU policy with the Lisbon Agenda of 2000 and the European Commission's Social Investment Package for Growth and Social Cohesion in 2013. Political contention came to center around social investment as a substitute for, rather than a complement to, social protection through cash transfers, or the extent to which the turn to social investment would make it possible to reduce welfare state expenditures.

In the Nordic countries, social investment had a long tradition, parallel to a generous cash transfer system. The Nordics were pioneers in early childhood education and care and leaders in investment in education and active labor market policies. In contrast, an early version of social investment as a substitute for employment protection and passive welfare state benefits was the Third Way charted by New Labour. Clinton's welfare state reforms were similarly justified in terms of activation. To various extents, the Third Way agenda was adopted by continental European countries also, as manifested for instance by the German Hartz reforms.

Social investment as practiced clearly has not been a panacea for the ills of the welfare state (Hemerijck 2017). Cutting social transfers has been politically very difficult, which in turn has kept limited the resources that were available for social investment. Beneficiaries of transfers clearly perceive losses and common interests in reversing them, whereas those who are to become beneficiaries of social investment lack the same group cohesion and awareness. Even in Sweden, resources devoted to active labor market policies declined. Critics of social investment pointed out that it did not help the most disadvantaged; members of middle-class households were better able to take advantage of childcare, education, and training opportunities than were the poor. Moreover, social investment is a long-term proposition, which makes it politically vulnerable. Politicians may have rather short-term horizons, depending on the party systems in which they operate, and as just mentioned, in times of austerity it is politically less costly to delay expenditures on social investment than to cut transfer benefits.

Much recent literature has focused on citizen preferences for redistribution as a driver of redistribution and thus of disposable income inequality. Some scholars inferred preferences from the degree or shape of inequality (Meltzer and Richard 1981; Lupu and Pontusson 2011), whereas others inferred them from occupational positions (Beramendi et al. 2015). Still others measured them directly and linked them to party choice (Häusermann and Kriesi 2015). However, preferences for redistribution are poor predictors of redistributive policy. There is general agreement that the political space has become multidimensional, with the emergence of a second dimension cutting across the class or state/market divide. This second dimension has been variously labeled materialism/post-materialism, liberalism/authoritarianism (Kitschelt 1994), green–alternative–libertarian (gal)/traditional–authoritarian–nationalist (tan) (Hooghe, Marks, and Wilson 2002), or universalism/particularism (Häusermann and Kriesi 2015). The political saliency of this second dimension has been promoted by new parties, the emergence of which has caused party system fragmentation in most countries. In a parallel development, voter volatility has increased due to the diversification of work and residential communities.

Party system fragmentation and voter volatility have in turn made the formation of stable pro-redistribution political coalitions and the implementation of major social policy reforms more difficult. Governmental coalitions have tended to include more parties or parties on either side of traditional ideological divides, thus making policy negotiations more complex and moving reforms toward incrementalism. Nevertheless, partisan politics left its imprint on social policy adaptations. Generally, left parties (including Social Democrats, Greens, and Socialists) supported social investment more than center or right parties did, based on differences with regard to values like gender equity and equal access to quality education. Moreover, social democratic parties increasingly embraced improvements of noncontributory social safety nets, such as minimum pensions and (in some countries) minimum incomes, to protect those left behind by changing labor markets. Where they were able to form majority governments, as for instance in Spain, social democratic parties made progress on these agendas. However, institutions continued to shape the translation of political support into policies. Constitutional dispersion of power from the central to subnational governments, along with presidentialism and bicameralism, slowed reform efforts and generated uneven outcomes among subnational units.

Theoretical Framework

Our explanatory focus will be on power in the labor market and politics (that is, on the power of labor vis-à-vis capital through organization and the institutional position of labor) and on partisan politics shaping the size and structure of welfare state programs. We shall focus on the ability of labor in established labor market institutions to protect wage and salary earners and keep rent-seeking elites in check. We shall examine the hypotheses on the causes of rising inequality outlined above as explanations of common trends, and our power-centered explanation—an updated version of Power Resources Theory (PRT)—will be our point of departure in the quantitative and case study analyses that follow.

Power resources theory was developed to explain differences between countries in redistributive policy, with a focus on the welfare state (Stephens 1979; Korpi 1983; Esping-Andersen 1985). The basic argument was that organization of labor in unions and left parties could serve as a counterweight to the power of capital in the economic and the political arena, thereby enabling the passing of more redistributive policies with more egalitarian outcomes. Over the long term, strong labor movements and left parties in government were able to construct generous and redistributive welfare states. Weak labor movements and weak or absent left parties, in contrast, resulted in residual or liberal welfare states. Labor movements, and left parties of intermediate strength and in competition with Christian democratic parties, tended to result in generous but less redistributive social policies. These power constellations, then, were at the root of the development of the three worlds of welfare capitalism: the social democratic or Nordic, the Christian democratic or continental European, and the liberal or Anglo-Saxon welfare states (Esping-Andersen 1990).

PRT has remained one of the dominant approaches in the study of welfare states in advanced capitalist democracies (Campillo and Sola 2020). It has been expanded to include the organizational power of women in women's movements and alliances with left parties to explain egalitarian gender policies (Huber and Stephens 2000). In quantitative studies, authors have included additional indicators of labor power, such as voter turnout (Brady 2009). It is a well-anchored finding in studies of political participation, going back to Verba, Nie, and Kim (1978), that membership in unions mobilizes people with low socioeconomic status into political participation. Thus, at the aggregate level union density will increase turnout among lower-skilled workers, and this higher turnout should keep politicians more responsive to the interests of these voters. We shall consider voter turnout as a PRT indicator here.

PRT was developed to explain the formation of welfare states. However, it can also be used to explain the defense of established welfare states. The period of welfare state expansion came to an end in the 1980s, as slower growth and higher levels of unemployment constrained the resource base and imposed greater burdens on the welfare state. However, even under the new politics of the welfare state (Pierson 2001), or the politics of retrenchment, the legacies of the power distributions in the formative period lived on through the mechanisms of the ratchet effect and regime legacies (Huber and Stephens 2001). The ratchet effect refers to the support for universalistic policies that affect a large proportion of the population after their introduction, which makes these policies the new point of reference for any discussion of welfare state reform. The regime legacies effect refers to the impact of policy regimes on the institutional strength of social actors and thus on their capacity to shape further welfare state developments. As we shall show here, PRT retains its explanatory power as the organizational and institutional strength of labor continue to exert profound influence on market income inequality, and the strength of left parties and voter turnout continue to shape welfare state generosity, which in turn crucially affects disposable income inequality.

A theory about domestic dynamics, PRT works well for the core countries in the world economic and political system. In our book on *Capitalist Development and Democracy* (Rueschemeyer, Stephens, and Stephens 1992) we expanded the theoretical frame to include international power constellations, as those were important to explain the weakness of democratic impulses in Latin America and the Caribbean. We similarly needed to expand our frame to include external pressures when dealing with the European semi-periphery, in our case Spain (Huber and Stephens 2012). The economic and social policy trajectory of Spain was profoundly shaped first by the country's integration into the EU and then by the sovereign debt crisis and the dictates of the Troika: the International Monetary Fund (IMF), the European Central Bank (ECB), and the European Commission. The prospect and then the reality of admission to the EU accelerated the opening and restructuring of the Spanish economy, which inflicted major hardship in the form of unemployment, but at the same time brought economic support and the European social model as a guide to redistributive policy reform. As of 2007, Spain had made significant progress in expanding social policy, but in the wake of the fiscal crisis much of this progress was reversed. The austerity imposed on Spain reversed some of the reforms and enormously reduced the government's capacity for redistribution.

Ultimately, redistribution happens through policy: through social transfers and the provision of services. Most of the tests of alternative prominent explanations of redistribution focus only on the direct effects of the master variables, such as the degree and structure of inequality (Lupu and

Pontusson 2011) or the structure of the electoral system (Iversen and Soskice 2006), on redistribution, leaving the role of policies unexamined. We shall operationalize the generosity of policy and look at the effects of the master variables on policy, the effects of policy on redistribution, and the remaining direct effects of the master variables on distribution.

Our approach runs counter to the exclusive emphasis in much of the recent literature on popular preferences and electoral politics. As we shall show, institutions continue to matter, as do partisan politics. Specifically, the institutional position of labor continues to shape minimum wages and thus market income poverty. At the other end of the income distribution, the institutional strength of labor matters for keeping the rent-seeking of the top 1 percent in check. When it comes to pre-distribution and redistribution, policy legacies shaped by long-term incumbency of political party families continue to matter. Of course current electoral politics matter, but party system fragmentation, higher electoral volatility, and the constraints of coalitions have significantly weakened partisan bases for sustained redistributive policies. Therefore, it is important to examine partisan politics in conjunction with the institutional strength of wage and salary earners and policy legacies.

Regime Typology

Throughout this book, we will refer to the typology of political economies shown in the figures in the appendices and table 1.1. The regime typology is a heuristic rather than an explanatory device. While all of the explanatory factors outlined above vary across countries and over time, the variations in labor market institutions and politics we favor as explanations are primarily across countries and cluster by political economy regimes.[3] Our regime typology is derived from Esping-Andersen's (1990) *Three Worlds* typology as amended by Leibfried (1993) and Ferrera (1996) to include a southern or Mediterranean regime. In his original regime typology, Esping-Andersen (1990, 144–61) notes the close affinity between welfare state regimes and labor market regimes. This affinity is clearly apparent in the first five rows of the political economy typology shown in table 1.1.

The three rows below the middle of the table—human capital spending, welfare generosity, and parental leave—show a sharp contrast in social and educational policy between regimes. These are the policy indicators used in this book; many more could be added which would show a similar

TABLE 1.1. **Typology of Political Economies**

	Nordic	Continental	Southern	Anglo-American
Union density %	65.6	31.5	29.9	34.0
Wage coordination 1 (most fragmented) to 5 (most centralized).	4.1	3.6	2.4	2.2
Contract coverage %	81.2	78.9	88.2	37.0
Works council rights 0 to 3 with 0 no works council and 3 indicating extensive powers	2.0	2.3	1.4	0.4
Employment protection legislation	2.1	2.2	3.2	0.8
Average left cabinet share 1960–2020 (e.g., left parties accounted for an average of 54% of parliamentary seats held by all governing parties in the Nordic countries, 1960–2020)	54.0	35.1	41.1	20.2
Average Christian democratic cabinet share	3.1	41.7	17.2	0
Average cabinet share of secular center and right parties	42.9	30.8	42.4	79.6
Human capital spending % GDP	9.3	6.6	4.8	5.9
Welfare generosity	25.4	24.5	17.1	13.4
Parental leave pay	52.2	39.4	29.4	13.4
Stock market capitalization % GDP	42.2	51.6	30.5	79.9
Corporate governance Hall and Gingerich (2009) index, varies from 0 (most LME) to 1 (most CME)	.70	.79	.87	.24

Except for corporate governance, averages for all country year observations in Brady, Huber, and Stephens (2020). Most data series begin in 1960. For more details on measurement and data sources, see table A.1.

contrast. The final two rows contain some indicators of corporate governance which Varieties of Capitalism (VoC) scholars (e.g., Hall and Soskice 2001; Hall and Gingerich 2009) use to distinguish Liberal Market Economies (LMEs) from Coordinated Market Economies (CMEs). Hall and Gingerich's "Coordination of Corporate Governance" index is an additive index of shareholder power, dispersion of control, and stock market capitalization. Arguably it is a good proxy for shareholder value corporate governance. The fit between VoCs and welfare state and labor market regimes has been noted often (e.g., Estevez-Abe, Iversen, and Soskice 2001; Huber and Stephens 2001), though it is less tight if only because the VoC typology is a dichotomy and the so-called mixed regimes, primarily southern Europe and France, are left out entirely or undertheorized.

A few further notes about the regime typology are in order before we proceed to an outline of the book. First, we chose regime labels that are partly geographic and, in any case, atheoretical. This contrasts to our 2001 book, in which we label the *Three Worlds* as Social Democratic, Liberal, and (departing from Esping-Andersen) Christian Democratic. This was consistent with our argument that it was long-term government by social democratic parties, Christian democratic parties, and secular center and right parties that shaped social policy and historically created the three worlds. Three of the four southern European countries—Portugal, Spain, and Greece—were not included in that book, and their inclusion in welfare state analyses and typologies makes it impossible to give a convenient and transparent "political origins" label to the regimes. Moreover, the political origins labels fit uncomfortably with some of the other cases, such as France, where the Christian Democrats were an unimportant political force after the advent of the Fifth Republic. This change in regime labels does not affect our analysis in any way. We use the regime classification to summarize our presentation of the data in tables, but we never enter the regime classifications in the quantitative analysis. We do use the regime typology to select our case studies for the qualitative analysis.

As noted, the hypothesized causal variables we group together under the categories of long-term economic transformation and globalization vary primarily through time, though some of the globalization variables do vary significantly across countries and are significantly higher, on average, among European countries. These variables are largely orthogonal to the political economy regime variables. The periodization in tables A.2–A.7 is primarily shaped by the process of European integration, as are such globalization variables as capital controls and trade openness. The first period ends with the enactment of the Single European Act; the second corresponds to the run-up to the introduction of the Euro; and the third ends with the Great Recession/Eurocrisis. The fourth period is the Great Recession/Eurocrisis, and the fifth is the post-crisis period. As we will see, European integration is notable for its second-order effects on inequality and redistribution, because it greatly constrained macroeconomic management. By contrast, long-term economic transformation in the form of deindustrialization, technological change, deregulation, and the transition to the knowledge economy have moderately strong direct effects on income distribution.

Methodology

As in previous works (Huber and Stephens 2001, 2012), we combine pooled time-series analysis of a near universe of cases meeting our scope conditions with comparative historical analysis of selected cases. This combination is what Tarrow calls triangulation, which he considers the research strategy that "best embodies the strategy of combining quantitative and qualitative methods" (2010, 108). Lieberman (2005) also recommends this combination. The combination of these two methods allows us to achieve generalizability and to establish causality by tracing links between events, actors' behavior, and policy changes in the historical narrative. Our scope conditions call for the inclusion of all democracies transitioning from industrial economies to knowledge economies. We include all countries with populations of at least 1 million.

In our comparative historical analysis, we select one country from each of our four regime types for in-depth historical interrogation: Sweden as a Social Democratic regime and a CME, the United States as a Liberal regime and an LME, Germany as a Christian Democratic regime and a CME, and Spain as a southern European regime. We do not claim that the four cases are representative of their regime types in the sense of being somehow average for their regimes. Rather, based on previous work (Huber and Stephens 2001 and 2012; Stephens, Huber, and Ray 1999), we compare them to other countries within their regime type. We find that the US is extreme on the measures of both inequality and its causes, though the UK is not far behind. Sweden moved from the least unequal of the four Nordic countries to the most unequal, both at the top due to the increased importance of capital gains and at the bottom due to a weakening of the safety net, though it remained in the Nordic group of countries with relatively low inequality, especially when the distributive effects of public services are included. Germany moved from one of the least unequal of the continental welfare states to one of the most unequal due to the expansion of low-wage and part-time and temporary work. Spain is for the most part quite close to Italy and the mean for the southern European countries in disposable income inequality and poverty; it improved its position during the boom but was hit harder by the post-2007 crisis than Italy in terms of poverty.

In chapters 2–7, we analyze pooled time-series data covering the period from 1960 (or from the beginning of the available data series) to 2018. The dependent variables are various measures of inequality and poverty. In discussions of the selection of statistical techniques in quantitative journal articles, the selection of the appropriate technique is often treated as an entirely technical problem that can be solved by reference to the latest technical innovation without reference to the hypothesized theory or even the nature of variation in the data at hand. This is a mistake and can lead to the selection of an inappropriate technique for testing the theory. In our case, much of the variation in some of our dependent variables is between countries. This is the case for the two wage dispersion variables, redistribution, poverty reduction, social policy generosity, and human capital spending. Given the theoretical concerns and the nature of variation in the data, it is less appropriate to employ a fixed-effects specification—that is, country unit dummies—as the main specification in the analysis. We do, however, provide country fixed-effects specifications as robustness checks in appendix C. We not only look at statistical significance, but pay particular attention to the substantive importance of the statistical associations between our independent and dependent variables.

By the same token, since a lot of the variation we explain in the statistical analysis is between countries, we forgo one advantage of the time structure of pooled time-series data—that is, using the time sequence in the data to make claims about causality. However, as in our previous work (Huber and Stephens 2001 and 2012), we do not make claims about causality based on the quantitative analysis. As we just noted, we make our claims of having uncovered causal relations by examining the historical sequence and causal mechanisms in the comparative historical analysis. The role of the quantitative analysis is to demonstrate that these relations hold over a large number of cases and over long periods of time, and to rule out alternative explanations. We agree with Hall (2003), who argues that causation in the real world is highly complex and is characterized by multiple paths to the same outcomes, complex interaction effects, path-dependent effects, reciprocal causality, and diffusion, and that one is not likely to uncover these causal processes with techniques like multivariate regression (or any other statistical technique, for that matter).

The very logic of multivariate regression is to estimate average associations of an independent with a dependent variable for all cases, holding potential alternative associated variables constant. Interaction terms will tell us the magnitude of the covariation of one independent variable with the dependent variable depending on the value of another independent variable. These tools are helpful in demonstrating general patterns of relationships among variables. Newer estimation techniques aim to establish actual causal relationships by building on the logic of experiments, such as in difference-in-differences and matching (Basu and Small 2020). Yet these analyses remain in the realm of average effects, everything else held constant. They cannot deal with multiple paths to the same outcome or complex interactions. Moreover, they remain at the level of covariation—they do not elucidate the causal mechanisms that produce this covariation. This is why mixed methods remain the most appropriate approach to the analysis of large-scale processes of social change.

We use the comparative historical analysis of our four cases to explore whether a posited causal factor actually exerts a causal effect on a specific outcome. If an intervening mechanism can be found, then we have confidence that the posited causal factor did indeed have the predicted effect (Mahoney and Terrie 2008, 747). Looking for mechanisms means going beyond relationships between variables to look for actors, their relationships, and the intended and unintended consequences of their actions (Hedström 2008, 320). For example, our posited causal factor for lower disposable household income inequality is prolonged left incumbency. Our intervening mechanisms are welfare state generosity and the passing of legislation on welfare state programs. In our case analyses, we show which parties expanded or defended, and which parties reduced, welfare state generosity. Similarly, we posit that labor strength has a causal effect on market income inequality and on redistribution. In our case analyses we can show the mechanisms: that is, unions promoted higher-level bargaining, or wage coordination, which reduces wage dispersion and thus market income inequality. We also find that unions influenced legislation that affects redistribution by strongly resisting cuts in welfare state generosity and supporting expansion of welfare benefits to labor market outsiders.

Overview of the Book

Part I of the book consists of six chapters analyzing quantitative data on distributive outcomes. Chapter 2 focuses on inequality in individual market income, measured by wage dispersion. Chapter 3 looks at household income inequality, from market income through redistribution to disposable income. Chapter 4 analyzes inequality at the top, measured by top 1 percent shares of national income. Chapter 5 explores inequality at the bottom, measured by relative poverty. Chapters 6 and 7 analyze the predictors of social policy generosity and the nexus between social investment and social consumption. Our analyses of household income are based primarily on data for which we have access to microdata on income distribution. This allows us to construct measures of market (pre-tax and transfer) income and poverty and disposable income and poverty, and therefore of governmental redistribution and poverty reduction. It also allows us to focus on the working-age population only, which is important since we are exploring the effects of technological change and globalization on labor markets and the countervailing effects of the institutional strength of labor. Moreover, including the elderly exaggerates the degree of redistribution through taxes and transfers in countries with generous mandatory pension systems.

Our main findings in Part I are that unemployment has very strong substantive effects on market and disposable household income inequality and poverty. Unemployment has become a particularly strong predictor of poverty since 2000. Technological change and globalization have comparatively weak direct effects on market income inequality, but to the extent that they caused deindustrialization and trade competition and thus drove up unemployment, they drove up inequality. The same argument can be made for the impact of capital market openness; to the extent that it reduced tax revenue and room for macroeconomic management, it reduced governments' capacity to combat unemployment and to provide social transfers.

However, the long-term structural and short-term cyclical pressures toward higher inequality and poverty have been mediated by labor market institutions and policies that have granted different degrees of power to labor and have shaped both market and disposable income distribution. Among the various institutions empowering labor (union density, contract coverage, wage coordination, works council rights, union participation in minimum wage setting, employment protection legislation) we shall show that the most robust and most widely important is union density. We shall show that union density has statistically highly robust and substantively important effects on wage dispersion, the share of the top 1 percent of income earners, redistribution of household income, and inequality in disposable household income. We shall show similar effects for some of these other institutions on different measures of inequality.

The most important policy for reducing market inequality and poverty is welfare state generosity. We shall show that social rights to generous compensation in case of loss of market income due to unemployment and sickness are highly robust and substantively large predictors of redistribution and poverty reduction and thus of poverty and inequality in disposable household income. However, this is not the only policy available to governments. Investment in human capital, from early childhood to adulthood, shows equally robust associations with market and disposable household income inequality. The takeaway is that governments do have options to counteract the inequality-enhancing pressures exerted by changing labor markets. These options go beyond social policy and include legislation to strengthen the position of labor, which then will counteract inequality in market income.

This brings us to the question of the conditions under which governments choose such options. We shall confirm an argument that is firmly established in the welfare state literature: that governments of the left are the most likely to adopt generous social rights and to invest in human capital. We shall further show that high voter turnout, which indicates higher turnout among lower socioeconomic groups, is a highly robust and important predictor of lower disposable household income inequality and poverty. In short, politics does make a big difference in how inegalitarian changes in labor markets are translated into inequality and poverty.

Part II consists of four chapters each presenting a case study of one country from each of our political economy regimes — Germany, Sweden, the United States, and Spain — and a chapter comparing these cases. We shall explore the role of governments and unions as they confronted the pressures on labor markets and budgets resulting from technological change and globalization, within the context of the structural conditions shaped by policy legacies. Germany, Sweden, and the US are widely seen as prototypical examples of continental CMEs and Bismarckian welfare states, Nordic CMEs and social democratic welfare states, and liberal CMEs and welfare states respectively. Spain's institutional configuration has been more fluid. The economy was shaped by an import substitution strategy under Franco and had to undergo a painful transition to an open economy. Nevertheless, the economy is closer to a CME than an LME, in particular with regard to the frequent use of tripartite social pacts. The Franco legacy for the welfare state was clearly Bismarckian, but its coverage was much more restricted than in the continental countries, which made it possible for social democratic governments to add universalistic elements during their fourteen years in power in the first two decades after the transition to democracy.

The overall pattern in Germany is one of starkly increasing inequality and poverty, turning one of the more equal continental European countries into the most unequal in this regime type. In the pre-1993 period, Germany was close to Sweden in the Gini of disposable household income and clearly lower in poverty (though, as we point out in chapter 10, the Swedish figure is largely due to the unusually high proportion of student households in Sweden). German unification contributed to deindustrialization, raised unemployment levels to unprecedented heights, and imposed a heavy financial burden on the government. After more than a decade, these issues prompted drastic labor market reforms that led to the growth of low-wage and part-time jobs and to cuts in unemployment insurance. At the same time that the low-wage sector expanded and fewer people had access to social insurance, the unemployment compensation system was made much less generous, all of which meant that redistribution and poverty reduction through the welfare state declined. In fact, disposable household income poverty almost doubled, from 5.6 percent to 10 percent of the working-age population. Union density declined steeply, centralized bargaining declined, and contract coverage saw an even greater decline. Influence of the Social Democratic Party (SPD) on labor market and social policy has been highly constrained. In the forty-three years since 1980, the party was the leading partner in a purely Red-Green coalition for only seven years; in four more of those years the pro-business Free Democratic Party (FDP) was a coalition partner, and for a dozen years the SPD was the junior partner in a grand coalition with the Christian Democratic Union/Christian Social Union (CDU/CSU). In contrast, the CDU/CSU was the leading party in government for thirty-two years. Finally, in the period of the great fiscal pressures and the labor market reforms of the Red/Green coalition, the CDU/CSU controlled the Bundesrat.

The overall pattern in Spain is one of comparatively high and strongly cyclical levels of inequality and poverty, with a strong upward trend beginning in 2007. Spain transitioned in the 1970s away from an authoritarian regime presiding over an uncompetitive economy with an anemic welfare state and a low degree of union density, and the economic opening resulted in rapid deindustrialization. The country started out with high levels of market and disposable income inequality and low levels of redistribution. In fact, disposable household income inequality in the pre-1993 period was very close to that of the United States, but it increased much less over the period and ended up significantly lower than in the United States. The share of the top 1 percent remained relatively modest, and as of 2015 the low-wage sector remained smaller than in Germany and the United States. Spain's key problems since the 1980s have been the high level of unemployment and the low overall level of employment. After a period of improvement during the boom years in the early 2000s, these problems were aggravated by the post-2007 recession. Spain greatly expanded social services and the social safety net, but the austerity measures imposed in the wake of the 2007 crisis limited the ability of the welfare state to counteract rising market income poverty effectively, such that disposable income poverty ended up being even slightly higher than in the United States. Union density remained constant and contract coverage even increased slightly, but the context of low employment and high unemployment restricted their effectiveness. The Partido Socialista Obrero Español (PSOE), the socialist party, was in power for twenty-six years between 1980 and 2023 and greatly modernized and expanded the welfare state, but the austerity policies under the conservative Partido Popular (PP) government from 2011 to 2018 wiped out much of the progress that had been made. The improvements in labor market policies and the safety net implemented by the PSOE since 2019 are not yet reflected in our data.

In the 1980s Sweden was the most egalitarian country in our case studies, but starting with the economic crisis of the early 1990s inequality there rose at both the top and the bottom end. The sharp rise in unemployment stimulated a reduction in the generosity of the unemployment insurance system—a reduction that was made worse by the bourgeois government of 2006–2014. Increasing stock market capitalization and the parallel increase in the impact of capital gains increased top income shares. Nevertheless, though the disposable household income Gini increased by 4.4 points, this increase was lower than the 5.5 points in Germany and the 6 points in the United States. At the same time, Sweden intensified its poverty reduction efforts and thus was able to keep disposable household income poverty essentially constant. High levels of employment, particularly among women, meant that dual-earner households have been the norm, which reduces the risk of poverty in the event one of the partners becomes unemployed. Union density declined by 18 percent, as much as in Germany, but from a much higher original level. Also, contract coverage even increased slightly, to 88 percent. Thus, continued high levels of union density and strong labor market institutions dampened the increase in market inequality and poverty. A continuation of high levels of public spending on human capital contributed to keeping these levels in check. The Swedish Social Democratic Workers Party (SAP) was in power for twenty-nine years from 1980 on and thus managed to break or reverse some of the welfare state cutbacks pushed through by the bourgeois governments in that period. As a result, Sweden remained among the least unequal countries, and the least unequal of our four cases.

In the pre-1993 period, the United States already had the highest levels of disposable income inequality and poverty of the countries examined in this book, and inequality also increased the most, by 6 points. In contrast, poverty reduction efforts intensified and thus could contain the increase in disposable household income poverty to 2 percent. The main inegalitarian dynamic has been the increase in the top 1 percent income share. This can be explained by labor market institutions that were initially weak and grew even weaker, and the absence of a social democratic party. Union density and contract coverage declined from already low levels to the lowest among our four countries, at barely 11 percent. Republicans held the presidency for twenty-four years, and Democrats remained constrained by conservative senators in their own ranks. We can add to this list of explanations an electoral system that enhances the role of money in politics, low voter turnout, a weak social safety net, and a decline in public investment in human capital going back to the 1970s.

As noted, our comparison of the four cases highlights that Sweden, Germany, and the United States all saw an increase in both market and disposable household income inequality; Spain saw an increase in market income inequality but essentially stability in disposable income inequality. The ordering of the countries, however, remained stable from 2000 on for redistribution and disposable income inequality, with Sweden showing most redistribution and least inequality, followed by Germany, then Spain, then the United States. We saw similar dynamics but with different weights: rising levels of unemployment and precarious employment depressed incomes at the bottom, a weakening of the position of labor left a greater share of wage earners unprotected, a particularly weak position of labor failed to restrain the top 1 percent, dualization of labor markets left fewer people with access to social insurance, social insurance was also made less generous, and social assistance remained insufficient to keep households out of poverty. Partisan politics remained important in that left parties made great efforts to protect the social safety net and social services, particularly in Spain and Sweden, though important cuts to the welfare state were passed by the Red-Green coalition in Germany and the Clinton administration in the United States. Conservative parties pushed for and implemented larger cuts, and in the United States they implemented major tax cuts.

Our concluding chapter summarizes the evidence and reiterates our key arguments that structural changes in the economy and globalization did change labor markets in an inegalitarian direction, but politics and policies continued powerfully to shape both market income distribution and redistribution and therefore disposable income inequality. The strength of labor and the generosity of the welfare state protected individuals and households at the bottom and restrained earnings at the top. Sustained investment in human capital facilitated adjustment to the knowledge economy and dampened income inequality. We end by speculating about the extent to which left parties could have done better in strengthening labor, maintaining the generosity of the welfare state, and investing in human capital. This leads us to a discussion of the constraints resulting from European integration as well as changes in party systems. We end with a number of policy recommendations for parties and governments concerned about rising inequality.

PART I
The Shapes and Determinants of Inequality
Broad Trends

PART I

CHAPTER TWO

Wage Dispersion

For most people the experience of inequality and poverty is one shared with other members of a family. It is shaped first by market income—that is, income from work, capital income, and private transfers. For most people, the most important among these is income from work, which in turn depends on the volume and the remuneration of work performed by family members. The actual experience of poverty and inequality is shaped by disposable household income, which is a result of the modification of market income through the tax and transfer system. Taxes are deducted from market income and all public transfers are added, from public pensions to unemployment compensation, social assistance, public scholarships, etcetera. We begin with an analysis of income from work in this chapter and turn to redistribution in the next chapter. To build an understanding of the factors that shape the distribution of income from work from the ground up, we analyze the distribution of income from work among full-time employed people, or wage dispersion. We shall follow the convention of measuring wage dispersion by the 90-50 and 50-10 ratios—that is, the ratio of earnings of a full-time employee at the 90th percentile to those of a full-time employee at the median, and the ratio of the earnings of a full-time employee at the median to those of a full-time employee at the 10th percentile. Patterns of wage dispersion have differed considerably across postindustrial societies, which calls for an explanation of these differences (Atkinson 2007 and 2008; Gottschalk and Smeeding 1997).

Theoretical Perspectives and Hypotheses

The transition from the industrial to the service and knowledge economy has changed skill requirements for jobs and thus the patterns of remuneration. It has increased skill requirements for many jobs and has destroyed relatively productive and well-paying industrial jobs for low-skill workers. Technological change has also destroyed routine white-collar business service jobs. Low-skill workers, both blue and white collar, have increasingly become relegated to low-productivity service jobs, such as personal services or the hospitality industry. This process, skill-biased technological change (SBTC), is an explanation of the rise in wage dispersion in the United States that has been favored in scholarly work on the topic by economists (Autor 2014; Autor, Katz, and Kearney 2008; Goldin and Katz 2001 and 2008; Acemoglu 2002), and, to a lesser extent in comparative work on wage dispersion (Goos and Manning 2007; Goos, Manning, and Salomon 2009).

Deregulation of the energy, transport, and communication sectors has contributed to the disappearance of secure and well-paying jobs for the low-skilled by replacing public-sector jobs with more precarious and lower-paying private-sector jobs. The growth sectors of the economy have been dynamic knowledge sectors—that is, sectors with a high contribution of information and communication technology (ICT) services to value-added growth, such as communications, financial intermediation, and business services. Figures A.10 and A.11 show the decline in industrial employment and in the regulation of these sectors; table B.12 shows the growth of employment in the dynamic knowledge sectors. We expect, then, that deindustrialization, technological change, deregulation, and the size of the dynamic knowledge sectors are all associated with higher levels of wage dispersion. All our variables and hypotheses are summarized in table 2.1; our variable definitions and sources are displayed in table A.1.

Globalization evolved in parallel with the transition to the knowledge economy. The extent of globalization is indicated by the increased flow of goods, capital, and labor across borders. Trade openness is assumed to reward capital-intensive production in advanced countries and to reduce labor-intensive production, thereby depressing wages of low-skilled workers. However, to the extent that trade is carried on between advanced countries, this mechanism will not operate. Therefore, we adopt a nondirectional hypothesis. Competition from third world imports and outsourcing of production and services to low-wage countries have decreased demand for low-skilled labor and placed downward pressure on wages of less skilled workers and of medium-skilled white-collar workers (Wood 1994). Threats to relocate production abroad have also arguably increased capital's power in wage bargaining. The free movement of capital across borders has made such relocations easier and the threats more credible. Therefore, third world imports, capital openness, and outward foreign investment are expected to increase wage dispersion. Increased cross-border mobility of labor has generated two kinds of immigration: people with highly specialized skills hired for specific jobs, and people with low skills (or at least low language skills) fleeing violence or poor life chances in their home country. The latter category of immigrants has competed for low-paying jobs with local low-skilled workers. Immigration of people with high skills has been much lower in volume than immigration of people with low skills. Accordingly, we expect trade openness, third world–manufactured imports, outward foreign investment, capital openness, and immigration all to be associated with higher levels of wage dispersion.

These general trends have manifested themselves differently in different countries, and different countries have been very unevenly prepared to meet these challenges. The key to meeting these challenges has been human capital. As Goldin and Katz (2008) showed, the United States has been falling behind in the race between technology and education. In contrast, the Nordic countries have kept up comparatively high investment in education at all levels and have therefore been able to adapt better to changing job requirements. The importance of human capital is underlined by Nickell's (2004) finding that skills dispersion, as measured by the ratio of test scores of adults at the 95th percentile to adults at the 5th percentile in the International Adult Literacy Survey (IALS), was a better predictor of wage dispersion than were labor market institutions.

The availability of comparable data on skill distributions is highly restricted. Accordingly, many researchers have used public expenditure on education as a proxy for human capital and a predictor for returns to skills, and we shall do the same here. Weisstanner and Armingeon (2020) found that public expenditure on education depressed the education premium, operationalized as the difference between the median wage of workers with and without tertiary education, in twenty-two OECD countries between the early 1990s and 2014. Making the leap to disposable household income, Busemeyer (2015) still found that public spending on all levels of education was negatively associated with inequality of disposable household income in postindustrial societies in the period from 1997 to 2008. The emphasis here is on public expenditure on education. Reliance on private expenditure on education, in contrast, increases inequality. Weisstanner and Armingeon (2020) showed a positive effect of private education spending on the education premium. Similarly, Busemeyer (2015) found that the private share of education spending at all levels was positively related to the Gini of disposable household income.

In our exploration of scores of fifteen-year-old students on the test of mathematical skills in all the waves of the PISA tests conducted between 2000 and 2015, we found that total education spending and public education spending raised the math scores of students at the 25th percentile and the mean, but that the effect of public spending was stronger. Moreover, the difference between the effects of total expenditure and public expenditure was larger for math scores at the 25th percentile than for math scores at the mean, which suggests that greater reliance on private spending is more likely to leave the bottom behind (Huber, Gunderson, and Stephens 2018). Finally, in our analysis of top 1 percent income shares, we found that the private share of total tertiary spending was strongly associated with greater top income shares (Huber, Huo, and Stephens 2019). So, the sources of education spending matter because they shape the (in)egalitarian nature of educational systems and, indirectly, the distribution of wages.

The formation of human capital extends to before and after the regular school years. It begins with early childhood education and care and with preschool or kindergarten. These early years prepare children to learn effectively during their school years. If coverage is very wide and attendance is free or subsidized for low-income parents, early childhood education and care and kindergarten can also reduce the gap in preparation for school between children from low- and high-income households, thus reducing the skills gap later in life. In the knowledge society, learning is a lifelong requirement, and public expenditures on adult training and retraining make such learning more widely possible. As critics of social investment have pointed out, though, adults with higher levels of skills are more likely to take advantage of such opportunities (Kilpi-Jakonen, Vono de Vilhena, and Blossfeld 2015), which underlines the importance of starting public investment early both to upgrade the overall quality of human capital and to reduce inequalities in the distribution of human capital. Accordingly, we expect human capital spending to be negatively associated with wage dispersion, and the private share of education spending to be positively associated with wage dispersion.

As noted, our primary variables of interest are politics and labor market institutions. We are building on power resources theory (Stephens 1979; Korpi 1983) that conceptualizes organization as a counterweight to wealth in democratic societies. Strong organization of labor in unions and political parties can increase the share of income going to labor directly through collective negotiations, and it can improve the overall position of labor in terms of rights and benefits indirectly through legislation. Where labor movements are able to organize a large share of employees and/or where they are able to coordinate wage bargaining at a high level, they not only improve the collective position of labor vis-à-vis employers but also reduce income differentials among employees. Similar effects are produced by laws or regulations that extend the coverage of collective agreements to sectors of the labor force that were not party to the negotiations. Such contract coverage extension can serve as a substitute for coordination of wage bargaining at a high level.

Other legal provisions that strengthen the position of labor and work against downward pressure on wages are employment protection legislation (EPL), union participation in minimum wage setting, and works council rights. Employment protection applies to both permanent and temporary employees. Protection of temporary employment, however (such as restrictions on renewals of temporary contracts), also serve to protect permanent employees from the spread of temporary work. Accordingly, employment protection legislation is a double-edged sword. On the one hand, it protects employed low-income workers from a race to the bottom in wages; on the other, it tends to depress overall levels of employment (Nelson and Stephens 2011 and 2013). Union participation in minimum wage setting, either in consultation or negotiation with the government and/or employers, elevates the reservation wage. Stronger works council rights also protect the employment and the wages of employees and thus can be expected to prevent a race to the bottom. Accordingly, we expect EPL, union participation in minimum wage setting, and works council rights to be negatively associated with wage dispersion, particularly in the lower half of the wage distribution.

Left governments were traditionally the key allies of unions and promoters of policies to strengthen the position of labor and to reduce poverty and inequality in society at large. Left parties have seen the center of gravity in their social base shift from blue-collar workers to white-collar employees, but they have retained a commitment to equity as a defining characteristic (Gingrich and Häusermann 2015). Among white-collar employees, particularly sociocultural professionals (that is, employees with relatively high education employed in sectors such as education, health care, and social work), tend to support left parties (Kitschelt and Rehm 2014). Sociocultural professionals express stronger support for social investment

TABLE 2.1. **Variables and Hypotheses**

	Hypothesized relation	
	50-10	90-50
Dependent variables		
Wage dispersion 50-10 ratio		
Wage dispersion 90-50 ratio		
Independent variables		
Power resource variables		
Left government	−	−
Union density	−	−
Wage coordination	−	−
Contract coverage	−	−
EPL	−	
Minimum wage setting	−	
Works council rights	−	
Long-term economic change		
Industrial employment	−	−
Total factor productivity change	+	+
Regulation	−	−
Dynamic service employment	+	+
Globalization		
Capital market openness	+	+
Outward FDI	+	+
Trade openness	−/+	−/+
Third world imports	+	+
Immigration	+	+
Other independent variables		
Unemployment	+	+
Human capital spending	−	−
Private education spending	+	+

See table A.1 for variable definitions and sources.

than do blue-collar workers, whereas blue-collar workers have stronger preferences for social transfers (Beramendi et al. 2015) and remain supportive of policies to protect the position of labor. As noted above, social investment reduces inequality through pre-distribution. Accordingly, both parts of the social base of left parties support policies to restrain inequality, and we expect long-term incumbency of left governments to be associated with lower wage dispersion in the top and bottom halves.

Political scientists have tested the effects of variables derived from power resources theory on wage dispersion. Wallerstein (1999) and Pontusson, Rueda, and Way (2002) identified high levels of union density, coordination of wage bargaining, coverage by collective contracts, and left governments as key factors associated with comparatively low levels of dispersion.

Rueda and Pontusson (2000) added varieties of capitalism to the analysis and showed stronger negative effects of coordination of wage bargaining on wage dispersion in coordinated market economies than in liberal market economies, and positive effects of right government in liberal market economies but an absence of such effects in coordinated market economies. Studies covering the more recent period confirmed the importance of union density as a factor constraining the growth of the top 10 percent income share (Jaumotte and Buitron 2015). We expect long-term incumbency of the Left along with all the variables indicating a strong labor position—union density, wage coordination, contract coverage, employment protection legislation, union participation in minimum wage setting, and works council rights—to reduce wage dispersion in the top and/or the bottom half. Our theoretical expectations are summarized in table 2.1.

Data, Measurement, and Statistical Estimation

Our dependent variables are the ratio of earnings of a full-time employee at the 90th percentile to those of a full-time employee at the median, and the ratio of the earnings of a full-time employee at the median to those of a full-time employee at the 10th percentile. The sources of the data are indicated in table A.1. The operationalization of our independent variables and our measurement decisions are explained in appendix C.

Our analysis covers twenty-one postindustrial democracies—the twenty countries in table 1.1 plus Japan. Japan is in the data analysis, but it cannot really be classified with any of the regime types in table 1.1 and therefore was left out of that table. The time period covered extends from the 1960s to 2019, though observations are sparse before 1980.

We use Prais-Winsten estimations in our statistical analysis. This estimation technique uses panel-corrected standard errors and correction for first-order auto-regressiveness. Our reasons for choosing this technique are explained in appendix D, and alternative statistical estimations are provided in appendix E.

Results

Table 2.2 shows the results of a cross-sectional analysis of the impact of skills inequality based on test scores in numeracy of adults from the

TABLE 2.2. **Skills Dispersion and Wage Dispersion**

	50-10 ratio			90-50 ratio		
	Model 1	Model 2	Model 3	Model 4	Model 5	Model 6
Union density	−.002		−.001	−.005 *		−.004 †
Contract coverage	−.004 **		−.003 *	.002		−.001
Numeracy 95-5 ratio		.310 **	.199 †		.356 **	.243 *
Constant	1.951 **	.990 **	1.452 **	2.105 **	1.070 **	1.495 **
R²	.37 *	.28 *	.45 **	.39 *	.42 **	.54 **
Observations	16	16	16	16	16	16

† Significant at the .1 level; * .05 level; ** .01 level.

PIAAC data on wage dispersion. Given the small number of cases, we report significance at the .1 level in addition to the more conventional levels. The skills dispersion variable and one of the two labor strength variables are consistently significant in the models for both dependent variables. Comparing adjusted R squares for the various models can give us an estimate of the inner and outer bounds of the effects of skills dispersion and labor market institutions. Models 2 and 5 show the outer bound for skills dispersion: 28 percent of the variation explained for the 50-10 ratio, and 42 percent for the 90-50 ratio. Comparing Models 2 and 3 gives the inner bound of the effects of skills dispersion for the 50-10 ratio as 17 percent; models 5 and 6 show the inner bound for the 90-50 ratio as 12 percent. For labor market institutions the outer bound is 37 percent for the 50-10 ratio and 39 percent for the 90-50 ratio. The inner bound is 8 percent for the 50-10 ratio and 15 percent for the 90-50 ratio.

Table 2.3 shows our results for wage dispersion in the lower half of the distribution, the 50-10 ratio. Model 1 contains our power resources variables: left incumbency and indicators of the organizational and legal power of labor. Together, these variables explain 62 percent of the variation—more than any of the other clusters of variables. Left government, union density, wage coordination, and employment protection legislation are all highly significant and are negatively associated with the distance between the mean and the 10th percentile. Model 2 contains our indicators of structural changes in the economy. Only regulation and employment in dynamic ICT-heavy service sectors are significant, regulation being negatively and employment in dynamic services being positively associ-

TABLE 2.3. Wage Dispersion (90-10 Ratio)

	Model 1	Model 2	Model 3	Model 4	Model 5	Model 6
Left government	-.004 ***					.101 ***
Union density	-.003 ***					-.005 ***
Wage coordination	-.020 ***					-.044 ***
Contract coverage	.000					
EPL	-.117 ***					-.158 ***
Minimum wage setting	-.005					
Works council rights	-.002					
Industrial employment		.006				
Total factor productivity change (10-year)		-.170				
Regulation		-.025 *				-.041 ***
Dynamic service employment		.016 *				-.031 ^
Unemployment		.000				
Capital market openness			.029 **			.009
Outward FDI			.004 **			.000
Trade openness			-.003 ***			.101 ***
Third world imports			.001			
Immigration			.008			-.001
Human capital spending				-.056 ***	-.053 ***	-.005
Private education spending					.085 ***	
Constant	2.075 ***	1.480 ***	1.647 ***	2.001 ***	1.885 ***	2.622 ***
Adjusted R²	.62	.06 ***	.14	.25	.39	.74
Observations	617	374	590	498	258	270

* Significant at .05; ** significant at .01; *** significant at .001; ^ significant at .100.
Model 6 includes period dummies.

ated with wage dispersion at the bottom. The explanatory power of all the structural change variables is very weak, with only 6 percent of the variation explained.

Model 3 enters all our indicators of globalization, which also have only weak explanatory power, with 14 percent of the variation explained. Capital market openness, outward foreign direct investment, immigration, and trade openness all reach statistical significance, the first three being positively associated with wage dispersion, and the last negatively associated. Model 4 enters human capital spending only, and this variable alone explains 25 percent of the variation—four times as much as the structural change variables, with many more observations in the model. As expected, human capital spending is negatively associated with wage dispersion. Model 5 enters the percentage of education spending that is private, in addition to human capital spending, and this variable is positively associated with wage dispersion. Together, human capital spending and the share of private education spending explain 39 percent of the variation.

Model 6 is our combined model. As expected, it has the best fit, with three-quarters of the variation explained. Union density, wage coordination, and employment protection legislation remain highly significant and correctly signed, as does regulation. Employment in dynamic services and trade openness remain highly significant but flip the sign; this is contrary to our expectation on employment in dynamic services, but for trade openness we adopted a nondirectional hypothesis.

Table 2.4 shows the same type of analysis for the upper half of the wage distribution, the 90-50 ratio. Again, our power resources cluster of variables has the best fit, explaining 44 percent of the variation. Union density, wage coordination, and works council rights are all significant and negatively associated with wage dispersion, as expected. Among the indicators of structural change in the economy, only total factor productivity change and regulation are significant; they also conform to expectations in that total factor productivity change is positively, and regulation negatively, associated with wage dispersion. The globalization variables have the poorest fit, explaining only 4 percent of the variation. Capital market openness is positively, and trade openness negatively, associated with wage dispersion.

Human capital spending in models 4 and 5 is highly significant and negatively associated with wage dispersion at the top. Private share of education spending is significant and positively associated. Our final model has three highly significant variables: union density, wage coordination,

TABLE 2.4. Wage Dispersion (90-50 Ratio)

	Model 1		Model 2		Model 3		Model 4		Model 5		Model 6	
Left government	-.001											
Union density	-.005	***									-.005	***
Wage coordination	-.037	***									-.025	**
Contract coverage	.000											
Works council rights	-.030	**									-.02	
Industrial employment			.002									
Total factor productivity change (10-year)			5.242	***							5.622	***
Regulation			-.042	***							-.026	*
Dynamic service employment			.003									
Unemployment			-.002									
Capital market openness					.038	**					-.045	^
Outward FDI					.003						.000	
Trade openness					-.001	***						
Human capital spending							-.054	***	-.046	***	-.012	*
Private education spending									.067	**		
Constant	2.169	***	1.891	***	1.839	***	2.190	***	2.090	***	2.275	***
Adjusted R²	.44		.10		.04		.18		.19		.39	
Observations	614		369		592		493		258		465	

* Significant at .05; ** significant at .01; *** significant at .001; ^ significant opposite hypothesized direction.
Model 6 includes period dummies.

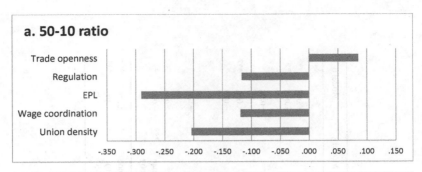
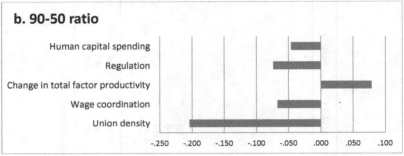

FIGURE 2.1. Effect of two-standard-deviation change in significant independent variables on measures of wage dispersion

and total factor productivity change. They are all signed as expected. Regulation and human capital spending also reach statistical significance and show the hypothesized association with wage dispersion at the top. The combined model explains less of the variation than do the power resources variables alone, but the composition of the observations is different because of variable availability.

Figures 2.1a and b show us the substantive importance of our significant variables. They show the effects of a two-standard-deviation change in the independent variables on the measures of wage dispersion. The figures are based on model 6, the combined model, in both tables. What is striking is the large substantive effect of union density for wage dispersion in both the lower half and the upper half. In the upper half it is the single most important variable; in the lower half only employment protection legislation has a larger effect. The next most important variables for wage dispersion at the bottom (of roughly equal importance) are wage coordination and regulation of energy, transport, and telecommunications. In the upper half of the wage distribution regulation has a slightly larger impact than wage coordination, though they are close. So, the extensive process of deregulation that occurred in all countries clearly contributed in important ways to greater wage dispersion. Next in importance are indicators of structural change in the economy. Total factor productivity has a strong inequality-enhancing effect on the 90-50 ratio, and trade openness has a similar effect for the 50-10 ratio. Finally, human capital spending only has a depressing effect on wage dispersion at the top, which suggests that an increase in the supply of skilled workers moderates wage increases at the top.

Table E.2 in appendix E provides alternative statistical estimations of our final models. As we argued at the beginning of this chapter, most of the variation in wage dispersion is across countries rather than over time. Therefore, we begin with the random effects estimations in models 2 and 5. Model 2 shows that the findings for union density, employment protection legislation, and trade openness for the 50-10 ratio shown in figure 2.1a are very robust. Model 5 shows that the findings for union density and regulation for the 90-50 ratio shown in figure 2.1b are very robust. The country fixed-effects estimations for the 50-10 ratio do show that EPL and trade openness explain variation over time (models 1 and 3). The EPL finding would appear to indicate that a weakening of temporary EPL did contribute to increasing inequality at the bottom end of the wage distribution. The country fixed-effects estimations for the 90-50 ratio do show that union density and trade openness explain variation over time. The union density effect supports the view that de-unionization contributed to increased wage dispersion in the upper half of the wage and salary distribution. The consistently negative effect of trade openness across all estimators is surprisingly strong evidence in support of Katzenstein's compensation hypothesis.

Discussion

Our analysis showed that two variables indicating labor strength—union density and wage coordination—were strongly negatively associated with wage dispersion both at the bottom and at the top. The same is true for regulation None of the other variables were highly significant for both parts of the income distribution. Thus, power and policy variables were more strongly and consistently associated with patterns of wage dispersion than were structural transformations of the economy and globalization.

Strong unions and high levels of wage coordination have been able to keep the bottom of the wage distribution from falling too far below the median and the top from rising too high above it. Strong unions are thus able to translate a commitment to solidarity into limits on wage dispersion. A high level of coordination of wage bargaining helps unions of any strength pursue the same goal. Another policy variable, employment protection legislation, was substantively very important for the bottom half. High levels of legal regulation of temporary work and of protection of permanent employees prevent the emergence of an underclass of poorly paid precarious workers.

Deregulation of the energy, transport, and communications sectors deserves additional discussion. While regulation is a policy and deregulation was a policy change, we have grouped the variable with structural transformations because we are dealing with a uniform trend largely initiated by technological change. Technological changes like cell phones and the emergence of private competitors to the postal service forced policy changes in these areas. In the European context, European Union rules put further pressures on governments to adopt uniform deregulation measures. Whereas liberal and coordinated political economies started with very different degrees of regulation in the 1960s, they ended up at essentially the same degree of deregulation by the 2000s. Partisanship did not play a role. As a result of widespread deregulation, secure and relatively well-paid public-sector jobs for low-skilled employees were lost and replaced by more precarious and poorly paid private-sector jobs for the low-skilled. This put pressure on remunerations at the 10th percentile. At the other end, privatization and competition based on technological advances increased the demand for and wages of highly skilled employees, which put upward pressure on remunerations at the 90th percentile.

The only other indicator of structural change in the economy that was significant in our final models was technological advance as indicated by the growth of total factor productivity. This indicator was positively associated with the 90-50 ratio. Technological change is another indicator of increasing demand for highly skilled workers, and commensurate upward pressure on wages at the top. Notably, the cluster of variables measuring structural change in the economy by themselves had little explanatory power for wage dispersion both at the bottom and at the top—explaining only 6 percent of the variation in the 50-10 ratio and 10 percent in the 90-50 ratio.

The same is true for the cluster of variables measuring globalization. By themselves, they explain only 4 percent of the variation in wage dispersion at the top and 14 percent of the variation at the bottom. The only variable that is significant in our final model is trade openness in the analysis of the 50-10 ratio. Trade openness here is positively associated with wage dispersion, suggesting downward pressure on wages of unskilled workers. It is not significant in the final model for the 90-50 ratio. Even for the 50-10 ratio, it has the weakest substantive impact among our significant variables.

In contrast, a strong public commitment to investment in human capital has considerable explanatory power for wage dispersion at both the top and the bottom of the wage distribution. This variable alone explains 25 percent of the variation in the 50-10 ratio and 18 percent in the 90-50 ratio. Once we introduce all the other variables in our final models, investment in human capital loses significance for wage dispersion at the bottom but remains significant for the top. If we assume that higher levels of investment in human capital—from early childhood education and care to preschool and school and on to labor market training and retraining—improve skills at all levels, we can conclude that better skills at the bottom pull up wages at the 10th percentile, and better and more abundant skills at the top keep wage pressures at the 90th percentile at moderate levels. It is important here to emphasize the public commitment. Not all sources of education expenditures have a moderating effect on inequality. Indeed, a high share of private education spending has a significant enhancing effect on the 50-10 and 90-50 ratios. This finding squares with Busemeyer's (2015) finding of the same effect on the Gini of household disposable income, Weisstanner and Armingeon's (2020) finding of the same effect on the education premium, and our finding on the effect of the private share of education spending on skills at the bottom (chapter 7, and Huber, Gunderson, and Stephens 2018).

The importance of investments in skills can be clearly seen in the cross-sectional analysis that includes the PIAAC scores, by far the best measure of the stock of skills of the adult population. Our analysis is suggestive and squares with Nickell's finding that the 95-5 skill ratio is actually a more statistically significant determinant of wage dispersion than are variations in labor market institutions. We find this to be true for the 90-50 wage ratio, and the skills distribution to be significant also in the case of the 50-10 wage ratio. The 95-5 skill ratio is driven by differences at the bottom: the correlation of numeracy scores at the 5th percentile and the 95-5 ratio is $-.93$. It is not surprising that the scores at the bottom are particularly high in countries that make large public investments in human capital, like the Nordic countries, and are particularly low in countries that do not, like the United States.

In sum, we have found some indication that structural transformations and globalization have tended to be associated with stronger wage dispersion. In particular, deregulation and trade openness have shown positive associations with wage dispersion at the bottom, and total factor productivity change and deregulation have shown positive associations with wage dispersion at the top. Shrinking numbers of public-sector jobs and increased trade competition have put pressure on the wages of the lowest-paid workers. Technological advances and deregulation have driven up wages at the upper end of the distribution.

However, we have also found that union density and wage coordination are strongly negatively associated with wage dispersion in both parts of the wage distribution, and that these variables have substantively stronger effects than do technological change and globalization. The problem is, of course, that union density has declined everywhere, as industrial and public-sector employment have shrunk and organizing workers in service-sector employment is very difficult. Still, great differences persist in the level of unionization across countries. Similarly, employers everywhere have pushed for the decentralization of collective bargaining and for exemption clauses. In the face of high levels of unemployment and in economic crisis situations unions tended to accept such exemption clauses, which weakened the reach and the protection offered by collective agreements.

Nevertheless, we are not dealing with an inexorable technological imperative. Governments have options to influence the distribution of market income, or pre-distribution. They can protect unionization efforts, promote bargaining coordination, and enhance employment protection, or they can make unionization difficult, promote decentralization of collective bargaining, and deregulate employment. In the former case, they will protect workers at the bottom from falling too far behind the middle, and keep workers at the top from leaving the middle too far behind. In the latter case, they will promote the opposite developments. As our case studies demonstrate, the former option has generally been preferred by left governments and the latter option by secular center and right governments, even though left governments also weakened employment protection in order to deal with unemployment.

Even with the shifting electoral base of left parties, consensus on these issues should not be too difficult to achieve. Both blue-collar and white-collar workers, routine workers and sociocultural professionals should see their common interest in the protection of unions, coordination of collective bargaining, and regulation of temporary work, given that all three factors contribute to moderating wage dispersion at both levels. Support for investment in human capital at all levels is another area of common interest. And a less unequal distribution of wages will take some redistributive pressure off the overburdened welfare state, where conflicts of interest are arguably more pronounced and are complicated by generational differences of interest.

CHAPTER THREE

Household Income Inequality

We began by analyzing wage dispersion, which is a measure of inequality in individual earnings from work, or market income. As noted, though, the experience of inequality for most people is shaped by the combined earnings of household members. Therefore, household composition and the volume of work performed by members of the household become additional important determinants of household income inequality. Moreover, the distribution of household income that is relevant for the lived experience of the members of the household is the distribution of disposable income. And for disposable income, the role of the state in the form of the tax and transfer system is crucial. Accordingly, in this chapter, we analyze household market income inequality, redistribution through the tax and transfer system, and household disposable income inequality for the working-age population.

As tables A.2 and A.4 show, both market and disposable income inequality increased in all four welfare state regimes distinguished in the comparative social policy literature. To be sure, some countries defied that trend, as one can see from the tables. Nevertheless, the overall trend is very clear: the correlation between time (year) and disposable income inequality is over .8 in six countries (Australia, Canada, Denmark, Finland, Germany, and the US); between .5 and .8 in seven more (Austria, Belgium, Italy, Netherlands, New Zealand, Norway, and the UK); not significant in Japan, Spain, Sweden, and Switzerland; and actually negative in France, Greece, Ireland, and Portugal.

We build and improve upon the analyses of Bradley et al. (2003) and Huber and Stephens (2014), two studies (and the only ones that we know of) that look at the determinants of disposable income inequality as a two-stage process, first examining the determinants of market income inequality and then examining the determinants of welfare state redistribution. We go beyond these previous studies in five major ways: First, we measure welfare state effort with social rights rather than expenditure. This allows us to separate the effect of policy from the underlying social risks, which jointly shape expenditure. Second, we bring the analysis up to date, covering some twenty more years than Bradley et al. and eight more years than Huber and Stephens, which allows us to compare our findings to those of the earlier studies. Third, we pool data from three sources—the Luxembourg Income Study (LIS), the Organisation for Economic Co-operation and Development (OECD), and Eurostat Statistics on Income and Living Conditions (SILC)—to almost three times the number of observations for analysis as Huber and Stephens, and four times the number in Bradley et al. Fourth, we leverage the much greater number of observations to test a broader range of possible determinants. Fifth, we use newer estimation techniques that deal better with serial correlation.

Theoretical Perspectives

Market Household Income Distribution

STRUCTURAL TRANSFORMATIONS IN THE ECONOMY AND GLOBALIZATION
We have already thoroughly discussed the impact of technological change—specifically SBTC, deregulation, and globalization—on domestic labor markets in the past few decades. We shall not revisit this discussion in detail here. Suffice it to remember that deindustrialization, SBTC, deregulation, and the growth of third world imports increased the demand for and the wages of skilled workers and decreased the demand for and wages of workers already at the low end of the income distribution, whereas immigration increased the supply of the latter (Wood 1994; Nam 2020; Acemoglu and Autor 2011; Emmenegger et al. 2012). Other aspects of globalization, such as capital market openness, outward direct foreign investment, and trade openness, have strengthened the hand of employers vis-à-vis labor through threats of outsourcing production. Employers have used their leverage to demand concessions on wages, working conditions, and bargaining arrangements. All these changes have had particularly negative effects on low-skilled workers and therefore have contributed to increasing inequality in earnings. Our variables and expected associations with the dependent variables are listed in table 3.1.

TABLE 3.1. **Variables and Hypotheses**

Dependent variables	Market income inequality	Redistribution
Market income inequality		
Redistribution		
Disposable income inequality		
Independent variables		
Power resources variables		
Left government	−	+
Union density	−	+
Wage coordination	−	
Employment protection legislation	−	
Contract coverage	−	
Minimum wage setting	−	
Works council rights	−	
Voter turnout		+
Other theories of redistribution		
Mean to median ratio		+
Proportional representation		+
Skew		+
Other political variables		
Christian democratic government		+/−
Women in parliament		+
Veto points		−/+
Long-term economic change		
Industrial employment	−	
Technological change	+	
Product market regulation	−	
Employment in dynamic services	+	
Policies		
Parental leave benefits		+
Social insurance generosity	+/−	+
Social assistance generosity	+/−	+
Globalization		
Third world imports	+	
Trade openness	+/−	+/−
Outward FDI	+	
Immigration	+	
Capital market openness	+	
Social risks		
Unemployment rate	+	+
% children in single-mother households	+	+
Employment	−	
Other		
Wage dispersion	+	
Human capital spending	−	
Average level of education	−	
Private share of education spending	+	

Variable definitions and sources in table A.1.

LABOR POWER AND LABOR MARKET INSTITUTIONS   As in chapter 2, we expect that the mobilization power of labor organizations (measured by union density) and institutional arrangements that guarantee labor representation, contract coverage, wage coordination, employment protection, and participation in minimum wage setting will be crucial factors in shaping the market household income distribution. We have shown that strong unions can lift up the bottom and restrain the top of the wage distribution, and we expect wage dispersion to be positively associated with household market income inequality. Another way in which unions can affect the income distribution is by mobilizing members to elect labor-friendly candidates. Social democratic parties in particular have historically implemented policies that are favored by their union partners. Here too, empirical findings suggest an egalitarian effect, especially at the bottom of the income distribution (Brady, Blome, and Kleider 2016).

CHANGING SOCIAL RISK STRUCTURE   Social risks refer to the economic and demographic factors that, by shaping the supply and demand for labor, determine workers' risk of displacement from the labor force. These risks, therefore, influence the volume of work that members of a household are likely to perform. Unemployment did not have a statistically significant effect on wage dispersion in our analyses, but it increases market income inequality among households by increasing the number of individuals with no market income. These cyclical dynamics are further compounded by the structural economic changes discussed above that have led to an increase in structural unemployment (Mocan 1999). Moreover, structural unemployment caused by increased skill obsolescence may in fact undercount the true number of unemployed individuals. For one thing, workers who ceased actively searching for work are not considered unemployed by most measures. Historic welfare policies that reclassified such displaced workers as retirees or disabled further led to an artificial reduction in the rate of unemployment (Ferrera 1996; Palier 2010). We therefore include measures of both employment and unemployment. High levels of employment in a society increase the probability that households will have more than one income earner, which provides a buffer against loss of earnings due to unemployment. Thus, whereas we expect high levels of unemployment to increase market household income inequality, we expect high levels of employment to have the opposite effect.

Household structure is another important predictor of market vulnerability. Demographic changes over the past few decades have increased the number of households led by a single parent, usually the mother, which are disproportionally at greater risk of poverty (Esping-Andersen 2003). One reason for this dynamic comes from the inability of single-parent households to compensate for a decrease or loss of income by increased employment (Kenworthy and Pontusson 2005). At the same time, single parents face greater difficulty in balancing their earnings and care responsibilities. Despite the common trend to outsource such activities to state or market actors, the high cost of such services in most countries hinders single parents' capacity for full or partial labor force participation and for skill acquisition (Orloff 2010). Finally, the very intersection of a pay gap and gendered households would produce greater income disparities. We therefore hypothesize that the proportion of single-mother households will be positively associated with market household income inequality.

POLICIES   So far, we have analyzed the impact of public and private education spending and the entirety of human capital spending on earnings inequality. We shall do so again with regard to the relationship between these policies and household market income inequality. Again, we expect strong public investment in education and the totality of spending from early childhood education and care through preschool, all levels of schooling, and training and retraining of adults to be associated with lower levels of inequality among households. We expect heavy reliance on private expenditure for education to show a statistically positive association with inequality. Heavy reliance on private education spending stratifies access to quality education and thus serves to reproduce income inequality intergenerationally. Strong public investment is crucial to enable more members of households to function better in the knowledge society. Investment in the education of children of all ages improves skill levels for young adults. In addition, increased access to early childhood education and care and to preschool can alleviate care responsibilities, increase employment, and, by doing so, decrease poverty rates (Hufkens et al. 2020). Active labor market policies serve to increase the productivity of workers at different career stages by investing in skills and market integration, unlike traditional social policies that preserve existing skills and earning levels through decommodification.

We shall also analyze the impact of the population's average level of education on household market income inequality. If we assume that higher average levels of education mean that workers at the bottom of the skill distribution have higher skills and that there are more workers at the top of the skill distribution, then wages at the bottom should be higher and wages at the top lower than in societies with lower average levels of education. In other words, the income distribution should be less unequal. Autor (2014) adds an additional, indirect mechanism through which education affects income distributions and shows that wage premiums are inversely associated with intergenerational mobility. This is far from surprising given that parental income and education are strongly correlated with workers' subsequent wages (Jencks 1972; Brady 2022). But Autor's point further implies that state support for mass education can dampen this effect by limiting the reproduction of unequal skill distributions. And indeed, public investment in education has a strong negative effect on both wage and skill disparities (Huber, Gunderson, and Stephens 2020).

Policy responses to the changing social risk structure just described are often classified as investment versus consumption or as relating to new versus old social risks (Beramendi et al. 2015; Armingeon and Bonoli 2007). While these dichotomies are at times tenuous due to the combined causal effects of most policies, it is nevertheless a helpful way to distinguish the main logics of different state efforts. In our analysis, we distinguish between social rights (which are the traditional welfare responses aimed at decommodification) and social investment policies (which serve to determine workers' skill levels and productivity).

"Social rights" refers to social transfers and regulations that under certain predefined conditions compensate individuals for withdrawal from the labor force or guarantee individuals and families a certain floor of income. These include the main social insurance policies that formed the basis of the postwar welfare state (Hicks 1999) and the totality of social assistance provided to individuals and families below certain income levels. Lacking suitable data, early studies of social rights relied on the expenditure-to-GDP ratio as a measure of the scope of state insurance. The problem with relying on expenditure data is that they reflect both generosity and risk, and the analyst cannot disentangle the two. Social rights data—indices that combine information on benefit levels and qualifying conditions—are unambiguous indicators of policy and thus are preferable to expenditure data. Such data have only been available for our set of countries in an annual time series since Scruggs put the first version of the Comparative Welfare Entitlements data in the public domain in 2004 (Scruggs and Tafoya 2022). We use Scruggs and Tafoya's (2022) index of generosity for sickness and unemployment compensation. For social assistance, we use the net minimum income benefit replacement rates provided by Wang and van Vliet (2016a). We analyze generosity of parental leave benefits separately, since taking parental leave is more often a choice, whereas getting sick, becoming unemployed, or being unable to earn a living wage are not.

The impact of policy generosity on market income has been a source of scholarly dispute. The orthodox economic approach in the "job search theory" views social insurance and social assistance as a form of moral hazard that disincentivizes workers from seeking employment. As a result, this frame expects generosity to increase unemployment, and consequently market inequality (OECD 1994b). The social policy literature and more recent economic scholarship take the opposite view and expect these policies to reduce market inequality by allowing individuals to refuse ill-suited positions, recover from illness, or avoid food insecurity or homelessness, thus helping to prevent scar effects during temporary spells of limited employment opportunities. Common to both views is the expectation that unemployment insurance increases workers' leverage in wage negotiations (Barth and Moene 2016).

Empirical findings generally lay somewhere between these two approaches, with the exact configuration playing a pivotal role. Arni, Lalive, and van Ours (2013) found that partial or full reductions in unemployment benefits lowered workers' subsequent wages. At the macro level, unemployment duration and replacement generosity have been linked to wage compression (Koeniger, Leonardi, and Nunziata 2007). Nelson and Stephens (2011) found that generosity of sickness benefits was related to higher employment levels. Farber and Valletta (2015) further found that extending the period of unemployment benefits did not increase the duration of unemployment; rather, it delayed people from exiting the workforce entirely. Overall, when combined with generous benefits, the duration of eligibility for unemployment insurance follows a nonlinear trajectory: whereas generous benefits of medium duration avoid scar effects of unemployment and thus are associated with higher levels of employment, very long duration of benefits is associated with lower levels of employment (Bradley and Stephens 2007).[1]

The expansion of minimum income schemes has been closely tied to activation. In fact, the very name of these schemes in many cases reflects that idea. For instance, the Spanish scheme was named Renta Mínima de Inserción, or Minimum Insertion Income, to reflect the intent of social integration, which entailed integration into the labor market. Typically, behavioral requirements are often stringent with regard to seeking and accepting employment. Also, as the number of working poor has increased, more social assistance has been going to working people. Accordingly, one would not expect any negative effects on employment.

Work-life reconciliation strategies have been one of the main areas of policy innovation in the past two decades. Rising female employment rates and changing family structures imposed new earnings responsibilities on working-age women, in the face of resilient gendered care expectations. With half of the working-age population at risk of partially or fully exiting the labor market due to this burden, various state responses yielded different rates of female participation and income inequality (Esping-Andersen 2003). The structure of parental leave benefits in particular proved pivotal for female participation and income levels in a manner analogous to traditional social insurance policies. Here too, studies have shown that policy designs involving unpaid, overly brief or overly long periods of leave suppress the rate of female participation (Jenson 2009; Gingrich and Ansell 2015; Thévenon and Solaz 2013). Inegalitarian leave policies targeting mothers but not fathers have further been argued to generate employment and qualification gaps for working women, thereby encouraging working parents to adopt a neoconservative career path with partial female employment (Pedulla and Thébaud 2015). Parental leave of at least six months with a high replacement rate and incentives for both parents to share the leave have the most egalitarian impact on women's work and pay trajectories in the long run. In the short run, of course, generous parental leave is likely to increase market household income inequality, because the parent on leave will have no pre-transfer income.

WAGE DISPERSION To comparative political economists not intimately familiar with the data analyzed in this book, it might seem almost tautological to hypothesize a (causal) relationship between wage dispersion and market household income inequality. In fact, the correlation between the 90-10 wage ratio and the market household income Gini is modest, .53, which is a tribute to the importance of the household composition, economic cycles, and long-term economic change factors discussed above. Nevertheless, we do expect a positive relationship between wage dispersion and market household income inequality.

Redistribution through the Welfare State

We now turn to determinants of redistribution (that is, the difference between pre- and post-tax and transfer income inequality as a percentage of pre- inequality). Redistribution then is a function of the social risks affecting market incomes and the adequacy of policy efforts to compensate for these risks. There is strong evidence that redistribution is directly connected to the magnitude of welfare state effort (Bradley et al. 2003; Huber and Stephens 2014). If we assume that the level of welfare state effort remains constant, then higher levels of social risk will result in more redistribution. We therefore expect the level of unemployment and percentage of children in single-mother households to result in more redistribution. By the same token, factors that lower social risks by increasing the probability of a second earner in the household cushioning reduction of household income, such as high levels of employment, will result in less redistribution. Again, our hypotheses regarding redistribution are summarized in table 3.1.

We use social insurance generosity and social assistance benefits, conceptualized and measured as social rights, to explore the extent of redistribution, whereas past work has mostly used welfare state expenditure (see for example Bradley et al. 2003). Social rights determine the size of and criteria for transfers and for access to services. Since our measures of pre- and post-tax and transfer household income only measure monetary income, we do not capture the value of services. We shall come back to this issue in the conclusion. Suffice it to say here that access to free or subsidized public services increases redistribution. To capture social rights affecting the redistribution of income among the working-age population, we consider the generosity of benefits workers receive when they lose income due to unemployment and sickness or when they are unable to earn a sufficient income. There is also evidence that generous parental leave benefits lower disposable income poverty, thus plausibly increasing redistribution. Misra, Moller, and Budig (2007) found that family allowances, generous parental leaves, and childcare provision lowered poverty among mothers and that the effect was particularly strong among *single* mothers. They further found that parental leave and childcare provision boosted maternal employment. We therefore expect social insurance generosity toward working-age people (that is, generosity of unemployment and sickness insurance), generosity of social assistance, and parental leave policies to be positively correlated with redistribution. All three of these components contribute to overall welfare state generosity.

Welfare state generosity is the outcome of a political process and is largely a function of partisan politics, since these benefit structures and institutions are typically built up and entrenched by governments over long periods of time. Civil society organizations, specifically organized labor, here take a secondary role to the political actors and institutions that may or may not be supportive of their goals. Nevertheless, civil society organizations on both sides, labor and capital, have profoundly shaped the fortunes of political parties, and they have shaped policies by exerting pressures on political actors. The historical development of the welfare state demonstrates that incumbent social democratic, Christian democratic, and liberal parties left distinct legacies with respect to both their social legislation and their redistributive patterns (Esping-Andersen 1990; Huber and Stephens 2001; Hicks 1999). Left parties in particular have long been strong supporters of redistribution and egalitarianism, and left partisanship is associated with lower levels of poverty and inequality (Brady 2009; Nelson 2012; Huber and Stephens 2014). Christian democratic parties have traditionally also strongly supported the welfare state (Huber and Stephens 2001; van Kersbergen 1995). However, they have historically valued egalitarianism less than social democratic parties have (Esping-Andersen 1990); they have been primarily concerned with poverty and the welfare of children. In two previous analyses we found that Christian democratic government was associated with *less* redistribution (Bradley et al. 2003; Huber and Stephens 2014). Therefore, we adopt a nondirectional hypothesis. Finally, a variable that figures prominently in many studies and can also be regarded as an indicator of working-class power is voter turnout. Kenworthy and Pontusson (2005, 459) argue that voter turnout is a proxy for electoral mobilization of low-income workers and conditions the responsiveness of government policy to market income inequality trends. Therefore, we expect voter turnout to be positively associated with redistribution.

Partisan differences have also shaped policy responses to new social risks. While social democratic parties were early adopters of gender-egalitarian policies, the religious Right remained tethered to the male breadwinner model for quite some time (Orloff 2010). One of the key contributing factors to this differentiation came from the feminization of the electorate and of party ranks, which generally skewed leftward. The need to attract female voters, though, eventually motivated Christian democratic parties to adopt more women-friendly policies as well (Morgan 2013). Beyond partisan politics, female legislators have been shown to have distinct agendas, placing greater importance on social policies and welfare issues than do their male counterparts (Wängnerud 2000; Little, Dunn, and Deen 2001). Female participation at different levels of government has further been linked to the expansion of various social policies including childcare (Bratton and Ray 2002) and parental leave (Atchison and Down 2009). Accordingly, we expect female representation as well as a stronger history of left government incumbency to be associated with more redistribution. Further, and in line with earlier work (Bradley et al. 2003; Huber and Stephens 2014), we expect this to hold true even when the various types of benefit generosity are held constant, since one cannot capture the full profile of benefit structure and institutions via generosity measures alone.

Arguably the most influential theory in the literature on redistribution is the one developed by Meltzer and Richard (1981), hereafter referred to as MR. They argue that a greater difference between the mean and the median income will result in bigger government and thus more redistribution, because the voter with median income is decisive under majority rule. Thus, redistribution is a function of the degree of inequality: the greater the degree of inequality of market income, the greater the degree of redistribution. This assumption runs directly counter to an understanding of policy as a result of power and interests as well as of a positive relationship between economic and political power. Nevertheless, since we are testing their theory, we are adopting their hypothesis of a positive relationship.

The partisanship explanation, which highlights the role of left parties in promoting redistribution, is basically a variant of Power Resources Theory (PRT). PRT predicts that the relationship between market income inequality and redistribution is precisely the opposite of what MR predict; greater market income inequality will be associated with lower redistribution. According to PRT, strong unions result in lower levels of market income inequality and also in longer periods of left government, which in turn results in larger and more redistributive welfare states. PRT also hypothesizes a direct causal link between market income inequality and (less) redistribution; more material resources concentrated at the top will translate into more political influence concentrated at the top.

Lupu and Pontusson (2011) propose a hypothesis focusing on the structure of inequality rather than its magnitude. They argue that the extent of redistribution is determined by the "skew" of the market income distribution: the distance between the middle and the poor in relation to the distance between the middle and the rich. The intuition behind this model is that greater income proximity between social classes will lead to an affinity with respect to their redistributive expectations. If the distance between the middle and the poor (the 50-10 earnings ratio) is smaller than the distance between the middle and the rich (the 90-50 earnings ratio), the middle class will have greater affinity to the poor and will consequently support redistribution. We test their hypothesis and therefore accept their prediction of a positive relationship.

Political institutions shape the policy-making process and its outcomes. Immergut's (1992) veto-points framework drew attention to how institutional structures could delay social policy expansion at the height of the Golden Age by giving minority actors sufficient intervention points to block such expansion. By the time of retrenchment the relationship grew more complex, with the same mechanisms now being used not just to block cuts to popular policies (Pierson 2001), but also to facilitate drift that reduced policy efficacy (Hacker 2005). Therefore, we adopt a nondirectional hypothesis.

Iversen and Soskice (2006) have argued that proportional representation (PR) electoral systems result in more frequent left government and more redistribution. Their reasoning is that if the middle classes have to decide between left and right in a majoritarian system, before an election they will choose the Right in order to prevent a situation where the Left taxes the rich and the middle classes to finance redistribution to the working class. In contrast, in PR systems, lower, middle, and upper classes vote for the parties that represent their interests, and after the elections the parties conclude coalition agreements. In these coalition negotiations, representatives of the middle classes can prevent that kind of situation and may form a coalition with the Left to tax the rich and redistribute to the middle and working classes. We adopt their hypothesis of a positive association between PR systems and redistribution.

Finally, we include the globalization variables that have been linked to welfare state generosity and thus redistribution. High levels of immigration have tended to generate anti-welfare state sentiments, or at least welfare state chauvinism—that is, attitudes that see social rights as rightfully extending to citizens only (Magni 2021). Capital market openness has been linked to welfare state generosity via financial constraints due to tax competition. Easy and quick movement of capital across borders has made it more difficult for governments to tax corporations and high-income individuals, and thus has restricted revenue available for welfare state expenditures. Outward foreign direct investment and imports from the third world also work against taxation and redistribution, as they increase the leverage of corporations vis-à-vis both governments and workers. The effects of trade openness are disputed in the literature. Katzenstein (1985) argued early on that governments in small, trade-open states were likely to compensate workers for the risks of unemployment resulting from exposure to foreign markets. More recent literature has emphasized the race to the bottom in wages and benefits generated by high exposure to world markets (Wood 1994). Accordingly, we expect the first four globalization variables to be associated with less redistribution, and we adopt a nondirectional hypothesis for trade openness.

Disposable Household Income Distribution

We expect disposable household income inequality (and poverty, the subject of chapter 5) to be shaped by a combination of the factors that shape market income distribution and redistribution through the tax and transfer system. However, a comparison of differences in market income inequality and poverty between countries (tables A.2 and A.5) with differences in redistributive efforts between countries (tables A.3 and A.6) shows that the differences in redistributive efforts are greater. This suggests that redistributive efforts will be more powerful in shaping the disposable household income distribution. Accordingly, we expect our policy variables, above all social insurance generosity, to have the strongest effects on disposable household income inequality and poverty. Empirically, we proceed by including all the variables that are significant in our final models for market income distribution and redistribution in our model for disposable household income distribution.

Data, Measurement, and Statistical Estimation

The main dependent variables here are the Gini index of market income inequality of individual working-age people, with or without children, nested inside households; redistribution effected by direct taxes and transfers among these households; and inequality in disposable income for those same people. We define working age as including those aged eighteen to sixty-four years old. As noted, we omit all households with elderly members, as this would exaggerate the market inequality rates in countries with generous pension systems. The reason we drop all households with elderly members rather than just households "headed" by the elderly is that it is not possible with the data we have to tell which household member is the "head" of household. We do not drop households on the basis of the presence of children.

Our measure of redistribution is calculated as the Gini of market income inequality minus the Gini of disposable household income inequality divided by the Gini of market income inequality. Again, our operationalization of the variables and the explanation of the harmonization of the data series are discusses in appendix C.

Our statistical estimation is the same as in the previous chapters: Vernby and Lindgren's (2009) dvgreg package for dynamic panel data models.

Results

Our statistical estimation, represented in table 3.2, shows our nine models for household market income inequality. Again, we enter our independent variables in theoretical clusters—politics and labor market institutions, wage dispersion (a result of politics and labor market institutions), structural economic changes, social rights, globalization, social risks, and education—and we carry the significant variables forward to the combined models 8 and 9.

In model 1, union density, wage coordination, and union participation in minimum wage setting are all significant and working in the predicted direction. In model 2, one of the results of these variables, the 90-10 wage ratio, is highly significant and positive. All of our variables indicating structural change in the economy in model 3 are significant and correctly signed. The same is true for two of our social rights variables in model 4; generosity of unemployment and sickness compensation along with generosity of social assistance are significantly and negatively associated with market income inequality. In model 5, capital market openness and third world imports are significant and correctly signed. All three social risk variables are correctly signed but the level of employment is not significant in model 6. Human capital shows a significant negative association in model 7.

In model 8, wage dispersion remains highly significant and positive, as one would expect. Union density and wage coordination flip their signs, but they become insignificant with more observations in model 9. Industrial employment is significant and negative, indicating that deindustrialization is associated with higher levels of inequality. The same holds for

TABLE 3.2. **Predictors of Market Income Inequality**

	Model 1	Model 2	Model 3	Model 4	Model 5	Model 6	Model 7	Model 8	Model 9
Left government	.064							.051	-.001
Union density	-.054***							1.051<	-.313
Wage coordination	-.783***								
Contract coverage	.002								
Employment protection legislation	-.284							.206***	-1.295***
Minimum wage setting	-.510*			-.002					
Works council rights	0.050			-.233					
Wage dispersion		2.679***						3.414***	
Industrial employment			-.253***					-.374**	-.044
Technological change			95.269**					-18.334***	106.944***
Regulation			-.609***					-.366**	-1.453***
Employment in dynamic services			.318***					.379	
Parental leave benefits								.046	-.014
Social insurance generosity									

TABLE 3.2. (continued)

	Model 1	Model 2	Model 3	Model 4	Model 5	Model 6	Model 7	Model 8	Model 9
Social assistance generosity									
Capital market openness				−.063**				−.037	−.107
Outward FDI					1.609***				
Trade openness					−.010			−1.518	
Third world imports					−.001				
Immigration					.231**			−.453^	−.094
Unemployment rate						.332***		.371***	.396***
% children in single-mother households						.777***			
Employment						−.040		−.037	−.024
Human capital spending							−.540***	−.774***	−.346**
Average level of education							.594^		
Constant	44.472***	31.910***	42.122***	47.549***	35.661***	30.257***	37.005***	36.767***	46.318***
Adjusted R²	.18***	.28***	.38***	.25***	.07***	.28***	.09***	.61	.48***
Observations	436	370	221	220	432	457	372	125	368

Models 8 and 9 contain period indicators.
* Significant at .05; ** Significant at .01; *** significant at .001; ^ significant opposite hypothesized direction.

regulation: deregulation is associated with higher levels of inequality. Employment in dynamic services is significant and positive, indicating that higher levels of demand for highly skilled workers increase inequality. Unemployment also shows a significant positive association with inequality, as expected. Finally, human capital spending is negatively associated with inequality, confirming that a better human capital base can moderate inequality.

In model 9 we drop wage dispersion, employment in dynamic services, and social assistance generosity because they are only available for a restricted number of country years. As a result, we almost triple the number of observations, and several independent variables become statistically significant. Regulation, unemployment, and human capital spending show the same associations as in model 8. Union participation in minimum wage setting is significantly and negatively associated with inequality, indicating that unions are able to keep the wage floor from falling too low if they are included in setting the minimum wage. Technological change—an alternative indicator to employment in dynamic services for structural economic changes—becomes significant in the expected direction. A second social risk variable, overall levels of employment, becomes significant and is negatively associated with inequality because a higher level of employment increases the probability of higher volumes of work being performed by households.

Figure 3.1a shows the substantive strength of our significant variables from model 9, measured as the effect of a two-standard-deviation change in the independent variable on the dependent variable. Clearly the strongest variable is regulation, indicating that deregulation of the energy, transport, and communication sectors had a major impact on market income inequality. A two-standard-deviation change in regulation is the difference between regulation in Germany in 1995 and 2005; in those ten years the regulation index dropped from 3.8 to 1.2. A similar drop occurred in Sweden from 1991 (index value 4.0) to 2013 (index value 1.4). Such a drop was associated with an increase in the Gini of close to 4 points. The next most important variable is the level of unemployment. A two-standard-deviation difference is 8 percent, which corresponds to the difference between unemployment in Sweden in 2015 (7 percent) and Spain in 2018 (15 percent). This difference is associated with a Gini more than 3 points higher. A two-standard-deviation difference in the index of union participation in wage setting is 1.7 (rounded to 2, since the index is measured in whole numbers), which is the difference between the United

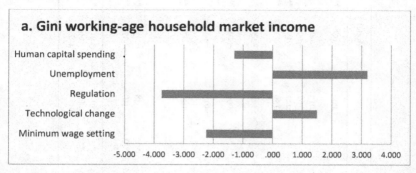
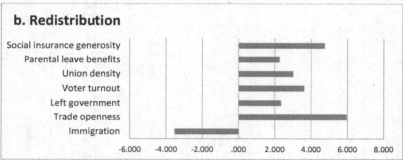
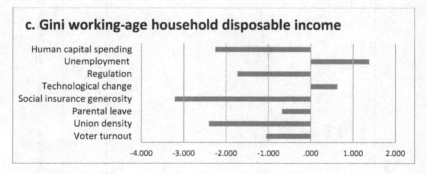

FIGURE 3.1. Effect of two-standard-deviation change in significant independent variables on inequality and redistribution

States and Spain before 1980 (index of 1) and Spain since 1980, as well as Germany and Sweden (indices of 3). This difference is associated with a Gini more than 2 points lower.

Table 3.3 contains our seven models for redistribution. Again, we enter the variables in theoretically meaningful clusters—power resources

TABLE 3.3. **Predictors of Redistribution**

	Model 1		Model 2		Model 3		Model 4		Model 5		Model 6		Model 7	
Left government	.069	*									.006		.088	**
Christian democratic government	.033										-.013		.002	
Women in parliament	.121	**									-.162		-.096	
Veto points	-.562	**									.222	***	.151	***
Voter turnout	.093	**									.156	***	.075	***
Union density	.137	***												
Mean to median ratio			-38.462	^										
Proportional representation			3.551	***							-2.120	^	-2.810	^
Skew			2.274											
Immigration					-.494	***					-.090		-.295	***
Capital market openness					.482						-.013		-.041	
Outward FDI					-.092	**								
Third world imports					-.064						.041	*	.079	***
Trade openness					.119	***								
Unemployment rate							-.083							
% children in single-mother households							.245							
Employment							-.039							
Parental leave benefits									.067	***	.048	***	.038	***
Social insurance generosity									.548	***	.416	***	.379	***
Social assistance generosity									.181	***	-.072	^		
Constant	10.857	***	62.997	***	22.917	***	26.476	***	4.674	*	-.610		3.916	*
Adjusted R²	.47	***	.42	***	.33	***	.00		.46	***	.66	***	.66	***
Observations	457		348		432		478		220		220		427	

Models 6 and 7 contain period indicators.
* Significant at .05; ** significant at .01; *** significant at .001; ^ significant opposite hypothesized direction.

and political institutions, the alternate hypotheses on redistribution, globalization, social risks, and social rights—and we carry the significant variables forward to the combined models. In model 1 all the power resources (union density, left government, and voter turnout) and political institutional variables except for Christian democratic government are significant in the expected direction, and together they explain close to half of the variation.[2] In model 2, which tests the alternative theories of redistribution, only proportional representation (the variable central to Iversen and Soskice's argument) is significant and correctly signed. In model 3, immigration and outward FDI are significantly and negatively associated with redistribution, in contrast to trade openness which is positively associated with redistribution. The three indicators of welfare state generosity in model 5 are all significant and explain almost half of the variation in redistribution. In the combined model 6, left government, women in parliament, and veto points lose significance. Voter turnout and union density remain significant in the predicted direction, just like generosity of social insurance and parental leave benefits. This suggests that political mobilization and union strength can pressure any kind of government and any parliament to adopt a variety of redistributive measures that are not captured by our indicators of social rights. Social assistance generosity no longer works in the hypothesized direction. Trade openness keeps its significance in a positive direction. In model 7, we drop social assistance generosity in order to double the number of observations. The results remain the same with two exceptions: left government and immigration reach significance again in the expected directions, suggesting that left parties in power do more to advance redistribution than pass generous social insurance and parental leave benefits, and that immigration does present an obstacle to redistribution.

Figure 3.1b, which is based on model 7 in table 3.3, shows that trade openness had by far the strongest substantive effect on redistribution. A two-standard-deviation change in trade openness effected a 6 percent reduction in the Gini. The differences in trade openness between countries are greater than differences over time within countries. A two-standard-deviation change corresponds to the difference between the United States in 1973 (imports and exports accounting for 13 percent of GDP) and Sweden in 2019 (90 percent of GDP) or Sweden in 1996 (67 percent of GDP) and the Netherlands in 2011 (142 percent of GDP). Generosity of social insurance for the working age and immigration had the next strongest effects, the former supporting and the latter working against redistribution.

TABLE 3.4. **Predictors of Disposable Income Inequality (Working-Age Population)**

	Model 1		Model 2	
Immigration	−.073		−.022	
Trade openness	−.009		−.002	
Left government	.410	^	.027	
Voter turnout	−.009		−.044	***
Union density	−.020		−.058	***
Parental leave	−.001		−.011	**
Social insurance generosity	−.149	**	−.257	***
Wage dispersion	2.231	***		
Minimum wage setting			.046	
Industrial employment	−.304	***		
Technological change			44.972	**
Regulation	−.099		−.662	***
Employment in dynamic services	−.105			
Unemployment rate	−.171		.173	***
Human capital spending	−.972	***	−.580	***
Constant	41.679	***	44.084	***
Adjusted R²	.86	***	.81	***
Observations	154		361	

All models contain period indicators.
* Significant at .05; ** significant at .01; *** significant at .001; ^ significant opposite hypothesized direction.

A two-standard-deviation change in generosity corresponds to the difference between Spain in 2012 (index of 18) and Sweden in 1993 (index of 30.5), or Spain in 2006 (peak of generosity with index of 22) and the United States in 2015 (index of 9.5). Such a difference was associated with a close to 5 percent reduction of the Gini. Union density, voter turnout, and left government, along with parental leave benefits, also had noticeable substantive effects, reducing the Gini by roughly 2.5 to 3.5 percent.

Table 3.4 shows the results of our analysis of household disposable income inequality. We took all the significant variables from our analyses of market income inequality and redistribution, specifically from models 8 and 9 in table 3.2 and model 6 in table 3.3. In model 1 we have all the significant variables from model 8 in table 3.2, but we lose too many observations, so in model 2 we have the significant variables from model 9 in table 3.2, where we dropped the variables responsible for the loss of observations. In model 1, social insurance generosity, wage dispersion, industrial employment, and human capital spending are all significant and correctly signed. Wage dispersion, industrial employment, and human capital spending all shape market income distribution, and generosity of social insurance is the key to redistribution. In model 2, generosity of social insurance and human capital spending remain significant, and in the absence of the variable wage dispersion, the factors that shape it—union density and regulation—become significant. In addition, the two political and policy variables of voter turnout and parental leave benefits become significant, as does the social risk factor of unemployment.

Figure 3.1c, the third one in the panel, demonstrates the substantive importance of our variables for disposable income inequality. We can see that social insurance generosity has by far the biggest impact, reducing the Gini for disposable household income inequality by more than 3 Gini points. It is followed by union density and two more policy variables: human capital spending and regulation. Unemployment is the next most important variable. Voter turnout and parental leave benefits follow next, reducing the Gini by 1 point or less, whereas technological change has an opposite effect of similar magnitude. We have provided examples above for a two-standard-deviation change in generosity of social insurance. Looking at union density, a two-standard-deviation difference corresponds to the difference between Germany in 2000 (24.6 percent of employed wage and salary earners organized) and Sweden in 2009 (64.2 percent organized). Such a difference is associated with a roughly 3-point lower Gini.

Finally, in table 3.5 we explore the question of whether the dynamics of disposable income inequality have changed over time. We analyze the time periods up to 2000 and after 2000 separately. We include all the significant variables from model 2 in table 3.4. Of course, we have many

TABLE 3.5. **Predictors of Disposable Income Inequality (Working-Age Population) by Period**

	Pre-2001		Post-2000	
	Model 1		Model 2	
Voter turnout	−.007		−.046	***
Union density	−.055	***	−.048	***
Parental leave	−.009		−.005	
Social insurance generosity	−.306	***	−.213	***
Technological change	37.882		72.242	***
Regulation	−.265		−.811	***
Unemployment rate	−.083		.198	***
Human capital spending	−.666	***	−.450	***
Constant	42.068	***	42.190	***
Adjusted R²	.82	***	.76	***
Observations	111		278	

All models contain period indicators.
* Significant at .05; ** significant at .01; *** significant at .001; ^ significant opposite hypothesized direction.

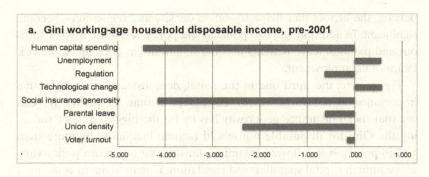

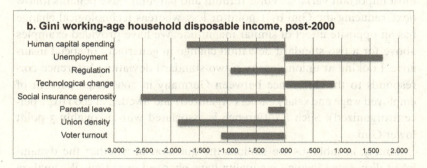

FIGURE 3.2. Effect of two-standard-deviation change in significant independent variables on disposable income inequality by period

fewer observations in the earlier period (111 compared to 278), so we have to compare the results with caution. Nevertheless, we observe a suggestive pattern that will also reappear in our analysis of poverty over time and that finds support in the evidence from our case studies. In the earlier period, only three variables are significant: union density, generosity of unemployment and sickness benefits, and human capital spending, all with a depressing effect on inequality. They remain significant in the second period as well, and in that period voter turnout, regulation, and unemployment also have significant effects. Unemployment emerges in the second period with a significant positive effect on disposable income inequality.

In figure 3.2 we plot the substantive effect of all the variables, not just those that are significant. In the earlier period, the three significant variables also have the strongest substantive effects: human capital spending had the largest, followed by generosity of unemployment and sickness benefits and then union density. In the post-2000 period, generosity of benefits retains the strongest effect, with human capital spending, union density, and unemployment tied for second. Unemployment was not significant and had a minimal substantive impact on inequality in the earlier period, but emerges as close to union density and human capital spending in substantive importance in the second period, driving up inequality. We interpret this to indicate that in the earlier period generosity of unemployment compensation managed to neutralize the impact of unemployment on inequality, but in the later period the problem pressure was greater than the welfare state response.

Table E.3 shows that human capital spending, unemployment, industrial employment, and regulation have significant effects on market household income in all alternative statistical estimations. Union density and social insurance generosity have significant effects on redistribution in all specifications, while parental leave generosity has significant effects on redistribution in the fixed effects and random effects estimations. Human capital spending, social insurance generosity, and voter turnout have significant effects on disposable household income inequality in all alternative estimations. In addition, union density and unemployment have significant effects in the random effects model, but since disposable income inequality varies primarily across countries, these independent variables should probably be considered robust as well.

Discussion

The pattern that emerges from our analyses of market income inequality, redistribution, and disposable income inequality underlines the importance of policies, labor strength, and the politics that shape unmeasured policies. Figure 3.1 nicely illustrates this pattern. Three policies appear as crucial: By far the substantively strongest variable predicting disposable household income inequality is the generosity of unemployment and sickness compensation, and it is also second in importance in driving redistribution. As noted, this result is highly robust for different estimation techniques. A generous welfare state that protects its population from loss of income due to unemployment and sickness is the most important defense against high levels of inequality. Deregulation of key economic sectors shows the strongest substantive effect on higher market inequality and an effect that is fourth in importance in predicting disposable household income inequality. Higher human capital spending is associated with lower market income inequality, and powerfully so with lower disposable household income inequality. Again, the results for deregulation and for human capital spending are highly robust. The debate about the extent to which deregulation was a real political choice or was forced upon governments by the disappearance of natural monopolies is ongoing, but the fact is that all countries underwent massive deregulation. The case for political choice in the amount of spending on human capital is clear. Our final significant policy variable, parental leave benefits, has the predicted effects on redistribution and disposable household income inequality. We shall explore the politics that produce generous social insurance, parental leave, and human capital investment policies in chapter 6.

Unions influence all three dependent variables. Union density has a strong and highly robust positive impact on redistribution and a strong negative impact on disposable income distribution. Union participation in minimum wage setting strongly moderates market income inequality. We demonstrated the highly robust and substantively important impact of union density on the 90-50 wage dispersion in chapter 2. Our findings here further underline the crucial role played by unions in shaping income distribution in an egalitarian manner. Finally, two political variables contribute to shaping redistribution and disposable household income—voter turnout and left government. Voter turnout is significantly and importantly associated with redistribution and with lower disposable household income inequality, even with generosity of social insurance, parental leave benefits, and human capital spending held constant. We interpret this as an indication that governments under pressure from mobilized lower-class voters pursue other measures to moderate inequality. Left government also retains a significant effect on redistribution, even with social rights held constant. We will show in chapter 6 that left government has a strong effect on all three policy variables: social insurance generosity, parental leave, and spending on human capital.

The social risk of unemployment shapes both market and disposable income distribution. Higher levels of unemployment are associated with higher income inequality both before and after taxes and transfers. As we have shown in our analysis of the two different periods, the result for disposable income inequality is powered by the situation in the more recent period. Welfare states have become less effective in compensating for higher levels of unemployment.

Technological change is only significantly associated with market income distribution, and the effect is substantively weak. This weak effect of technological change suggests that the consequences of structural changes in the economies for disposable household income inequality are counteracted to a large extent by policies such as investment in human capital and welfare state generosity. To the extent that the consequences of structural changes in the economies entail higher levels of unemployment, though, they have had an indirect effect on higher disposable income inequality since 2000.

Among our indicators of globalization, trade openness and immigration are significant only for redistribution. However, their effects are substantively strong. Surprisingly, trade openness has the strongest substantive effect; a two-standard-deviation change in openness increases redistribution by some 6 percent. Immigration is tied with voter turnout for third in importance, behind social insurance generosity, but working in the opposite direction. The effect of trade openness on redistribution is clearly driven by the small European countries, the Nordic countries, the Netherlands, Belgium, and Austria, joined in the most recent period by Ireland. They all have long had highly open economies and generous welfare states. The only outlier is Switzerland, with very high trade openness but a very weak redistributive effort.

Surprisingly, our other indicator of social rights, social assistance generosity, while highly significant in the regression on redistribution when entered without variables other than social rights indicators, did not remain significant in our combined models. One possible interpretation is that the reason may be a combination of the number of people and the generosity of benefits. The countries that rely heavily on means-tested social assistance also tend to have liberal residual welfare states, where social assistance benefits are low and thus not very effective in reducing inequality. The countries with more comprehensive welfare states and more generous social assistance also tend to have more services to support people's integration into the labor market and thus into universal and social insurance-based programs, so that fewer people are relying on social assistance.

CHAPTER FOUR
Top Income Shares of National Income

In this chapter and the next we shall focus on dynamics at the top and the bottom of the income distribution, respectively. Both these dynamics contributed to the overall increase in inequality, to different degrees in different countries. In this chapter we shall ask what accounts for the steep rise in the share of the top 1 percent of income earners in some countries and for restraints on this rise in others. We shall argue that the increase in stock market capitalization and in reliance on stock options for executive compensation were drivers of the increase in the top 1 percent share, and that the overall decline in union density facilitated it. We shall demonstrate the importance of various dimensions of labor power in restraining the share of the top 1 percent. We shall also emphasize policies and the politics driving them. Thus, we shall again highlight the explanatory power of PRT.

The growth of incomes at the very top has attracted much political and academic attention in recent years. The "Occupy Wall Street" movement has politicized the steeply rising income shares of the top 1 percent of income earners in the United States. In academics, the debate was fueled by the monumental data collection efforts of Thomas Piketty and his colleagues, who assembled a large comparative and historical database on the top income shares in almost all current postindustrial democracies as well as a number of other countries (Alvaredo et al. 2015; Atkinson 2005; Atkinson and Piketty 2007 and 2010; Piketty 2001 and 2003). This scholarly work was crowned by the publication of Piketty's *Capital in the Twenty-First Century* (2014), which became a worldwide best seller.

Atkinson, Piketty, and Saez (2011) note that the rise in top incomes is primarily an Anglo-American phenomenon, a view supported by figure A.1.

There is some increase in top incomes in a number of other countries, so a complete account would explain these modest increases as well as the sharp increase in the Anglo-American countries. When we first began to work on the rise of top income shares with Jingjing Huo in 2015 (Huber, Huo, and Stephens 2015, updated as Huber, Huo, and Stephens 2019), to our knowledge there were only two pooled time-series analyses of the determinants of the top income shares, and neither of these focused on the recent rise in top income shares (Scheve and Stasavage 2009; Roine, Vlachos, and Waldenström 2009). In this chapter we revisit our earlier analysis, restructuring the quantitative analysis of the determinants of top 1 percent income shares to make it comparable to the other pooled time-series analyses of inequality in this book. We think that the past half-century merits close examination not just because it saw the tremendous increase in top income shares, but also because it has been the period of globalization and transition to the knowledge economy—transformations that figure prominently in economic explanations of the rise of the top 1 percent share (Hager 2021).

We build on the literature on inequality in advanced industrial democracies outlined in chapter 1, keeping in mind that the share of the top 1 percent is a special case that may not have determinants identical to those of Gini coefficients, poverty, or wage ratios (e.g., Bradley et al. 2003; Brady 2009; Huber and Stephens 2014; Brady and Leicht 2008; Pontusson, Rueda, and Way 2002; Wallerstein 1999). Nevertheless, political power distributions and institutions that have been shown to shape household income distribution and wage dispersion can be expected also to shape the top 1 percent share. Our insistence on politics, labor market institutions, and policies as explanations for the growing concentration of wealth at the top of the income distribution is an important corrective to a number of economic theories that explain and essentially justify the rise of the top 1 percent share with reference to the presumably rising productivity of top managers (see for example Kaplan and Rauh 2013). We find little evidence supporting these explanations.

We agree with Soskice (2014, 661), who argues that an account of the rise of the top income shares has to begin with an account of why the Anglo-American countries stand out in that respect. Thus, we begin with an examination of the political economies of the Anglo-American compared to the Nordic and continental European countries. These are liberal market economies, in contrast to the coordinated market economies in continental and northern Europe. They have undergone particularly steep declines in union density, have labor market institutions that do not extend contracts to non-union members, and have neglected investment in public education.

Based on our PRT framework, we expect strong unions, high levels of wage coordination, and a high level of union contract coverage to constitute checks on the rise of the 1 percent share. In contrast, we expect center-right incumbency to be associated with a larger share of income going to the top 1 percent, because center-right governments pass policies that support income concentration at the top, such as low marginal tax rates and deregulation. We shall indeed show that union density, wage coordination, and contract coverage, along with the partisan composition of government and policies like marginal tax rates, are the crucial determinants of the top 1 percent share, trumping economic developments like globalization and the transition to the knowledge economy. The distribution of income is an inherently political issue. Explanations based on economic laws like supply and demand determining the price, or in this case the supply and demand of talent shaping the top 1 percent share, ignore the fact that supply is politically determined and that price is also potentially subject to political constraints.

Long-Term Economic Change and Globalization

Among economic determinants of top 1 percent income shares, the literature identifies the distribution of assets (wealth and skills), economic growth, the share of the financial sector, and expansion of scale due to globalization and the ICT revolution. These are closely related and in many cases identical to our clusters of variables indicating long-term structural change in the economy and globalization associated with rising inequality outlined in chapters 1 and 2. Kaplan and Rauh (2013) and Mankiw (2013) argue that the recent increase in the income share of the top 1 percent in the United States has been largely a product of the normal operation of competitive markets resulting in compensation in line with the marginal productivity of holders of marketable assets, capital, or skill. They are particularly intent on justifying the high incomes of top managers and entrepreneurs, arguing that globalization and technological change, especially the ICT revolution, enable "highly talented individuals . . . to manage or perform on a larger scale, applying their talent to greater pools of resources and reaching larger numbers of people . . . [and thus receiving] higher compensation" (Kaplan and Rauh 2013, 35). Interestingly, both

Kaplan and Rauh (2013) and Mankiw (2013) approvingly cite Goldin and Katz (2008) about the effects of skill-biased technological change, contrasting it to the "political" sources of rising inequality cited by leftist critics (Mankiw 2013, 23). In fact, skill-biased technological change is only half of Goldin and Katz's argument; the other half is very political—the failure of the US government to invest sufficiently in education to keep the human capital stock increasing at a pace that matches technological change. If the arguments of Kaplan and Rauh (2013) and Mankiw (2013) are correct, one should expect top income shares to be related to measures of globalization (capital market openness, outward foreign direct investment, and trade openness); technological success, especially in ICT (total factor productivity change and dynamic service employment); economic growth; export competitiveness (trade surplus); and other indicators of the transition to the knowledge economy (deindustrialization and deregulation).

An examination of the Nordic model (and to a lesser extent the continental European CMEs to the south of them) suggests a diametrically opposed set of hypotheses. These economies are highly globalized; they have been highly trade-open for a long time, and they run trade surpluses. They have also been highly successful in technological innovation in ICT. Yet they have seen only moderate increases in the top 1 percent shares, and their levels of the top 1 percent shares are among the lowest. Accordingly, we adopt nondirectional hypotheses for most of our globalization and technological change variables. The Nordic model shows a different picture of the race between technological change and educational investment. In contrast to the Anglo-American countries, the Nordic countries intensified their public investment effort in education over the past half-century, which helped to dampen increases in inequality (Huber and Stephens 2014).

At its core, Piketty's (2014) explanation for the resurgence in top inequality in the twenty-first century is increasing wealth in relation to national income: when economic growth slows down, wealth (through savings and hence capital accumulation) increases relative to output, pushing up the income of the very wealthy. His measure of wealth concentration is the ratio of total wealth to national income. Although extremely elegant, this explanation leaves some unanswered questions in both empirics and theory. Empirically, Bonnet et al. (2014) and Soskice (2014) highlight that Piketty's measure of wealth does not parse out the inflationary effect of housing prices, and may therefore overstate inequality. This suggests that, in addition to testing Piketty's total wealth ratio, one should also test the wealth ratio with housing wealth subtracted from the numerator. In earlier work on the top 1 percent share, we found no support for Piketty's explanation (with or without housing included), so we do not revisit it here (Huber, Huo, and Stephens 2015 and 2019).

Atkinson, Piketty, and Saez (2011) identify the expansion of scale associated with globalization and advances in information technology as potentially important determinants of top shares. Roine, Vlachos, and Waldenström (2009) find that periods of high economic growth and a higher share of the banking and stock market sectors in the economy are associated with an increase in the income share of the top 1 percent. Krippner (2011) has argued that the "financialization" of the US economy has contributed to rising inequality, and Volscho and Kelly's (2012) time-series analysis of US data supports her argument. We analyze all of these relationships.

Power, Politics, and Policies

Power Relations in Domestic Society and Polity

To begin with the liberal political economies, analyses of the steep rise of the top 1 percent share in the United States highlight political determinants. Volscho and Kelly (2012) find that rightward shifts in Congress, declines in union power, and reductions in marginal income and capital gains taxes all helped fuel the recent rise of the super-rich in the US. In a similar vein, Kristal (2013) finds that the decline in union bargaining power is the crucial channel through which technological innovation in the US drove up the capital share of income since the late 1970s.

According to Enns et al. (2014), the failure of US governments to take steps in addressing widening top inequality reflects a majoritarian "status quo bias" built into US political institutions such as the Senate, which causes policies to drift out of sync with income inequality realities in society. As the authors point out, the impact of such institutional veto points may be especially sharp when Democrats and Republicans are polarized in their policy disagreement, and when top inequality is already substantial in society. Similarly, Hacker and Pierson (2010) suggest that the rise of the super-rich in the US reflects a "winner-take-all" effect of US political institutions. In particular the authors highlight policy drift in industrial relations, where the erosion of union power removed one of the key antidotes to managers' drive toward top compensation. While Hacker and Pierson believe that the root of policy drift is political (mobilization by business interests), Kenworthy (2010) suggests that policies to avert top inequality are also thwarted by the evolution of the US economy, such as changing corporate practices, rise in stock values, and the downward economic cycle following the burst of the subprime bubble.

In contrast to these studies with a focus on the United States, Scheve and Stasavage (2009), in their study of thirteen countries over the period 1916–2000, conclude that political factors and labor market institutions have had little influence on the evolution of income inequality over the long run and suggest instead that income inequality has been driven by underlying economic forces such as the race between technology and education or economic crises. They do not test these hypothesized alternatives. We shall test these alternatives and show that for the steep recent increase in the top 1 percent share the lack of union strength was indeed of crucial importance. We shall also examine the impact of works councils. Many countries do not have legally sanctioned works councils, and in the countries where they exist their powers vary widely, from a simple right to information through consultation all the way to codetermination. Works councils with more extensive rights can be expected to restrain the income of top executives. Even where they only have a right to consultation, their presence works as implicit regulation, as we shall discuss below.

We also test the partisan incumbency hypothesis. Traditionally PRT has focused on organized labor and left parties to explain welfare state development, labor market policies, and income distribution. This is entirely appropriate because they are the main actors actively promoting policies that favor labor and lower-income households. Here we remain within the power resources framework but focus on the main actors actively promoting opposite agendas. We focus on organized labor as a protector of workers' income and on secular center and right governments as active promoters of policies that weaken labor and favor their business and high-income core constituency. Starting again from the experience of the Anglo-American countries, the right-wing governments of Reagan and Thatcher stand out for their radical attacks on unions and their slashing of top marginal tax rates. Huber and Stephens (2001) showed that long-term incumbency of secular center and right parties has been historically constitutive of liberal welfare states, which have been built in the same countries that are classified as liberal market economies in the Hall and Soskice (2001) typology. Thus, we hypothesize that long-term incumbency of secular center and right parties has supported the rise of the top 1 percent income share.

Among the policies associated with top 1 percent income shares, top marginal tax rates are central. They figure prominently in Volscho and

Kelly's (2012) study of the US; Roine, Vlachos, and Waldenström's (2009) cross-country study from a century-long perspective; and Atkinson, Piketty, and Saez's (2011) overview of findings. We adopt the hypothesis that higher marginal tax rates reduce the pre-tax income share of the top 1 percent. As to the mechanisms, the literature identifies three options. First, the increased tax rates may stimulate more tax avoidance and evasion, so the tax returns show lower incomes. Second, higher tax rates may do the opposite of what lower tax rates are assumed to do—that is, the opposite of improving work incentives of top managers and thus stimulating entrepreneurial innovation and raising marginal productivity (Feldstein 1995). Third, they may reduce the incentive for top income earners to bargain aggressively (Alvaredo et al. 2013).

The first of these mechanisms can be observed, for instance, in certain spikes in declared income before announced increases in tax rates. An example is the spike in Norway visible in figure A.1. Its extent over the longer run will depend on the quality of the tax code in the form of the absence of opportunities for tax avoidance (Piketty, Saez, and Stantcheva 2014). If the standard work incentives argument were correct, then we would see higher growth in countries with lower top marginal tax rates. In their study of three elasticities, Piketty, Saez, and Stantcheva do not find such a result. However, their evidence is consistent with the third interpretation, the incentive for aggressive bargaining on the part of top income earners.

As noted, the literature on the consequences of skill-biased technological change for income inequality emphasizes the importance of investment in education. Long-term strong investment in public education increases the supply of skilled employees and thus reduces the return to education. However, Atkinson, Piketty, and Saez (2011, 58) rightly observed that most heads of household not only in the top 1 percent but also in the top 10 percent now have a college education, thus the "skill-bias explanation has little to say directly about why the top percentile has increased relative to the top decile." This ignores variation in skill—and credentials and networks—among those who have tertiary education. It is well known that there is huge variation in the quality of tertiary education in the US. Prestigious colleges and universities not only arguably impart greater skills, but also carry greater market value as a credential and make it more likely that the degree holders become embedded in social networks that land them in jobs that carry greater compensation.

Like the US, the other liberal countries, along with Japan, are characterized by high levels of private tertiary education spending, which plausibly is related to variations in the quality of tertiary education and the value of credentials. Indeed, the correlation of top income shares with private tertiary education spending as a percentage of total tertiary education spending is moderately high (r = .51), as is the correlation between private tertiary education spending and secular center and right government (r = .59). Thus, we hypothesize that the private share of tertiary education spending will be related to the income share of the top 1 percent.

Finally, Weisstanner and Armingeon (2020) have argued that a state that collects high taxes, particularly high marginal income taxes and social security contributions, and provides generous redistributive welfare policies reduces the material incentives and attitudinal motivation of highly qualified workers to exploit their strong position in the labor market, which in turn reduces the education premium. Similarly, Roine, Vlachos and Waldenström (2009) test the hypothesis that the size of government affects the top income share. Their hypothesis is that increased government size will have a negative effect on top income shares. They find that the simple correlation between the two variables is negative and significant, but in the multiple regressions it is wrongly signed and insignificant. We agree with Weisstanner and Armingeon that size of the welfare state is a theoretically more plausible mechanism for reducing top income shares than simple size of government because of its effects on attitudes. Accordingly, we test the hypothesis that size of the welfare state, in both social security transfers and total government revenue, reduces top income shares.

Our models will thus test effects of power resources alone and in combination with specific policies and competing explanations. Of course, besides the specific policy mechanisms we measure, there are various other mechanisms through which power resources affect top incomes. These mechanisms can be conceptualized on the basis of a variety of studies, to which we will turn next. Although we cannot test all mechanisms in a single chapter, we do cite empirical evidence for these additional mechanisms from the existing literature. Our variables and hypotheses are summarized in table 4.1.

Conceptualizing Union Effects on Top Income Shares

Linking declining union strength (as indicated by a decline in union density), contract coverage, and wage coordination, to increasing top 1 percent income shares is not straightforward.[1] For the top 1 percent, it is not a plausible assumption that their compensation is determined through the

TABLE 4.1. **Variables and Hypotheses**

Dependent variable	Hypothesized relation to top income shares
Top 1% income shares	
Independent variables	
Power resource variables	
Secular center and right government	+
Union density	−
Wage coordination	−
Contract coverage	−
Powers of works councils	−
Policies	
Top marginal tax rates	−
Civilian government employment	−
Social security transfers	−
Public education spending	−
Private tertiary education spending	+
Financialization	
Financial sector size	+
Stock market capitalization	+
Long–term economic change	
Industrial employment	−
Total factor productivity change	+
Regulation	−
Employment in dynamic services	+
Globalization	
Trade surplus	−/+
Capital market openness	+
Outward FDI	−/+
Trade openness	−/+
Other	
Economic growth	−/+

Variable definitions and sources in table A.1.

collective bargaining process. In our dataset, contract coverage exceeds 95 percent in only two country years, so it is reasonable to assume that the compensation for the top 1 percent is not directly subject to union wage bargaining. For this reason, we highlight some more subtle mechanisms through which union strength shapes top income shares.

IMPLICIT REGULATION Analyzing 1,049 corporations and 1,688 CEOs from 1974 to 1986 in Forbes's Executive Compensation Surveys, Jensen and Murphy (1990) find that each $1,000 of variation in shareholder wealth is associated with only $2.50 variation in CEO stock options compensation ($3.50 in total compensation including stocks, bonuses, and cash pay). Instead of being pegged strictly to performance, CEO pay leaves considerable room for rent bargaining between managers and their shareholders. Because CEO pay is by law public information in the United States, managerial labor contracts are not "private" (to managers and their shareholders); instead they are open to public scrutiny and pressure. As a result, third parties such as labor unions or journalists play an important role in constraining executive pay, a dynamic the authors refer to as "implicit regulation." For example, although CEO pay is not directly subject to union *wage bargaining*, it is affected by union *presence*, because when unions actively publicize information on "what the boss makes" (Jensen and Murphy 1990, 254), they influence worker demand for their own pay as well as worker morale.

Several other scholars echo Jensen and Murphy's "implicit regulation" thesis. For example, citing Joskow and colleagues' finding that CEO pay is lower in more regulated industries (Joskow, Rose, and Shepard 1993; Joskow, Rose, and Wolfram 1996), DiNardo, Hallock, and Pischke (2000, 4) suggest that union presence is "akin to regulation," safeguarding the welfare of those company "stakeholders" outside the circle of shareholders and executives. When executive pay is perceived to be excessive, unions may voice their equity and fairness concerns not only directly through industrial disputes, but also indirectly through local stewards, public awareness campaigns, and shareholder activism by union-controlled pension funds to constrain executive pay via expensing, future repricing, or performance-based vesting conditions (Gomez and Tzioumis 2011; Katz et al. 2003). For example, Ertimur et al.'s (2011) study of 1,198 compensation-related shareholder proposals between 1997 and 2007 finds that 48.2 percent of these proposals stem from union pension funds. In a similar vein, DeAngelo and DeAngelo's (1991) study of labor-corporate negotiation in the US steel industry finds that, in industrial disputes, unions often make CEO pay a visible issue, which forces the management to take its own pay cut before negotiating pay concessions from workers. Because inequity aversion lies at the heart of "implicit regulation" by unions, one distinct implication is that union presence may be associated with pay compression not only across labor and management, but also *for management, across firms*. Consistent with this implication, Gomez and Tzioumis's (2011) study of more than one million CEO compensation packages (1992–2001) from Standard and Poor's Executive Compensation database finds that the cash pay Gini coefficient for

CEOs is .317 for union firms and .381 for non-union firms (and .311 and .337 respectively for non-CEO executive pay).

RESOURCE CONSTRAINT While the "implicit regulation" mechanism allows unions to increase a company's political and publicity cost of giving high management pay, unions can also reduce the company's financial resources for high executive compensation. Because neither executive nor worker pay is pegged strictly to marginal product, the surplus is divided between workers and management. As unions enable workers to negotiate for better pay, working conditions, and other benefits, more surplus is redistributed to workers at the expense of management (Addison and Hirsch 1989; Chiles and Stewart 1993). Consistent with this notion of management-labor contest for firm surplus, Clark (1984) finds that profits are lower in unionized firms, and Abowd (1989) finds that union wealth increases dollar-for-dollar with the decline of shareholder wealth. Similarly, Fallick and Hassett (1999) find that the impact of union certification in such surplus contests is equivalent to a doubling of the firm's profit tax (Banning and Chiles 2007). Besides contestable surplus, unions may also constrain resources for top executive pay through their influence on stock prices, and hence the valuation of stock options compensation for executives. This channel of influence is important because stock valuation depends on financial market performance, and financial markets tend to react negatively to union presence. For example, Abowd (1989) finds that share price movements in the US react negatively to union activity, and Ruback and Zimmerman (1984) find that the decline in firm equity after union victories in National Labor Relations Board elections is three times as large as in the case of union defeats (Gomez and Tzioumis 2011). Although an increased union presence may reduce firm market valuation, it does not necessarily reduce firm productivity. As Gomez and Tzioumis point out, because steep stock options compensation distorts management incentives (toward short-term valuation at the expense of long-term investment and production), union constraint on stock valuation may mitigate such allocative inefficiency.

Unlike the "implicit regulation" thesis, the "resource constraint" interpretation understands lower executive pay as an indirect consequence of union presence rather than a direct union objective. To this extent, unions may actually be willing to compensate for lower *level* of executive pay with lower *risk* (variation) in executive compensation. Consistent with this implication from the "resource constraint" mechanism, both Banning and Chiles (2007) and Jensen and Murphy (1990) find empirically that executive compensation variability is lower when union presence is stronger.

ORGANIZATIONAL CONSTRAINT   Finally, union presence may also constrain top executive pay by affecting the firm's organizational strategy, which in turn affects the firm's demand for CEO services. Unlike production workers, the main responsibility of management is supervision. The greater the need for supervision, the more complex the firm's hierarchy, and the higher the pay for top executives (Garicano 2000). However, when union activism allows workers to increase their own pay, conditions, and autonomy on the job, monitoring by management becomes less necessary for enforcing high workforce performance (DiNardo, Hallock, and Pischke 2000; Acemoglu and Newman 2002). Extensive laboratory evidence (Bartling et al. 2012; Fehr et al. 2013) shows that higher worker autonomy and pay are complementary in raising workforce motivation and performance, a finding also echoed by the knowledge-intensive employment literature (Arundel et al. 2007). In turn, as Garicano and Rossi-Hansberg (2006) prove formally, higher worker performance leads to a flatter firm hierarchy, where managers comprise a smaller fraction of the workforce and pay at the top is less steep.

Although the "organizational" interpretation is similar to the "implicit regulation" and "resource" interpretations in predicting lower executive *pay*, it is distinct in its implication that union strength will also reduce the proportion of managers *employed*. Furthermore, with fewer positions in higher corporate tiers, there will be less room for firms to change the number of managers, placing more weight on management pay as the main margin of adjustment to reduced demand for supervision services. In other words, the pay impact of union strength should be sharper for higher-level executives. Consistent with these implications, DiNardo, Hallock, and Pischke's (2000) study of corporate employment in sixteen OECD countries between 1970 and 1993 finds that a 10 percent increase in union density reduces the fraction of managers hired by up to 0.9 percent, management pay by up to 0.7 percent, and CEO pay by more than 2.5 percent.

We have outlined three mechanisms through which unions may affect top incomes, each backed by empirical evidence from the literature. While each mechanism has some distinct aspect, they are complementary in reinforcing two arguments central to how we hypothesize the impact of unions on top inequality. First, because executive pay is not directly subject to collective bargaining, union constraint on top inequality may be more effectively understood through union *presence* (i.e., union density) than through bargaining institution characteristics. Second, because executive pay leaves considerable room for rent-seeking (see evidence in Jensen and Murphy 1990), top income share will not be strongly driven by genuine economic or knowledge growth, and to this extent union density's impact on top income share can be understood as an "implicit tax" on rents.

Conceptualizing Partisan Effects on Pre-Tax and Transfer Income

There are many channels through which secular center and right governments may influence the pre-tax, pre-transfer income share of the top 1 percent. As Kelly (2005) points out, partisan governments not only shape post-tax, post-transfer inequality by influencing redistribution of income, but also exert a comparable impact on pre-tax and transfer income by conditioning markets in labor, finance, and products. In fact, as we have laid out above, top marginal taxes, as a key redistributive instrument, have important effects in curtailing the pre-redistribution income share of the 1 percent. Besides top marginal income tax rates, Atkinson (2014) lists myriad other taxes that may affect the top 1 percent, such as inheritance, capital gains, and wealth taxes, which secular center and right governments tend to cut (Volscho and Kelly 2012).

At a general level, we can identify two ways in which center and right governments can support an increase in the income share of the top 1 percent: they can increase the bargaining power of top earners, and they can weaken the countervailing power of workers (Hacker and Pierson 2010b; Volscho and Kelly 2012; Enns et al. 2014). We tap directly into these two broad partisanship mechanisms through the effect of, respectively, top marginal taxes and union density. The decline of top marginal taxes (favored by secular right governments) increases the bargaining power of top earners, just as the decline of unions (also favored by the right) undermines union power to countervail top management pay. However, right government partisanship continues to have a clear beneficial effect for the top 1 percent, even after we parse out the influence of top marginal taxes and union density in the empirical analysis. Here, we outline various additional forms these partisan mechanisms may take.

As noted earlier, workers tend to be especially successful in forcing down CEO pay during the course of collective bargaining, because the firm's stakeholders often agree that managerial sacrifice is a necessary condition for concessions by labor (DeAngelo and DeAngelo 1991). Various right governments have used labor legislation to directly erode the wage bargaining power of unions. For example, in 1975, President Gerald

Ford vetoed Democratic legislation that would have legalized common situs picketing. Three later Democratic attempts to amend the National Labor Relations Act (NLRA) (in particular, to ban the hiring of permanent replacement workers during strikes) were defeated by Republicans (Block 1997). In Britain, the Thatcher Conservative government used similar labor legislation tactics to (among other things) abolish union recognition in the process of collective bargaining, remove statutory immunities for workers involved in industrial action, and weaken protection against unfair dismissals (Towers 1989).

According to the "resource constraint" literature, when pay and conditions for workers improve, more of the firm's surplus is redistributed to workers at the expense of top-paid managers (Addison and Hirsch 1989; Chiles and Stewart 1993). In this light, secular right governments have also cemented top income shares by directly reducing workers' wages. For example, the Thatcher government not only restricted the tripartite Wages Councils' ability to set minimum wage rates, but also abolished the statutory provision for workers to lodge pay comparability claims (whereby they could apply for legally enforced awards based on arguments that they were paid less than generally prevailing rates—Towers 1989). Similarly, the Reagan and Bush administrations in the US froze the federal minimum wage at $3.35/hour for a decade (1980–1990), triggering the largest and longest continuous fall (by 30 percent) in the real value of the minimum wage in postwar US history (Morris and Western 1999, 642).

Many of the above policy changes under secular center and right governments also directly enhanced the bargaining power of top earners. For example, industrial deregulation and the decline of unions allowed the shareholder value revolution to take hold in firm management practices (Fligstein and Shin 2007), which was in turn a key driver behind the subsequent sharp increases in options-based CEO compensation (Hall and Liebman 1998; Frydman and Saks 2010). As Hacker and Pierson (2010a) and Kenworthy (2010) point out, corporate governance practice, including the compensation of CEOs through stock options, is an important driver of top income share. Many corporate governance institutions, in turn, can be affected by government legislation, such as mandated supervisory boards with labor representation, assignment of joint governance rights by firm and labor over pension funds, and restrictions on bank shareholding (Perotti and Thadden 2006, 160). Closely related to this theme is government deregulation of the financial industry, which, as Philippon and Reshef (2012) document, increases wealth concentration at the top. Another channel is high interest rates (favored by anti-inflationary conservative governments—see Volscho and Kelly 2012, 683), which raise the return on savings, and in turn the return on capital income. Furthermore, as Atkinson (2014) points out, excessive return on capital (relative to labor) may reflect a fundamental underinvestment in knowledge-intensive human capital, and secular center and right parties tend to shun spending on public education, one of the most important means of human capital investment in a knowledge economy (Iversen and Stephens 2008).

Measurement and Statistical Estimation

Our dependent variable is the share of total national income going to the top 1 percent of income units—individuals or households, depending on the tax laws of the country and period. Saez and Veall (2007) present evidence for Canada that treating individuals as the unit of taxation increases the level of measured inequality, so in earlier work on the top 1 percent share we controlled for the unit of analysis with a methodological dummy variable for individuals (Huber, Huo, and Stephens 2015 and 2019). This variable was insignificant in all models, so we do not include it here. The data come from the World Inequality Database (Alvaredo et al. 2015). They are derived from tax returns and capture pre-tax and transfer income. The countries in our analysis are the eighteen advanced industrial democracies in figure A.1. We cover the period from 1960 to 2019. The operationalization of all our independent variables is explained in appendix C.

As in chapters 2 and 3, we display Vernby-Lindgren dynamic panel estimates in all of our models in table 4.2. Top 1 percent shares vary significantly both between countries and between years, so both country fixed-effects estimators and random effects estimators are equally relevant robustness checks for this dependent variable (see table E.4).

We noted that Roine, Vlachos, and Waldenström (2009) interpolate a number of data points for stock market capitalization for the 1960s and early 1970s. To examine whether this affected the results, we reran the models without those data points. The results were substantially the same, so we retain those interpolated data points in our analysis.

Results

Table 4.2 displays the results of our analysis. Model 1 contains the power resource variables, all but one of which are significant and correctly signed.

TABLE 4.2. **Predictors of Top 1% Income Shares**

	Model 1	Model 2	Model 3	Model 4	Model 5	Model 6	Model 7
Secular center and right government	.025						.011
Union density	-.044 ***						-.021 ***
Wage coordination	-.265 ***						-.438 ***
Contract coverage	-.027 ***						-.029 ***
Powers of works councils	.023						
Top marginal tax rates		-.090 ***	-.088 ***				-.017 **
Government revenue		-.097 **	-.116 **				.041 ^
Social security transfers		.090 ^	.162 ^				
Public education spending		-.329 ***	-.172 ***				
Private % of total tertiary education spending			.670				-.421 ***
Financial sector size				.365 ***			
Stock market capitalization				.017	-.038		.009 ***
Industrial employment					76.123 ***		46.628 ***
Change in total factor productivity					-.911 ***		-.516 ***
Regulation					0.133 **		
Employment in dynamic services						-.104 ***	-.004
Trade surplus						1.119 ***	-.039
Capital market openness						0.048 **	-.012
Outward FDI						-.014 *	.005
Trade openness						.063	.002
Economic growth							
Constant	12.807 ***	17.384 ***	15.389 ***	5.064 ***	10.610 ***	7.034 ***	14.053 ***
Adjusted R²	.48	.30	.42	.24	.37	.24	.68
Observations	762	545	214	521	444	635	470

* Significant at .05; ** significant at .01; *** significant at .001; ^ significant but contrary to directional hypothesis.
Model 7 includes period indicators.

Together they explain 48 percent of the variation in top 1 percent income shares. Models 2 and 3 display the results of our policy variables. The top marginal tax rates, government revenue, public education spending, and private tertiary education variables are correctly signed and significant. Together they explain 42 percent of the variation in top income shares. As noted earlier, the OECD public versus private tertiary education series begins in 1995, so we lose many observations in these models. Thus, we do not carry this variable forward to the combined model.

Both of the financialization variables included in model 4 are significant and correctly signed and explain 24 percent of the variation in top income shares. Three of the four long-term economic transformation variables included in model 5 are significant and together explain 37 percent of the variation. We will show in chapter 5 that industrial employment, the one economic transformation variable that is not significant in model 5, is an important explanatory factor at the opposite end of the income distribution, for market income poverty. Model 6 contains our four globalization variables and economic growth, all of which are significant.

We combined all of the variables that were significant in models 1–6 except private tertiary education, which we omitted due to the dearth of data for that variable. We dropped employment in dynamic services and financial sector size—both of which were insignificant—from the final combined equation in model 7, in order to increase the number of observations from 349 to 470. One striking finding of the combined model is that none of the globalization variables are significant, and economic growth is also not significant. This means that the data offer almost no support for the arguments of Kaplan and Rauh (2013), Mankiw (2013), and others that link the top 1 percent share to globalization and economic success. By contrast, the significant effect of long-run total factor productivity change does support the view that skill-biased technological change is related to rising top income shares.

The OECD measure of regulation in the telecom, electricity, gas, post, rail, air passenger transport, and road freight industries has robust negative effects on top income shares in the combined models. Or, to be more precise about the over-time dynamics, the process of deregulation in these industries (which is strong in every country in our analysis—see figure A.10) resulted in rising top income shares.

As we did in chapter 3, in order to compare the substantive strength of the independent variables that were significant in our combined models (in this case model 7) we present the effect a two-standard-deviation

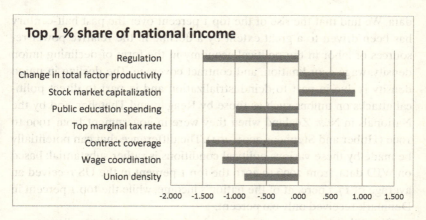

FIGURE 4.1. Effect of two-standard-deviation change in significant independent variables on top 1% share of national income

change in the independent variables on the dependent variable in this chapter, the top 1 percent share of national income, in figure 4.1. Not surprisingly, together the power resource variables are associated with the largest substantive changes in top income shares. The effect of (de)regulation is also very large. Finally, the effects of long-term technological change and stock market capitalization, taken together, are moderately large and positively related to top income shares. The two policy variables, top marginal tax rate and public education spending, are moderately large and negatively related to top income shares.

Table E.4 shows that most of the results shown in figure 4.1 hold with alternative statistical estimators. Union density, contract coverage, stock market capitalization, and long-term change in total factor productivity are significant in all models. Again we find a highly robust result for the importance of labor power as an antidote to inequality. In addition, regulation, public education spending, and wage coordination are significant in the random effects specification.

Conclusion

In our previous analyses of the top 1 percent share of national income (Huber, Huo, and Stephens 2015 and 2019), we emphasized the importance of power resource variables, which still holds in this revisiting of the data. We find that the rise of the top 1 percent over the past half-century has been driven to a great extent by a decline in the relative power resources of labor in the political economy in the form of declining union density, wage coordination, and contract coverage. The decline in union density is due in part to deindustrialization and in part to direct political attacks on unions such as those by Reagan and Thatcher, and by the Nationals in New Zealand when they were in government from 1990 to 1996 (Huber and Stephens 2001, 294). The difference that can potentially be made by these various political conditions is rather substantial: based on WID data, from 2006 to 2010 the top 1 percent in the US received an average of 17.7 percent of the nation's income, while the top 1 percent in Denmark received only 6.0 percent.

Given that top 1 percent income shares are not subject to direct wage bargaining between unions and employers, the strong effects of union density, wage coordination, and contract coverage on top 1 percent income shares shown in figure 3.1 are striking. We have argued that the industrial relations and sociology of work literature points to three mechanisms—implicit regulation, resource constraint, and organizational constraint—that account for this effect.

In contrast, we find little support for explanations of income concentration at the top based on increasing marginal productivity of top managerial talent. Top income shares do not rise with trade flows and investment flows that increase market size, capital market openness, or trade surpluses. We found some evidence that financialization, particularly in the form of increased stock market capitalization, is associated with higher top income shares. Stock ownership is very concentrated at the top in all of these countries, so increasing stock market capitalization resulted in increasing top income shares. Also, increasing reliance on top executive compensation in the form of stock options helps account for the rising share of income of top income groups. In the CMEs, the period since 1990 witnessed a trend from bank to stock market financing of business investment and thus significant increases in stock market capitalization, which arguably was associated with an increase in the top 1 percent shares.

In related work with Bilyana Petrova, we found that the effect of financialization was contingent on the strength of labor and works council powers: where labor was very strong (10–12 on the 12-point index of labor strength used in that article) or works councils very powerful (3 on our measure of works council rights), financialization had no effect on the shares of national income of the top 1 percent of income earners

(Huber, Petrova, and Stephens 2022). Hope and Martelli (2019) have a similar finding with regard to the effect of the expansion of the knowledge economy on inequality: they find that the expansion of the knowledge economy increases inequality overall, but has no effect on inequality (measured by both top income shares and wage dispersion) at the highest levels of labor strength.

We also found that two aspects of long-term economic change—deregulation and long-term increases in total factor productivity—increase top income shares. The total factor productivity finding might be interpreted as evidence of skill-biased technological change. The exact mechanism by which this results in increased top income shares is less straightforward than in the case of our finding for the 90-50 ratio in chapter 3. There the usual argument put forward by proponents of the SBTC hypothesis (that SBTC replaced routine manual and non-manual jobs while increasing the demand for highly skilled and educated labor) seems eminently reasonable. The loss of routine jobs would appear to have little effect on the top 1 percent, though an increase in demand for skills at the very top seems at least plausible.

The effect of deregulation on top income shares appears more straightforward and a direct extension of our discussion of deregulation in earlier chapters. Even short of actual privatization, deregulation could open up markets for highly skilled managers, scientists, and engineers. With privatization, top managers could reward themselves with stock options and promote shareholder value principles of corporate governance, thus further enlarging their income share.

The effect of centralized bargaining by strong unions on wage inequality has long been an established finding in the comparative political economy literature. Union solidarity results in both wage restraint at the upper end and protection for workers at the lower end. Our findings here suggest that this mechanism holds throughout all ranks, including the CEO level, which is well above the 50-10 or 90-50 ratio that is normally analyzed in the literature on wage dispersion. Our findings further suggest that the emphasis on cooperation between strong unions and employers in CMEs that is prominent in the Varieties of Capitalism literature (Hall and Soskice 2001) has to be tempered with the insight that the struggle over distribution of income continues. Management-labor cooperation on the input side (such as skill training) does not necessarily imply the lack of continuing fundamental conflict on the output side (such as dividing the firm's surplus). Because firm and worker inputs are complementary (machinery, financial capital, and labor), cooperation on the input side can be rationalized. On the output side, however, the two sides draw from the same pot of revenue for compensation, so competition is a more normal outcome. Therefore, a strong labor movement may not only cooperate more often with management in production; it may also, as our finding implies, win more often in the contest for the share of the nation's income, which reinforces the central message of classic PRT.

CHAPTER FIVE

Poverty

One of the reasons inequality is of wide concern is its relationship to poverty. Normatively, many find inequality objectionable because of considerations of fairness, whereas others see it as tolerable or even necessary, as long as all members of a society have a chance to engage in efforts to improve their position. Poverty, however, is precisely the condition that hampers people's efforts to improve their position, as it entails being deprived of the means to participate as full members of society. Thus, political support for alleviating poverty has been stronger than has support for reducing inequality. In particular, religious center and right parties have pursued policies of poverty alleviation along with left parties, whereas inequality reduction has been the exclusive concern of left parties. Yet, at any given level of societal affluence, higher inequality is likely to result in higher poverty, unless we assume that inequality increases because of a shift of income exclusively from the middle to the top of the income distribution.

In this chapter, we analyze the factors that drive levels of market income poverty, poverty reduction, and disposable income poverty in our set of postindustrial societies. Our focus remains on households made up of working-age people, with and without children. As in our analysis of inequality, including households with elderly members would result in an overestimate of market income poverty and poverty reduction in countries with generous public pension systems. We follow LIS, OECD, and European Union (EU) convention to analyze relative rather than absolute poverty, thus making our study comparable to almost all other comparative studies of poverty in postindustrial countries. We expect the same theoretical clusters of factors to shape differences in poverty that we found to be important in our analyses of inequality. Within those theoretical clusters, we naturally expect those variables to be of particular importance that affect the bottom of the income distribution.

As our tables A.5 to A.7 show, market income poverty and disposable income poverty rose in all our political economy regime types from the pre-1993 period to the 2010s. The only two countries that defied the trend to higher market income poverty are Switzerland (where it remained at the lowest level among all countries) and New Zealand (where it was already comparatively high in the pre-1993 period). Switzerland also saw a decline in disposable household income poverty over this period, as did France. This squares with the trajectory of disposable household income inequality, which also declined in these two countries over the same period. The trajectories of poverty reduction efforts differed somewhat; they rose from the pre-1993 period through the 1990s in the Nordic, western European continental, and Anglo-American countries and declined everywhere from the 1990s to the most recent year for which data are available.

We can build and improve upon an earlier analysis of poverty and poverty reduction (Moller et al. 2003). We improve upon this earlier study by measuring welfare state effort with social rights rather than expenditure, in order to differentiate the effect of policy from the effect of need, both of which shape expenditure. We are able to extend our coverage by some ten to fifteen years, allowing us to compare changes over time in welfare state efficacy and in the importance of partisan incumbency. And pooling data from our three sources—LIS, SILC, and the OECD—allows us to almost triple our number of observations compared to the earlier analyses.

Theoretical Perspectives

Market Household Income Poverty

Brady (2019) distinguishes three theoretical approaches to poverty—behavioral, structural, and political. Behavioral theories focus on behaviors of the poor as shaped by incentives and culture to explain poverty. We are interested in macro-level processes; thus we focus only on the structural and political theories outlined in previous chapters. As before, we group our variables into the theoretical clusters of power resources, political institutions and processes, policies or social rights, long-term structural change in the economies, globalization, and social risks.

We have essentially the same expectations for the impact of our independent variables that we had for wage distribution and inequality. We expect the power resources variables to be associated with lower market income poverty, greater poverty reduction, and lower disposable income poverty. The minimum wage level is of particular importance for market income poverty. Union involvement in minimum wage setting pushes the minimum wage upward and improves the income position of workers at the bottom, lowering the probability of poverty among households with fulltime workers. Strong unions can also raise wages at the bottom through collective bargaining, thus reducing market income poverty. Contract extension and employment protection legislation should help to protect wages and employment at the bottom as well. We expect works councils to use their rights to protect all workers, including those at the bottom of the pay scale. One may also expect a smaller 50-10 wage ratio to be related to lower market income poverty, given that we are using a relative poverty threshold.

We expect the different policy variables we use to have different effects on market income poverty. Parental leave benefits are designed to make it possible for parents to take off from work, so generous parental leave benefits should increase the proportion of people without income from work, and thus should also increase market income poverty. Generosity of social insurance and of social assistance, in contrast, should have the opposite effect. By protecting people from falling into or staying in disposable income poverty, they also protect people from scar effects like loss of skills and thus from future inability to earn a market income sufficient to keep them out of market income poverty (Gangl 2004; DiPrete and McManus 2000; DiPrete 2002; Bradley and Stephens 2007; Nelson and Stephens 2011). Our expectation, then, runs counter to the argument of mainstream economics that generous social policies raise the reservation wage and thus create more market income poverty. Nevertheless, in light of the mainstream economics view we adopt a nondirectional hypothesis.

The long-term changes in economic structure and globalization should influence market income poverty through the same mechanisms that influenced market income inequality by making the situation of low-skilled workers more difficult. Loss of relatively well-paying jobs for low-skilled workers due to deindustrialization, deregulation, skill-biased technological change, third world imports, outsourcing in the form of outward direct foreign investment facilitated by open capital markets, and immigration should all contribute to higher levels of market income poverty. In the case of trade openness we are again agnostic and adopt a nondirectional hypothesis.

We also expect our social risk variables to relate to market income poverty in the same way that they relate to market income inequality. Higher levels of unemployment mean less volume of work available and more people without any market income, or with only intermittent and low market income, who are therefore at risk of poverty (Kalleberg 2011). In contrast, higher levels of employment mean a higher probability that households will have more than one income earner, which can keep a household out of poverty even in the case of loss of one earner's income. A greater proportion of children living in single-mother households implies a greater proportion of households that have a low volume of work and are therefore at risk of poverty (Kenworthy and Pontusson 2005).

Finally, we would expect human capital spending over the long run to result in fewer workers with low skills and therefore less market income poverty. We also analyze the prevalence of low skills in a more direct way by measuring the proportion of the population who have not completed secondary education. We expect a higher proportion of the population with less than complete secondary education to result in higher levels of market income poverty.

Poverty Reduction

Poverty reduction through the tax and transfer system is primarily politically determined and therefore shaped by power resources, other political variables, and policies themselves. The policies are crucial; poverty reduction is directly linked to generosity of benefits (Moller et al. 2003; Lohmann 2009; Gornick and Smeeding 2018). Misra, Moller, and Budig (2007) found that family allowances, generous parental leave, and childcare provision lowered poverty among (particularly single) mothers. With generosity of the key transfer benefits held constant, higher social risks will result in more poverty reduction. Globalization variables may shape politics mainly in ways that undermine poverty reduction efforts.

Let us begin with our power resource variables. Unions can pressure governments to implement a variety of poverty alleviation measures, and left governments are most likely to take such measures, so we expect union density and left incumbency to be positively associated with poverty reduction. The finding of a left incumbency effect on disposable household income poverty is well established (Brady 2009; Nelson 2012; Brady, Blome, and Kleider 2016). As noted, Christian democratic parties have traditionally also pursued anti-poverty policies (Huber and Stephens

2001; van Kersbergen 1995), so we have the same expectations for Christian democratic incumbency as for left incumbency. High voter turnout, signifying high mobilization of lower-income voters, can also be expected to lead to stronger anti-poverty efforts by all kinds of governments. Women's representation in parliaments should contribute to poverty reduction because women promote measures to support families and women's employment, such as generous parental leave, free or subsidized childcare, and child or family allowances. Atchison and Down (2009) have shown this for women's representation in cabinets. Our variables capture generosity of parental leave and social assistance, but not free or subsidized childcare or child and family allowances that are not means-tested, so we expect to see an effect. We include proportional representation in our analysis because Iversen and Soskice (2006) have linked it to more redistribution, which should also lower disposable income poverty levels. Finally, veto points can obstruct efforts to promote poverty reduction, but they can also obstruct efforts to cut existing benefits that contribute to poverty reduction, so we adopt a nondirectional hypothesis. We include our globalization variables but adopt nondirectional hypotheses. On the one hand, these variables may increase need if our hypotheses regarding their effect on market income poverty are correct. On the other, they may reduce government capacity to respond to this need. All our theoretical expectations are summarized in table 5.1.

TABLE 5.1. **Variables and Hypotheses**

Dependent variables		
Market income poverty		
Poverty reduction	Market income poverty	Poverty reduction
Independent variables		
Left government	−	+
Christian democratic government		+
Women in parliament		+
Veto points		+/−
Union density	−	+
Wage coordination	−	+
Works council rights	−	+
Minimum wage setting	−	+
Parental leave benefits	+	+
Social insurance generosity	+/−	+
Social assistance generosity	+/−	+
Third world imports	+	

continues

TABLE 5.1. (*continued*)

Dependent variables Market income poverty Poverty reduction	Market income poverty	Poverty reduction
Trade openness	+	
Outward FDI	+	
Immigration	+	
Capital market openness	+	−
Unemployment rate	+	+
% children in single-mother households	+	+
Industrial employment	−	−
Employment	−	
Human capital spending	−	
Low education	+	

See table A.1 for variable definitions and sources.

Disposable Household Income Poverty

As we noted in chapter 3, we expect disposable household income distribution—and therefore disposable household income poverty—to be shaped by a combination of the factors that shape market income distribution and redistribution through the tax and transfer system. We further expect our policy variables, above all social insurance generosity, to have the strongest effects on disposable household income inequality and poverty. Empirically, we proceed by including in our model for disposable household income poverty all the variables that are significant in our final models for market income poverty and poverty reduction.

Data and Measurement

Dependent Variables

Our main dependent variables are market income poverty rates of individual working-age people (ages 18-64), with or without children, nested inside households; and poverty reduction effected by direct taxes and transfers among these households. As in our analysis of inequality, we drop all households with elderly members, as this would exaggerate market poverty rates in countries with generous pension systems. We first create a relative poverty line of 50 percent of median (disposable) household income; then we drop all households with elderly members; then we calculate the percentage of households whose income falls below this threshold, weighted by the number of working-age household members. This provides the percentage of the working-age population whose household income falls below the relative (disposable household income) poverty line.

We use the standard International Labor Organization (ILO) recommended equivalency scale, in which a household's income is divided by the square root of the number of household members (*Household Income / √# Household Members*). As just noted, we define the working-age market income poverty rate as the percentage of working-age people whose household market incomes fall below 50 percent of the median disposable household income level. We use a relative poverty rate centered around disposable household income so that we may study poverty reduction using the same poverty line. Our measure of poverty reduction is calculated as the (working-age) market income poverty rate minus the (working-age) disposable household income poverty rate, divided by the market income poverty rate. We are again using a combination of LIS, SILC, and OECD data, harmonized as we explained in chapter 3.

Independent Variables

Our independent variables are the same as in the analysis of market income inequality and reduction of inequality, with two exceptions. First, since we are focusing on the bottom of the income distribution, we are measuring wage dispersion with the 50-10 rather than the 90-10 ratio. So, we are measuring the ratio of wages of a full-time worker at the median to those of a full-time worker at the 10th percentile. Second, instead of operationalizing stock of human capital as the average years of education in the population, we focus on the lower end of the human capital distribution and measure the percentage of the population with low education. We operationalize this variable as the percentage of the adult population who have not completed secondary education. This variable also comes from the Barro and Lee (2013) educational attainment dataset. Measurement of the remaining independent variables is explained in appendix C. We use the same estimation technique as in the previous chapters and as explained in appendix D.

Results

Our model-building strategy remains the same as in the previous chapters. We enter the variables in theoretically coherent clusters of politics and labor market institutions, wage dispersion (a result of politics and labor market institutions), structural economic changes, social rights, globalization, and social risks and education, and we carry the significant variables forward to the combined models. Where we lose too many observations, we show the combined models with and without the variable that is the reason for the loss of observations.

Table 5.2 shows our results for market household income poverty. In model 1 union density, minimum wage setting, and works council rights are all significant and correctly signed. Union participation in minimum wage setting and works council rights remain significant in the combined model, indicating that these rights institutionally granted to labor play an important role in protecting low-income workers from falling into poverty. In contrast, the 50-10 wage dispersion is not significant, which indicates that the relationship between the wages of full-time workers at the median to the wages of full-time workers at the 10th percentile is not related to poverty. Household composition and the volume of work are clearly more important than the distance between the median wages of full-time workers and the wages of those at the 10th percentile.

Among the indicators of long-term structural change in the economy, only industrial employment is significant, but in the combined model even this variable loses significance. This contrasts with our analysis of market income inequality, where deregulation and technological change were significantly associated with higher inequality in the final model. The effects of deindustrialization, deregulation, and skill-biased technological change on poverty are most likely to work through higher levels of unemployment. Among our globalization variables, capital market openness and trade openness are significant and positively associated with poverty in model 5, but only trade openness retains significance in the combined model 8. This squares with our results for market income inequality, where globalization had no significant impact.

Among our social rights indicators, parental leave benefits and generosity of unemployment and sickness insurance are significant (as expected), the former increasing the number of people without market income and therefore in poverty, the latter depressing it. In the final combined model, only parental leave benefits retain significance. We interpret this as an effect of generosity of unemployment and sickness benefits that works through levels of employment. Generous benefits make it possible for people to recover from sickness and to retrain during unemployment, thus maintaining their employment status. Generosity of social assistance fails to reach significance. Unemployment and children in single-mother households both have significant effects that drive up market income poverty

TABLE 5.2. **Predictors of Market Income Poverty**

	Model 1	Model 2	Model 3	Model 4	Model 5	Model 6	Model 7	Model 8
Left government	.098 ^							
Union density	−.021 *							.020
Wage coordination	−.204							
Employment protection legislation	.966 ^							
Contract coverage	.047 ^							
Minimum wage setting	−1.994 ***							−1.579 ***
Works council rights	−1.491 ***							−.939 ***
Wage dispersion 50-10 ratio		.777						
Industrial employment			−.345 ***					−.011
Total factor productivity change (10-year)			14.313					
Regulation			−.284					
Employment in dynamic service			−.094					
Parental leave benefits				.010 ***				.036 ***
Non-aged welfare state generosity				−.174				.020
Social assistance generosity				.038				
Capital market openness					1.192 **			
Outward FDI					−.059 ^			
Third world imports					.027			
Trade openness					.030 ***	.305 ***		.022 ***
Immigration					−.129 ^	.609		
Unemployment rate						−.158 ***		.275 ***
% children in single-mother households								.102
Employment								−.214 ***
Human capital spending						.232		
Percentage with no secondary degree							.025	
Constant	20.190 ***	16.813 ***	25.528 ***	18.447 ***	15.062 ***	18.328 ***	16.136 ***	31.189 ***
Adjusted R^2	.17 ***	.00	.19 ***	.07 ***	.08 ***	.28 ***	.00	.50 ***
Observations	454	373	222	221	433	458	416	425

Model 8 contains period indicators.
* Significant at .05; ** significant at .01; *** significant at .001; ^ significant opposite hypothesized direction.

in model 6, but only unemployment remains significant in the combined model. Overall levels of employment are significantly associated with lower poverty in model 6 and retain significance in the final combined model. Finally, in model 7 neither human capital spending nor the percentage of the population with low education reach significance.

The combined model 8 shows significant labor market institution (minimum wage setting and works council rights), social rights (parental leave benefits), social risks (employment and unemployment), and globalization (trade openness) variables. The top panel in figure 5.1, based on model 8, displays the substantive effects of these variables, again measured by the effect of a two-standard-deviation change in the independent on the dependent variable. Clearly, the level of employment in a society is the strongest driver of market income poverty. It is closely followed in importance by union participation in minimum wage setting. Thus, the combination of the volume of work performed by households and the floor of remuneration for this work is the key to the level of market income poverty. The former reduces poverty by over 3 percentage points and the latter by slightly less than 3 percentage points. As noted in chapter 3, a two-standard-deviation difference in employment is 15 percentage points, which corresponds to the difference between employment levels in the United States in 1983 (65 percent) or Germany in 2005 (66 percent) and Sweden in 2018 (80 percent). A two-standard-deviation difference in the index of union participation in wage setting is 1.7 (rounded to 2, since the index is measured in whole numbers), which is the difference between the United States and Spain before 1980 (index of 1) and Spain since 1980, Germany, and Sweden (indices of 3).

The substantive effect of trade openness rivals that of union participation in minimum wage setting, but it works in the opposite direction. Since our model controls for employment and unemployment, one can assume that this effect works mainly through downward pressure on wages at the bottom rather than through displacement of low-skilled workers. The graph indicates that union participation in minimum wage setting should be able to counteract this effect. Works council rights work in the same direction as union participation in minimum wage setting to lower poverty. Works councils often work with management to protect working time and pay during economic downturns, and our result suggests that this protection works in favor of low-paid workers who would be at risk of poverty. Finally, as expected, generous parental leave benefits enable parents temporarily to drop out of paid work and thus have their market income drop

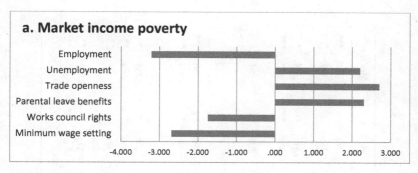
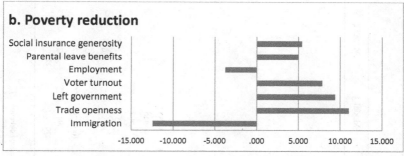
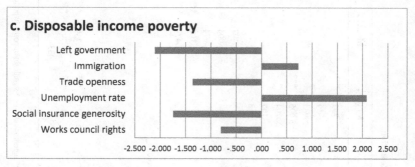

FIGURE 5.1. Effect of two-standard-deviation change in significant independent variables on poverty and poverty reduction

below the poverty threshold. And unemployment drives up market income inequality, as expected.

The results of our analysis of poverty reduction are displayed in table 5.3. In model 1, all but two of the power resources and other political variables are significant in the expected direction. Left and Christian democratic government, voter turnout, and union density all enhance poverty reduction, whereas the presence of veto points hinders such efforts. Of the

TABLE 5.3. **Predictors of Poverty Reduction**

	Model 1		Model 2		Model 3		Model 4		Model 5		Model 6	
Left government	.293	***							.214		.352	***
Christian democratic government	.214	***							-.135		-.219	^
Women in parliament	-.023											
Veto points	-3.865	***							-2.710	**	-1.108	*
Voter turnout	.164	*							.489	***	.327	***
Proportional representation	-.167											
Union density	.178	***							.051		-.094	
Capital market openness			-1.207									
Outward FDI			-.004									
Third world imports			.074									
Trade openness			.197	***					.085	*	.146	***
Immigration			-1.472	***					-.649	**	-1.039	***
Unemployment					-1.258	^						
% children in single-mother households					.628							
Employment					-.764	***	.185		-.467	**	-.255	*
Parental leave benefits							.958	***	.096	**	.084	**
Non-aged welfare state generosity							.351	***	.391	**	-.431	**
Social assistance generosity							5.232		-.274			
Constant	27.473	***	51.236	***	100.971	***			46.715	***	29.846	**
R²	.41	***	.29	***	.04	***	.35		.64	***	.54	***
Observations	458		433		479		221		221		436	

Models 5 and 6 contain period indicators.
* Significant at .05; ** significant at .01; *** significant at .001; ^ significant opposite hypothesized direction.

globalization variables in model 2, only immigration and trade openness are significant, the former negatively and the latter positively associated with poverty reduction. Of the social risk factors in model 3, only employment is significant, in the expected direction. Unemployment is actually significant and negative. We did find that long periods of high unemployment in a society tend to result in reductions of unemployment benefits (Huber and Stephens 2001). We shall come back to this point in our analysis of different time periods. All three of our social rights variables are highly significant and correctly signed, and together they explain more than a third of the variation in poverty reduction.

Model 5 contains all the significant variables from models 1–4, as does model 6, but the coverage of our data for social assistance generosity is so restricted that we are down to 221 observations in model 5. When we drop this variable, model 6 is based on 436 observations. In this model we have significant and correctly signed variables from each of the four theoretical clusters: left government, voter turnout, and veto points (politics); immigration and trade openness (globalization); parental leave benefits and generosity of unemployment and sickness benefits (social rights); and employment (social risks).

The middle panel in figure 5.1 illustrates the substantive importance of these variables. Somewhat surprisingly, the two globalization variables show the strongest association with poverty reduction. The effect of immigration is plausible, as immigrants often do not have the same access to social benefits as citizens and thus are not reached by efforts at poverty reduction. As a reminder, we found a similar effect on inequality reduction. The effect of trade openness on the reduction of both poverty and inequality is not as intuitively plausible. As noted, the compensation hypothesis has a long pedigree in the literature, but we would expect compensation to work through generosity of welfare state benefits or human capital spending, which we analyze. Part of the effect may work like a social risk or need variable. We saw that trade openness increases market income poverty, so with welfare state generosity and political variables held constant it also increases poverty reduction. A two-standard-deviation difference in trade openness corresponds to the difference between the United States in 2010 (28 percent of GDP) and Denmark in 2015 (104 percent of GDP). This difference is associated with a roughly 11 percent greater reduction of poverty. A two-standard-deviation difference in immigration is 12 percent, which corresponds to the difference between Spain in 2002 (6 percent, before the influx of immigrants during the boom years, which doubled that

TABLE 5.4. **Predictors of Disposable Income Poverty**

Minimum wage setting	.248	
Works council rights	−.422	*
Parental leave benefits	−.003	
Working-age social insurance generosity	−.139	***
Unemployment rate	.258	***
Employment	−.012	
Trade openness	−.018	***
Immigration	.061	**
Left government	−.079	***
Voter turnout	.024	^
Constant	9.589	***
Adjusted R^2	.60	***
Observations	436	

Period indicators are included.
* Significant at .05; ** significant at .01; *** significant at .001;
^ significant opposite hypothesized direction.

level) and Sweden in 2018 (18 percent). This difference is associated with a roughly 12 percent lower reduction of poverty.

Voter turnout and left government have strong effects on poverty reduction, even with our two generosity variables held constant. The effect of the generosity variables is expected. Parental leave benefits compensate parents for income they lost because they opted to take leave, and unemployment and sickness benefits compensate workers for loss of income due to these two involuntary states. The fact that an effect of left government and voter turnout remains when generosity of benefits is held constant indicates the use by governments, particularly governments of the left but also governments of all stripes when under pressure from mobilized lower-class voters, of additional anti-poverty policies that we do not have measures for.

Finally, we turn to disposable household income poverty. Table 5.4 shows our model with all the variables that were significant in our analysis of either market household income poverty (model 8 of table 5.2) or poverty reduction (model 6 of table 5.3). The bottom panel of figure 5.1 shows the substantive effects of the significant variables in the model for disposable household income poverty. Left incumbency shows the strongest association with poverty, having a dampening impact, even with generosity of social insurance held constant. This is not surprising, given its large positive impact on poverty reduction. Unemployment has the next strongest impact, followed closely by generosity of unemployment and sickness benefits.

These effects are as expected, given the strong effect of unemployment on market income poverty and the effect of generosity on poverty reduction.

The negative effect of works council rights on market income poverty is replicated on disposable income poverty. Also expected is the positive effect of immigration on disposable income poverty, given its rather large negative effect on poverty reduction efforts. However, among the variables that shape disposable income poverty, immigration has the weakest substantive effect.

Table 5.5 shows the results of our analysis of the dynamics of disposable income poverty in the two time periods. We include all the significant variables from our model of disposable income poverty. The variable left government is measured here as the average over the past fifteen years, not a cumulative average. Only three variables are significant in the period up to 2000: generosity of social insurance and left government are associated with lower disposable income poverty, and immigration with higher poverty. In the post-2000 period, generosity of social insurance and left government retain their significant and positive effects, but immigration fails to reach significance. Instead, unemployment shows a significant effect on higher levels of disposable income poverty, and works council rights and trade openness show a significant effect on lower levels of poverty.

Figure 5.2 shows the very strong substantive effect of generosity of unemployment and sickness insurance on poverty in the earlier period. Generosity of benefits remains substantively important in the more recent period, but the unemployment rate has a considerably stronger effect than

TABLE 5.5. **Predictors of Disposable Income Poverty by Period**

	Pre-2001		Post-2000	
	Model 1		Model 2	
Works council rights	.047		−.426	*
Working-age social insurance generosity	−.262	***	−.151	***
Unemployment rate	.018		.369	***
Trade openness	−.012		−.017	***
Immigration	.117	***	.031	
Left government	−.100	*	−.197	***
Constant	13.772	***	12.450	***
Adjusted R^2	.61	***	.61	***
Observations	139		296	

All models contain period indicators.
* Significant at .05; ** significant at .01; *** significant at .001; ^ significant opposite hypothesized direction.

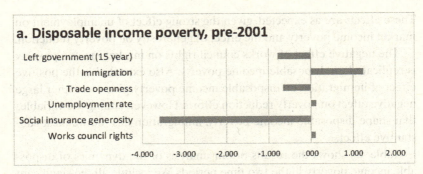

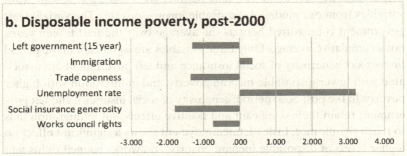

FIGURE 5.2. Effect of two-standard-deviation change in the independent variables on disposable income poverty by period

does generosity. This is in stark contrast to the earlier period, where unemployment was not significant and had a substantively negligible effect. So, we see a pattern similar to that for inequality: unemployment did not drive disposable income poverty and inequality in the earlier period, but it has done so since 2000. Welfare state efforts have fallen short of neutralizing the impact of higher levels of unemployment on poverty and inequality.

Trade openness in the more recent period has the third strongest effect on disposable income poverty—behind the unemployment rate and generosity of unemployment and sickness benefits, and about equal in substantive important to the direct effect of left government. This squares with the strong positive effect on poverty reduction. The fact that the substantive effect of trade openness was much smaller and not statistically significant in the earlier period suggests that the small and historically highly trade-open European countries with generous welfare states (the Nordic countries plus the Netherlands, Belgium, and Austria) were better prepared to deal with European integration and the more globalized world economy.

Table E.5 shows that only unemployment has significant effects on market income poverty in all statistical estimations. Industrial employment and capital market openness have significant effects on market income poverty in all of the alternative statistical estimations, but they were not significant in the final model of table 5.2. The table shows that social insurance generosity, employment, and voter turnout have significant effects on poverty reduction in all statistical estimations. Finally, social insurance generosity, works council rights, unemployment, and immigration have significant effects on disposable income poverty in all models. In addition, voter turnout has significant effects on disposable income poverty in all of the alternative statistical estimations, but it was not significant in the final model of table 5.4. In short, our findings regarding the importance of unemployment and its antidote in generous unemployment benefits for poverty reduction and disposable income poverty are highly robust.

Discussion

In many ways, the patterns for poverty and poverty reduction are similar to those for inequality and inequality reduction. Politics and policies, and unemployment levels, powerfully shape both market and disposable household income inequality and poverty. Politics and policies, of course, are crucial for reduction of both inequality and poverty, and are closely related. As we shall demonstrate in chapter 6, left government has the largest substantive effect on the generosity of unemployment and sickness benefits and the second largest effect on parental leave benefits, as well as an important effect on human capital spending. Christian democratic government has smaller but still significant effects on parental leave and on unemployment and sickness benefits. The direct effects of politics—specifically of left government and voter turnout—that we see on inequality reduction and poverty reduction in the final models with policies held constant indicate that a strong Left and highly mobilized low-income voters make governments adopt tax and transfer policies other than those for which we have measures. Ideally, our measure of generosity of social assistance would capture those other policies, but the restricted temporal coverage of that measure makes it difficult for us to test its impact. Moreover, from case studies we know that social assistance varies quite substantially between subnational units, whereas the measure we have is based on national guidelines or specific subnational units. Also, this measure does not include family allowances or housing subsidies. Nor do we have a measure for the structure of the tax system. As we explained in chapter 1, the bulk of redistribution takes place on the expenditure side, but tax systems nevertheless do vary in their distributive impact.

Employment and unemployment have powerful effects on both market income poverty and inequality. As noted, employment is the most powerful variable predicting market income poverty. A larger share of the population employed means a lower risk of people falling into poverty. Employment levels are partly shaped by demand factors rooted in economic structures. However, supply is also important, and supply is shaped by politics and policies. As we showed in chapter 1, overall employment levels are very highly correlated to women's labor force participation. And women's labor force participation can be greatly enhanced by the provision of free or subsidized child and elderly care services. This process is exemplified by the development of the social democratic service states starting in the 1970s (Huber and Stephens 2000).

Unemployment remains important for disposable income poverty and inequality, with generosity of unemployment benefits held constant. It is among the substantively more important variables for poverty and among the substantively less important variables for inequality. This difference is understandable, since the Gini measures inequality throughout the income distribution, whereas poverty measures what is going on at the bottom, where the loss of paid work can easily push household income below the poverty line. On average, then, over time and across countries, the generosity of unemployment compensation is not sufficient to protect all households with unemployed members from falling into poverty. As our analysis of different time periods has shown, and as our case studies will show, this result is driven by the more recent period, as benefit generosity has not kept pace with need in the face of long-lasting high levels of unemployment; on the contrary, some governments have reduced the generosity of unemployment compensation to deal with the financial pressures resulting from higher need.

The institutional position of labor is important for poverty and for inequality, but different provisions are important at different stages. Union participation in minimum wage setting is substantively important for both market income poverty and inequality. Having a strong floor of market wages keeps both market income poverty and inequality in check. Works council rights further reduce market income poverty, with union participation in minimum wage setting held constant. For disposable income poverty, of the two variables only works council rights matter. For disposable income inequality, the relevant variable is union density. Based on our analysis of top income shares and our case studies, we would interpret this in the following way: Works councils are important for protecting volume and remuneration of work of all workers, including the lowest paid and thus those most at risk of poverty. Strong unions do more than protect low-income workers; they also restrain high income from growing disproportionately, and thus they have a moderating impact on inequality.

Trade openness has a large positive impact on market income poverty and on poverty reduction. Since we are holding politics and policies constant in the analysis of poverty reduction, we can interpret this as the effect of a need variable. Trade openness puts pressures on the incomes at the bottom and pushes people into poverty, and with generosity of benefits held constant results in greater poverty reduction. However, trade openness retains a large negative effect on disposable income poverty, so it does more than repair the damage it creates in market income poverty. Our analysis of the drivers of social rights in chapter 6 will show a large positive effect of trade openness on generosity of unemployment and sickness benefits, with partisan politics held constant. We interpret this as a result of nonpartisan political support for compensating those hurt by trade openness. Greater trade openness means that a larger share of the population is exposed to its negative effects, and thus that the consensus to compensate them is stronger. Again, this consensus and the measures taken go beyond generosity of unemployment and sickness compensation, so that we see a direct effect of trade openness on disposable income poverty after we control for generosity of benefits.

High levels of immigration apparently generate the opposite outcome. Immigration has a negative effect on redistribution and on poverty reduction, and it drives up disposable income poverty. It also has a negative effect on our three measures of social policy, as we shall see in chapter 6. Right-wing nationalist parties have made the issue highly salient, which has arguably pushed the established parties to restrict access to benefits as well. The direct effect of immigration on disposable income poverty, then, with generosity of benefits controlled, can be interpreted as a result of lack of (unmeasured) generous social assistance and/or restriction of access to benefits to non-immigrants.

Human capital spending had the expected effect on market income inequality, and a large moderating effect on disposable income inequality. However, it was not significant in our analyses of market and disposable income poverty. We interpret this to mean that on average human capital spending does more to lift the overall supply of skills in a society than to lift up the bottom specifically. A higher supply of skills will in turn reduce the skill premium and thus inequality in earnings, but it may not do much for earnings at the bottom and thus for poverty levels. Clearly, the unmeasured composition of human capital spending is crucial here. The concentration of expenditures on early childhood education and care and on primary and secondary education should do more for the quality of skills at the bottom, and thus poverty, whereas high expenditures on tertiary education should do more for lowering the skill premium and thus inequality. This is clearly a subject for future research.

CHAPTER SIX

Social Policy

In previous chapters we found strong effects of labor strength, variously measured, on market income inequality; strong effects of social policy on redistribution; more modest effects of social (educational) policy on market income inequality; but few effects of partisan government on distributive outcomes, at least in our combined models including all significant variables. In this chapter we complete the picture by showing that partisan government has very large effects on our policy variables, and thus large indirect effect on the distributive outcomes analyzed in this book.

Quantitative Literature on Welfare State Generosity

Quantitative studies of the causes of variation in welfare state generosity can be subdivided into those which use social or government spending as a measure of welfare state generosity and those which use social rights. These two groups can be subdivided into cross-sectional analyses and pooled time-series analyses. The rough historical sequence is that the early studies were cross-sectional studies of spending (e.g., see Wilensky 1975 and 1981; Stephens 1979; Castles 1982; Korpi 1983); they were followed by pooled time-series analyses of social spending (Pampel and Williamson 1988 and 1989; Hicks and Swank 1992; Hicks 1999; Huber and Stephens 2001; Swank 2002). With the exception of Myles (1984), studies using social rights as welfare state effort measures basically awaited data development by the Swedish Institute for Social Research's large project (later named the Social Citizenship Indicators Project, SCIP). These data were the basis for Esping-Andersen's (1990) book, though he did not take advantage of the pooled data. Early publications that did conduct pooled analyses with the SCIP data were Korpi (1989), Palme (1990), and Kangas (1991).

However, the SCIP data did not enter the public domain until 2007, which slowed progress on the analysis of social rights with pooled data. In the meantime, Scruggs put the first version of his social rights data, an annual time series beginning in 1971, in the public domain in 2004, and this led to the publication of a large number of pooled analyses (e.g., see Allan and Scruggs 2004; Scruggs and Allan 2008; Huo, Nelson, and Stephens 2008; Barth and Moene 2016; Jahn 2018; Loftis and Mortensen 2017).

The quantitative debate of the past five decades about determinants of welfare state development has been carried out between proponents of three different theoretical approaches: the "logic of industrialism," "state-centric," and "political class struggle" (or PRT) approaches. More recently, feminist scholars have made important contributions to the debate, moving from early critiques of the welfare state as reinforcing patriarchy to more nuanced assessments of the differential effects of different welfare state regimes on the status of women and of the role of women as actors in welfare state development. We have already discussed in some detail the PRT explanation, which is our favored explanation of welfare state development (Huber and Stephens 2001); we draw our control variables from these competing explanations. We begin with a brief exposition of the logic of industrialism, state-centric, and feminist contributions, as well as several other hypotheses about welfare state expansion and retrenchment that do not lend themselves to easy classification.

According to the logic of industrialism explanation, both the growth of the welfare state and cross-national differences in "welfare state effort" are by-products of economic development and its demographic and social organizational consequences (Wilensky 1975; Pampel and Williamson 1989). This suggests that GDP per capita and demography should be important causes of welfare state variation. Those insisting on a state-centric approach have focused on the policy-making role of bureaucrats (who are assumed to be relatively impervious to social forces), on the capacity of the state apparatus to implement welfare state programs, on the effects of state structure (e.g., federalism), and on the influence of past policy on new social policy initiatives (Heclo 1974; Orloff 1993; Weir, Orloff, and Skocpol 1988; Skocpol 1988; Immergut 1992).

The contributions to the welfare state literature from a feminist perspective have mostly focused on the consequences of the welfare state for women's material position and for gender relations more broadly. Comparative studies of the role of women as active promoters of gender interests in shaping welfare states in the post–World War II era were initially scarce. Since the mid-1990s, though, there has been a proliferation of work on the role of women's movements in shaping the welfare state (e.g., see Hill and Tigges 1995; Hobson and Lindholm 1997; Jenson and Mahon 1993; Lewis 1994; O'Conner, Orloff, and Shaver 1999; Stetson and Mazur 1995; Wängnerud, 2000; Little, Dunn, and Deen 2001; Bratton and Ray 2002; Atchison and Down 2009). Virtually all of these studies confirm that women, acting as independent women's movements, within established political parties (particularly leftist parties) and within state agencies, have been important actors promoting what Hernes (1987) calls women-friendly policies, but that they were only successful when they had allies.

There are two other lines of argument in the literature about the expansion of and cross-national differences in the aggregate size of welfare states that cannot really be classified as theoretical schools as they focus on one particular causal dynamic and are compatible to various degrees with the logic of industrialism and the power resources approach. The first holds that economic openness causes domestic vulnerability to external fluctuations and thus provides the incentive for the establishment of social safety nets for those affected by such external trends or cycles (Cameron 1978; Katzenstein 1985). Since smaller countries tend to be more open to international trade than larger ones, they are more likely to develop comprehensive systems of social protection as compensation for the victims of industrial adjustment. Recent contributions to the retrenchment literature turn this thesis on its head, arguing that increasing openness of financial as well as goods markets leads to cuts in the generosity of social policy, particularly in the most advanced welfare states.

A second line of argument is that the strength of political Catholicism has led to the development of generous welfare states, though until recently there was no attempt to set this in a clear theoretical frame. Stephens (1979, 100, 123–24) argues that political Catholicism leads to welfare states almost as generous but less redistributive than those developed under social democratic auspices. Wilensky (1981) presents cross-national data showing that Christian democratic cabinet share is the most important determinant of his measure of social spending. Based on a variety of indicators of welfare state patterns, Esping-Andersen (1990) argues for the existence of a distinctive type of "conservative" though generous welfare state regime created largely by European continental Christian democratic parties. Van Kersbergen (1995) provides a quantitative and an in-depth case study analysis and a power resources interpretation for the development of the Christian democratic welfare state.

Hypotheses

Dependent Variables

Our policy variables are generosity of social insurance benefits for the working-age population, parental leave benefits, and human capital spending. Generosity of social insurance benefits for the working-age population is operationalized using an index of sickness and unemployment benefits taken from Scruggs and Tafoya's (2022) Comparative Welfare Entitlements Project. Parental leave benefits come from Gauthier's (2011) Comparative Family Policy Database and our own coding from country sources for 2011–2019, and are operationalized as the average replacement rate of parental leave benefits in the first year. Human capital spending is spending on daycare, public education at all levels, and active labor market policy as a percentage of GDP.

Political Variables

Based on our previous research (Huber, Ragin, and Stephens 1993; Huber and Stephens 2000 and 2001; Huo, Nelson, and Stephens 2008), we expect long-term left government to have a strong effect on all three of our policy measures (table 6.1). In Huber and Stephens (2001), we argued that the dominant parties in government in a given country over the long run—left parties, Christian democratic parties, and secular center and right parties—determined which of Esping-Andersen's (1990) three worlds a country ended up in, and we presented both quantitative and comparative case study evidence to support that view.[1]

With regard to Christian democratic government, we expect modest positive effects on unemployment insurance and sick pay generosity, ambiguous effects on parental leave, and negative effects on human capital spending. We expect ambiguous effects on our parental leave measure because Christian democratic parties typically favored parental leave, but with low pay. We expect a negative effect on human capital spending because daycare is much less developed in continental (often Christian democratic-governed) countries compared with the Nordic model due to the dominance of the male breadwinner model in the former. Led by coalitions of social democratic and agrarian/center parties, the Nordic countries universalized and de-tracked secondary education and later greatly expanded access to public tertiary education. By contrast, Christian dem-

TABLE 6.1. **Variables and Hypotheses**

	Social insurance generosity	Parental leave benefits	Human capital spending
Dependent variables			
Social insurance generosity			
Parental leave benefits			
Human capital spending			
Independent variables			
Politics and political institutions			
Left government	+	+	+
Christian democratic government	+	+/–	–
Women in parliament	+	+	+
Veto points	+/–	+/–	+/–
Proportional representation	+	+	+
Voter turnout	+	+	+
Globalization			
Capital market openness	–	–	–
Third world imports	–	–	–
Trade openness	+/–	+/–	+/–
Outward FDI	–	–	–
Immigration			
Long-term economic change			
Technological change			+
Employment in dynamic services			+
Social risks			
Unemployment rate	+/–		
% children in single-mother households		+	
Other control variables			
Military spending (% GDP)	–	–	–
GDP per capita	+	+	+

Variable definitions and sources in table A.1.

ocratic governments pushed back social democratic and union demands for expanded and de-tracked secondary and expanded public tertiary education (Österman 2017).

Our expectations for women in parliament are clear: a strong positive association with all three policy indicators, but especially parental leave and human capital investment. However, the effect of women in parliament is trickier to interpret causally because it is highly correlated to left government (r = .78). Historically, left governments promoted gender-egalitarian policies and all left parties—social democratic, Green, and left socialist—instituted quotas for women in party affairs, including parliament representation. As we have argued in earlier works (Huber and Stephens

2000 and 2001), this initiated a feedback loop in which women, particularly politically activated women, increased their support for the Left and demanded more gender-egalitarian policies, like work and family reconciliation policies, and greater incorporation into policy making, including parity in representation in parliament and in the cabinet. Disentangling this feedback loop in quantitative analysis is simply not possible. We expect higher voter turnout to be positively associated with all three of our social policy variables. As noted in earlier chapters, high voter turnout is mainly driven by mobilization at the bottom and thus can be grouped with power resources variables.

The state-centric approach to welfare state development argues that political institutional variables affect variations in welfare generosity. We measure this with two variables: veto points and proportional representation. Our hypotheses on their effects are the same as for the effects for redistribution outlined in the last chapter. Our original finding on veto points—that they retarded welfare state development—was on data that primarily covered the period of welfare state expansion (Huber, Ragin, and Stephens 1993). Later research, primarily case studies, indicated that opponents of welfare state cutbacks could use constitutional structure veto points to retard retrenchment. Thus, we adopt a nondirectional hypothesis for veto points. In chapter 5 we found that there was no direct effect of proportional representation, and that it was necessary to show that proportional representation effects social policy generosity or left government or both to find support for Iversen and Soskice's (2006) hypothesis. We expect a positive effect of proportional representation on social policy generosity.

Globalization

Our hypotheses for the globalization variables are also the same as in previous chapters. We expect all of them except trade openness to have a negative effect on social policy generosity, as they strengthen the hand of capital in negotiation with governments and labor. As we explained earlier in this book, there are competing hypotheses with regard to the effect of trade openness: the conventional race-to-the-bottom hypothesis is counterposed by Katzenstein's (1985) "compensation" hypothesis, which contends that in very open economies such as the small countries of northern Europe labor is compensated for the vagaries of rapid change by generous social policy.

Long-Term Economic Change, Social Risks

We hypothesize that long-term economic change will create a demand for human capital investment because it creates demand for more skilled and educated workers. We do not expect it to affect the other two policy variables. We also expect the effects of social risks to be specific to the three dependent variables. We hypothesize that greater proportions of children in single-mother families will increase the demand for generous parental leave. Arguably, unemployment will affect unemployment insurance generosity, but it is unclear what direction this might take. For instance, in the mid-1970s Switzerland moved from virtually no unemployment to very modest levels of unemployment. The government responded by replacing an almost nonexistent system in 1974 with one with benefits at the 90th percentile on Scruggs's unemployment generosity index. On the other hand, governments in Denmark, the Netherlands, Finland, and Sweden responded to sustained periods of high unemployment with cuts in unemployment insurance generosity.

Other Controls

Past quantitative studies of welfare state development have included level of affluence (measured by GDP per capita) and demographic structure, usually measured by the percentage of the population over sixty-five years of age, as operationalizations of the logic of industrialism theory (Wilensky 1975; Pampel and Williamson 1989). Many decades before the formulation of the logic of industrialism theory in the 1960s, in the late nineteenth century, the German economist Adolph Wagner formulated a thesis, which became known as Wagner's Law. His thesis states that as the national income increases, the government's share of national income will rise as well, as the government's role in the economy (including the provision of welfare) expands. We measure national economic affluence as GDP per capita. We do not include aged population as a control variable because our measure of social insurance generosity excludes pensions and our household disposable income variables data exclude elderly households. Following many quantitative studies of variations in welfare generosity (e.g., see Hicks 1999; Huo, Nelson, and Stephens 2008), we control for military spending to account for a possible guns-versus-butter trade-off. The measurement of these variables and data sources is explained in appendix C and summarized in table A.1.

Results

Again, our statistical estimation is the same as in the previous chapters: Vernby and Lindgren's (2009) dvgreg package for dynamic panel data models. Table 6.2 displays our analysis of the causes of variation in generosity of social insurance for the working-age population as measured by an additive measure of Scruggs's sick pay and unemployment insurance indexes. As before, we enter our independent variables in theoretical clusters—politics and political institutions, globalization, and other controls—and we carry the significant variables forward to the combined model 4. Model 1 contains all of the political variables, four of which are correctly signed and significant. Together they explain an impressive 50 percent of the variation in social insurance generosity. Model 2 contains the globalization variables. Three of the five are correctly signed and significant, and together, they explain 30 percent of the variation in social insurance generosity. Two of the control variables in model 3 are significant and correctly signed, but the model only explains 5 percent of the variation.

TABLE 6.2. **Predictors of Social Insurance Generosity**

	Model 1		Model 2		Model 3		Model 4	
Left government	.220	***					.288	***
Christian democratic government	.081	***					.034	**
Women in parliament	.003							
Veto points	.397	***					1.033	***
Proportional representation	3.546	***					1.610	***
Voter turnout	−.047	^						
Capital market openness			.247					
Third world imports			−.427	***			−.772	***
Trade openness			.117	***			.090	***
Outward FDI			.028					
Immigration			−.168	***			−.231	***
Unemployment rate					−.238	***	−.089	*
Military spending (% GDP)					.917	^		
GDP per capita					.032	*	.038	
Constant	13.125	***	14.028	***	22.105	***	8.999	
Adjusted R²	.50	***	.30	***	.05	***	.65	***
Observations	957		882		926		846	

Model 4 contains period indicators.
* Significant at .05; ** significant at .01; *** significant at .001; ^ significant opposite hypothesized direction.

SOCIAL POLICY

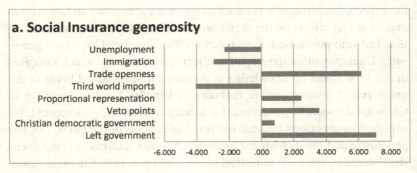

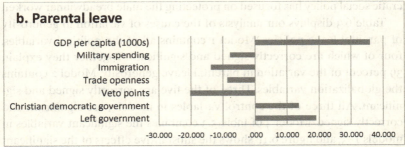

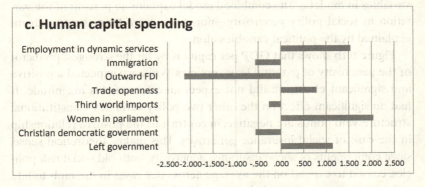

FIGURE 6.1. Effect of two-standard-deviation change in significant independent variables on social policy

Model 4 combines the significant variables in models 1–3, and figure 6.1a shows the substantive effects of the significant variables in model 4. The combined model explains 65 percent of the variation in social insurance generosity. Left government and trade openness clearly have the strongest effect on generosity, which supports PRT and Katzenstein's compensation hypothesis, respectively. The other two globalization variables have the expected negative effects on social insurance generosity and have moderately strong effects on the dependent variable. Proportional representation and veto points both have *positive* effects on social insurance generosity. Unemployment has negative effects on generosity, which indicates, in our view based on knowledge of the cases, that sustained bouts of unemployment often stimulate cutbacks in benefits. Finally, the effect of Christian democratic government is much smaller than we expected. We expected larger effects because the two components of the index, sick pay generosity and unemployment insurance benefits, address the "old social risks" faced by the male industrial worker, and generally Christian democratic social policy has focused on protecting the male breadwinner worker.

Table 6.3 displays our analysis of the causes of variation in generosity of parental leave policies. Model 1 contains all of the political variables, four of which are correctly signed and significant. Together they explain 39 percent of the variation in parental leave generosity. Model 2 contains the globalization variables. Three of the five are correctly signed and significant. All three of the control variables in model 3 are significant and correctly signed. Model 4 of table 5.3 combines the significant variables in models 1–3, and figure 6.1b shows the substantive effects of the significant variables in model 4. The combined model explains 40 percent of the variation in social policy generosity—not much more than the 39 percent explained by the political variables alone.

Figure 6.1b shows that GDP per capita is by far the strongest predictor of the generosity of parental leave policies. While we expected a positive and significant effect, we did not expect an effect of this magnitude. It had no significant effect on the other two policy variables. Constitutional structure veto points are negative, in contrast to the positive relationship in the case of social insurance generosity. This makes theoretical sense, since components of social insurance generosity, both old social risk policies, ceased to expand on the average across our cases in the mid- to late 1980s, so it was a matter of blocking cutbacks. By contrast, parental leave continues to expand on the average up to the most recent time points, so veto points served to block expansion.

The effect of left government is stronger than that of Christian democratic government, as hypothesized, though we expected a larger difference in magnitude, since the way we measured parental leave taps work and family reconciliation, which was not favored by Christian democrats until very recently, and even then not by all Christian democratic parties (Morgan 2013). Immigration again has a negative effect on parental leave

TABLE 6.3. **Predictors of Generosity of Parental Leave Policies**

	Model 1		Model 2		Model 3		Model 4	
Left government	.967	***					.815	***
Christian democratic government	.917	***					.587	***
Women in parliament	.321	***					-.121	
Veto points	-5.385	***					-5.906	***
Proportional representation	-1.609							
Voter turnout	-.460	^						
Capital market openness			5.614	^				
Third world imports			1.469	^				
Trade openness			.119	**			-.087	**
Outward FDI			-.359	**			-.086	
Immigration			-1.283	**			-.912	***
% children in single-mother households					1.045	***	.203	
Military spending (% GDP)					-3.839	***	-2.874	***
GDP per capita					.586	***	1.158	***
Constant	54.076	***	30.349	***	14.228	***	11.747	***
Adjusted R^2	.39	***	.11	***	.18	***	.40	***
Observations	1231		879		1122		933	

Model 4 contains period indicators.
* Significant at .05; ** significant at .01; *** significant at .001; ^ significant opposite hypothesized direction.

generosity, as does trade openness, consistent with the race-to-the-bottom rather than the compensation hypothesis. Finally, as expected, military spending has a small but statistically significant negative effect on variations in the generosity of parental leave policies.

Table 6.4 displays our analysis of the causes of variation in human capital spending—spending on daycare, public education, and active labor market policies. Again, we enter our independent variables in theoretical clusters—politics and political institutions, globalization, and other controls—and we carry the significant variables forward to the combined model 4. There are a lot of missing data for employment in dynamic services, so we drop that variable in model 5.

Model 1 contains the political variables, three of which are significant. The model explains an impressive 56 percent of the variation in human capital spending. Four of the globalization variables in model 2 are significant. The remaining controls are included in model 3. As mentioned, model 4 contains all of the significant variables in models 1–3, and model 5 drops employment in dynamic services, which results in the addition of 255 observations. Figure 6.1c shows the substantive effects of the significant

TABLE 6.4. **Predictors of Human Capital Spending**

	Model 1		Model 2		Model 3		Model 4		Model 5	
Left government	.054	***					.036		.046	***
Christian democratic government	-.020	***					-.012	*	-.021	***
Women in parliament	.078	***					.085	***	.089	***
Veto points	-.032									
Proportional representation	-.114									
Voter turnout	.003									
Capital market openness			.706	^						
Third world imports			-.105	**			-.569	***	-.053	*
Trade openness			.019	***			.025	***	.007	***
Outward FDI			-.024	*			-.013	*	-.012	*
Immigration			-.024	*			-.014		-.036	***
Technological change					-64.058	^				
Employment in dynamic services					.223	***	.263	***		
Military spending (% GDP)					-.317	*	.165			
GDP per capita					-.032				.127	
Constant	3.750	***	4.509	***	6.411	***	1.992	***	3.740	***
Adjusted R²	.56		.14		.12		.68		.60	
Observations	675		585		361		345		600	

Models 4 and 5 contain period indicators.
* Significant at .05; ** significant at .01; *** significant at .001; ^ significant opposite hypothesized direction.

variables based on the coefficients in model 5 except for dynamic services, which is based the coefficient in model 4.

Though we expected outward direct foreign investment to have a negative effect, we did not anticipate that its substantive effect would be the largest of the significant variables (though it was followed closely by the percentage of parliamentary seats held by females). The two cabinet variables were significant and signed as predicted. As we noted earlier in this chapter, left government and female percentage of parliamentary seats are highly correlated ($r = .78$). If one drops female parliamentary seats from the model, left government becomes the strongest variable, with a two-standard-deviation increase in left government resulting in a 2.5 percent increase in human capital spending. This is not to imply that female parliamentary representation is somehow spurious or even that the overlap in variation explained should be assigned to left government. Rather, we argue that the two are so closely causally entwined that it is not possible to separate the effects of the two statistically.[2] Our results indicate that employment in dynamic services, a measure of the expansion of the knowledge economy, created a demand for more investment in human capital; a two-standard-deviation increase in dynamic service employment results in a 1.5 percent increase in human capital spending. Trade openness is now positive, while the other two globalization variables are negative but not particularly strong.

Just as we did in chapter 5, we explored whether the dynamics of expansion of social rights differed from the earlier to the later period. We compared the periods before and after 1990 for generosity of social insurance and of parental leave, and before and after 1996 for human capital spending, because of the scarcity of observations for human capital spending before 1990. The politics of social rights expansion remained remarkably stable across periods for all three social rights, so we do not include the additional table. The one notable exception is that immigration was not significant in the earlier period and became highly significant and negative in the later period for all three social rights variables.

Unemployment was significantly and negatively associated with generosity of unemployment and sickness benefits in both periods. This is a result we have seen and shall see repeatedly in our case studies: in the face of high levels of unemployment, governments tightened eligibility conditions and reduced replacement rates for unemployment compensation. The only variable that shows a consistent difference in impact between the two periods is immigration. It is not significant in the earlier period for generosity of social insurance and for parental leave, and marginally significant and positive for human capital spending. In the later period, it becomes highly significant and negative on all three social rights indicators. Immigration before the 1990s came mainly in the form of workers (and eventually their families) from the southern European countries, so immigrants were largely seen as productive members of society. As immigration from other countries increased, anti-immigrant sentiment was politically mobilized and immigrants were frequently portrayed as relying on public support rather than earning their keep, which in turn could be used as political cover by politicians intent on restraining welfare state benefits.

Table E.6 shows that unemployment, trade openness, and third world imports have significant effects on social insurance generosity in all statistical estimations. In addition, left government and Christian democratic government have significant effects in the random effects model, but since social insurance generosity varies primarily across countries, these independent variables should be counted as robust. The table shows that left government and GDP per capita have significant effects on parental leave for the working-age population in all statistical estimations. Veto points have significant effects on parental leave in the two country fixed-effects models. Finally, left government, third world imports, and women's share of parliamentary seats have significant effects on human capital spending in all models.

Discussion

In this chapter we demonstrated that partisan government had a strong effect on variations in our social policy indicators. Left government had the largest effect of any independent variable on variations in social insurance generosity for the working-age population, the second largest on parental leave, and the third largest on human capital spending. Moreover, female representation in parliament, which is causally entwined with left government, had the second largest effect on variations in human capital spending. The strong role of partisanship in shaping the welfare state helps explain the geographic clustering of the regimes, with the social democratic regimes developing in the social democratic-dominated Nordic countries, the Christian democratic/conservative regimes developing in the continental European countries, and liberal regimes developing in the secular center- and right-governed Anglo-American countries. From table A.3

and A.4 one can see that government redistribution and disposable income distribution closely follow this regime typology, and we argue that variations in long-term partisan government are the primary reason for that.

Tables A.3 and A.4 show that the southern regimes effect the least redistribution and have the most unequal disposable income distributions. Table 1.1 indicates that this is not due to their values on the power resource, labor market institutions, and partisan government variables. Southern regimes are very similar to the continental group on all of these factors. They are distinctly lower on the three policy variables, which seems puzzling given their similarity to the continental group on power resources, political institutions, and partisan government. We can look to Ferrara's original 1996 article, in which he first argued for the existence of a distinct southern regime, for a solution to this puzzle. He argues that the southern regime has four distinct features: (1) dualism—holes in coverage of social insurance, pension-heavy, not much spending on youth and working-age population;[3] (2) clientelism as a basis for distribution of some transfers, especially in Italy and Greece; (3) familialism—reliance on the family to do what the welfare state does elsewhere (at least in Europe); and (4) national health services established in the 1970s, but more reliance on private spending than in the Nordic countries and Britain. Ferrara links this to distinctive features of the development of these countries, and above all to late democratization (except Italy) and incomplete development of Fordism due in turn to late economic development.

It is certainly not surprising that partisan politics and political institutions have substantively larger impacts on all three social rights variables. As we discussed, welfare state construction has been a profoundly political affair, and political institutions (proportional representation and veto points) shape the translation of partisan and nonpartisan (from women representatives) political pressures into actual policies. What deserves some more discussion is the differences in the impact of globalization variables on our three social rights indicators.

Trade openness has a positive and large effect on generosity of unemployment and sickness benefits, as well as a positive but relatively less important effect on human capital spending, but a moderate negative effect on parental leave benefits. Outward direct foreign investment has a strong negative effect on human capital spending. Assuming that business acts as an interest group in promoting its advantages in global markets and at home, we can propose the following interpretations: In highly trade-open countries, a large proportion of the population is exposed to possible negative effects from foreign markets and competition, so support for generous unemployment benefits is likely to be wide. Business will go along with this support for compensation in order to maintain political support for trade openness. Exporters also need a skilled labor force to be competitive in export markets, so we can expect them to support human capital spending. On the other hand, parental leave benefits do not directly contribute to support for trade openness or to competitiveness on export markets, and they can create problems for business not only in costs but also in missing staff, so business opposition to generous parental leave benefits is more probable. Business sectors that rely heavily on direct investments abroad and on outsourcing of much of their production of goods and services do not have much interest in human capital spending at home, and accordingly can be expected to oppose such spending.

Immigration has a medium-strength negative effect on all three social policy indicators. Immigration can be and has been instrumentalized by opponents of generous social policy by fueling anti-immigrant sentiment through messaging alleging that idle immigrants take advantage of social benefits paid for by hard-working citizens. However, it is unclear whether these opponents were successful in undermining public support for the welfare state. Brady and Finnigan (2013) found only very limited support for a negative effect of immigration on support for social policy, and Breznau et al. (2022) found inconclusive results as well. This leads us to interpret the immigration effect in much the same way we analyzed the unemployment effect. The problem pressure in combination with fiscal constraints induced politicians to introduce policy changes that have tightened eligibility conditions and reduced generosity of social insurance.

CHAPTER SEVEN

Social Investment versus Social Consumption?

We have firmly established that the social policies generally labeled social investment are indeed strongly and robustly associated with lower market and disposable income inequality. This is particularly true for education at all levels, from early childhood education to training and retraining of adults, but also for policies that facilitate the simultaneous pursuit of raising a family and engaging in paid work. We have also established that the key is public investment in education. It is also firmly established that societies with greater inequality have lower social mobility. Here we want to bring these facts into the discussion of social investment and social consumption, and we want to elucidate the mechanism that works through the distribution of human capital.

In chapter 2 we showed that high inequality in skills among adults, measured by the 95-5 ratio in numeracy scores on the PIAAC tests, is significantly associated with higher wage dispersion. We also showed that human capital spending, a measure including public spending on education, daycare, and active labor market policies as a percentage of GDP, is strongly negatively associated with both the 90-50 and the 50-10 ratios of wages of full-time employees. With all the controls entered, human capital spending remained significantly associated with the 90-50 wage ratio, indicating that a higher supply of human capital reduces wage inequality in the upper half of the income distribution. Finally, we showed that the share of total education spending that is private is strongly positively associated with both wage ratios—so, reliance on private education spending increases wage dispersion. Our findings in chapter 4 mirrored the findings on the egalitarian impact of public education expenditures and the inegalitarian impact of reliance on private education spending. We showed that public education expenditure is highly significantly negatively associated with the share of the top 1 percent and that the private share of tertiary education spending is strongly positively associated with that share. Our analyses in chapters 3 and 5 showed that human capital spending is strongly associated with market and with disposable household income inequality, but not with household income poverty. So, human capital spending reduces wage dispersion in the upper half of the income distribution and household income inequality as measured by the Gini, but is less closely associated with wage dispersion in the lower half and with poverty.

In this chapter we shall try to throw some light on this difference by exploring further the role of human capital spending in different contexts, as well as the link between human capital spending and the distribution of skills. Our findings regarding the effect of human capital spending on income inequality strongly support the arguments of the pre-distribution agenda (Chwalisz and Diamond 2015). The key prescription of this agenda is to improve the distribution of market income rather than relying entirely on taxes and transfers to repair the inequalities created by markets. Investing in human capital throughout the life cycle and providing social services that enable individuals to remain productively employed throughout their working-age lives took center stage, but reforms of the financial system, corporate governance, labor market institutions, and product market regulation were also part of this agenda (Chwalisz and Diamond 2015, 5–6). The agenda had precursors in the Nordic countries but became internationally prominent with the 2000 Lisbon agenda that proclaimed as a goal turning Europe into the "most competitive and dynamic knowledge-based economy in the world, capable of sustainable economic growth and more and better jobs and greater social cohesion" (Hemerijck 2017, 4).

The academic debate about social investment centered around the relative value of the active versus the passive welfare state and around the distributive implications of an emphasis on investment in human capital. In addition, the rapidly growing literature on redistributive preferences explored differences among socioeconomic groups regarding their support for transfers relative to expenditures on social investment, with an emphasis on necessary trade-offs (Beramendi et al. 2015). Advocates of social investment correctly argued that new labor markets and family patterns made risks less predictable and therefore less amenable to social insurance than were the risks characteristic of the past industrial society with the male breadwinner family. In addition, an aging society required higher employment, improvements in productivity, and faster economic growth in order to sustain a generous welfare state. Therefore, welfare state efforts should focus on labor market integration of the current generations of working age and on the future productivity of children by investing in education at all levels and all stages of life, by socializing care work in order to free women to join the labor force, and by assisting individuals in entering and remaining connected to the labor force. Higher levels of employment would in turn reduce the burden on the passive welfare state, and higher levels of human capital would reduce poverty and inequality.

Whereas academic advocates of social investment explicitly warned that the policy they were promoting should not be seen as an alternative to or replacement of a transfer-based safety net (Esping-Andersen 2003), some participants in the political debate painted social investment geared toward labor market integration of individuals as an alternative to this safety net for working-age people. The Introduction to the OECD (2008b) report *Growing Unequal?* does not explicitly state that the safety net should be cut, but the implications are rather clear: "Relying on taxing more and spending more as a response to inequality can only be a temporary measure. The only sustainable way to reduce inequality is to stop the underlying widening of wages and income from capital. In particular, we have to make sure that people are capable of being in employment and earning wages that keep them and their families out of poverty. This means that developed countries have to do much better in getting people into work, rather than relying on unemployment, disability and early retirement benefits, in keeping them in work and in offering good career prospects" (OECD 2008b, 16).

Academic critics pointed out that social investment was being oversold: the conceptual distinction between passive social spending and social investment spending was not sharp, and empirical evidence that social investment was working was scarce (Nolan 2017). Moreover, much social investment helped upper income earners more than the truly disadvantaged; for instance, full-time formal childcare use was significantly higher in the top quintile than in the bottom quintile in most countries with high levels of use, and participation in higher education was much more likely for children of parents with higher education than for children of parents without (Bonoli, Cantillon, and van Lancker 2015). Moreover, emphasizing the economic justification—the payoff of social investment for productivity and economic growth—risked losing sight of the essential goals of producing social returns to social spending (Nolan 2017).

We agree with the critique of the view that social investment should be prioritized at the expense of social consumption, or that there should be a political trade-off between the two, and we shall show that indeed social investment and social transfers have to work in tandem in order for social investment to have the intended effects. Specifically, we shall show that poverty and inequality in the parents' generation profoundly affect human capital in the children's generation, above and beyond investment in human capital. We shall also show that public education spending is crucial for skill levels in the population, and that higher skill levels in the adult population are associated with a lower education premium. Finally, we shall show that higher public education spending reduces the education premium, whereas greater reliance on private education spending increases it.

Data and Measurement

Comparable data that measure the distribution of skills among current students and among the adult population are very scarce. For current students we have test results from the Programme for International Student Assessment (PISA), which is a program of the OECD. These tests are given triennially to fifteen-year olds in OECD and partner countries to evaluate reading, mathematical, and scientific literacy. The scores are standardized to have an OECD average of 500, with about two-thirds of scores between 400 and 600. We use the results for mathematical skills, because they are generally more comparable cross-nationally than literacy skills (Hanushek et al. 2015). We are interested in both the country mean scores and the scores at the 25th percentile, because they measure the central tendency as well as the performance of low achievers. We use the aggregate national-level scores for all the waves of the PISA test conducted between 2000 and 2015.

To measure the distribution of skills among the adult population, we use scores from the Programme for the International Assessment of Adult Competencies (PIAAC), also a program of the OECD. These tests were given to a nationally representative sample of adults (age 16–65) in the period 2011–2012, and we only have data from this single wave. We also use the numeracy scores and the mean scores, and the scores at the 25th percentile. There are considerable cross-national differences in literacy-related non-responses. The data we use here are adjusted for these non-responses, following the method used by the OECD to adjust the published mean scores.[1] Australia, Belgium, Greece, Portugal, and Switzerland lack usable data for skills in the PIACC studies.

To measure the education premium, we use the Weisstanner and Armingeon (2020) data, as in earlier chapters (appendix C). There are no data for New Zealand and Portugal.

Similarly, as in earlier chapters, we use human capital spending as a percentage of GDP. For the analysis of PISA data, we use the average total and public education spending as a percentage of GDP from 1990 or 1995 to the year of the test score observation. For the analysis of the PIAAC data we use the average of human capital spending from 1985 to 2010. Our measures for poverty and inequality are also the same as in earlier chapters: they are for disposable household income of the working-age population. For the analysis of PISA data, or students, we use poverty and inequality levels in the year of the observation. For the analysis of PIAAC data, or adults, we use average poverty and inequality levels in the pre-1990 period, when these adults were of school age. The variables, data sources, and hypotheses are listed in table 7.1.

TABLE 7.1. **Variables and Hypotheses**

	Definition	Test scores	Education premium
Dependent variables			
Math mean score	Mean score on PISA's mathematical literacy component		
Math 25th percentile score	25th percentile score on PISA's mathematical literacy component		
Numeracy adjusted scores	25th percentile and mean numeracy score adjusted for literacy-related non-responses, Study of Adult Skills		
Education premium	The percentage difference between the median wage of full-time workers with tertiary education and the median wage of individuals without tertiary education (pre-tax)		
Independent variables			
Poverty in the 1980s	Percentage of working-age households below 50% of median disposable income in the 1980s	–	
Gini in the 1980s	Gini index of working-age households in the 1980s	–	
Human capital spending	Public spending on education, daycare, and active labor market policies as a % of GDP	+	

continues

TABLE 7.1. (*continued*)

	Definition	Test scores	Education premium
Working-age poverty	Percentage of working-age households below 50% of median disposable income	–	
Working-age Gini	Gini index of working-age households	–	
Public education spending	Total general (local, regional, and central) government expenditure on education (current, capital, and transfers), expressed as a percentage of GDP	+	–
Private education spending	Education expenditure provided by private sources, expressed as a percentage of GDP		+
Union density	Net union membership as a percentage of employed wage and salary earners	–	
Mean literacy score	Mean literacy score in the Study of Adult Skills adjusted for literacy-related non-responses		–
Numeracy adjusted scores	25th percentile and mean numeracy score adjusted for literacy-related non-responses, Study of Adult Skills		–
Total factor productivity	Total factor productivity (TFP) level at current PPPs (USA = 1)		+
% with tertiary education	Percentage of the population aged 25 and over with any tertiary schooling		–
Unemployment	Harmonized unemployment rate, the number of unemployed persons as a percentage of the civilian labor force		+

Results

Given the cross-sectional nature of the data, and the small number of observations in the case of the PIAAC data, we begin with simple correlations and then proceed to two-variable OLS regressions. The correlations between the mean numeracy score of the population in the PIAAC tests and public education spending, human capital spending, and poverty and inequality in the parents' generation range from .65 (public education spending) to −.93 (Gini in the pre-1990 period). The correlations are almost the same for the numeracy scores at the 25th percentile (table 7.2). The correlations of the scores with human capital spending are higher than those with public education spending, which is understandable because human capital spending is a more inclusive measure. Accordingly, we use human capital spending in our regressions.

The regressions reflect these correlations and the greater strength of

TABLE 7.2. **Correlations of PIAAC Scores, Human Capital Investment, and Inequality in the Parental (1980s) Generation**

	25th percentile	Mean
Public education spending	.63	.65
Human capital spending	.72	.71
Gini in the 1980s	−.92	−.93
Poverty in the 1980s	−.82	−.80

TABLE 7.3. **PIAAC Scores, Human Capital Investment, and Inequality in the Parental (1980s) Generation**

	Numeracy 25th percentile adjusted score			
	Model 1		Model 2	
Human capital spending	3.650	**	.822	
Gini in the 1980s			−3.018	***
Poverty in the 1980s	−2.987	**		
Constant	230.127	***	308.485	***
R^2	.79		.87	
Observations	13		13	
	Numeracy mean adjusted score			
	Model 3		Model 4	
Human capital spending	3.503	*	.718	
Gini in the 1980s			−2.880	***
Poverty in the 1980s	−2.752	**		
Constant	265.822	***	341.929	***
R^2	.75		.84	
Observations	13		13	

association with the poverty and inequality variables as compared with the spending variables. Our models in table 7.3 show that human capital spending is significant and positively associated with the numeracy scores at both the 25th percentile and the mean when we control for poverty in the parents' generation, but the variable loses statistical significance when we control for inequality in the parents' generation. Poverty and inequality in the parents' generation are consistently significant and negatively associated with the skill measures. This indicates that human capital spending does indeed improve the skill levels of the population, including in the lower half, whereas poverty and inequality in the parents' generation work in the opposite direction, lowering skill levels. High levels of inequality overpower the effects of human capital spending.

TABLE 7.4. **PISA Scores and Public-Private Mix in Education**

	Math 5th percentile score			
	Model 1	Model 2	Model 3	Model 4
Total education spending	5.566 **			
Public education spending		9.581 ***	7.884 ***	7.710 ***
Working-age Gini			−.952	
Working-age poverty				−1.557 **
Constant	310.223 ***	294.198 ***	333.990 ***	321.294 ***
Adjusted R²	.08 **	.21 ***	.25 ***	.28 ***
Observations	101	98	76	75

	Math mean score			
	Model 5	Model 6	Model 7	Model 8
Total education spending	5.122 **			
Public education spending		8.519 ***	3.380	4.599 **
Working-age Gini			−2.267 ***	
Working-age poverty				−2.475 ***
Constant	468.607 ***	455.607 ***	549.589 ***	498.844 ***
Adjusted R²	.08 **	.19 ***	.29 ***	.32 ***
Observations	101	98	76	75

* Significant at .05; ** significant at .01; *** significant at .001.

We perform a similar analysis of the impact of education spending and of poverty and inequality on the performance of fifteen-year-old students on the mathematical part of the PISA tests (see table 7.4). In these data and in the education premium data in table 7.5 we have data at multiple time points, so we use dynamic panel estimates, as in previous chapters. Here we want to explore the effect of total education spending, public and private, compared to public education spending alone. As noted, we have data on private education spending starting in 1995, so we are able to do this in the analysis of PISA data but not the PIAAC data. Our dependent variables are the aggregate national-level scores at the mean and at the 5th percentile for mathematical skills in all the waves of the PISA tests between 2000 and 2015. Since one would not expect spending in the year of observation to affect test results, we use the average of education spending from 1990 (for public education spending) or 1995 (for total—i.e., public and private combined—education spending) until the year of the test score observation.

Models 1, 2, 5, and 6 in table 7.4 show that both total and public spending on education are positively associated with math skills at the 5th percentile and the mean, but the association is stronger and the variation explained greater for public education spending. So, for the lowest-performing students and for the mean, public education spending is crucial. We control for inequality in models 3 and 7, and for poverty in models 4 and 8, in regressions of public education spending on math skills. Poverty among the working-age population is highly significant and negatively associated with math skills at both levels. Inequality among the working-age population is highly significant for the mean scores and is correctly signed, but does not reach significance for the scores at the 5th percentile. Public education spending remains significant and positive when controlling for poverty. Public education also remains significant in model 3, when controlling for inequality in the regression on the scores at the 5th percentile, but it loses significance in model 7 where we control for inequality in the regression on the mean scores. The summary picture from these analyses, then, suggests that public education spending does make a significant difference in the skill levels of fifteen-year-old students, but that poverty and inequality in society also have a significant negative impact on these skills. Indeed, high levels of inequality can overwhelm the positive impact of public education spending on average skills.

As a next step we want to show that higher skill levels in the adult population are associated with a lower education premium—that is, a smaller difference between the wages of workers with and without tertiary education. Our scatterplot with the mean numeracy score in PIAAC and the education premium shows Italy as a big outlier, with a much smaller education premium than expected on the basis of the mean skill level of the population (see figure 7.1). Therefore, we exclude Italy from the regressions shown in table 7.5. Our results demonstrate that the mean numeracy scores and the mean literacy scores are significantly negatively associated with the education premium, even with controls for union density (one of the key determinants of wage dispersion). However, numeracy skills emerge as more important because they explain more of the variation. This finding is in line with work by Hanushek et al. (2015). The numeracy scores at the 10th, 25th, and 75th percentiles also show significant and negative associations with the education premium, whereas the scores at the 5th percentile are not significant. This is not surprising, given that we are looking at returns to tertiary education.

Finally, we want to explore the relationship between public and private education spending, respectively, and the education premium. We showed

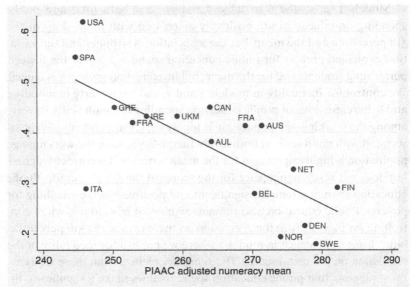

r = -.73, -.86 without Italy

FIGURE 7.1. Numeracy mean scores and the education premium

TABLE 7.5. **Adult Skills and the Education Premium**

	Model 1		Model 2		Model 3		Model 4	
Mean numeracy	−0.009	***			−0.006	**		
Mean literacy			−0.01	**			−0.005	***
Union density					−0.003	**	−0.004	**
Constant	2.802	***	3.026	**	1.322	*	1.822	*
R^2	.71		.42		.81		.72	
Observations	13		13		13		13	

	Model 5		Model 6		Model 7		Model 8	
Numeracy 5th	−0.002							
Numeracy 10th			−0.004	*				
Numeracy 25th					−0.005	**		
Numeracy 75th							−0.006	**
Union density	−0.004	**	−0.003	*	−0.002	*	−0.003	**
Constant	.788	***	1.204	**	1.712	***	2.215	**
R^2	.69		.74		.80		.79	
Observations	13		13		13		13	

* Significant at .05; ** significant at .01; *** significant at .001.

TABLE 7.6. **Public-Private Mix and the Education Premium**

	Model 1		Model 2		Model 3	
Public education expenditure	−.086	***			−.072	***
Private education expenditure			.083	**	.045	*
% with tertiary education	.005	^	.003	^	.004	^
Total factor productivity	.099		.172	*	.102	
Unemployment	.002		.013	*	.007	*
Constant	.650	***	.056		.505	***
Common ρ	.90		.80		.90	
R^2	.52	***	.30	***	.60	***
Observations	68		64		64	

* Significant at .05; ** significant at .01; *** significant at .001; ^ significant but incorrectly signed.

in chapter 4 that a higher share of private tertiary education spending is associated with a greater income share for the top 1 percent. Here we analyze the relationship between total public and private education spending and the education premium, broader measures of both the independent and the dependent variables. We have more observations than for our analyses with adult skills, so we can control for variables that may plausibly shape the education premium: the percentage of the population with tertiary education, total factor productivity as an indicator of technological advance, and the level of unemployment. The three models in table 7.6 show that public education expenditure is highly significant and negatively associated with the education premium, whereas the share of education expenditures from private sources is significant and positively associated with the education premium. These results again drive home the importance of public investment in education, for both skills acquisition and outcomes in terms of income inequality.

Conclusion

Our purpose in this chapter was to delve deeper into the relationship between social investment and income inequality. We established the link via skills by looking at the effect of education and human capital expenditures on skills in the population and the effects of these skills on inequality in earnings, measured by the education premium. In analyzing the effects of education expenditures, we showed that public education expenditures are crucial for more egalitarian outcomes. We also showed that social investment cannot replace the traditional social safety net or—in the language of the debate about welfare state policy—social consumption. Our admittedly very limited data consistently suggested that high levels of poverty and inequality among parents depress skills among students and adults alike, and that they may neutralize the effect of social investment. Human capital spending and income support policies have to work in tandem to achieve full effectiveness. Our data also suggested that public education spending is more important than private spending for skill levels, and that public education spending depresses earnings inequality whereas reliance on private education spending enhances it.

Our findings in this chapter help us to interpret our findings in previous chapters that human capital spending reduces wage dispersion in the upper half of the income distribution and household income inequality as measured by the Gini, but is less closely associated with wage dispersion in the lower half and with poverty. Indeed, human capital spending may benefit those in the middle and upper levels of the income distribution more than those at the very bottom. Our results in this chapter suggest that poverty levels depress the math skills of fifteen-year-old students at the 5th percentile and the mean, and poverty and inequality levels in the parents' generation depress numeracy skills among adults at the 25th percentile and the mean, regardless of spending on education or on human capital more broadly. In fact, in some of our models the inclusion of controls for inequality rendered education and human capital spending insignificant. Given the intergenerational reproduction of educational attainment, we can assume that children and adults at the 5th and 25th percentiles, respectively, also came from low education and therefore low-income households. This background prevented them from benefiting from educational opportunities to the same degree as offspring of better-off families. Thus, in order to work most effectively, education and human capital spending need to be accompanied by policies directly targeted at lowering poverty and inequality.

PART II
A Closer Look at Four Trajectories
Germany, Spain, Sweden, and the United States

PART II

CHAPTER EIGHT

Germany

In the next four chapters, we complement the quantitative analysis with in-depth case studies of four countries: Germany, Spain, Sweden, and the United States. As noted in chapter 1, our methodological strategy is to establish generalizability with the quantitative analysis of the near universe of cases that meet the scope conditions of our theory, which applies to democracies transitioning from industrial economies to knowledge economies. We establish cause through comparative historical analysis of our four focal cases (Germany, Spain, Sweden, and the United States), and strategic but partial comparisons with nine others which we have researched over the past three decades. Comparative historical analysis combines two distinct methods: (1) process tracing, examining the historical record to uncover the links between actors, policies, and policy outcomes; and (2) formal comparative analysis as exemplified by Ragin's (1987) qualitative comparative analysis and Skocpol's (Skocpol and Summers 1980; Skocpol 1984) analytical comparative history.[1] The aspects are complementary: for example, process tracing alone is not very effective at uncovering the effects of institutional arrangements that do not vary much over time, like aspects of the constitutional structure or labor market institutions. This is true especially for labor market institutions other than union density, which our quantitative analysis also found to strongly affect distributive outcomes.

The overall pattern in Germany is one of starkly increasing inequality and poverty. Up to the late 1980s Germany was one of the most equal continental European countries, but by 2016 it had become the most unequal among them. German unification raised unemployment levels to unprecedented heights and imposed a heavy financial burden on the government. After more than a decade, these issues prompted drastic labor market reforms that led to the growth of low-paid and part-time jobs and to cuts in unemployment insurance. At the same time, core manufacturing industries remained competitive in export markets, relying in part on strategies of outsourcing and working with their permanent workforce through unions and works councils to smooth cyclical downturns. Outside of these industries unionization and contract coverage declined massively, and precarious employment became more prevalent. This also meant that fewer people had access to contributory social insurance and had to rely on less generous social assistance. As a result, redistribution through the welfare state declined and disposable income poverty and inequality increased markedly after 2000.

Changes in the labor market greatly weakened the economic and political power of organized labor, and thus its capacity to stem rising inequality. Union density declined to 17 percent by 2017 and contract extension to 54 percent (Visser 2019), but even workers covered by contracts were affected by derogation clauses accepted by unions in order to trade wage restraint for job protection. On the positive side, the institutional position of labor at the enterprise level in large enterprises, in the form of cooperation between works councils and unions, kept the shareholder value model of corporate governance (and thus executive compensation and the share of the top 1 percent) in check.

Partisan differences in policy positions persisted. The Social Democratic Party (SPD) consistently advocated for stronger protection for workers and low-income groups. However, extreme fiscal pressures and opposition control of the Bundesrat pushed the Red/Green coalition government reelected in 2002 to implement the consequential Hartz reforms that deregulated the labor market and cut unemployment benefits. As a result, the SPD lost support among organized workers, and in subsequent years, even when participating in government, coalition constraints reduced the ability of the Left to shape policy. One remarkable area of success was the implementation of a minimum wage as a result of the 2013 coalition negotiations with the Christian Democratic Union (CDU) and the increase of the minimum wage to twelve Euros under SPD Chancellor Scholz in 2022.

The first watershed was German unification; the second watershed was the period from 2004 to 2006. As noted, Germany before unification had a level of inequality that was comparatively low within the continental European context, but by 2016 disposable household income inequality had risen to levels above those of the other continental European countries (table A.4). During the Golden Age, union density was at an intermediate level, with around 35 percent of the labor force organized, but contract coverage was as high as in Sweden, at 85 percent (tables B.17 and B.18). Unemployment was relatively low, though higher than in Sweden, and overall employment was lower than in Sweden; industrial employment was high, and bargaining and wage coordination took place at the industry level. Though the percentage of the population with tertiary education was much lower than in the Nordic countries or the United States, the system of vocational education provided the workforce with important skills. These labor market institutions produced a pattern of wage dispersion that was intermediate between the Swedish and the US levels (table B.1). Top income shares were twice as high as in Sweden, though as of 1986 clearly below US levels. Redistribution and the Gini of disposable household income similarly occupied an intermediate position: in the period before 1993, the German welfare state reduced inequality by an average of 28 percent, compared to 35 percent for the Swedish and 18 percent for the US welfare state, and the Gini of disposable household income was 25, compared to 23 in Sweden and 32 in the United States (tables A.3 and A.4).[2]

Unemployment increased in the wake of unification from 5 percent in 1990 to a high of 11 percent in 2005. Poverty and inequality followed the same trajectory as unemployment. From 1989 to 2004, the pre-tax and transfer household income Gini of the working-age population increased from 35 to 42. Pre-tax and transfer poverty increased dramatically as well, from 10 percent in 1989 to 23 percent in 2005. The burden on the welfare state was enormous. The tax and transfer system reduced the Gini by 35 percent and poverty by 66 percent in 2004. Nevertheless, post-tax and transfer poverty rose from 5 percent to 8 percent and the disposable household income Gini for the working-age population from 25 to 27 (tables A.3–A.7). If the entire population is included, the post-Gini rose to 28 in this period (Caminada and Wang 2011). By comparison, poverty reduction in 2004 in Sweden was 70 percent and inequality reduction 40 percent, resulting in disposable income poverty of 5 percent and a disposable income Gini of 23. Thus, the German welfare state was less effective in reducing poverty and inequality than was the Swedish, but not by much.

After 2005 unemployment declined, and it fell back to 4 percent by 2017. At the same time employment levels rose from 66 percent in 2005 to 77 percent by 2017 (tables B.7 and B.8). However, the drop in unemployment and the increase in employment were not reflected in a parallel drop in inequality and poverty. The pre-tax and transfer Gini remained roughly stable, at 42 in 2004 and 41 in 2015, but the post-tax and transfer Gini increased from 27 to 31 in the same period. Pre-tax and transfer poverty declined from 23 percent to 18 percent, but post-tax and transfer poverty increased from 8 percent to 11 percent. The tax and transfer system continued to reduce both poverty and inequality by considerable amounts, but the degree of reduction declined rather dramatically. The first steep drop occurred between 2004 and 2006, when the reduction of the Gini fell from 35 percent to 27 percent and the reduction of poverty from 66 percent to 47 percent. Thereafter, poverty reduction continued to fall gradually, to 41 percent by 2015, and inequality reduction to 25 percent (tables A.3 and A.6). In other words, the capacity of the German tax and transfer system to reduce poverty and inequality declined markedly.

The increase in inequality is due more to the growth of low-income groups than to the pulling away of the top 1 percent. As our data show, and as Dell (2007) also shows, the top 1 percent was already receiving a comparatively large average share of total income before unification, with around 10-11 percent, comparable to the United States. However, in contrast to the United States and other liberal countries, that share stayed roughly constant from 1990 to 2005, and then increased to around 14 percent by 2008, where it remained (table B.2 and figure A.1). At the same time, the low-wage sector came to account for some 20 percent of employment, and low-income groups grew, as is apparent in the increase in poverty. Thus, the task is to explain why low-income groups, both pre- and post-tax and transfer, grew after unification. The answer lies in structural changes in the economy and the accompanying dualization of the labor market, decline of trade union density and centralized bargaining, and—crucially—the weakening of social protection.

Changes in the Economy and the Labor Market

In addition to the pressures from technological change and globalization shared by other postindustrial countries, reunification in 1990 imposed a great added burden on the German labor market and the welfare state. In order to prevent massive internal migration, the government and its labor market partners extended the welfare state and collective contracts to the east. The increase in labor costs left East German industries noncompetitive and led to a steep increase in unemployment. Manufacturing jobs declined steeply, from 34 percent in 1989 to 22 percent in 1997, and they kept falling, reaching 20 percent in 2004 (table B.6). The response was a mix of active and passive labor market policies, expenditures for which were covered by a combination of tax increases and government borrowing. A good part of the tax increases was levied on labor costs, which disadvantaged job creation (Jackson and Sorge 2012). This massive support continued for more than two decades. As late as 2007, per capita social transfers were 20 percent higher and income taxes paid were 50 percent lower in the east, and about 3.5 percent of the East German GDP consisted of transfers from West Germany to East Germany (Ragnitz 2009).

The recession that followed the tightening of monetary policy by the Bundesbank in 1992 further contributed to an increase in unemployment, in both the western and the eastern parts of Germany. A temporary recovery at the end of the decade was followed by another cyclical downturn in 2001, and unemployment reached 11 percent in 2005. This put an ever-increasing fiscal burden on the federal and the Länder governments, prompting an intensive search for ways to reduce welfare state expenditures and to raise employment levels. Indeed, overall employment had fallen to 66 percent by 2005, compared to 74 percent and 72 percent in Sweden and the United States, respectively. The Hartz reforms of 2003–2005 (to be discussed below) were designed to address these problems, but despite increases in employment levels these reforms also reduced the state's efforts in redistribution and thus resulted in rising poverty and inequality.

Technological change contributed to problems matching demand for and supply of skilled labor, and thus to increasing returns to high skills. Goos, Manning, and Salomon (2009) show a trend toward job polarization in Europe, with the lowest-paying occupations growing their employment share slowly between 1992 and 2006, middling occupations losing employment share, and the highest-paying occupations increasing their employment share. Germany shows a very pronounced pattern of polarization, with the lowest-paying occupations growing employment share by 3 percent, middling occupations declining by 9 percent, and the highest-paying occupations growing by 6 percent. Using a much more fine-grained classification of occupations according to their skill level (using 145 categories instead of 21 for Germany) and different surveys, Oesch (2013, 72) argues that actually the trend was toward occupational upgrading. According to his figures for Germany, the employment share of low-skilled occupations fell by 23 percent from 1990 to 2007, and the employment share of mid-skilled occupations fell by 11 percent. In contrast, the employment share of high-skilled occupations grew by 53 percent. Despite their disagreement on trends at the bottom, these two studies concur that the demand for skilled labor increased very strongly. Wage returns to skill in Germany by 2011–2013 were third highest, behind the United States and Ireland (Autor 2014; Hanushek et al. 2015). Returns to tertiary education were third highest also by 2013, behind the United States and Spain, and tied with Canada (Weisstanner and Armingeon 2020). This is not surprising, considering that in 2010 16 percent of the over-twenty-five population in Germany had completed tertiary education (tables B.21 and B.23).

As noted, the share of the top 1 percent increased but did not reach 14 percent until 2007, remaining clearly below the level of the liberal countries. A number of factors contributed to keeping it there. First, as of 2007, stock market capitalization in Germany had remained much lower than in our other three countries. The average in the period 2000–2007 reached 51 percent of GDP, compared to 86 percent in Spain, 111 percent in Sweden, and 137 percent in the United States (table B.15). Indeed, the increase in the top 1 percent share with capital gains included was one percentage point or less (table B.2). Second, the shareholder value model of corporate governance was kept in check by the stronger institutional position of labor at the enterprise level and by legislation that watered down European rules to limit hostile takeovers, and thus to limit pressures on companies to prioritize their share prices (Fauver and Fuerst 2006; Hall 2021). Third, Germany's top marginal tax rate changed very little between the 1960s and the early 2000s, remaining at 48 percent. This contrasted sharply with the large reductions of the top marginal tax rate during this period in the US and the UK (Piketty, Saez, and Stantcheva 2014).

Wage dispersion, as measured by the 90-50 and 50-10 ratios, remained remarkably stable, increasing slowly from 1985 to 2018—from 1.7 to 1.9 and from 1.7 to 1.8, respectively (table B.1). The share of the top 10 percent of income earners, though, rose rapidly from 1995 on, from 31.4 percent to 39.5 percent of total income in 2008, in line with the high returns to skills (Autor 2014—table B.3). As noted, wage ratios underestimate earnings inequality, because they are based on earnings of full-time workers, and the German labor market created lots of part-time jobs, particularly jobs with less than half-time work. From 2005 on, 21 percent of total employment was part-time (defined as less than 30 hours per week), and 38 percent of women's employment. This is a much higher share than in Sweden and

Spain, with 11–14 percent of total and 18–23 percent of female employment. Moreover, as of 2008, 57 percent of German part-timers worked less than 20 hours per week, and 38 percent of part-time jobs were low-paying (Eichhorst and Marx 2012).

Germany did not make the same breakthroughs to information technology as Sweden (Thelen 2021). Rather, Germany persisted in maintaining a comparative advantage in diversified quality production, or high-end advanced manufacturing. However, as Sorge and Streeck (2018) argue, Germany particularly excelled in combining non-routinized with routinized operations, and in switching from one to the other. The shock of unification, the context of the international pressures for liberalization, and the relocation of production activities by many enterprises to recently opened eastern European countries, drove unions and works councils to accept more opening clauses (that is, local departures from collective agreements) to trade more wage restraint for jobs preservation. On their part, enterprises reduced vertical integration and outsourced service activities in particular to firms with different or no labor contracts or to firms using contract labor from East Germany. Thus, German export production became cost-competitive again even in more routinized operations (Sorge and Streeck 2018). Dustmann et al. (2014) concur that competition-weighted relative unit labor costs in Germany declined relative to the United States, the UK, France, Italy, and Spain between 1994 and 2012. Their figures also suggest that the costs of this reduction were borne mainly by lower-income workers, as real wages in West Germany at the 15th percentile remained essentially stagnant after 1990 and declined markedly after 2003, real wages at the median increased moderately until 2003 and then declined slightly, and real wages at the 85th percentile increased steadily from the mid-1990s on.

The mix of more and less routinized production operations in Germany may also have contributed to significantly lower average employee involvement in decisions at the workplace compared to Sweden, as indicated by data from the 2015 European Working Conditions Survey (Kirchner and Hauff 2019). Employee involvement describes employees' opportunities to personally influence decisions about work organization or other aspects of the work environment. However, this study included employees from the manufacturing and service sectors, so the results may also be driven by the difference in the overall employment regime, which in Sweden is more supportive of non-core employees. A further important difference that is relevant to the difference in employee involvement in decisions is in education, which in Sweden combines a strong vocational system and an extensive higher education system, compared to Germany's strong vocational system and elitist higher education system.

Deregulation of services and product markets has also been linked to rising inequality in our quantitative analyses. In Germany, deregulation of energy, transportation, and communications was extensive. The OECD index of total regulation, which is the simple mean of sectoral regulation indices in airlines, telecom, electricity, gas, post, rail, and road, shows that in the 1970s Germany regulated these sectors more than average among twenty-two advanced industrial countries, and regulated them less than average by the post-crisis period. The index ranges from 0 to 6; Germany started at 5.2 compared to an average of 5.1, and ended up at 1.1 compared to an average of 1.6 (table B.14). These sectors ended up even less regulated in Germany than in the United States. This implied the disappearance of stable and decently remunerated public-sector jobs and their replacement with less stable and lower-paying private-sector jobs, and the opening up of opportunities for new highly paid positions in the private sector.

Changes in Labor Market Institutions and Policies

As noted, the core of the German economy remained the high-quality manufacturing export sector. However, since this sector faced increasing competition internationally, labor costs became a key issue. In this situation, both employers' associations and unions supported a continuation of the tradition of sectoral coordinated bargaining and contract extension (Thelen 2014). Nevertheless, plant-level supplementary agreements between management and works councils, typically trading wage restraint for employment protection, became more common. This was the case particularly during the 2008 crisis, but the practice had started in the 1990s to prevent corporations from moving production offshore. According to the figures from Visser's database, contract extension fell to 54 percent economy-wide in 2018. Baccaro and Howell (2017) give slightly different figures, with industry-level collective bargaining coverage having dropped to 49 percent economy-wide, and 67 percent in manufacturing establishments with more than 250 workers, by 2013. Outside of manufacturing, union density and contract coverage have been much lower.

As noted, overall trade union membership had fallen to just 17 percent by 2017 (table B.17). Also, employers' associations lost member firms that were unwilling to implement collective agreements, and therefore began to offer memberships without the obligation to adhere to collective agreements (Bosch 2018, 214–16). Unionization rates in manufacturing were still around 50 percent, but in services only 10–20 percent. In particular, the growing personal service sector was and remains poorly organized, and service-sector employers have strongly resisted contract extension, instead pushing for more flexible labor markets. Contract extension can happen if at least 50 percent of all employees in an industry work in firms that are covered by an industry contract, and if a majority of the central collective bargaining committee (with equal numbers of representatives from the unions and employers' associations) petitions the government to declare the contract universally binding (Bosch 2018, 217). Since 2000 the national employers' association in retail has blocked extensions, and in the hospitality industry only a few regions have extension clauses—and those that exist do not include wages. As of 2013, some 50 percent of service-sector workers were not covered by any kind of contract (Baccaro and Howell 2017, 115).

Even those workers covered by collective agreements are subject to derogation clauses. In a 2004 agreement, unions approved the use of derogation clauses to protect employment. Under derogation clauses, wage and working hours agreements reached in collective negotiations may be undercut in economic emergency situations by agreements for individual enterprises. In the wake of the 2008 financial crisis, such clauses were used very widely. Working hours were shortened in order to protect employment, and this practice was much more widespread in Germany than in any other EU country (Bosch 2018, 240). Government subsidies for short-term work, paid to employers who use them in part to cover social security contributions and in part to compensate workers directly, made up for part of the lost wages and helped to shelter jobs in the core manufacturing sectors (Thelen 2014, 132–33).

Works councils play an important role in German industrial relations. They are elected by all employees in an establishment as representatives to protect the interests of the employees. In companies with more than 2,000 employees they have parity representation on the supervisory board; in companies with fewer employees they have one-third of the seats on supervisory boards. In companies with 200 or more employees, one works councilor is released completely from work to carry out such duties, and that number increases with the size of the company. Works councils have strong rights to economic information and to codetermination on social and personnel issues, and they monitor compliance with labor laws and collective agreements. For the most part, they work closely with the unions; more than two-thirds of works councilors are union members (Bosch 2018, 221). However, only 38 percent of companies with 50–100 workers have works councils, and in smaller enterprises the percentage is even lower. Thus, representation through works councils in wholesale and retail trade covers only about a quarter of employees, and in hotels and restaurants it is below 15 percent (Bosch 2018, 222). Overall, in 2014 about a quarter of companies with more than 5 employees had neither a works council nor a collective agreement in western Germany, compared to close to half in eastern Germany (Bosch 2018, 224).

The decline in collective agreement coverage led to a rise in pay inequality, and particularly to the increase in the share of low-wage jobs. Germany did not have a legal minimum wage until 2015, relying on collective agreements to set floors. Thus, the wage floor outside the sectors covered by these collective agreements fell to particularly low levels. A further development contributed to declining contract coverage and the proliferation of low-wage jobs: as former public services, such as public transportation, communications, and postal services were opened up to private competition, new firms were formed that refused to join collective contracts in order to compete in these sectors on the basis of lower labor costs (Bosch 2018, 228).

Throughout the 1990s, unemployment had remained at high levels and had generated a discussion about the cost of production in Germany. In particular, non-wage labor costs were held responsible for the slow growth of jobs in personal services (Scharpf 1997), and high total labor costs were an incentive for moving production offshore. Unification had been financed in part by increased taxation and higher social security contributions borne by employers and employees, and in part by government deficit spending. As Sorge and Streeck (2018) put it, the structural problems and state debt, combined with the collapse of the internet boom, meant that Germany was approaching a financial collapse of the welfare state, at least as it existed in 2002. Baccaro and Höpner (2022, 249) specify that the budgetary situation of the municipalities was particularly disastrous because they were responsible for paying the social assistance for the long-term unemployed. Under these immense pressures, the red/green government led by Schröder from 2002 to 2005 introduced a series of very important labor market reforms. Before the 2002 election, unemployment stood at 8.7 percent and was the most salient issue in the campaign. A scandal in the Federal Labor Authority (FLA), with false numbers of job placements, added urgency to the reform. Chancellor Schröder fired the head of the FLA and appointed the Hartz Commission (named after its chair), which reported one month before the elections with plans to make the FLA into an efficient job-placement organization—referring workers to training or temporary job agencies—and plans to lift earnings ceilings in mini-jobs (Carlin et al. 2015). Mini-jobs are low-wage, part-time work without the usual social insurance contributions and benefits. Earnings below a certain limit (450 Euros as of 2020) are exempt from social security taxes, whereas employers pay a lump-sum tax.

The reforms called Hartz I–IV were enacted from 2003 to 2005 with support of the CDU, which had a majority in the Bundesrat and had actually advocated for deeper reforms. In addition to instituting reforms in the administration of job placement and unemployment benefits that shifted the financial burden for long-term unemployed from the municipalities to the federal government (Baccaro and Höpner 2022, 249) and that expanded mini-jobs, they also deregulated agency work (that is, the use of temporary workers) and supported self-employment (Jackson and Sorge 2012). Hartz IV, arguably the most controversial and consequential of these reforms, reduced the duration of social insurance-based earnings-related unemployment benefits from up to 36 months (depending on age and work history) to 12 months for those under fifty-seven, and 18 months for those over fifty-eight years of age. Importantly, it eliminated the second tier of unemployment benefits, which were tax-based and lower than the contribution-based benefits but still income-related and with essentially unlimited duration. After the reform, once the social insurance-based benefits were exhausted, the recipients transitioned to social assistance— that is, a tax-financed, means-tested, flat-rate benefit, combined with supplements to guarantee a minimum household income. Recipients of social assistance who could work three hours a day and fifteen hours a week were transferred into a work scheme. They were required to accept jobs with lower qualifications and pay and in different locations, with stricter sanctions for noncompliance. As of 2012, two-thirds of unemployed people received the low social assistance benefits (Jackson and Sorge 2012).

The key impetus for the cut in benefits was fiscal pressure. However, the Grand Coalition government led by Merkel (2005–2009) then reduced unemployment insurance contributions by workers and employers: from 6.5 percent to 4.2 percent in 2007, and further to 3.3 percent by 2008. The conflict between the unions and the SPD over the reforms was deep, and the SPD paid a price in the 2005 elections. Hartz IV also threatened insiders who might lose their jobs and were union members. In fact the Linke was founded by trade union representatives; about half of the members of parliament from the Linke were former officials from IG Metall and the service-sector union Ver.di. The voter base of the Linke in the west is concentrated among blue-collar workers with medium skills, not outsiders. Much of the SPD's losses in 2005 were to the Linke, whereas other former SPD voters abstained or voted for other parties (Carlin et al. 2015). Fervers (2019) shows that the announcement of the Hartz IV reforms had a negative effect on satisfaction with democracy and on propensity for political participation, as well as a positive effect on propensity to vote for non-established parties, among respondents interviewed in the two months after the announcement.

With the Hartz reforms, the use of temporary employment spread (even within the manufacturing sector), and with it the division between insiders with stable jobs and outsiders with temporary or part-time employment. Agency workers who can be hired for unlimited duration have wages that are 25 to 30 percent lower than those of permanent employees (Eichhorst and Marx 2012). Initially, unions did not oppose the increase of temporary work in the manufacturing sector, because under German labor law workers in a firm who perform the same tasks have a right to the same pay, unless they are covered by a separate contract. However, smaller Christian unions began to bargain for these workers, and employers had an incentive to negotiate separate contracts with them (Thelen 2014).

As of 2010, the proportion of low-wage workers was 64 percent in hotels and restaurants, 45 percent in agriculture, 34 percent in wholesale and retail trades, and 32 percent in other (not education and health) social and personal services (Bosch 2013). Particularly affected were employees under twenty-five (51 percent low-wage), on fixed-term contracts (46 percent), women (30 percent), and foreigners (32 percent). Women made up 64 percent of low-wage workers. Moreover, 71 percent of low-wage workers did have vocational qualification, so the vocational training system was no longer a ticket into good jobs. Foreigners made up only 11 percent of low-wage workers, so the problem cannot be attributed to immigration. Nor is the problem confined to part-time and temporary employment: close to half of low-wage workers worked full-time, and 79 percent had open-ended contracts; 28 percent were in mini-jobs, and 24 percent in part-time jobs with social insurance (Bosch 2013). The overall picture then was of a substantial rise in precarious employment, largely as a result of a combination of the decline in unionization and the changes in labor market policy (Brady and Biegert 2017).

As noted, Germany did not have a statutory minimum wage, and the powerful industrial unions were opposed to one based on the principle of autonomous collective bargaining between employer associations and trade unions. However, as Marx and Starke (2017) argue, the effects of the Hartz reforms combined with a vigorous campaign in 2006 by service-sector unions that highlighted low-wage workers in poverty generated a public opinion backlash against rising poverty and inequality. This in turn galvanized other unions into action. In 2007, the umbrella organization of unions (Deutscher Gewerkschaftsbund or DGB) picked up the campaign and began pushing for a minimum wage. By their 2010 federal congress, all unions supported a statutory minimum wage. As a result, the SPD adopted the minimum wage as a key platform issue and used its leverage in the Grand Coalition negotiations with the CDU in 2013 to get the law passed in 2014 and enacted in January 2015. It was a combination of fear of low-wage competition from outsiders through outsourcing (Meyer 2016) and adherence to the principle of solidarity (Marx and Starke 2017) that motivated the unions to depart from their traditional insistence on autonomy from state intervention into collective bargaining. The minimum wage is set by a commission controlled by employer and union representatives; it started at 8.50 Euros and was to be adjusted every two years, the benchmark for any increases being the average increase in collective bargaining agreements (Bosch 2018, 245). In the 2021 election campaign, the SPD promised to raise it to 12 Euros.

Reflecting and further contributing to the dualization of the labor market in Germany has been the narrowing of the path into good jobs for people without upper secondary education through the apprenticeship system. In the 1990s the number of apprenticeship positions began to shrink. Youths who fail to secure apprenticeship places have no options to receive this training later, which means that there is a compounding of (dis)advantages on the job market. Moreover, new models of apprenticeships were created through an upgrading of skill requirements and the creation of profiles for emerging jobs that demanded more or less training. The more demanding training models required better education as a condition of entry. Traditionally, recruitment to apprenticeships came from non-Gymnasium tracks, but increasingly firms began to recruit people with Abitur, the general higher-education entry certificate. This is particularly true in business services, such as banking and ICT, but it has become common even in manufacturing. For instance, about half of Volkswagen employees in Germany have completed the Abitur (Thelen 2014, 89). In 2008 about a third of students with an Abitur were headed to vocational education and training, not university. In contrast, fully 50 percent of students completing the lowest educational track only (Hauptschule) failed to find apprenticeship positions (Thelen 2014).

The system of vocational education has also become more segmented. Traditional vocational training followed occupational profiles that were nationally standardized and embodied in specific curricula. A typical apprenticeship lasted three years and included both on-the-job and in-school training, thus conveying skills that were portable beyond the company that provided the training. Just as new and upgraded profiles and curricula were developed, so were watered-down versions of vocational training. In 2003, the Social Democratic/Green coalition government agreed to the introduction of two-year apprenticeships in order to address the high levels of youth unemployment. Firms can decide after two years whether to offer the apprentice additional training (Thelen and Busemeyer 2011). Moreover, firms have increasingly demanded and been given more flexibility in the training curricula, in order to orient them more toward the production processes in the firm and to reduce the costs of training (Thelen and Busemeyer 2011). Accordingly, labor training has become more differentiated and has come to resemble the stratified educational system, rather than correcting for its inegalitarian effects.

The dualization of the labor market with the growth of a low-wage sector and increasing returns to skills was accompanied by parallel developments in social protection in the form of increasing distance between people with social insurance and others on social assistance. Not surprisingly, these trends also raised household inequality, though the impact was moderated to a considerable extent because the majority of low-wage jobs are filled by women. With the increase in women's labor force participation, the proportion of households with two earners increased. To the extent that low-wage work is performed by second earners in households with a member of the core workforce, its growth does not necessarily drive up poverty and inequality. However, the growth of low-wage work clearly drives up poverty in households where the sole earner is a low-wage worker.

Demographic changes added to the fiscal burdens on the welfare state. The percentage of the population 65 and older rose from 16 to 20 percent in the period 1980 to 2007. Fertility was very low, with a total fertility rate of 1.4 holding steady during that period. The percentage of children living with a single mother increased from 6 to 16 percent, which constituted a new social risk confronted by households. Moreover, the decline in industrial employment from 28 to 21 percent of the working-age population between 1980 and 2007 reduced the number of households that even had the option of relying on the old male breadwinner model.

Immigration was very comparable in speed and extent to the processes in Sweden and the United States until 2010. In 1990 she immigrant share of the German population was 7.5 percent, a level Sweden and the United States had reached in 1980. By 2010, all three countries had reached somewhat over 14 percent. In the following five years, immigration grew very moderately in Germany and in the United States, whereas growth accelerated in Sweden (table B.16). Much of the immigration into Germany up to 2015 was a result of demand for foreign workers, who then over time were able to bring their families. The big influx of refugees seeking asylum came in 2015 and thereafter, as a result of the Syrian civil war. Traditionally, refugees and asylum seekers did not have access to the labor market and survived on the basis of social transfers, but this policy changed in 2016, which led to a dramatic increase in the number of job-seeking people. However, qualification levels were mostly low, which made labor market integration difficult even after acquisition of basic language skills (Färber and Köppen 2020). As of 2019, immigrants had a 7.4 percent lower employment rate and a 3 percent higher unemployment rate than did native-born Germans (OECD 2020), which aggravated the burden on the tax and transfer system.

Human Capital

Germany has maintained a tiered system of secondary education and an elitist system of tertiary education, in conjunction with a comparatively well-developed system of vocational education and training. Various Länder have experimented with de-tracking secondary education and facilitating the path to the Abitur, the exam that qualifies for university entrance; but these efforts have not resulted in massive increases in the percentage of people who hold university degrees. Moreover, as we discussed above, the capacity of the system of vocational education and training to provide young people without higher secondary education an entry into well-paying jobs has greatly declined. The two studies of adult skills—the IALS study of the mid-1990s and the PIAAC study of the mid-2010s—show German adults scoring in the middle of the sixteen countries participating in the IALS and the eighteen countries participating in the PIAAC study. In the IALS study, German scores at the 5th percentile were the second highest, just slightly lower than the best scores in Sweden (208 versus 216) and much higher than the scores in the United States (133). At the 25th percentile and the mean, Germany (255 and 285) ranked right below Sweden (274 and 304) and the other Nordic countries, and well above the United States (234 and 275). In the PIAAC study, Germany's relative performance at the 5th percentile had declined to fifth place, and the difference between Germany and the top scorer (Finland) had increased (from 168 to 193). At the 25th percentile and the mean, Germany ranked eighth. Accordingly, returns to skills measured by the PIAAC scores were high, with .235 compared to .121 in Sweden; they were even higher than in Spain (.228), though not quite as high as in the United States (.279) (Hanushek et al. 2015 — tables B.20 and B.21). Clearly, the high scores at the 5th and 25th percentile and the mean in the IALS test reflected the wide reach of vocational education and training, and the relative decline over the twenty years in the PIAAC test scores seems to reflect the declining coverage of this education.

Enrollment in tertiary education has remained comparatively low, and the education premium high. In tertiary education, German unification and internationalization of higher education, specifically Europeanization, gave rise to numerous reforms that led to greater differentiation, competition, and transparency (Welsh 2010). In 1999 Germany signed the Bologna Accord, which created the European Higher Education Area; subsequently, the structure of university education was reformed to replace the traditional diploma with the BA and MA degrees. Though authority over education has continued to rest with the Länder, the federal government assumed increasing importance by providing funds for increasing enrollment and through seed money and competitive grants (Busemeyer, Garritzmann, and Neimanns 2020). The Excellence Initiative introduced in 2005 provided funds to universities on the basis of their strength in research and teaching in specific areas. Along with strengthening the international competitiveness of these universities, the initiative also began to stratify and differentiate universities. Still, in comparative perspective, Germany as of 2005 devoted a below-average amount of resources to tertiary education, with 1.1 percent of GDP compared to an OECD average of 1.5 percent.

The elitist nature of the university system is reflected in the high education premium in Germany, measured as the percentage difference in median wages between full-time workers with tertiary education and full-time workers without. As of 1995, the German education premium was below average among twenty-two postindustrial democracies; by 2007 it had risen to the average, and by 2013 it was clearly above average. In fact, between 1995 and 2013 Germany experienced the largest increase in the education premium, ranking second (with Canada) behind only the United States and Spain (Weisstanner and Armingeon 2020).

The issue of tuition payments for university students has been controversial, and opinions have followed party lines, with FDP supporters being least opposed and supporters of the Linke most opposed (Busemeyer, Garritzmann, and Neimanns 2020, 164). Still, a majority of the population opposes tuition payments, and the few attempts to introduce them met with strident opposition and were abandoned. In contrast, there is majority support and little partisan disagreement regarding the desirability of subsidies for low-income students. As of the second decade of the twenty-first century, some 16 percent of university students received such subsidies (Busemeyer, Garritzmann, and Neimanns 2020, 165).

The area of education where the most significant innovation has occurred is early childhood education and care (ECEC). The federal government has consistently provided discretionary funds to the Länder to support infrastructure investment and operational funds for ECEC facilities. The overall number of places available for children under three years of age in formal daycare institutions rose from 360,000 in 2008 to 660,000 in 2014 (Busemeyer, Garritzmann, and Neimanns 2020, 171). Along with the financing came federal standards for the quality of ECEC, to be enforced by local governments. While this expansion has been impressive, the availability of places in ECEC still falls short of demand. The alternative is home daycare, which is also supported by public financing. The combination of formal institutional and home daycare has made work/family reconciliation a lot easier, and thus has contributed to the increase in female labor force participation. Whether the educational component will improve educational skills at the bottom remains to be seen.

Changes in Social Policy

Starting in the 1990s and intensifying after 2000, a series of reforms in work/family policies were adopted designed to facilitate the entry of women into the labor force. Blome (2016) argues that a change in attitudes toward working mothers, particularly among women and the better educated, and intensifying political competition account for these policy innovations. In 1992–1993 the Christian democratic government passed an entitlement to publicly provided or subsidized childcare for three- to six-year-olds. However, this right could not really be enforced, as the facilities and personnel were insufficient. Moreover, for the rest of the decade, family policy legislation remained focused on tax credits and child allowances (Häusermann 2018). On the other hand, long-term care insurance introduced in 1996 eased the burden on working-age women of caring for the elderly. Between 2000 and 2004 the Red-Green government passed legislation to expand childcare places and introduce a right to care for children under the age of three, and it significantly expanded parental leave. The Grand Coalition in 2007 then further extended parental leave and provided incentives for high-income couples to share such leave. From 2008 on, the government consistently pursued mixed policy packages, combining support for childcare with expansion of child allowances and benefits for stay-at-home mothers (Häusermann 2018). Thus, German family policy became a hybrid of employment-oriented and traditional familial elements, and it continued to be modified, generally in a more generous direction. By 2017, childcare for children under three covered nearly 38 percent.

Since 2007 German parents have been entitled to fourteen months of paid leave, as long as they shared the leave, with one parent not exceeding twelve months. The replacement rate was originally 67 percent of previous income; this was later reduced to 65 percent, up to a ceiling of 1,800 Euros per month. For low incomes, the replacement rate could go up to 100 percent; parents who did not work before the birth could get 300 Euros per month. Parents had the option of working part-time and drawing half the benefit for twice the duration. If the family had other small children, they got a sibling bonus; if they had twins or triplets, they got extra funds. Finally, as of September 1, 2021, if the child was born six or more weeks prematurely, the parents got up to four months of additional paid leave (Bundesministerium für Familie, Senioren, Frauen und Jugend 2021).

Women's labor force participation increased, which kept employment levels steady at 65 percent, despite the rising unemployment rates from 1990 to 2005; employment levels continued rising to reach 77 percent by 2017 (tables B.7 and B.9). But much of this employment has been part-time and low-income. For instance, as noted, over 60 percent of low-paid workers are women, followed by pensioners and students. In 2010, 6.8 million workers were paid less than the 8.50 Euros that the German unions were demanding as a minimum wage, and 2.5 million earned less than 6 Euros per hour (Bosch 2013, 340–41).

Two parallel developments, then, contributed to increasing poverty and inequality. Social policy in the employment-based programs (unemployment compensation, sickness pay, pensions) became less generous (tables A.5 and A.6) and the proportion of the population with access to these programs declined, leaving more families dependent on a variety of social assistance programs. Our non-aged generosity index based on Scruggs's data, which combines measures for the generosity of unemployment and sickness benefits, declined from 27 in 1980 and 26 in 1990 to 23 by 2007, after the Hartz reforms, and though it recovered to 25.6 by 2019, it has not reached pre-1990 levels again.

Post-tax and transfer poverty in Germany rose despite stability in the net minimum income replacement rates of means-tested social benefits. According to Wang and van Vliet (2016a), the net minimum income benefit replacement rate, defined as the ratio of net minimum income benefits to the net average production wage, and calculated as an average of three household types, remained stable at about 37 percent in Germany between 1990 and 2009. Their calculation of the net minimum income includes social assistance and related minimum income benefits—such as child benefits and refundable tax credits—available to households lacking work income and entitlements to contributory benefits. This put Germany right between Spain (34 percent) and Sweden (39 percent) in 2009; the replacement rates in both these countries had fallen from much higher levels in 1990.

During the same period, the share of total social benefit expenditures going to means-tested benefits rose from 5.5 percent to 9 percent in Germany, compared to an average of 4.8 percent in the Nordic countries (Kuivalainen and Nelson 2010, 23). This suggests that larger numbers of households became dependent on social assistance. Just looking at pensioners, the value of the minimum noncontributory pension is certainly very low, with only 20 percent of average earnings (OECD 2011, 109). As our figures show, poverty reduction through taxes and transfers rose to a high of 65 percent in 2005 but then plummeted to 47 percent in 2006 and kept falling after that to a low of 36 percent in 2014, before recovering to 41 percent in 2015 (table A.6).

Demographic trends contributed to increasing poverty and inequality. First, the share of persons who are the only adult in a household increased from roughly 15 percent in 1993 to some 23 percent in 2012 (Brülle 2016,

768), which meant that more households were left without a buffer in case of loss of earnings. Second, the relationship between education and labor force participation became stronger and the educational levels of couples became more similar. Therefore, the gap between work-poor and work-rich households widened and household buffers in the form of earnings from others became more unequally distributed across the educational spectrum (Brülle 2016).

Single mothers are particularly vulnerable to poverty in all countries, and Germany is no exception. In fact, according to the LIS figures, 37 percent of children living in single-mother households were in poverty in 2007 after receiving child benefits—a slightly higher proportion than in Spain (32 percent) and clearly higher than in Sweden (10 percent) in 2005. The main reason for this high poverty rate was the high rate of non-employment among single mothers: 34 percent of single mothers were not in employment, compared to 23 percent in Spain and 20 percent in Sweden (Van Lancker, Ghysels, and Cantillon 2015). The deficit in publicly supported childcare was clearly a major reason for this high rate.

Deviating from its traditional heavy orientation toward the elderly, the German welfare state by 1990 was spending 2.5 times more on the non-elderly than on the elderly. This ratio was just slightly higher than in Sweden, though one has to keep in mind that Sweden spent more on both groups. For Germany, this was a big increase from 1.5 times in 1980. Clearly, this reorientation was originally forced by the high levels of unemployment. Over the period up to 2015, the ratio of spending on the non-aged to spending on the aged remained between 2.2 and 2.3, exceeded among our four countries only by the United States with 2.8. Continued high levels of unemployment account for this ratio, as do the expansion of active labor market policies, parental leave, and day care on the one hand, and reductions of pension benefits on the other.

A brief comment on pension reform is in order, even though its impact is not visible in our data on the working-age population. The need for pension reform had been clear before unification already, and a limited reform was passed in 1989, to be effective in 1992. After the Golden Age, mature pension systems in all postindustrial democracies began to experience financial pressures. They were all built on the pay-as-you-go defined benefits principle, where currently working people pay for the retired people whose benefits are calculated based on their years of contributions and their pay during their working years. As wage growth and the ratio of working to retired people declined (due to decreasing fertility and increasing longevity), it became increasingly difficult to maintain existing levels of benefits under the current rules. Countries first used a variety of gradual reforms, such as raising contributions, changing the formulas for calculating benefits, and raising the retirement age. In many cases, these first reforms were followed by structural reforms to the systems, introducing mandatory or optional funded tiers. In order to reduce political backlash, these reforms were mostly phased in over long periods.

In Germany, in addition to these common problems, fiscal pressures mounted rapidly in the wake of unification due to the widespread use of early retirement to deal with the unemployment problem. The share of pension benefits funded by federal subsidies from general taxes increased from 23 percent in 1995 to 37 percent in 2004 (Streeck 2007). The combination of the rise of non-wage labor costs and the fiscal pressures on the federal budget broke up the agreement between the political parties and employers about the German social model and led to a series of unilateral reforms (Trampusch 2009 and 2020). Chancellor Kohl passed a reform in 1996 that essentially ended the early retirement program and cut sickness benefits. The Red-Green government that won the 1998 elections then changed parts of the reforms passed by the CDU/CSU/FDP government in 1997, specifically to improve pension coverage for the marginally employed. The big change came in 2001 with the move from a defined benefit to a defined-contribution scheme and the introduction of a voluntary capitalized individual savings plan supported by tax incentives, the product of a complex compromise (Häusermann 2010). Yet this was not the end of the reforms; the intense fiscal pressures prompted further cutbacks by the Red-Green government in 2004 and finally a long-avoided increase of the retirement age from sixty-five to sixty-seven by the Grand Coalition in 2007. The various aspects of the pension reforms were phased in over many years, but over all they resulted in a projected drop from a 74 percent net replacement rate by the mandatory system for a worker with an average wage who was newly retired in 1995 to a 56 percent net replacement rate for a worker starting her working career in 2008 (OECD 2011). If the take-up in the tax-subsidized voluntary scheme were to reach 100 percent, this replacement rate would rise to 78.6 percent (OECD 2011, 127). However, take-up rates in voluntary schemes are always higher for higher-income groups, so this reform will further aggravate inequality.

After the 2001 pension reform, strong unions negotiated occupational pensions and overall occupational pension coverage increased. However, about a decade later, only about half of workers in the private sector were covered by occupational schemes. Predictably, coverage varied considerably between sectors, with low coverage in the poorly unionized service and retail sectors (Seeleib-Kaiser 2016). Thus the occupational pension system emulated the dualization of the labor market.

Impact of the Tax System

Germany has relied on a comparatively large share of payroll and consumption taxes, in typical Bismarckian fashion (Kenworthy 2011, 78–85). The country increased its tax revenue from the 1960s to the twenty-first century without markedly changing the tax mix. The increase in total tax revenue was comparatively moderate, and total tax revenue in 2007 was on the lower end among the continental countries. Nevertheless, according to Wang and Caminada's (2011) data, in 2004 Germany effected the third highest reduction of the Gini for the whole population, including pensioners, through the tax and transfer system, behind Belgium and Finland. Of this reduction, 25 percent was a result of direct taxation, which compares to an average of 15 percent for the 36 countries in their study. Consumption taxes were not included in these calculations. Nevertheless, this means that 75 percent of redistribution was achieved through transfers. These figures clearly reflect the generosity of the pension system at the time. As noted, the pension reforms were being phased in over long periods. As our table A.3 shows, Germany ranked much lower in redistribution among the working-age population in the period from 2000 to 2007, behind all the Nordic countries and Austria, Belgium, and France, as one would expect based on the comparatively (among continental countries) low total tax revenue. It fell further in the rankings between 2008 and 2016, falling behind the Netherlands, Ireland, and the UK as well, with a Gini reduction of 26.5 percent.

If we just look at the average payroll tax share from 1979 to 2007, Germany ranks with France, Spain, and the Netherlands among the highest postindustrial countries (Kenworthy 2011, 85). As discussed above, payroll taxes emerged as a major issue in the political debate about labor costs, international competitiveness of German industry, and job creation in the 1990s. The Grand Coalition government led by Merkel (2005–2009) reduced unemployment insurance contributions by workers and employers from 6.5 percent to 4.2 percent in 2007, and further to 3.3 percent by 2008, a reduction preceded by the reduction in generosity of unemployment benefits under the Hartz IV reforms. By 2015, the contribution for unemployment insurance was down to 1.5 percent.

Germany had a comparatively high top marginal tax rate of 49 percent on incomes exceeding 55,000 Euros per year before 2004. Germany, Switzerland, and Spain are the only postindustrial countries that did not lower their top marginal tax rate between the 1960s and the first decade of the 2000s (Piketty, Saez, and Stantcheva 2014). In 2004, this rate was lowered to 42 percent, but at the same time the income threshold was lowered to 52,151 Euros. In 2007, a new tax rate of 45 percent came into effect on incomes over 250,000 Euros per year (Jessen 2016). Consistent with our analysis in chapter 4, we can argue that this rate contributed to keeping the top 1 percent share from rising even more. After 2002, the lowest marginal tax rate was reduced from 19.9 to 14 percent (Jessen 2016).

Germany also had a comparatively high combined corporate income tax rate. Like the United States, Germany had both national and subnational corporate taxation. In the 1980s, the combined rate was at 62 percent—higher than in Sweden. In the 1990s it dropped in several steps to slightly above 50 percent, and then in the early 2000s it dropped steeply to below 40 percent and then, by the end of the decade, to 30 percent, where it has stayed. By 2020, Germany had the highest combined corporate income tax rate among our four countries, but by a small margin (figure B.1).

Germany also had a personal net wealth tax, levied annually on all personal wealth, including financial wealth, equity interests, real estate, and other property, with liabilities and debts deducted. After World War II the rate was set at 0.75 percent, and after gradual increases it had reached 1 percent when it was abolished in 1997 because the Federal Constitutional Court declared the unequal treatment of real estate and financial wealth unconstitutional. Surprisingly, the SPD/Green coalition government from 1998 to 2005 did not follow through with its initial plans to bring new wealth tax legislation into conformity with constitutional provisions (Hilmar and Sachweh 2022).

Comparable data on the impact of consumption taxes are not widely available. It is generally agreed that they are regressive. Warren (2008) confirms that they are regressive and calculates based on data from around 2000 that in the countries in our analyses consumption taxes made up between 25 and 35 percent of total tax revenue, with Portugal and Sweden being higher by 2 or 3 percent. The increase in the Gini of disposable household income when indirect taxes are taken into account ranged from 5 to 12 percent, except for Denmark, where it was 15 percent. However, this increase did not change the ordering of the countries: the Nordic countries remained the most equal, and Greece, Italy, Portugal, and the United States the most unequal (no data for Spain). In Germany, the proportion of total tax revenue coming from consumption taxes was at the lower end of the range, at 27 percent, and the increase in the Gini was about 7 percent, leaving the country in the group of medium inequality. Blasco, Guillaud, and Zemmour (2023) come to the same basic conclusions with a new method of estimating the inequality impact of consumption taxes: they are regressive, they reduce the redistributive effect of the tax and expenditure system on average by one-third, but they do not change the ordering of countries. The United States, Greece, Spain, the United Kingdom, Italy, and Australia remain the most unequal countries (in this order), and Sweden, Norway, Iceland, the Netherlands, Denmark, and Finland the least unequal.

We should keep in mind that, given the progressive structure of direct taxes, tax systems as a whole are generally slightly progressive or proportional (e.g., Decoster et al. 2010). What is important to keep in mind is that high tax revenue from proportional taxation can finance highly redistributive transfers and services.

Impact of Social Services

Marical et al. (2006) estimate the distributive effect of public spending on health, education, and housing, and they show that all postindustrial countries reduce inequality significantly if the value of the services used by these households is taken into account. The effect is greater if inequality is measured by the ratio of the income of the top 20 percent of households to the bottom 20 percent than if it is measured by the Gini, because the Gini is more sensitive to changes in the middle rather than the extremes of the income distribution. This effect is larger for countries with greater inequality of household income; it is especially large for Spain, Portugal, and the United States. However, the ranking of the countries does not change significantly when the quintile ratio includes public services (Marical et al. 2006, 37).

Germany has fewer publicly funded social services than the Nordic countries and some continental countries, such as France. Accordingly, estimates of the distributive effect of social services rank Germany comparatively low (Kenworthy 2011, 76). The 80-20 ratio of household income is reduced by .84 in Germany, which is the smallest reduction among the continental countries. However, Germany follows the general pattern in that its ranking on the 80-20 ratio does not change; as of 2000 it remained the fifth most equal of the countries in the analysis, behind Denmark, Sweden, Austria, and the Netherlands, and ahead of Finland, France, Belgium, and the southern and Anglo-American countries (Marical et al. 2006, 37). As our table A.4 showed, after 2000 Germany became markedly more unequal.

CHAPTER NINE

Spain

The overall pattern in Spain is one of comparatively high and strongly cyclical levels of inequality and poverty, with a strong upward trend beginning in 2007. Spain started out with high levels of market and disposable income inequality and low levels of redistribution, comparable to US levels. By the early 2000s, before the onset of the crisis, household market income inequality had fallen to a very low level, close to the Swedish level. However, redistribution remained low, even somewhat lower than in the United States, despite higher levels of spending. As a result, household disposable income inequality was clearly higher than in Sweden and Germany, but lower than in the United States. The crisis then drove up market income inequality to very high levels, and the redistributive effort increased to a level higher than in the United States, so that the ordering of the four countries on disposable income inequality remained stable: highest in the United States, followed by Spain, Germany, and Sweden (tables A.2–4).

Spain's main problems underlying inequality and poverty have been the high levels of unemployment and the low levels of employment, particularly among women, and the austerity conditions imposed by the Troika—the International Monetary Fund (IMF), the European Central Bank (ECB), and the European Commission—in the wake of the 2007 financial crisis. The legacies of Francoism (in the form of poor human capital and subordination of women on the one hand, and the structure of the economy with the core growth sectors in construction and tourism on the other) stood in the way of the development of a labor market capable of creating and filling a sufficient number of jobs paying above poverty wages to keep poverty and inequality at moderate levels in the European context. A trend toward improvement during the growth phase from the late 1990s to 2007 was cut short by the economic crisis. The Socialist governments (Partido Socialista Obrero Español, or PSOE) of 1982–1996 and 2004–2011 had made strong efforts to modernize the Spanish welfare state and bring it closer to EU norms, but the austerity measures imposed in the wake of the crisis constrained the ability of the welfare state to counteract rising market income poverty and inequality effectively.

In the Spanish case, we actually saw a moderate increase in union density between 1980 and 2010, but by 2018 it was back down to the low 1980 level of 13 percent. Moreover, the union movement remained politically divided, which weakened its economic and political power. Contract coverage remained at 80 percent as of 2018, though opt-out clauses became increasingly common, just as in Germany. Also, the high level of temporary employment means that effective contract coverage was much lower than the 80 percent figure suggests.

Partisan differences in policy were stark, with the PSOE governments leading the expansion and redistributive thrust of the Spanish welfare state, universalizing health care and establishing tax-financed social safety nets for outsiders in its first two periods in office. The conservative Partido Popular (PP) governments, in contrast, introduced no major improvements in the earlier period and imposed deep cuts under the general austerity program after they returned to power in 2011. When the PSOE returned to power in 2018, the government renewed efforts to protect the most vulnerable, and these efforts intensified under the coalition government of the PSOE and Podemos. Education was a major battleground; the PSOE strengthened public education and tried to make it more accessible, and the PP kept supporting Catholic education and early tracking.

What distinguishes the Spanish case from our other three countries is the influence of external forces. Spain is the only one of our four countries that suffered a sovereign debt crisis and had to ask for support from the IMF and ECB, and thus had to comply with harsh externally imposed austerity. It is important to note that this crisis resulted from the government bailing out a financial system that had collapsed due to private overlending, not from the government's own fiscal irresponsibility. Indeed, the government ran surpluses from 2005 to 2007, and the debt was well below the level stipulated in the Stability and Growth Pact. The austerity conditions destroyed the political support for the PSOE government under Zapatero and opened the way for the election of the PP, led by Rajoy, in 2011. The Rajoy government then proceeded not only to double down on austerity but also to impose a number of legal changes that weakened collective bargaining and protection for workers.

Looking at the extremes of the income distribution, the share of the top 1 percent remained relatively modest, between 8 and 9 percent as of 2005 (though with capital gains included it rose to 11 percent—Alvaredo and Saez 2010, and see our table B.2). On the lower end, as of 2015 the low-wage sector remained smaller that in Germany and the US, with 15 percent compared to 20 percent and 25 percent respectively (table B.5). Spain's key problems since the 1980s have been the high levels of unemployment, particularly among young people, and the low overall levels of employment (tables B.7–8). Unlike the rest of western Europe (with the exception of Portugal and Greece), Spain did not enter the 1980s after a "Golden Age" of economic growth, union strength, and welfare state expansion. Rather, Spain transitioned from an authoritarian regime presiding over an uncompetitive economy with an anemic welfare state to a democratic regime that attempted to catch up with the rest of Europe.

Once democracy was consolidated and the PSOE under Felipe González had won the election in 1982, the government faced three major challenges: modernizing the economy, modernizing the welfare state, and managing regionalization. It faced these challenges in the context of inflation that was running at an annual rate of 16 percent, an external current account that was US$4 billion in arrears, and foreign exchange reserves that had become dangerously depleted. The economy under Franco had been based on an import substitution industrialization (ISI) model, with high tariffs and a large public enterprise sector. The welfare state had been built on the ISI economy, with an employment-based male breadwinner insurance model, and it was not generous at all. Guillén and León (2011, 5) aptly characterize it as an underdeveloped version of the Bismarckian model. Social security and welfare expenditure in 1970 amounted to no more than 8.6 percent of GDP, and public health spending was at 2.3 percent. Post-tax and transfer poverty in 1980 was 10 percent. Moreover, education under Franco was underfunded and highly stratified. Modernizing the economy and the welfare state, including education, was a prerequisite for catching up with Europe and becoming a member of the European Union. By the same token, membership in the European Union provided incentives to follow recommendations for reforms to foster social inclusion.

Modernizing the economy entailed lowering tariffs and privatizing state enterprises. Many industrial enterprises were forced to downsize their labor force radically. Industrial employment overall declined from 35 percent of the labor force in 1980 to 31 percent in 2000, but in several sectors the decline was much more radical. The growth model then was based on tourism and construction, which limited improvements in productivity and exposed the economy to strong cyclical fluctuations. In 1985 unemployment stood at 21 percent of the labor force. It fell to a low of 8 percent in 2007, at the height of the boom, and rose back up to 27 percent in 2013, before declining steadily to the still very high level of 20 percent in 2018. Pre-tax and transfer household poverty followed a similar trajectory, rising from 19 percent in 1990 to 24 percent in 1995, falling to a low of 16 percent in 2006, and rising again to 27 percent in 2015. Employment levels also fluctuated, but rose from 50 percent in 1990 to 63 percent in 2018, still some 15 and 17 percentage points below employment levels in Germany and Sweden, respectively.

Modernizing the welfare state entailed a move from the corporatist employment-based model to a more universalistic orientation, including an expansion of health services and the social safety net to cover previously excluded groups. Major progress was made in these areas through the universalization of health coverage and the introduction of noncontributory pensions in 1990 under the PSOE. Overall benefits in Spain improved and welfare state effort in spending on the non-aged rose to Swedish levels by 2010, with 17 percent of GDP (table B.28). Redistribution significantly and consistently lowered poverty and inequality, and it cushioned the impact of the crises of the early 1990s and 2008 on both, but given the high pre-tax and transfer poverty and inequality, redistribution was insufficient to bring disposable income poverty and inequality down to the average of the original EU member countries. In fact, post-tax and transfer levels of poverty have remained comparable to levels in the United States, even surpassing US levels slightly by 2013. The post-tax and transfer Gini, in contrast, remained lower than in the United States. The pre-tax and transfer Gini is higher in the United States, which is due to the much higher share of the top 1 percent—18 percent in 2007, which was twice the Spanish share in that year. Also, the redistributive effort in the form of non-aged social spending was higher in Spain for the entire period under consideration here, and from 2007 on inequality reduction was higher in Spain than in the United States (tables A.2–7).

The expansion of health care, education, other social services, and social assistance was complicated because it became intertwined with the larger process of transfer of power to the regions. Spain has changed from the highly centralized unitary system under which Franco governed into a quasi-federal system. The Constitution of 1978 devolved authority for social services and social assistance to the regions, while preserving social security as a national-level program. Between 1982 and 1993, the regions established systems of social services in a concerted effort to get as much autonomy as possible, in the context of a tripartite system of financing from the national, regional, and municipal levels. The territory was divided into seventeen regions, though originally only the three historical regions (Basque Country, Catalonia, and Galicia) would become Autonomous Communities (ACs). After 1985 all regions had a directly elected regional parliament and an administration independent of any veto by the central government. Seven regions followed a fast route (the historic three plus Andalucía, Canary Islands, Navarra, and Valencia) to higher levels of issue jurisdiction, but even among them there are asymmetries. Different regions have different degrees of autonomy in different issue areas. For instance, the Basque Country and Navarra collect all the taxes and pay a quota to the central government; the national government does not levy any taxes in their regions. A 1992 law gave the ten regions on the slow course most of the same powers as regions on the fast track, and by 2000 the transfer to the regions of responsibility for health and undergraduate education was completed. The regions also have a large role in other social services, such as childcare, elderly care, and social assistance. Since there are considerable differences in the affluence and the political makeup of the regions, the generosity of the social safety net and the quality of social services vary greatly.

Changes in the Economy and the Labor Market

As noted, the change of the economy from an ISI orientation to an open economy that would be ready to join the EU in 1986 was a difficult process. It caused an overall reduction of industrial employment, and a particularly drastic one in some sectors. Labor force reductions between 1982 and 1991–1996 reached 79 percent in public shipbuilding, 69 percent in small firms in shipbuilding, 64 percent in integrated steel, 46 percent in common steel, 51 percent in chemicals, 49 percent in home appliances, etcetera (Etchemendy 2011, 158). Workers could get unemployment benefits for anywhere from two months to three years, depending on previous contributions. In addition, there was the option of early retirement or participation in employment promotion funds. Thus, these workforce reductions drove up unemployment and put enormous pressure on the budget. Unemployment stood at 15 percent of the labor force in 1982, rose to 20 percent in 1985, and after a decline to 14 percent in 1990, climbed still further, to 21 percent in 1994 as a result of the economic crisis of 1992–1994. Employment followed a similar trajectory, rising from 47 percent in 1982 to 50 percent in 1990 and dropping again to 46 percent in 1995. So, workers displaced from industry were not absorbed by an expanding service sector, but largely relegated to inactivity. Accordingly, labor market policy became and remained a priority for the government.

The structural changes brought about by the opening of the economy were aggravated by the types of technological change experienced in other postindustrial economies. The employment structure changed in a U-shaped way in the period from 1990 to 2008: In particular, the decline of routine jobs, both manual and mental, as a result of technological change was very steep, and it was not counterbalanced by the creation of non-routine cognitive jobs at middle skill levels. Compared to Germany, routine manual jobs accounted for a larger share of the workforce in 1990 but fell to roughly the same level as Germany by 2020. In the same period, non-routine manual jobs grew more in Spain than in Germany, but non-routine cognitive jobs lagged far behind (Garritzmann, Häusermann, and Palier 2022). Figures from Oesch (2013, 71–73) add more detailed information: the employment share of non-routine service and manual occupations, such as childcare assistants, waiters, builders, and taxi drivers grew by 31 percent, and the employment share of non-routine analytical and interactive occupations, such as engineers, managers, and psychologists, grew by 41 percent. In contrast, mid-level routine cognitive and manual occupations, such as secretaries, cashiers, and mechanics, declined by 41 percent between 1990 and 2008 (Oesch 2013, 71). Data from Goos, Manning, and Salomon (2009) show low growth in employment share of the lowest-paying occupations between 1993 and 2006, with about 1 percent (compared to 3 percent in Germany and 2 percent in Sweden); considerable decline of middling occupations with 7 percent (the same as in Sweden and 2 percentage points less than in Germany); and considerable growth of the highest-paying occupations with 6 percent (the same as in Germany and 1 percentage point more than in Sweden). In other words, an upgrading of skill demands of jobs occurred, which relegated low-skilled workers increasingly into lower-paying service jobs—a sector that did not grow sufficiently to absorb all the available workers in the first place. Data for about 2005–2010 show between 16 and 18 percent of workers in low-paying jobs—lower than in Germany, but higher than in any other European country.

Educational levels of the Spanish population as of 1985 were very low, with only 7 percent of the adult population having completed secondary education and only 5 percent tertiary education. This ranked below Germany for secondary education (12 percent) and the same level for tertiary education; the figures for Sweden and the United States were 37 percent and 40 percent for secondary and 11 percent and 22 percent for tertiary education. By 2010, the gap in completed secondary education had widened and the ordering of the countries changed, with 19 percent in Spain compared to 36 percent in the United States, 48 percent in Sweden, and 57 percent in Germany. For completed tertiary education, the gap had narrowed and the ordering remained the same, with Germany and Spain at 16 percent and 17 percent, Sweden at 19 percent, and the United States at 31 percent (tables B.22–23). Accordingly, returns to skills measured by test scores in 2011–2013 were fourth highest in Spain, behind the United States, Ireland, and Germany (Hanushek et al. 2015). Returns to tertiary education in 2013 were even higher than in Germany (Weisstanner and Armingeon 2020, 8; and see our table B.21).

As noted, the share of the top 1 percent remained moderate, between Swedish and German levels, both with and without capital gains (table B.2). As in Sweden and the United States, the share reached its high point in 2007, with 11.2 percent, compared to 10 percent in Sweden and 23.5 percent in the United States. By 2012 it had dropped to 8.6 percent in Spain, essentially the same as in Sweden. Actually, average stock market capitalization in the period 2000–2007 was higher than in Germany, with 86 percent of GDP compared to Germany's 51 percent, but clearly below the levels of Sweden and the United States (table B.15). However, as in Germany, the spread of the shareholder value model of corporate governance was restrained by the institutionalized position of labor at the enterprise level in the form of factory councils, and average CEO compensation—especially the stock-based component—remained comparatively low in Spain in 2001–2008 (Croci, Gonenc, and Ozkan 2012). Also, the top marginal tax rate had not changed since the 1960s, and it was close to the German rate in the 2000s, at 45 percent.

Wage dispersion in Spain in 1995 was closer to the United States than to Germany and Sweden. The 90-50 ratio was 2.1, and the 50-10 ratio was 2.0 (table B.1). However, whereas the 90-50 ratio increased in the United States to 2.4, the Spanish ratio came down to 1.8 by 2016; the 50-10 ratio remained stable in the United States, but in Spain it also fell to 1.8 in this period. Both ratios increased by 0.1 point in Germany but remained stable in Sweden. So, as of 2016, wage dispersion as measured by these two ratios was the same in Germany and Spain. As noted, wage dispersion ratios underestimate earnings inequality because they measure wages of full-time workers. This is less a problem for Spain than it was for Germany, because part-time employment has been relatively low in Spain. Before 2000, part-time employment was in the single digits; by 2015 it had risen to 15 percent of total employment, just one percentage point above Sweden and clearly below Germany's 22 percent. The big problems in Spain have been temporary employment (fluctuating between 25 and 35 percent of total employment between 1995 and 2015, compared to around 15 percent in Germany and Sweden) combined with high unemployment and low levels of employment (tables B.10–11). So, more people were moving in and out of employment, and household poverty was higher than in Germany despite identical wage dispersion ratios.

Levels of employment in Spain were traditionally very low among women. In 1980, only 28 percent of women were in the labor force—half the level of the United States, and less than half that of Germany and Sweden (table B.9). Though women's labor force participation doubled to reach 56 percent in 2017, it remained very clearly below the levels of the United States, Germany, and Sweden. The weight of traditional gender roles combined with the lack of public childcare and the economy's sluggish pace of job creation to keep female employment rates so low. This in turn meant that fewer households had a buffer against poverty in the form of a second earner.

In terms of economic transformation, Spain made neither a breakthrough to information technology, as Sweden did, nor a leap to advanced diversified quality production, as Germany did; rather, its growth up to 2007 had been fueled by construction and tourism and thereafter remained based on domestic demand. As of 2008, on the eve of the crisis, exports accounted only for 26 percent of GDP, compared to 44 percent in Germany. Given the small size of the export sector, the structural adjustment demands aimed at lowering unit labor costs and thus making production more internationally competitive and bringing about an export-led recovery (which had worked in Germany) in fact deepened and prolonged the recession by depressing domestic demand in Spain (Scharpf 2021, 179–80). As a result, unemployment remained at 20 percent or above in the 2010s.

As in Germany, deregulation of energy, transport, and communications was extensive. The OECD simple mean of sectoral regulation indices in airlines, telecom, electricity, gas, post, rail, and road shows that Spain regulated these sectors even more highly than Germany in the 1970s, and regulated them at the levels of Sweden and the United States by 2013. Spain started at 5.7 compared to an average of 5.1, and ended up at 1.4 compared to an average of 1.6 (table B.14). As in the other countries, deregulation contributed to the disappearance of stable and decently remunerated public-sector jobs and their replacement with less stable and lower-paying private-sector jobs.

Changes in Labor Market Institutions and Policies

The union movement in Spain has been split between the Communist Workers' Commissions (CCOO) and the General Confederation of Workers (UGT), which was extremely close to the PSOE and participated in a variety of pacts after the transition (Royo 2000). Spain inherited a dual system of representation from the Franco period, with factory councils serving as bargaining agents and having the ability to call strikes. If a union obtains a majority of seats on the factory council in the elections held every four years, then the union becomes the bargaining agent (Burgess 2004). Union density was comparatively very low, with 13 percent of wage and salary earners belonging to unions in 1980—a figure that rose very slowly to 18 percent by 2010 and fell back to 13 percent by 2018. However, contract coverage rose from 83 percent in 1980 to 93 percent in 1995, and union mobilization capacity reached much further than the membership. Contract coverage declined very gradually over the next two decades, but remained at 80 percent in 2018 (tables B.17–18). However, opt-out clauses became more widely used and rendered effective coverage much more limited. And union rivalry weakened the power of organized labor because it often prevented the articulation of a coherent position of the labor movement.

In the early 1980s, two tripartite social pacts were designed to support efforts to reduce inflation, the budget deficit, and unemployment: the Acuerdo Nacional sobre el Empleo (1981–1982) and the Acuerdo Económico y Social (AES, 1984–1986—Pérez and Rhodes 2015). The AES was not signed by the CCOO, and it contained a variety of provisions responding to the priorities of the government, employers, and unions. It secured wage moderation to support the PSOE government's fiscal and monetary adjustment program; it increased the coverage of the unemployment benefit system; and it extended the use of temporary work contracts, part-time employment, and exemptions to the minimum wage for workers under eighteen years old (Pérez and Rhodes 2015). However, conflicts over further social policy issues, such as the 1985 pension reform, alienated the UGT from the government. The CCOO called for a general strike to protest the pension reform; the UGT did not join the strike, but it opposed the reform. When the 1988 budget did not show the increase in social expenditures that the UGT had demanded, the union officially broke with the government and joined a general strike in December 1988 to protest a youth employment plan (Burgess 2004). Nevertheless, the government and both union confederations agreed on a package in 1990 that created a universal means-tested noncontributory pension and indexed the contributory pensions to the consumer price index.

In 1992 the Spanish economy was hit by a deep recession, which was answered by successive devaluations of the currency in 1992, 1993, and 1995. The result was a renewed upward trend in unemployment, prompting efforts at cost control in the welfare state. Unemployment replacement rates and duration were reduced and qualifying periods were lengthened. The unemployment generosity index had risen from 9.6 in 1983 to 11.5 in 1992, but then declined to 9.5 in 1994, before slowly recovering to 10.8 in 1999. This meant that a larger number of unemployed had to rely on unemployment assistance with yet lower benefits. The government also intensified active labor market policies, with subsidies for hiring young people, those over forty-five, and the long-term unemployed, and for part-time employment; and it authorized nonprofit private employment agencies to operate. Since regions were in charge of administering active labor market policies, their effectiveness varied greatly. In particular, employment agencies in many areas had very low placement success rates.

The new conservative Partido Popular (PP) government sought new social pacts, and in 1996 the unions agreed to a social pact that promoted the creation of open-ended contracts, put part-time and temporary contracts on the same basis as permanent contracts with regard to social security rights, and reduced severance payments (Guillén 2010). In other words, the previously rigid labor market with high employment protection legislation was made more flexible, but these reforms also facilitated an ever more widespread use of temporary contracts. In the boom years from 2000 to 2007, the temporary employment share of total employment was

32–34 percent (Pérez and Rhodes 2015). A pact signed in 1997 strengthened national sectoral-level bargaining and established procedures to extend collective bargains across sectors (Pérez and Rhodes 2015). Nevertheless, contract coverage continued to decline from a high of 93 percent of employees in 1995 to 80 percent in 2018. This was below the Swedish level of 88 percent, but clearly above the German level of 54 percent. However, as noted, enforcement of these contracts was weakened by opt-out agreements at the enterprise level, particularly after the end of the boom.

After the mid-1990s, Spain entered an impressive growth cycle. Particularly after the country joined the Eurozone in 1999 and interest rates declined, private borrowing escalated and the construction boom accelerated. Male and female employment rose steeply, reaching 77 percent for males and 57 percent for females in 2007, while unemployment declined to 8 percent. However, when the construction bubble burst, banks hit by bad debts cut back lending, growth and government revenue collapsed, and government debt rose rapidly because the government bailed out the banks and engaged in countercyclical spending. This exposed the Zapatero government to intense pressure from financial markets and the Troika (the European Commission, European Central Bank, and International Monetary Fund) to discontinue its countercyclical stimulus measures. As the economy went into a steep decline, the employment gains were wiped out. Between 2007 and 2011 male employment dropped to 64 percent and female employment to 53 percent; employment in construction fell by 57 percent (Pérez and Rhodes 2015).

As discussed above, the share of non-routine service and manual occupations, such as childcare assistants, waiters, construction workers, and taxi drivers, had increased significantly (Oesch 2013, 71). Clearly, construction and tourism, the two growth sectors, accounted for much of the job creation in that category, and they were hit badly by the economic crisis. Unemployment jumped from 9 percent in 2005 to 20 percent in 2010 and 22 percent in 2015.

After first responding with countercyclical measures—among them a new benefit for the unemployed who had exhausted their contributory or noncontributory unemployment benefits, and voluntary contributions to unemployment insurance for the self-employed—the Zapatero government, under intense outside pressure, imposed austerity measures. Among them was the replacement of a six-month special unemployment support program for people over forty-five who had exhausted their unemployment benefits with an individual retraining program (Moreira et al. 2015). Salaries of public employees were reduced by some 5 percent, and public employment was reduced (León, Pavolini, and Guillén 2015). The austerity measures encountered massive popular resistance from the union movement and social movements alike. The *indignados* emerged in May 2010 and became the most visible social movement mobilizing against austerity. The unions called a general strike in 2010 to protest cuts in public-sector employment and compensation, along with reforms reducing severance pay and opening opt-out clauses from higher-level agreements to conclude company agreements (Molina and Godino 2013). They also opposed Zapatero's proposal for a pension reform that would raise the retirement age from sixty-five to sixty-seven, reduce replacement rates, and tighten conditions for accessing early retirement. Nevertheless, this reform was implemented in August 2011.

Despite strong opposition, reforms of labor market institutions also continued. A further important decree of June 2011 gave precedence to company collective agreements over provincial collective agreements, unless a national, sectoral, or regional agreement explicitly prevented this (Clauwaert and Schömann 2012). This opened the way for deviations downward in pay, working hours, leave, etcetera, and eroded the effectiveness of the comparatively high levels of contract extension.

The PSOE lost the November 2011 elections, and the PP government under Rajoy imposed even harsher austerity packages. In June 2012 Spain asked Eurozone governments for a massive bailout to rescue its banking system, and the government did get an ECB loan. The austerity measures affected all areas of public life, particularly public employment in health and education, and they also forced regional governments to cut their expenditures, including in all social services. In 2012 the government lowered unemployment compensation after six months of benefits from a 60 percent to a 50 percent replacement rate (Moreira et al. 2015).

The Rajoy government also undertook a number of measures to make the labor market more flexible, which eroded security for labor market insiders and weakened labor at all levels. A decree law in February 2012 further reduced the costs of layoffs, including compensation for unfair dismissal. By 2013, the OECD employment protection index for Spain for workers with regular contracts was below the average of fifteen EU countries. In contrast, the employment protection index for temporary employment remained much higher than for the EU fifteen. This is important, considering that the share of temporary employment in Spain remained at about a quarter of total employment—twice as high as in Germany. At the same time the reduction of the workforce in the public sector contributed to an increase in the share of labor market outsiders (León, Pavolini, and Guillén 2015).

The February 2012 decree law also extended the trial period for new hires to a year, expanded the scope of employer discretion in the workplace, and permitted the unilateral rejection of existing collective bargaining agreements for reasons related to a firm's economic, technical, organizational, or production needs, subject to a court's review. It removed the option for provincial collective agreements to supersede company collective agreements that the 2011 legislation had protected (Clauwaert and Schömann 2012). The law also restricted to one year the provision for agreements to remain in force pending negotiation of a new one. In addition, the government restricted the authority of the labor inspection service, engaged in regulatory forbearance, and limited collection and reporting of data on the effects of reforms (Cioffi and Dubin 2016). Again, unions called for protest demonstrations across the country, but the legislation stuck.

In an analysis of data for 2014 Muñoz de Bustillo and Hernández (2018, 499–503) found that firms that negotiated and reached agreements at the level of the firm had higher levels of wage inequality than firms whose agreements were reached at a higher level, controlling for a long list of variables. Accordingly, the decentralization of collective bargaining promoted through the 2012 reforms was likely to increase wage inequality. The same analysis showed that firms that relied more heavily on employees with temporary contracts had higher wage inequality.

After returning to power in 2018, the PSOE intensified efforts to reduce the dualization of labor markets. In the first two years the government was not able to pass major legislation, with the exception of an increase of 22 percent in the minimum wage for 2019. Labor market reforms then were part of the coalition agreement reached by the PSOE and UP in January 2020. The government immediately initiated talks with the unions and employer organizations aimed at essentially reversing Rajoy's labor market reforms of 2012. The pandemic delayed these talks, but an agreement was finally signed in December 2021 (Branco et al. 2023). Among the provisions were restrictions on the use of temporary contracts, stipulations that subcontracted workers should be covered by the sectoral collective agreement of the main company, partial recentralization of bargaining, an extension of the duration of collective agreements if not replaced by a new one, and a recognition of delivery workers for digital platforms as paid employees (Branco, Miró, and Natili 2023). Yearly increases of the minimum wage continued, totaling 47 percent for the period 2018 to 2023 (Branco, Miró, and Natili 2023). As of this writing, it is too early to measure the effects of these policy changes on poverty and inequality, but one can certainly expect both to be beneficial.

During the boom years, immigration accelerated massively. Between 2002 and 2007 the net number of immigrants increased each year by at least 600,000, compared to between 250,000 and 300,000 in Britain and between 55,000 and 100,000 in Germany. In 1996, Spain had no more than 500,000 foreign residents; by 2007 the number had grown to more than 5 million. In 2008, the share of foreign-born in the labor force was almost 16 percent. Initially, around half of the non-EU immigrants had no residence permits (Laparra 2011, 216). The PP government concentrated on security and control measures, but when the PSOE came back to power in 2004 the focus shifted to social integration.

Overall, the share of foreign-born in the population increased from only 3.6 percent in 2000 to 14 percent by 2019. This is the largest increase among our four countries, even though the levels in 2019 were the same in the United States and somewhat higher in Germany at 16 percent and in Sweden at 19.5 percent (table B.16). Until 2006 Spain kept permissive family reunification rules and work permits for sectors with labor shortages. In addition, irregular immigration in the 2000s was estimated to account for close to half of non-EU migration. This irregular immigration was facilitated by Spain's black-market economy, where irregular migrants could find work. In contrast to Germany and Sweden, the employment rate of immigrants in 2019 was roughly the same as that of the native-born; in Germany it was 7 percent lower and in Sweden 15 percent lower than the rate of the native-born (OECD 2020). An additional reason for this difference is language competency: Spain saw heavy immigration from Latin America, which made integration into the labor market easier. As of 2010, some 40 percent of immigrants originated from Latin America, mainly Colombia and Ecuador, and roughly 20 percent each came from eastern Europe and Africa (Mooi-Reci and Muñoz-Comet 2016, 732). The new PSOE government passed legislation in 2004 to facilitate regularization and integration of migrants. It established a support fund that was dispersed to ACs and town and city councils and it gave all immigrants access to health care, education, and other social services. By 2007 the share of irregular migrants had been reduced to an estimated quarter (Laparra 2011). During the crisis unemployment rose much more among the immigrant population, and as of 2019 unemployment was still 6 percent higher for immigrants. Also, immigrants generally had low educational levels (Oesch 2013, 95). Thus, immigration contributed to keeping wage levels low (Molina and Godino 2013).

Demographic changes also weighed on the welfare state. The portion of the population that was aged rose from 11 to 19 percent between 1980 and 2018. Fertility was very low, dropping from 2.2 in 1980 to 1.3 in 1990 and staying at that level through 2017. Both of these indicators were very close to the German figures. The percentage of children living with single mothers increased from 3.5 to 11 percent from 1980 to 2016—lower than the German rate of 16 percent, but still a major increase.

Human Capital

A comparatively low level of skills in the population has contributed to the high levels of inequality and poverty. Wage returns to skills in 2011–2013 were fourth highest among twenty-two countries, behind the US, Ireland, and Germany (Hanushek et al. 2013). The Francoist legacy was a highly stratified educational system with low accessibility and quality for many and strong reliance on private (mainly Catholic) institutions. The Constitution of 1978 guaranteed a system of mixed provision, with some form of subsidies to private schools, subject to certain conditions (Boyd-Barrett 1995, 8). Efforts to universalize educational access and lengthen compulsory schooling ran up against a problem of capacity in the public sector, such that a law passed in 1985 recognized the obligation of the state to finance compulsory education on the basis of a dual system where private institutions received subsidies from the state under the condition that they were nonprofit institutions, made confessional practice voluntary, and adhered to state-defined norms. Subsidies indeed increased greatly under the PSOE government of González.

By the mid-1990s, about a third of students at the pre-university level went to private schools, whereas universities were overwhelmingly public (Boyd-Barrett 1995, 8). Fully private schools (i.e., non-subsidized schools) accounted for no more than 3 to 4 percent of students. This pattern remained stable for many years but varies greatly among the Autonomous Communities (Gallego and Subirats 2011). Education in state-subsidized schools was generally free, though "supplementary charges of dubious legality were sometimes demanded" (Boyd-Barrett 1995, 9). In regions that tend to have higher quality education systems in terms of teacher/student ratios and percentages of pass/fail at each level, public education typically accounts for a larger part of the system. In some regions, there is no public involvement at all in preschool education (Gallego and Subirats 2011).

A major reform introduced in 1990 extended compulsory comprehensive education to age sixteen, eliminating the early separation of students into academic and vocational streams. The goal was to increase spending to the European average of 6 percent of GDP, but that goal fell victim to the economic problems of the early 1990s, which also slowed the implementation of the reform. Educational policy remained controversial between the Left and the Right. The PP government under Aznar strengthened the role of the Catholic church in education again in 2002 with tax exemptions, the right to appoint and dismiss religious teachers in public schools, and the reestablishment of religious education in all public schools (Chaqués-Bonafont, Palau, and Baumgartner 2015). The reform also reintroduced an early division between an academic and a vocational track. In 2006 the Zapatero government reversed course again by making religious education voluntary and introducing citizenship education. By 2010 this government had also doubled the amount of money spent on scholarships in 2004 (del Pino 2013).

The Zapatero government also initiated a major expansion of early childhood education and care, shortly before the onset of the economic crisis. The goal was to increase the available childcare to accommodate 300,000 more children younger than three years. However, this initiative was essentially eliminated under the austerity program of the PP government under Rajoy after 2011 (Busemeyer, Garritzmann, and Neimanns 2020). The cuts introduced by the Rajoy government fell hard on education in general. Teaching positions and teachers' salaries were cut, along with financial support for students.

The Rajoy government also continued the ideologically inspired conservative education reforms favoring private schools and educational segregation. They lowered the tracking age from sixteen to fifteen and introduced a lower-quality vocational certificate. They allowed publicly subsidized schools with curricular specializations to select up to 20 percent of students based on ability. They also attempted to introduce external examinations at the end of primary, lower secondary, and upper secondary levels, the effect of which would have been to increase the segregation of the educational system. However, the external examinations ran into a storm of protests not only from teachers but also from students and parents, and was ultimately abandoned after the PP lost its parliamentary majority in 2015 (Busemeyer, Garritzmann, and Neimanns 2020).

Vocational education in Spain is largely school-based. The Rajoy government attempted to introduce a dual model of vocational training, under which one-third of training would have been done through placements in commercial businesses. The hope was that this would increase trainees' employment chances and thus help reduce rampant youth unemployment. However, despite general support for the idea from political parties, employers, and unions, the program's progress lagged far behind target levels. Essentially, vocational education still carries the stigma of being for low achievers, and the government and employers have not been willing and able to make the significant investments needed to spur a significant expansion of a dual training system (Busemeyer, Garritzmann, and Neimanns 2020).

Tertiary education in Spain is predominantly public, but students do pay tuition, and those levels vary across the ACs. According to figures from the European Commission (Busemeyer, Garritzmann, and Neimanns 2020, 303) for the 2016-17 academic year, average fees were 1,100 Euros for first-cycle programs and 1,991 Euros for second-cycle programs—clearly more than a nominal amount. Roughly one-fifth of students received some financial help, but overall higher education remained the domain of the better-off. The percentage of the adult population with completed higher education degrees in 2010 was 17, just barely above Germany's 16.1 percent and below Sweden's 19 percent.

Interestingly, returns to education calculated by Weisstanner and Armingeon (2020) in 2013 showed clearly higher values in Spain than in Germany (.61 compared to .46), despite the comparable level of people with completed tertiary education. However, their measure compares workers with tertiary education to all workers without, so the educational achievements of the rest of the population are important too. And here we see a major difference. In 2010, only 19 percent of the Spanish population had completed secondary education (as the highest level, not counting those with tertiary education), compared to 57 percent in Germany, 48 percent in Sweden, and 36 percent in the United States (tables B.22–23). So, Spain still suffered from the legacies of the Franco period among the older generations, as well as from the limited progress of reforms under the democratic governments.

The data from the Program for the International Assessment of Adult Competencies (PIAAC) also drive home the legacy of the deficiencies in

Spain's educational system. The mean numeracy scores, which are most comparable across countries, show Spain and the United States over 30 points lower than Sweden (250 and 253 compared to 284—table B.20). Among the sixteen participating postindustrial countries, Italy is the only other one with such a low score. If we look at the percentage of adults classified as low literacy, Spain's is the highest at 28 percent (again matched by Italy). Despite significant reform efforts in democratic Spain, the performance of the educational system has remained problematic. In 2010 the rate of students dropping out of high school without a degree was 28 percent—double the EU-27 average of 14 percent.

Still, there are signs of improvement. The mean math PISA scores in 2000 were the lowest in our group of countries, at 476, compared to 510 in Sweden. Only Portugal, Italy, and Greece were lower in that year. At the 25th percentile, Spain was also lower than our other three countries, though Germany was close, and at the 5th percentile Germany was even lower. By 2015 Spain had switched places with the United States (i.e., students had the second-lowest math scores at the mean, the 25th, and the 5th percentile). Indeed, at the 5th percentile the scores were the same as in Sweden, and at the 25th percentile they were just slightly behind Sweden (table B.20).

Changes in Social Policy

The first major attempts to modernize the welfare state were a series of pension reforms carried out between 1983 and 1986, under the first Socialist government. These reforms lengthened the minimum contributory period from ten to fifteen years, reduced the replacement rate, capped contributory pensions at an amount of 4.7 times the 1986 minimum wage, and introduced a means-tested minimum pension supplement (Guillén, Álvarez, and Adão e Silva 2003; Aguilar-Hendrickson and Arriba González de Durana 2020). Another major reform adding an important universalistic element expanded the welfare state in 1986 by establishing a national health system with universal coverage and services, to be provided by the regions and coordinated by the central state. A policy of drift (that is, nonadjustment of the value of a benefit inherited from the Franco period) let the value of family allowances paid to male breadwinners through the social security system deteriorate to insignificance by 1990 (Naldini 2003, 162). A reform in 1990 introduced noncontributory child allowances for low-income families. The PSOE platform in 1989 had promised reforms in work-family reconciliation, including maternity leave and childcare. Childcare was initially framed as a women-friendly policy and later as an educational policy to reduce social inequality in preparation for school (Naldini 2003). In 1994 paid maternity leave was expanded from fourteen to sixteen weeks and the replacement rate was raised to 100 percent of salary (Bürgisser 2022).

By the early 1990s, the government had achieved important changes in the pension system, such as reducing the difference between maximum and minimum benefits and establishing the noncontributory pensions (Chuliá 2011). Nevertheless, the reforms had done little to make the pension system more sustainable, so a tripartite agreement, the Toledo Pact of 1995, changed the indexing rules and increased the number of years for calculating the replacement rate, and it separated the financing of contributory income support from noncontributory transfers and health care and other social services, the former to be financed by contributions and the latter by general revenue. At the same time, the value of minimum pensions for widows and orphans was raised (Guillén, Álvarez, and Adão e Silva 2003). The reforms also improved the situation of workers with a long history of temporary contracts in the calculation of pension benefits (Guillén 2010).

As of 2011 Spain still had one of the highest net replacement rates from mandatory pensions for workers newly starting their careers among advanced postindustrial countries, with 85 percent, compared to 56 percent in Germany, 73 percent in Sweden, and 44 percent in the United States (OECD 2011). The weight of the pension system in the Spanish welfare state becomes clear if we look at the ratio of non-aged spending to spending on the aged. As of 1990, this ratio was 1.7 in Spain, the same level as in the United States, compared to 2.4 and 2.5 in Sweden and Germany, respectively. Spending on the non-aged increased as a result of the economic crisis, so in 2010 this ratio stood at 2.2, roughly the same level as in Germany and the United States. However, by 2015 the ratio had returned to the 1990 level of 1.7, clearly lower than in the other three countries.

While dualization of the labor market deepened, the government made major efforts to improve social policy for outsiders (that is, those without long-term employment). Pressure from the unions was important in driving these reforms. After the general strike of December 1988, the CCOO and the UGT agreed on a programmatic accord addressed to the government and all ACs in which they proposed the expansion of noncontributory programs in pensions, unemployment, and social assistance, including the introduction of a comprehensive minimum income. This scheme was to be introduced by the central government, with opportunities for the ACs to introduce regional improvements (Natili 2019). The government introduced noncontributory means-tested retirement and disability pensions in 1991; supplements to minimum pensions grew; and family allowances for poor families became universal in 1990. The minimum income was left to the regions. The regions began to introduce minimum income schemes and linked them to efforts at integrating recipients into the labor market (Guillén, Álvarez, and Adão e Silva 2003) and to region-building efforts. Unions continued actively to support the noncontributory pensions and these minimum income schemes and negotiated with regional governments to promote their introduction (Guillén 2010). In some regions, Catholic groups like Caritas were important supporters as well (Natili 2019). By 1995, all of the Autonomous Regions had introduced at least rudimentary minimum income schemes, but they remained residual and underfunded for the next decade (Natili 2019). The conservative government of Aznar had other priorities, and the economic boom that began in the second half of the 1990s expanded employment and relieved some of the pressure on unemployment compensation and social assistance.

The other side of the coin was cuts in unemployment benefits. Unemployment coverage had been expanded to reach 82 percent of the unemployed by 1992, but during the recession of the early 1990s, replacement rates and duration of benefits were reduced and qualifying periods were lengthened. These cuts were followed by an intensification of active labor market policies, with subsidies for employment of young people, those over forty-five, and the long-term unemployed. At the same time, unemployment assistance was expanded for groups with low, expired, or no contributory unemployment benefits. However, this assistance remained targeted at specific risk groups according to age, family status, and other factors, and means-tested (Aguilar-Hendrickson and Arriba González de Durana 2020). The minimum income schemes were tied to labor market integration, but the services in most regions were lacking or inadequate. Also, access to the schemes was subject to administrative discretion and budgetary constraints, coverage and benefits were very low, and behavioral requirements were strict. Benefit levels varied tremendously between regions, as did coverage. Only three regions—Catalonia, Madrid, and Navarra—made the minimum income scheme a rights-based program (Natili 2019). Thus, the Spanish social protection system remained highly fragmented, with problems of coordination between different programs and between the national and the regional governments.

After the PSOE's return to power in 2004, reform efforts intensified. Further reforms of the labor market and of pensions were reached through negotiations with unions and employers' associations. The position of women in the labor market and the social security system was improved in the pursuit of gender equality. In 2006 a national system of care was established for all people in need of it, mainly the elderly (Guillén 2010). In 2007, legislation improved the work/life balance by introducing paid paternity leave of thirteen days at 100 percent pay and by improving maternity leave for more vulnerable groups (Bürgisser 2022). Also, childcare coverage expanded greatly after the 1990s, so much so that almost all children ages three to five were in preschool and care for children under three had reached 38 percent of coverage by the second decade of the twenty-first century (Guillén and Pavolini 2015). Also in 2007 the government introduced a major "baby bonus" for the birth or adoption of a child, but this reform became an early victim of the post-crisis austerity and was suspended in 2011.

As discussed in the analysis of changes in the labor market, the PSOE government at first reacted to the onset of the economic crisis with an expansion of unemployment benefits in 2009, but by 2010 it had accepted austerity policies. The center-right government that followed it imposed even harsher austerity on pensions, unemployment compensation and assistance, and social services. The government significantly reduced national social transfers to regional and local authorities. In this context, demands on the regional minimum income schemes intensified greatly and these schemes expanded in coverage and partly in generosity of benefits, as an increasing share of regional budgets was devoted to minimum income schemes (Natili 2019, 110). However, coverage and generosity of benefits in these programs continued to show dramatic regional differences. For instance, in 2017, spending on the Minimum Insertion Income as a percentage of GDP in the Autonomous Community ranged from 0.02 percent in Castilla-La Mancha to 0.66 percent in the Basque Country; and beneficiaries as a percentage of people at risk of poverty ranged from 2.8 percent to 37.9 percent in these two communities (Rodríguez et al. 2020).

The Wang and van Vliet (2016b) dataset provides data for minimum income benefits in Madrid, one of the more generous locations. The minimum income replacement rate (that is, the minimum income net benefit), averaged for three household types as a percentage of the net average production wage, was one of the highest in 1990 among the twenty-four countries for which they have data, at 51 percent. This was well above the

35 percent and 37 percent in the United States and Germany, respectively, though some 10 percentage points below the Swedish level. This replacement rate fell to 40 percent in 1995 and 34 percent in 2000, where it stayed until 2009. The German rate remained stable, but the US rate fell to 22.5 percent by 2009 and the Swedish rate to 39 percent. So, Spain and Sweden saw the sharpest erosion of the value of minimum income benefits, and in Spain this happened in one of the most generous jurisdictions.

More important for means-tested social assistance in Spain than minimum income schemes, both in number of recipients and in expenditure, are minimum pension supplements and unemployment assistance. According to figures for 2017, provided by Aguilar-Hendrickson and Arriba González de Durana (2020, 561), 2.4 million people received minimum pension supplements, 1.1 million received unemployment assistance, and only 313,000 received a minimum income benefit. Expenditures for minimum pension supplements were close to 7 bn Euros, for unemployment assistance 6.4 bn, and for minimum incomes 1.5 bn. Means-tested child benefits went to 1.3 million people but were very low, so total expenditure reached only 358 million Euros. Social assistance for working-age people, then, is a real patchwork, with great variation across Autonomous Communities.

Austerity also hindered the expansion of childcare coverage and the implementation of the long-term care program. Public funding for childcare services was greatly reduced in 2013. The long-term care system was to be built as a services-based, universalistic, tax-financed public care system, with mixed financing by the central and regional governments and user fees. The system got a slow start, with months-long determinations of eligibility, and with austerity after 2011 there was no expansion of services. On the contrary, spending cuts between 2012 and 2015 even reduced services and payments to families. Family care allowances were supposed to be exceptional, used only in case of non-availability of professional services, but they became widely used. By the end of 2017, some 30 percent of people approved for services received the family care allowance. This allowance could be used to purchase services on the market, where there was widespread availability of mostly migrant gray-market caregivers (Aguilar-Hendrickson 2020).

The combination of increasing need and increasing spending effected an increase in poverty reduction among the working-age population, from an average of 27 percent in the 2000–2007 period to 37 percent in 2008–2016. Nevertheless, the increase in spending was not sufficient to fully counteract the increase in market income poverty, with the result that disposable income poverty among the working-age population increased from 12 to 16 percent between the two periods (Alper, Huber, and Stephens 2021). Essentially, the safety net of last resort, consisting of noncontributory pensions and unemployment benefits and of minimum income schemes, is too much of a patchwork, with benefits too low and regional variation too extreme to be effective in keeping families out of poverty. It mitigates the severity of poverty without lifting all who need it above the poverty line.

The coalition government between the PSOE and Podemos that was formed in January 2020 addressed the problem of the deficient and uneven social safety net by introducing a number of new programs. They instituted a new means-tested unemployment benefit for those who had exhausted all others, they restored contributory unemployment benefits to pre-2012 levels, and they extended unemployment benefits to household workers (Branco, Miró, and Natili 2023). Importantly, they launched a national minimum income scheme in June 2020. This initiative was part of the government program, and its implementation was accelerated because of the COVID pandemic. It set a national minimum standard that for a single person is equivalent to 34 percent of standardized median income and increases with household size. Regional programs are supplementary to the national one; that is, the national program provides for the benefit floor. The effect of this new program will clearly depend on the effectiveness of reaching eligible households (which now is very low in many regions) and on the reaction of regional governments in terms of treating the national program as a substitute for or supplement to their own programs. By itself, the new program will be insufficient to lift households out of poverty, but it will reduce the poverty gap (Hernández, Picos, and Riscado 2022).

Impact of the Tax System

The modern income tax was established in 1979, and joint taxation was mandatory for married couples. Before then, Spain had relied on high consumption and payroll taxes, but the overall tax burden had been extremely low. The average payroll tax share in the 1979–2007 period was comparatively very high—close to 40 percent, comparable to the German share (Kenworthy 2011, 85), though the trajectory of this share was downward as the overall level of taxation increased. As of 2007, Spain was very comparable to Germany both in overall tax revenues as a percentage of GDP and in the mix, with payroll and consumption taxes accounting for roughly twice the share of income taxes (Kenworthy 2011, 72). Blasco, Guillaud, and Zemmour (2023) estimate an increase in the Gini of slightly over .03 points, just ahead of Sweden at .03, and .01 points more than Germany and .02 points more than the United States. Yet, as noted in the discussion of Germany, taking into account indirect taxes does not change the ordering of the countries in disposable income inequality.

From 1984 to 1987 the top marginal tax rate was 66 percent; however, the ceiling of the average tax rate could not exceed 46 percent. In 1988, under the PSOE government, the top marginal tax rate was lowered to 56 percent, but the 46 percent limit was eliminated. In 1989 the Constitutional Court decided that the obligation for married couples to file jointly would be unconstitutional. In the 1998 tax reform, the PP government lowered the top marginal tax rate to 48 percent and eliminated the 0 percent rate for the lowest incomes (Alvaredo and Saez 2010). Still, the 48 percent top marginal tax rate arguably had the same dampening effect on the rise of the top 1 percent share that it had in Germany. During the boom years the top marginal tax rate was temporarily lowered to 43 percent, only to rise again slowly, beginning in 2011, to end up back at 43.5 percent in 2017.

Between 1978 and 1991 capital gains were taxed as regular income. From 1992 to 2005 a distinction was made between short-term (less than one year) and long-term capital gains; the former were added to the main income and taxed at regular rates, whereas the latter were taxed at greatly reduced rates. Under the PP government the tax rate for long-term capital gains was progressively lowered from 20 percent in 1999 to 15 percent in 2003. According to Alvaredo and Saez (2010, 484, 501), the 1994 wealth tax reform passed under the PSOE government initiated an erosion of this tax. It exempted from the wealth tax gains from stocks of businesses where the individual owned at least 15 percent (or the family 20 percent) and where the individual received over 50 percent of his labor and business income from this business. Wealthy business owners were able to reorganize their ownership and activities to take advantage of this exemption, and the share of business-exempt wealth grew tremendously over the next eight years (the period covered under their analysis).

The corporate tax rate was already very low in the early 1980s and remained at 35 percent until the crisis. By 2010 it had been reduced to 30 percent, and it was then reduced again, to about 25 percent. Spain's corporate

rate was the lowest among our four countries until 1990, when the Swedish tax rate dropped to 30 percent. Sweden has remained the country with the lowest corporate tax rate, but the distance between the countries narrowed greatly (figure B.1).

Impact of Social Services

As noted earlier, Marical et al. (2006) and Verbist, Förster, and Vaalavuo (2012) estimate the distributive effect of public spending on social services, and they show that all postindustrial countries reduce inequality significantly if the value of the services used by households is taken into account. Because public service spending does not vary greatly between quintiles within countries, the reduction in inequality is greater in absolute terms in more unequal countries (though not in relative terms).

A more detailed examination of the effect of public social services in Spain in 2007 shows that total public health expenditures reduced the Gini by 9.7 percent, whereas total public education expenditures reduced it 9.2 percent (Verbist, Förster, and Vaalavuo 2012, 59). Unfortunately, the authors do not provide estimates broken down by level of education, but Marical et al. (2006, 49) show that pre-primary and primary and secondary spending are fairly evenly distributed across the income quintiles, with the top quintile receiving somewhat less than a 20 percent share, whereas tertiary education spending is heavily skewed to the top quintile. In 2000, the top quintile received 47.8 percent of the tertiary education spending while the bottom quintile received only 7.4 percent. Comparable figures for Germany were 30.7 percent and 19.3 percent, respectively. So, the primary and secondary education system in Spain still fails to channel children from lower-income backgrounds into higher education, and the costs of public higher education are far from negligible, with the result that the public higher education system benefits primarily those from higher-income backgrounds.

Overall spending on social services did not change Spain's ranking in 2007 as the least unequal of the southern countries and as less unequal than the Anglo-American countries, except Ireland. However, this was the end of the boom period, and inequality rose as a result of the crisis and austerity, so that in the 2013–2019 period Spain ranks second only to the United States, and tied with Ireland, in the level of inequality once social services are taken into account.

CHAPTER TEN

Sweden

Even more so than the other Nordic countries (with the possible exception of Norway), Sweden has been considered the purest expression of the social democratic model and the exemplar of the achievements of European social democracy. The Social Democratic Party led the government from 1932 to 1976, with the exception of a hiatus of 100 days prior to the 1936 general elections, and again from 1982 to 1991. Union density was very high and the union confederations highly centralized and thus capable of coordinated action. The development of the welfare state and the levels of inequality and poverty prior to the great Nordic recession of the early 1990s reflect this Social Democratic political hegemony and trade union power. Wage dispersion and overall market income inequality were kept low by low unemployment and highly centralized bargaining. The level of welfare state effort in Sweden at this point was among the highest, on various indicators, of any of the rich democracies in our dataset. The levels of household disposable income inequality and poverty were among the lowest of any these rich democracies.

The situation began to change after 1991. Inequality rose in Sweden at both the top and the bottom end, although drivers of inequality were different at the two ends. At the bottom, propelled by the sharp rise in unemployment in the wake of the crisis of the early 1990s, both political blocs reduced the generosity of the unemployment insurance system. However, this had only a marginal effect on disposable income poverty until the bourgeois government took office in 2006. At that point, disposable income poverty at about 5 percent was no higher than it had been before the crisis. It was the very substantial cuts to the system carried out by the bourgeois government that moved poverty close to the average for all countries we consider here.[1]

At the top end, increasing stock market capitalization and the parallel increase in the impact of capital gains raised the share of the national income received by the top 1 percent of income earners as well as the share received by the next 9 percent. Deregulation and the transition to the knowledge economy, and the consequent skill-biased technological change, appear to have increased inequality in the upper half of the income distribution but had much less impact on the bottom. The continued high levels of union density and strong labor market institutions certainly dampened the increase in inequality, as did the escalating levels of public spending on human capital.

The quantitative results presented in this book are consistent with the highly egalitarian outcomes shown in Sweden prior to 1990 (see tables B.17–19): high union density; high union contract coverage; and high levels of wage coordination, centralized employers' associations, and bargaining should have resulted (and did result) in low levels of wage dispersion as measured by the 90-50 or 50-10 ratios (figures A.2–3, table B.1). Moreover, investment in human capital in the form of active labor market policies (ALMP) and expansion of general education contributed to the improvement of the overall human capital stock, most probably especially at the bottom. We don't really have good measures of skill distribution until the OECD (2000) International Adult Literacy Survey affirmed that the average level of skill in the Nordic countries, led by Sweden, was the highest among the fourteen countries participating in the study (see table B.20 for PIAAC [replication of IALS scores]), but it does seem probable that these differences across countries existed fifteen years earlier. The gap between the Nordics and the other countries was particularly great at the bottom of the skill distribution. In turn, the low levels of wage dispersion along with rising (women's) employment levels, low levels of single-parent households (at least until the 1970s), low unemployment, and high levels of industrial employment (fourth behind Switzerland, Germany, and the UK) contributed to low levels of household market income inequality. The expansion of the welfare state under Social Democratic auspices led to increasing redistribution and thus to more equality in the distribution of disposable income. As we saw in chapter 4, the Swedish configuration of labor market institutions is also a restraint on top income shares. In addition, the stock market was of limited consequence for distributive outcomes in Sweden in this period, as one can see from the small differences between the top 1 percent income share with and without capital gains (table B.2). In the late 1970s, stock market capitalization was less than 10 percent of GDP in Sweden (table B.15).

Tables A.2–7 and figures A.1–3 show that the decline in inequality in all measures in Sweden, and for the most part in all four Nordic countries, continues into the early 1980s. At this point the four Nordic countries are the most egalitarian countries on almost every measure, and Sweden is the most egalitarian on most measures. Previously (Huber and Stephens 2001), we argued that the period up to the mid-1980s was still the era of welfare state expansion; only the UK under Thatcher had made serious cuts to the welfare state by this point. Reagan talked a neoliberal line, but he faced a Democratic Congress and was unable to implement much of his antiwelfare state agenda (Pierson 1994). So, the "Golden Age" of the welfare state and equality did not end in the mid-1970s as the "Golden Age" of postwar growth did; rather, it extended another decade. There is no question that the decline in growth along with globalization (mainly capital market liberalization) caused a rethinking of the welfare state in this period among its biggest supporters, the Social Democrats in Sweden and elsewhere (e.g., the French Socialist U-turn of 1981–1983), but this manifested itself mainly in macroeconomic policy, not welfare state or wage policy.

Changes in the Economy and the Labor Market

The long-term changes in the structure of the economy included a decline of industrial employment from 30 percent of the working-age population in 1965 to 14 percent in 2015 (table B.6, figure A.12). In a parallel transformation with similar causes, manual work declined in relation to nonmanual work. This is reflected in the decline of LO, the blue-collar central union confederation, relative to the white-collar confederations. In 1965, 75 percent of union members were in LO and only 20 percent in TCO, the main white-collar confederation. By 2010 the LO proportion had declined to 47 percent, with TCO accounting for 34 percent and SACO, the confederation for employees with university degrees, accounting for 16 percent.

Table B.7 shows that employment as a percentage of the working-age population rose until the crisis of the early 1990s. As one can see from table B.9, this is largely due to the rise in female employment levels. Moreover, female employment increasingly became full-time employment (82 percent by 2017), so that the dominant family pattern became a dual-earner household. Over the period under examination, Sweden shifted from a Fordist industrial economy to a postindustrial knowledge economy with a highly competitive ICT sector. With this shift, the nature of work changed profoundly.

Product market deregulation in Sweden, as in all other postindustrial countries, was far-reaching. In part, deregulation was a product of technological change; for example, the advent of cell phones eroded national telecommunications monopolies. However, it was the European integration process that was responsible for the widespread deregulation in Europe. So it was under the control of governments—but not *national* governments. All of the postindustrial democracies massively deregulated energy, transportation, and communications after the 1970s. Sweden was no exception. On the OECD measure of product market regulation in seven non-manufacturing sectors (telecoms, electricity, gas, post, rail, air passenger transport, and road freight), which varies from 0 (no regulation) to 6 (most regulation), 14 of the 21 countries in our data analysis scored over 5 in the 1970s. The figure for Sweden in this period is 4.77. By the end of the data series in 2018, the average on the regulation index for the 21 countries declined to 1.50; for Sweden the 2013 figure is 1.42. It seems likely that product market deregulation did contribute to the increase in equality in Sweden. The fact that deregulation occurred regardless of partisan government would seem to indicate that it was inevitable, but Mudge (2018) and others have argued that it is a manifestation of the conversion of the Left to neoliberalism. We will return to this question in the conclusion.

Kristensen and Lilja (2011) document the transformation of work in the Nordic countries in *Nordic Capitalisms*. All four Nordic countries had made new adaptations to their economic models to take advantage of the shift to the knowledge economy, with the breakthrough to ICT in Finland and Sweden being the most dramatic, resulting in annual per capita growth rates of over 3 percent in those two countries in the 2000–2007 period—well above the average of 2.3 percent for all advanced economies. Moreover, as the authors point out (p. xii), this shift was quite unexpected from the point of view of the Varieties of Capitalism (VoC) perspective on comparative political economy. According to Hall and Soskice (2001), coordinated market economies (CMEs), like the Nordic economies, are supposed to be adept at "incremental innovation" (incremental improvement of current product lines) and not "radical innovation" (dramatic breakthroughs in new product development). One reason for this is that the financial systems of CMEs were characterized by strong bank-industry links, which provided firms with patient capital but locked capital into existing firms. The role for stock markets and venture capital in financing investment was limited in CMEs.

Kristensen and Lilja (2011, 19) argue that the shift into the high-technology knowledge economy was accompanied by a shift toward high-performance work organizations characterized by "(a) leveling of hierarchical distinctions; (b) an interpenetration of units designed to enhance the integration and maximize the coordination of previously autonomous functions; (c) a dramatic increase in the amount of behavior that is not rule-bound; (d) hiring and promoting people who are creative and have a feel for the job; (e) shifting assignments in and out of flexible work teams; and (f) more widespread access to information within and across organizations." Without citing actual figures, the authors indicate at several points that the prevalence of this type of work organization can be indexed by the European Working Conditions Survey measure of "discretionary learning employment." The fourth European Working Conditions Survey distinguishes discretionary learning employment from traditional, taylorist, and lean production employment (Lundvall and Lorenz 2011). Discretionary learning jobs are jobs that involve high levels of problem-solving and learning on the job and high levels of freedom for the workers to organize their work activity. Lundvall and Lorenz (2011) show that the Nordic countries and the Netherlands have a high percentage of employees in discretionary learning employment. The Swedish figure is 53 percent.

This transformation of work was caused and accompanied by skill-biased technological change, and indeed furthered that change, as it manifested itself in the Swedish case. As in the rest of northern Europe and North America in the post-1990 period, the ICT revolution resulted in declining demand for routine manual (e.g., Fordist assembly line) and non-manual (clerical) work and rising demand for non-routine work, both manual and non-manual (Autor, Levy, and Murname 2003). This was accompanied by an individualization of wage setting especially among white-collar workers organized in TCO and SACO. That this skill-biased technological change did not lead to greater increases in wage dispersion is certainly due to increased public investments in skill development, above all the huge expansion in tertiary education in the 1990s (see below). This is consistent with the results of Berglund, Håkansson, and Isidorsson's (2022) analysis of occupational change in Sweden from 2000 to 2015, which shows that the predominant pattern was upgrading. The result has been that the skill wage premium estimated with PIAAC data on skills is the lowest among any of the countries analyzed by Hanushek et al. (2015, 110; also see Autor 2014, 845). Similarly, Weisstanner and

Armingeon (2020) show that the tertiary education premium in Sweden is the lowest of the twenty-three countries in their study, followed closely by Denmark and Norway (see tables B.20–21). Circa 2007, the tertiary education wage premium in Sweden was .17, which was less than half the average of the countries in their study.

The final long-term change in the Swedish economy has been the development of the stock market. As noted, stock market capitalization was only 5–10 percent of GDP in the 1970s, rising to 60 percent in the mid-1990s, seeing a bubble of 147 percent in 2000, and then falling back to 80–125 percent afterward (table B.15). It is very clear that the expansion of the stock market from the 1970s to the present increased the importance of capital gains in the income of the top 1 percent. As one can see from table B.2, when the top 1 percent share reached a low point around 1980, there were small differences (0.2 percent) between the figures with and without capital gains (table B.2). The capital gains share rose to 2–3 percent by 1997, fluctuating year to year. The correlation (for Sweden only) of stock market capitalization and top 1 percent share with capital gains is .84. In fact, the capital gains share in the top 1 percent share is percentagewise (though not in absolute terms) the largest for any country in this analysis, including the United States. Expansion of the stock market is not the only factor that caused the rise in top incomes, though, because the figures for top 1 percent income shares without capital gains increased from 4 percent in 1982 to 7 percent in 2012.

The increases in stock market capitalization and the growing importance of capital gains for top income shares suggest that one might find a similar pattern for other measures of inequality once capital gains are included. Two recent studies have indicated that the inclusion of capital gains does increase the Gini for disposable income to 32 (as compared to 28 for recent years in our data—table A.4). Moreover, as we showed for top income shares above, inclusion of capital gains made very little difference in inequality in the early 1980s (Jämlikhetskommissionen 2020; Hammar, Roth, and Waldenström 2021), so a significant portion of the increase in the Gini over the past forty years is due to the increasing impact of capital gains.

The studies just mentioned have the drawback that they include the whole population, not just the working-age population, and thus their Ginis are not comparable to ours in chapter 4 or table A.4. LIS collects information on capital gains, but only for a small subset of the country years in our analysis for which it has information on disposable income

(61 of 287—see table B.4). Unfortunately, as one can see from the table, it is not a representative sample, with only two observations from the continental European countries and none from southern Europe. Though it is based on only three country-year observations, the difference between the disposable income Gini with and without capital gains in Sweden is the largest of eight countries in table B.4. The average for the Gini with capital gains in the table is close to the figure reported in Jämlikhetskommissionen (2020) and Hammar, Roth, and Waldenström (2021). As one can see from the table, with the inclusion of capital gains, Sweden is now the most unequal of the Nordic countries. With data only for France in the table, it is not possible to draw firm conclusions about Sweden's rank relative to the continental European countries, but it seems likely that it is now slightly more unequal than two or three of them (see the last column in table A.4).

To outline the development of the economic policy underpinning the Swedish production regime in the Golden Age, we have to return briefly to the 1930s for the institutional foundation of later policy. After the reelection of the Social Democrats to a second term in 1936, the Swedish Employers Federation (SAF) abandoned its attempt to defeat the labor movement and entered into negotiations with LO, the manual worker trade union confederation, resulting in the Saltsjöbaden agreement of 1938. Korpi (1983, 47–48) characterizes the long-term effects of this "historic compromise" as an agreement by both parties to cooperate in creating economic growth: the labor movement would gain greater influence over the results of production; and employers would retain the right to control the production process and the direction of investment. The cooperative arrangement paved the way for labor peace and later for the centralization of collective bargaining at the national level.

Changes in Labor Market Institutions and Policies

The contours of this policy emerged in the famous Rehn-Meidner model named for the two LO economists who developed it (Meidner and Öhman 1972; Pontusson 1992, 57–96). The model called for LO to demand equal pay for equal work across the economy—the so-called solidaristic wage policy. This wage policy would force labor-intensive, low-productivity enterprises to rationalize or go out of business. The displaced labor would then be moved to high-productivity sectors through the active labor market policy. Wages in high-productivity, often export-oriented sectors would be restrained to facilitate international competitiveness. By reducing structural unemployment, the active labor market policy would further facilitate wage restraint and thus reduce the trade-off between unemployment and inflation, moving the Phillips curve down and to the left.

In 1956, LO and SAF struck a wage agreement that covered virtually all of the manual workers in the private sector. These centralized wage agreements continued until 1983. Scholars of Swedish industrial relations often attribute further wage compression beyond the equal-pay-for-equal-work policy prescribed by the Rehn-Meidner model to the development of centralized bargaining. By extension, the very modest (especially at the low end) rise in wage dispersion after 1983 might be attributed to the end of highly centralized bargaining (see table B.1).

Vartianen (2011, 333–34) offers a five-point corrective to this point of view: (1) Even in the period of centralized bargains, there was no direct control of wage levels. Market forces (wage drift) also affected the level and distribution of wages. (2) With the exception of setting minimum wages, most central pay settlements took the existing distribution of wages and salaries as a starting point. (3) The basic mechanism in all Nordic wage agreements across countries and over time is that unions get minimum wage adjustments in return for a peace agreement, and local-level bargaining occurs without the threat of conflict. (4) The Rehn-Meidner model called for solidaristic wages as a means to a macroeconomic goal—industrial transformation—and as a means to compress wages. (5) Since local bargaining is carried on without the threat of industrial conflict, it is fundamentally different from market-based wage bargaining as carried out in decentralized Anglo-American industrial relations systems.

Vartianen (2011) stresses the similarities between the Nordic industrial relations systems and continuity through time within the four countries. The structural characteristics of the system—very strong trade unions and high (and increasing) dependence on exports—meant that the system must produce moderate wage increases that maintained the competitiveness of the export sector with the consent of the strong unions. While employment in manufacturing declined, manufacturing exports as a percentage of GDP increased in all four countries, in Sweden rising from 18 percent of GDP in the Golden Age to 34 percent. Thus, the economy was more dependent on manufacturing exports than ever.

We are convinced by Vartianen's (2011) arguments questioning how much the decentralization of bargaining contributed to (modestly) rising wage dispersion. Nevertheless, it is important to try to account for the changes in the wage-bargaining system because it is clear in retrospect that the bargaining system was malfunctioning from the end of centralized bargaining in 1983 to the industrial agreement (*industriavtalet*) of 1997. One can see the instability of wage coordination in this period in table B.19.

The instability in wage bargaining was in large part a product of macroeconomic instability, and indeed outright mismanagement by both Social Democratic and bourgeois governments. Two large devaluations in the beginning of the 1980s boosted profits in the export sector and—combined with a tight labor market—encouraged employers to offer wages above the negotiated levels. The government's continued expansion of public-sector employment in this context aggravated the situation. Above all, the deregulation of credit markets was poorly timed. This was done in 1985 when there were still generous tax deductions for consumer interest payments, and it fueled an unprecedented credit boom and consumer spending orgy at a time when the economy was already beginning to overheat. Part of this credit boom was accounted for by cross-border flows of loans, clearly an effect of deregulation of international capital flows. As the Rehn-Meidner model would predict, this boom of export profits and of credit, combined with the decline of centralized bargaining, made wage restraint impossible. With wage increases far above productivity increases, Swedish export industries did become uncompetitive. Yet the government and its bourgeois successor refused to float the crown until the fall of 1992, when the economy was already in deep recession and much damage in terms of failed businesses, lost markets, and lost jobs had been done.

In the early 1990s, both Social Democratic and bourgeois governments continued to follow policies that inadvertently had strong pro-cyclical effects on consumer behavior, this time in the context of a deep recession. The combination of a reduction of the tax rate on capital income, falling inflation, and stable nominal interest rates resulted in a substantial increase in real after-tax interest rates. The bust after the real estate boom added to the situation by reducing the wealth position of many households, probably below the desired level. All this contributed to a household savings rate of 10 percent in 1993, by far the highest level in over two decades, and a correspondingly depressed level of personal consumption in the midst of a depression (OECD 1994b, 16–17). On the side of the banks, this same set of circumstances—the asset boom and bust caused by speculation in the wake of financial deregulation—left many banks holding sufficient bad debts that they became insolvent. The government bailout operation cost the public coffers 74 billion crowns (5 percent of GDP) in 1991 and 1992 alone, thus adding to the already spiraling budget deficit (OECD 1994b, 129).

When the Social Democrats returned to office in 1994, they began to right the policy errors of the previous ten years. In 1994, the economy showed positive growth: it experienced average per annum growth rates of 3.7 percent from 1994 to 2000.[2] By 1996, inflation had been brought down to below 1 percent. Renewed growth and a combination of tax increases and budget cuts enabled the government to cut the deficit from 7.3 percent of GDP in 1995 to a surplus in the 1998–2001 period. The austere budgets and the falling deficit brought down both interest rates and the crown-German mark interest rate differential substantially in the same period, stimulating investment and further growth. Renewed growth and active labor market policies resulted in a fall of open unemployment to 7.2 percent for the year 1997, and to 5.6 percent by January 2000. That, however, was the sticking point (see table B.8). Another area of concern at the time was wage inflation, as the 1995 bargaining round (in which negotiations were carried out at an industry-wide level) failed to produce wage moderation. With macroeconomic stability restored, reform of wage bargaining was on the agenda.

The industrial agreement of 1997 ushered in a new era of stability in Swedish industrial relations; after fluctuating following the end of centralized bargaining in 1983, the values for Sweden on our wage coordination measure are completely stable from 1998 on. The system was one in which unions, both white- and blue-collar, and employers in the entire exposed sector coordinated bargaining, and their agreement provided a pattern for the rest of the labor market. In 2000, this system was complemented by legislation establishing a National Mediation Office. As Vartianen (2011) points out, this system of coordinated industry-level bargaining with wage leadership exercised by the export sector reliably produced moderate wage increases and is functionally equivalent to centralized bargaining. As he underlines, both systems do not centrally fix wages and allow for local-level variation, especially among white-collar employees (organized in TCO) and employees with academic degrees (organized in SACO). LO, though much less influential than in the era of centralized bargaining, has continued to promote the interests of low-wage workers, mainly women working for municipal governments, with some success. That success is no doubt partly due to private-sector employers and their confederations not being involved in these wage negotiations.

In otherwise differing accounts, Baccaro and Howell (2017), Thelen (2014), and Vartianen (2011) all agree that wage formation has become more localized and more individualized in Sweden in the wake of the *industriavtalet* of 1997, mainly in the white-collar private sector and in the public sector. Baccaro and Howell (2017) see this as a result of a fundamental shift in power relations from employees and their unions to employers and employer organizations. As noted, Vartianen emphasizes continuity with the past. Our view is that Baccaro and Howell do not take into account the huge changes in the nature of work in the post-Fordist, postindustrial Nordic knowledge economies as outlined by Kristensen and Lilja (2011). These changes would appear to necessitate (or at least facilitate) the changes in wage bargaining.

The very small changes (+ 4–5 percent) in wage dispersion at the bottom (the 50-10 ratio) support the view that Swedish wage-bargaining arrangements are characterized by continuity. The larger increases (+ 8–10 percent) in wage dispersion at the top (90-50 ratio) make sense in light of the much greater localization and individualization of wages in the white-collar ranks. Moreover, the modest effect of wage dispersion on market income of the working-age population and market income poverty of the working-age population (tables 4.2 and 6.2) indicates that changes in bargaining are unlikely candidates to explain the much larger increases in market income inequality measures in Sweden. Union density did decline in Sweden (see figure A.8), and this decline arguably contributed to rising market income inequality, but the other indicators of union influence (coverage, wage coordination, works council rights) held up, which helps to explain why Sweden remained among the least unequal countries. Much more likely candidates for the increases in market household income inequality are the increases in unemployment, deindustrialization, the increasing proportion of children in single-mother families, product market deregulation, and increasing temporary employment (see table 4.2 in chapter 4).

Alm, Nelson, and Nieuwenhuis (2020) present compelling evidence that the post-1990 rise in unemployment and cutbacks in the welfare state (see below) disproportionately interacted with household composition to push many single-parent households and single-without-children households into poverty. They summarize their findings: "In a dual-earner society like Sweden, we show that the return of mass unemployment in combination with the retreat of a generous and inclusive welfare state have substantially increased the poverty risks of single-adult households" (p. 198).

While industrial employment and household structure are largely beyond the reach of public policy, governments do have policy levers to effect unemployment and temporary employment. Both have witnessed a significant increase in Sweden since the crisis of the early to mid-1990s. We have already discussed the development of unemployment in the period after the crisis. We should add here that even Social Democratic governments have been unwilling to return to the levels of public-sector employment characteristic of the pre-crisis period, arguably out of concerns about budget deficits. Changes in the OECD index for temporary employment protection legislation are shown in table B.13. The OECD label is something of a misnomer, because most components of the index (other than the requirement that temporary employees be paid the same as permanent employees) do not protect temporary workers. Rather, they protect permanent employees by limiting employers' rights to hire temporary workers. It is clear from the table that the crisis stimulated the bourgeois government of 1991–1994 to cut temporary employment protection, and that this was continued by the Social Democratic governments of 1994–2006 and further intensified by the bourgeois government elected in 2006. By the end of the deregulation process, Sweden had the lowest value on the OECD index of any of the Nordic countries. Indeed, it was closer to the Anglo-American LMEs. As a result, temporary employment increased substantially in Sweden and was higher there than in three-quarters of postindustrial knowledge economies. Berglund, Håkansson, and Isidorsson (2022, 937–38) show not only that temporary employment is concentrated in the bottom occupational quintile, but also that the temporary work of workers in that group is heavily "on-call work," which has the lowest pay, hours, and opportunities to advance of any type of temporary work.

In his comparative study of unemployment in Austria, Sweden, Denmark, and the Netherlands, Lindvall (2010, esp. 109–36) argues that a major reason for the persistence of high unemployment in Sweden beginning with the 1990s crisis is that the Social Democrats reordered their economic priorities, de-emphasizing the fight against unemployment and prioritizing low inflation and budget balances. In interviews with Lindvall, Ingvar Carlsson and Allan Larsson—the Social Democratic prime minister and finance minister, respectively—at the time contested the view that the party had prioritized fighting inflation over fighting unemployment (p. 112). Both Carlsson and Larsson argued that it was necessary to keep inflation low in order to combat unemployment. In truth, this was not new to the Swedish macroeconomic model, nor was budget balance. The Rehn-Meidner macroeconomic prescriptions included low inflation and tight fiscal policy, both of which were intended to facilitate wage restraint and thus export competitiveness (Huber and Stephens 1998, 367–68). What was new was that Sweden, like all other European countries, but especially the small open economies, had far fewer tools to combat unemployment than they did during the Golden Age due to globalization and European integration. In particular, open capital markets made it impossible for individual countries to set their own monetary policies. In a fashion parallel to the way in which wage increases became constrained by the EU norm, interest rates became constrained by the rate set by the ECB. All of the small northern European economies faced similar constraints, of course, and the unemployment performance in Sweden with 6.5 percent in 2000–2007 was worse than in Denmark (4.6 percent) or the Netherlands (4.5 percent)—though we hasten to add that employment performance in Sweden (79.8 percent of those aged sixteen to sixty-four employed) was better than the Netherlands (76.0 percent) or Denmark (74.5 percent).

Immigration contributed to the unemployment problem, and thus directly to rising inequality and poverty. In addition, it had an indirect effect by eroding support for parties that had historically promoted welfare state policies. As in many other countries, immigrants in Sweden are disproportionately represented among the low-skilled and unemployed. In 2011, the unemployment rate among immigrants in Sweden was 2.63 times the rate among native-born Swedes (Gordon 2019, 962). Whether immigration has weakened support for the welfare state and redistribution is disputed (Breznau et al. 2022). What is not disputed is that immigration has led to a rise in support for the anti-immigrant and nationalist Sweden Democrats, who entered the parliament for the first time in 2010 with 5.7 percent of the vote, and increased their vote share to 12.9 percent and 17.5 percent in the 2014 and 2018 elections, respectively. Some of these votes have probably come at the expense of the Social Democrats. What is clear is that, since 2010, it has become impossible for the left bloc (or the center-right bloc, for that matter) to form a government with majority support in parliament.

Human Capital

Our quantitative analyses showed that human capital investment affects wage dispersion and household market income distribution. Active labor market policy, the main program for retraining adult workers, fits squarely into the LO's wage policy of solidarity. The transformation of the system of public education was a joint project of the Social Democrats and the Agrarian Party, which continued after they ended their governmental coalition in 1957. Given the voting base of these two parties, expansion and de-tracking of the educational system to open up educational opportunities for the sons and daughters of workers and family farmers was common ground. This was accomplished with regard to secondary schools by the end of the 1960s, and with regard to tertiary education by a decade later. Another large expansion of university education took place in the second half of the 1990s, in the wake of the economic crisis.

A second set of social investment policies came as a result of the Social Democrats' efforts to promote gender equality. The two central policies aimed at reconciliation of work and family were early childhood education and maternal (and later parental) leave. The Nordic countries were world leaders in both policy areas, and Sweden was the first mover among the Nordic countries. By the beginning of the 1990s, Swedish parents were entitled to sixty-four weeks of leave with a 90 percent replacement rate. By the same time, Sweden was spending almost 2 percent of GDP on early childhood education.

It might be tempting to credit the Social Democrats with incredible foresight in anticipating the development of the knowledge economy. This would be giving them too much credit: as of 1990, the digital cell phone was in its infancy, the World Wide Web had just been made widely accessible, and the use of laptops was very limited. In truth, each of these three legs of Swedish human capital policy had additional goals besides improving human capital: in the case of educational expansion and de-tracking, it was improving the educational opportunity of the offspring of workers and farmers; in the case of ALMP, it was enabling the solidaristic wage policy; and in the case of early childhood education, it was gender equality. In the course of the 1990s, the government did recognize that the knowledge economy was emerging. The huge expansion of university education in the mid- to late 1990s mentioned previously was motivated by that recognition, as was the extensive but short-lived adult education initiative (*kunskapslyft*) (Thelen 2014, 189). As Jenson (2012, 70) points out, emblematic of the change in thinking was the government's movement of early childhood education from the social ministry to the Ministry of Education in the mid-1990s.

Changes in Social Policy

For our measures of disposable income inequality, it is clear that the welfare state and tax and transfer redistribution, and reduction in inequality, are of paramount importance. We have found that long-term left government results in large and very redistributive welfare states (chapter 6; Huber and Stephens 2001 and 2014; Bradley et al. 2003). The Social Democrats were the leading party in government in Sweden for most of the period of welfare state expansion, from 1932 to 1976 and from 1982 to 1991. The Gini index for 1981 for disposable income among the working-age population in Sweden, 20.2, is the lowest in our dataset. Three factors shape redistribution: the size of the welfare state, the distributive profile of taxes and transfers, and need (e.g., unemployment, proportion of children in single households). Sweden before the economic crisis, when social risks skyrocketed, was the second (to Finland) most redistributive welfare state in our dataset.

We have covered the period of welfare expansion in Sweden elsewhere (Huber and Stephens 2001, 117–31). Tables B.24–25 and figures A.4–6 show that welfare state generosity rose right up to the beginning of the 1990s economic crisis. The figures in the tables are Scruggs's indices of the generosity of unemployment benefits and sickness pay (Scruggs and Allan 2006). They are meant to update and correct Esping-Andersen's decommodification indices for unemployment benefits and sickness pay.

The table shows that the generosity of sickness pay, and more so unemployment insurance, declined (though not continuously) from 1990 until the end of the data series in 2019. In large part, the year-to-year declines in unemployment benefits were not the result of legislated cuts. Rather, there was a ceiling on the replacement rates that was not indexed to wages or inflation, so failure to adjust the ceiling resulted in falling replacement rates for all but the lowest paid (Ferrarini et al. 2012, 36). This is illustrated in figure A.5. Up to 1990, parliament (Riksdagen) regularly adjusted the ceiling using the development of wages of industrial workers as a guideline. Since the beginning of the crisis of the 1990s, the ceiling has been raised only three times, each time by Social Democratic governments: 1997, 2002, and 2015. In 2001, the Social Democratic government also raised the ceiling for the first 100 days of unemployment. As a result of the failure of most governments to adjust it, the ceiling has fallen from over 80 percent of an average industrial worker's wage in 1990 to less than 75 percent in 2005.

By contrast, the ceiling and the replacement rate for sickness pay are indexed to inflation, but they have still fallen because, over the long run, wage growth has exceeded inflation. Ferrarini et al. (2012, 35) show that the ceiling has fallen from over 140 percent of an average industrial worker's wage in 1985 to somewhat less than 80 percent in 2010. Scruggs's data show that the average replacement rate for a production worker was fairly stable at about 80 percent from the early 1990s on.

The lack of adjustments to the ceiling is a form of retrenchment by "drift" (Hacker 2005). There were actual cuts in benefits by the government, and not just drift, beginning with the Social Democratic government in 1990 and intensifying with the bourgeois government of 1991–1994. By the time that government left office the replacement rates in unemployment insurance, sick pay, work injury insurance, and parental leave had all been reduced from 90 to 80 percent. The Social Democrats supported most of this legislation and did not reverse it once in office. In fact, they reduced the replacement rate in unemployment insurance in 1996 to 75 percent, only to reverse themselves and raise it back to 80 percent the next year in response to protest within the party and from LO.

The bourgeois coalition, the Alliance, led by the Conservatives won the 2006 and 2010 elections, resulting in the longest period of bourgeois government since the 1920s. The government promptly restored the ceiling for the first 100 days of unemployment insurance and cut the replacement rate to 70 percent after 200 days (100 days for youth aged sixteen to twenty-four), and eliminated the possibility of limiting one's job search geographically and professionally for the first 100 days. These cuts resulted in a replacement rate of 60 percent (in 2014, the last year the bourgeois government was in office), just above the OECD average of 56 percent, and, along with cuts in qualifying conditions, a score on Scruggs's unemployment generosity index of 7.8 in 2014, substantially below the OECD average of 9.8 for that year. The cuts in sickness pay insurance were less extensive, so the replacement rate of 80 percent for the average production worker remained significantly above the OECD average replacement rate of 65 percent, and the Swedish figure of 16.2 on the sickness pay generosity index was also substantially above the average of 9.8 for 2014.

The changes the bourgeois government made in the financing of the unemployment system had huge effects on both union membership and coverage of unemployment insurance. Sweden has the Ghent system, in which unions provide unemployment insurance. Countries with Ghent systems—Sweden, Finland, Denmark, and Belgium—have high levels of union density, and it is reasoned that unemployment insurance is a selective incentive to join unions (Rothstein 1992). In an analysis of pooled time-series data, Rasmussen and Pontusson (2018) have recently shown that it is not the introduction of Ghent that stimulates union organization; rather, it is the later increases in state subsidies and benefit generosity that result in rising density.

The bourgeois government substantially reduced state subsidies to the union-run unemployment funds, raised individual contributions, and abolished the tax deductibility of union dues and fund fees. Kjellberg (2011) argues that these changes resulted in a 6 percent decline in union membership (from 77 percent in 2006 to 71 percent in 2008) and a 10 percent decline in membership in union-run unemployment insurance funds. The government also introduced regulations that made the employees' fees vary by the risk of unemployment in their occupation. Thus, the fund fees were highest for LO unions, then TCO unions, and lowest for SACO unions.[3] As a result, the declines in union density and fund membership were highest for the LO unions, then the TCO unions, and there was an increase in membership and fund membership for SACO unions. Berglund and Esser (2014, 108) show that the percentage of the unemployed not receiving unemployment insurance benefits varied between 20 and 30 percent from 1990 to 2006 and then moved up steeply under the bourgeois government, reaching over 70 percent by 2012. Arguably this increase was in large part due to the changes in the unemployment insurance system introduced by the bourgeois government.

The generosity of social assistance in Sweden also declined in the post-1990 period. Wang and van Vliet's (2016a) measure of net minimum income benefit replacement rates declined from 61 percent in 1990 to 39 percent at the end of their series in 2009. The timing of the cuts does not suggest a partisan divide on the issue.

Tables A.3, A.4, A.6, and A.7 show that the effect of the bourgeois governments' legislation on disposable income inequality and poverty, and on redistribution and poverty reduction, was quite dramatic. Poverty reduction declined, and at the end of our series, disposable income poverty in Sweden, at 10.3 percent, was close to the OECD average of 10.5 percent, so no longer exceptional![4] Redistribution also declined, and the Swedish Gini index of disposable income, though still lower than the OECD average, has moved toward the average, and is probably close to the average if capital gains are included for all countries (see our discussion above).

In light of the cuts to unemployment insurance shown in table B.24 and figure A.4, it is rather surprising that they are not reflected in the rise of household disposable income poverty prior to the advent of the bourgeois government in 2006. In fact, disposable income poverty in Sweden was *lower* in 2005 than it had been prior to the economic crisis of the 1990s (even more so if one adjusts for the large number of student households in Sweden—see below). This might be explained by the fact that the union confederations—first SACO and TCO, and then LO—negotiated top-ups to the legislated systems that effectively negated the ceiling in the system and brought their members back up to an 80 percent replacement rate. However, most of these agreements were made after the 2006 election (Lindellee 2018, chapter 5). It is important to note that the change in the unemployment insurance systems introduced by the bourgeois government went far beyond the replacement rate, radically reducing the coverage of the system by reducing union employment fund membership, as we just noted. This arguably was responsible for the spike in poverty after 2005, which one sees in table A.7, and the decline in poverty reduction after 2005 seen in table A.6.

Tables A.5 and A.7 show surprisingly high levels of poverty in Sweden in the 1980s, particularly when one takes into consideration that unemployment was very low then, between 2 and 3 percent of the labor force. As is known to many students of Swedish income distribution, an unusually large proportion of Swedish university students form their own households due to the fact that university students in Sweden not only pay no tuition, but also receive a modest stipend of about US$250 per month. This allows many of them to form their own households. To correct for this, we calculated poverty rates with the LIS data for households aged 25–64, which should exclude most student households. The overall poverty rate for this group in all countries is 8.6 percent, compared to 9.2 percent for households aged 18–64, whereas the poverty rates are 4.6 percent and 8.6 percent respectively for Sweden. The figure for Sweden for the first period in table A.7 (8.6 percent) is 4.0 percent for the 25–64 group.

As we pointed out in earlier chapters, public pensions do not affect our figures on household income inequality, poverty, and redistribution in chapters 3 and 5, because we have excluded the elderly from our calculations with the microdata. However, as noted, mature PAYGO pension systems do put pressure on the public purse due to demographic and economic change. The problems facing the Swedish system were largely solved by a pension reform in the 1990s in which the Social Democrats and the four bourgeois parties agreed to replace the old PAYGO system with a combination of a main tier of notional defined-contribution PAYGO accounts and a smaller fully funded (but compulsory) individual accounts tier.

Impact of the Tax System

Up to the 1980s, income taxes in Sweden were steeply progressive. The Social Democrats had already moved away from supporting that structure of income taxation in the 1970s and supported a proposed tax reform of the Center-Liberal government of 1981-82 that lowered the marginal tax rates in the middle and high brackets. This prefigured the 1989-90 "tax reform of the century" in which the Social Democratic government, in cooperation with the Liberals, reduced the rates of marginal taxation for those in higher income brackets, cutting them to 50 percent. Along with lower tax rates, the reform eliminated many deductions and taxed many company benefits (e.g., the use of a company-owned car) as income. Child allowances were increased at the same time. Government simulations showed that the reform package as a whole was distributionally neutral, a claim that was supported by an independent simulation study (Schwartz and Gustafsson 1991). The public perception at the time, particular 1y on the left, was otherwise. The fact that our disposable household income Gini shows little change at this point in time supports the view that these reforms did not have large distributive consequences. As a response to the revenue shortfall during the economic crisis of the 1990s, the top marginal rate was raised to 55 percent, where it remained.

The "tax reform of the century" also lowered corporate income tax rates, which had reached a high of 60.1 percent in 1989.[5] The corporate tax rate was lowered to 40 percent in 1990, 30 percent in 1991, and 28 percent in 1994. Further cuts in the corporate tax occurred in 2009 (26.3 percent) and 2013 (22 percent) (Henrekson and Stenkula 2015, 22). It was subsequently lowered slightly several times, the last being in 2021 (20.6 percent). Sweden had an inheritance tax until 2005 and a wealth tax until 2007. Neither was a significant source of revenue.

The differential between the corporate and the individual income tax rate established by the 1991 tax reform created incentives for tax filers to redefine labor income as capital income. The increasingly favorable rules for the taxation of closely held corporations (the 3:12 rules), especially after the 2006 reform of these rules, resulted in many more high-income individuals setting up corporations in order to convert their labor income into lower-taxed capital income (Alstadsæter and Jacob 2012).

As noted earlier, indirect taxes do increase inequality in all countries studied by the OECD, but have little effect on the ranking of countries in terms of the degree of inequality (Warren 2008). Sweden's reliance on indirect taxes was average for European countries in Warren's study (p. 53), and the increase in the Gini of disposable income once indirect taxes were included was moderate, from 23.7 to 26.7. Blasco, Guillaud, and Zemmour (2023) showed Sweden in 2005 as the least unequal in disposable income among eighteen countries, after including indirect taxes, though figures for the other countries are for 2010 or 2013.

Impact of Social Services

We calculated how the inclusion of spending on the public provision of social services would affect distributive outcomes in various countries including Sweden. The results showed that Sweden had the most equal disposable income distribution in 2007 and that the inclusion of public services slightly increased the distance between Sweden and Norway, the next most equal country. However, this table ignores capital gains. Table B.4 indicates that, if capital gains were also included, distributive outcomes in Sweden would be the most unequal of the Nordic countries, and possibly more unequal than France.

A more detailed examination of the effect of public social services in Sweden in 2007 shows that total public health expenditures reduced the Gini by 11.9 percent, whereas total public education expenditures reduced it 10.9 percent (Verbist, Förster, and Vaalavuo 2012, 59). As noted earlier, the authors do not provide estimates broken down by level of education, but Marical et al. (2006, 49) show that pre-primary and primary and secondary spending are somewhat more progressively distributed across the income quintiles than in Germany and Spain, with the top quintile receiving around 12 percent of total spending and the bottom quintile receiving around 23 percent. The distributive impact of tertiary education spending contrasts sharply with Germany, and even more so with Spain. In 2000, the top quintile received 16 percent of the tertiary education spending while the bottom quintile received 43.1 percent. This dramatic difference is certainly partly explained by the fact that, as noted previously, university students in Sweden not only pay no tuition, but also receive a modest stipend of about US$250 per month, which allows many of them to form their own households.

CHAPTER ELEVEN

United States

The long-term patterns of inequality in the United States are similar to those in Europe: a U-shaped curve with high levels of inequality before World War I, followed by decline until the 1960s or 1970s and then rising inequality up to the present (Piketty 2014; Atkinson and Piketty 2007). However, in the pre-1993 period the United States already had the highest level of disposable income inequality of the countries examined in this book (table A.4).

Not only did the United States begin the postindustrial period as the most unequal of any of the countries in this study; inequality in the US also increased the most, particularly at the top end.[1] At the bottom end, as indicated by the figures on market income and disposable income poverty, the US has been less of an outlier. Canada and three of the four southern European countries have had levels of poverty similar to the US. In terms of redistribution and poverty reduction (tables A.3 and A.6), Switzerland claims the dubious distinction of effecting the lowest levels of reduction, followed by the US, Canada, and some of the southern European countries.

Given the statistical results in chapters 2–7, the fact that economic inequality, already high in the United States in 1980, increased more than in any of the other postindustrial democracies in our study is not at all surprising. The US was a "perfect storm" on every causal and intervening variable identified in those chapters, either starting unequal and staying there or moving toward greater inequality: (1) labor market institutions (union density, contract coverage, wage coordination, employment protection laws, and works council rights); (2) partisan government (no social democracy, dominance by center and right political parties); (3) deregulation of financial markets and financialization (growth of the financial sector and the stock market); (4) deregulation of energy, transportation, and communications sectors; (5) low voter turnout; (6) minimal welfare state; (7) high and increasing immigration; and finally (8) declining public investment in human capital (decline in public education spending and low levels of early childhood education and active labor market policy) and high levels of private education spending.

The American Golden Age labor market institutions—moderate union density, union contract coverage tracking density, low levels of wage coordination, and decentralized unions, employers' associations, and bargaining—resulted in moderately high levels of wage dispersion as measured by the 90-50 or 50-10 ratios. However, Goldin and Katz (2008) argue that universal secondary education and expanding tertiary education should have restrained inequality, as it restrains the education wage premium by increasing the supply of highly educated workers. On the other hand, our statistical results argue that a high share of private tertiary education—a characteristic of the United States—should have worked in the opposite direction. Likewise, the stratification of school quality at the primary and secondary level (due to reliance on local property taxes and socioeconomic segregation) and the very low levels of early childhood education certainly contributed to poor skills at the bottom of the distribution.

In turn, the moderately high wage dispersion along with high levels of single-parent households (compared to Europe), high unemployment, and low levels of industrial employment (compared to northern Europe) contributed to high levels of household market income inequality. As is well known, the US is a welfare state laggard compared to western Europe, so taxes and transfers reduced income inequality less than they did in Europe, on average. As we saw in chapter 3, the US configuration of labor market institutions is not a restraint on top income shares. In addition, the stock market capitalization was high enough (50–60 percent of GDP) in the 1960s and 1970s to be consequential for distributive outcomes. Nonetheless, though inequality in the US, variously measured, was the highest among industrial democracies, it was not an extreme outlier in this period—but it increasingly became one.

Employers in the United States took a much more anti-union position than employers in northwestern Europe, and they enjoyed strong political backing from the Republican Party. Union density reached its peak of 35 percent in 1954, and its decline thereafter was aggravated by restrictive legislation, beginning with the Taft-Hartley Act of 1947. Such legislation facilitated aggressive union-busting techniques pursued by employers, extending over the decades all the way to Amazon in the third decade of the twenty-first century.

Partisan politics played a role as well, though one cannot characterize the Democratic Party as a left party, given its great internal heterogeneity. All major innovations in social policy were passed under Democratic presidents, from Roosevelt's Social Security Act to Johnson's Great Society and Obama's Affordable Care Act. In contrast, Republican presidents, from Ronald Reagan to George W. Bush and Donald Trump, prioritized tax cuts, particularly for the wealthy. However, the frequency of divided government and the lack of ideological consensus within the Democratic Party obstructed redistributive reforms and instead created deadlock and thus erosion of the redistributive capacity of the welfare state.

Indeed, the very high degree of inequality in the United States is self-reinforcing through the political process. American political institutions, particularly the single-member district electoral system and permissive campaign finance legislation, put a premium on the fundraising capacity of individual candidates and thus afford a large role for money in politics. Based on a mixed-methods design combining an analysis of twenty years of congressional speeches (1995–2016) with case studies of policy making on financial regulation and the minimum wage, Witko et al. (2021) demonstrate compellingly how the advantages of business and the wealthy in deploying resources get translated into congressional attention and action that privilege the interests of these groups. Kelly (2020) and Hacker and Pierson (2010, especially chapter 7) similarly argue that rising economic inequality and political inequality are mutually reinforcing, resulting in what Hacker and Pierson term "winner take all politics."

Changes in the Economy and the Labor Market

Industrial employment as a percentage of the working-age population in the United States declined from a high of 22 percent in 1969 to 13 percent in 2018. Employment also shifted from manual to non-manual work and from Fordist assembly line work to the knowledge economy. There is no question that long-term technological change was skill-biased in the US. A number of scholars have argued that skill-biased technological change (SBTC), especially in the wake of the widespread use of computers in the workplace, has led to increased inequality because it has increased the demand for high-skilled workers and reduced the demand for medium-skilled routine work (e.g., assembly line or clerical work) and left demand for low-skilled non-routine work (e.g., hotel and restaurant, personal services) unchanged (Goldin and Katz 2008, chapter 3; Autor, Katz, and Kearney 2008; Autor, Goldin, and Katz 2020). Building on the insights of Tinbergen (1974), Goldin and Katz point out in their 2008 book *The Race between Education and Technology* (RBET) that SBTC will only result in greater inequality if the government fails to invest in education to increase the supply of high-skilled workers. As we discuss below in the social policy section, they contend that the US did make such investment for the first 200 years of the republic and then failed to do so beginning in the last quarter of the twentieth century.

Unlike northwestern European CMEs, the US economy was already dualized between an industrial large business and largely unionized core in the 1960s and the poorly unionized small and medium enterprises and private services. Deindustrialization and de-unionization increased dualization, as did the rise in female employment and (more recently) the increase in the gig economy.

In the quantitative analysis, we found that high employment levels had an equalizing effect, while unemployment increased inequality. Unemployment followed different rhythms in the United States and Europe, but outside of southern Europe unemployment was not decisively higher in either region (table B.8). Employment levels have been consistently high in the US and the Nordic countries (table B.7), but this has translated only weakly into wage equality because of the weakness of American unions.

Stock market capitalization increased two-and-a-half-fold from the late 1970s to the early 2000s, after the dot-com spike and before the Great Recession (figure A.9). In itself, this would have increased inequality because stock ownership is much, much more concentrated at the top than income. In interaction with the change in management practices, the increase in inequality was magnified. Industrial deregulation and the decline of unions allowed the shareholder value revolution to take hold in company management practices (Fligstein and Shin 2007),[2] which was in turn a key driver behind the recent sharp increases in stock options-based CEO compensation (Hall and Liebman 1998; Frydman and Saks 2010). The stock buybacks drive up shareholder value, which in turn drives up CEO pay under the current shareholder value system of corporate governance. We discuss taxation policies below. Financial deregulation, which occurred under both Republican and Democratic administrations

(Hacker and Pierson 2010, 184–86) beginning as early as the 1960s, according to Krippner (2011), and culminating in the repeal of the Glass-Steagall Act in 1999, also drove up inequality.

The United States illustrates the perversity of the shareholder value revolution, and not just for rising inequality. Following a new conception of the firm as a set of tradable assets and a new definition of its goals as maximizing shareholder value, corporate management shifted from an emphasis on investment and innovation to a focus on short-term increases in stock prices (Davis 2009; Fligstein and Shin 2007). To attain such increases, firms resort to cost-cutting, which puts downward pressure on wages, as well as to financial maneuvers like stock buybacks, which divert resources from investments in physical and human capital (Lazonick 2014). Accompanying this change in corporate governance was a shift to greater reliance on stock options as a form of managerial compensation. Thus, CEO compensation became closely tied to the value of the company's stock, resulting in maximal incentives for CEOs to drive up the value of the company's stock through stock buybacks and cost-cutting measures.

In addition to the deregulation of labor markets and financial markets, the United States, like all other postindustrial economies, deregulated the energy, transport, and communication sectors. This has contributed to the disappearance of secure and well-paying jobs for the low-skilled by replacing public-sector jobs with more precarious and lower-paying private-sector jobs. At the top end, it has opened up opportunities for top managers to earn CEO pay. While the US was less deregulated in these sectors at the outset, it did subsequently experience very significant deregulation (figure A.10, table B.14). In our quantitative analysis of all countries, regulation had significant effects on many of our inequality measures, including very large effects on the Gini of household market income inequality and the top 1 percent share of national income, so it is very probable that it contributed to the rise in inequality in the US.

The timing of the large increases in top 1 percent shares, which were particularly steep in the 1980s and 1990s, argues that financial deregulation and the shareholder value approach to corporate governance were the critical developments in the rise of top 1 percent shares. Rising stock market capitalization certainly contributed to the rise in the top 1 percent share. Piketty points out that one of the main transformations of the composition of the top 1 percent is that they were rentiers 100 years ago and now they are primarily CEOs and other top managers, which is confirmed in a more detailed analysis of the composition of the top 1 percent of income earners in the United States by Bakija, Cole, and Heim (2012). One can see from table B.2 that most of the top 1 percent income is not capital gains.

Changes in Labor Market Institutions and Policies

Scholars of US industrial relations agree that the long-term decline of union strength and bargaining coverage have contributed to rising wage dispersion (Goldin and Katz 2008, 53; Thelen 2014, 43; Western and Rosenfeld 2011—see tables B.17–19, figure A.8). The decline in union density began before the series in figure A.8 begins. Union density in the United States peaked at 35 percent of wage and salary earners several decades before it began to decline in other liberal and continental European countries (Mayer 2004). The decline was arguably at least partly due to the passage of the Taft-Hartley Act in 1947, which made it harder to certify unions by making elections rather than card checks a requirement for certification[3] and weakened unions by banning wildcat strikes and closed shops, among other measures.

Though state-level "right to work" (RTW) laws, which make union shops illegal, predated Taft-Hartley in a few states, the act facilitated the passage of them, and currently twenty-seven states, mainly in the south and west, have RTW laws. The conventional wisdom on the effect of RTW, following the classic analysis of Olson (1965) in *The Logic of Collective Action*, is that they make it possible for non-union workers to get a "free ride" on union-negotiated benefits, thereby weakening unions. In a recent quantitative analysis of US panel data from 1968 to 2019, VanHeuvelen (2023) shows that the passage of RTW laws has the immediate effect of weakening unions and lowering the union wage premium and that RTW laws have additional long-term institutional effects establishing local- or regional-level high inequality political economies (e.g., weak unions, hostile public opinion, conservative government). A caveat here is that the effects of RTW laws are clearly context dependent, as Sweden with no union shops and nonetheless very high levels of union membership shows (Kjellberg, personal communication, October 5, 2023).

Thelen (2014, 39) argues that there was never a real CME-style accommodation between US unions and employers "not in the manufacturing core, and not even at the height of postwar capitalist growth." Whereas Swedish unions and employers responded to heightened international competition of the post-Golden Age era with a new set of wage-bargaining arrangements that would deliver wage increases compatible with export success, US employers responded with redoubled efforts in the 1970s and 1980s to destroy unions if possible, and if not, to greatly curtail their influence on wage formation. Led by the Business Roundtable, American employers managed to defeat an attempt by the AFL-CIO early in the Carter administration, when the Democrats controlled both houses of Congress and the presidency, to revise US labor legislation in a more pro-labor direction. The bill passed the House but was defeated by a Republican filibuster in the Senate. The advent of the Reagan administration unleashed another round of attacks on unions, culminating in Reagan's successful attempt to break the strike of the air traffic controllers in 1981.

The result of the anti-union offensive as well as long-term changes such as deindustrialization can be seen in the decline in union density shown in figure A.8. While continental European countries have also experienced a decline in union density, it has been much more debilitating to US union influence on wage formation because the US is lacking in other labor market institutions (tables B.18–19), like high contract coverage, centralized bargaining, high levels of wage coordination, and strong works council powers, which help offset low union density. In addition, the decline of union density was much more important for the US because so many benefits (e.g., health care, supplementary pensions) are not provided by the welfare state.

The US federal minimum wage peaked in its real value in 1968, and while Congress has periodically raised it since, the long-term trend is downward; in 2018, its value was 61 percent of its 1968 value (Payne-Patterson and Maye 2023). There is consensus among scholars studying US wage dispersion that the decline of the minimum wage is one reason for the increase in low-end inequality in the US as measured by the 50-10 wage ratio or the OECD low pay measure (less than two-thirds of the median wage—table B.5; see Goldin and Katz 2008, chapter 3; Autor, Katz, and Kearney 2008; Autor 2014).

The result has been steeply rising inequality, as tables A.2, A.4, A.5, and A.7 and figures A.1–3 show. Given the rise in the share of national income accruing to the top income earners, it is not surprising that the median household has hardly benefited at all from economic growth since 1979 (Nolan, Roser, and Thewissen 2016).

Table B.13 shows that Employment Protection Legislation (EPL) has always been very weak, meaning that it has always been easy for US employers to fire workers. Low EPL is certainly the reason temporary work is low in the US, as the fragmentary figures in table B.11 show.

Human Capital

Most of the proponents of the SBTC explanation for increased wage dispersion in the US do not claim that it is a complete explanation, and generally also point to declining union density and the declining real value of the minimum wage as additional causes of increasing inequality (see for example Autor 2014) without attempting to measure the strength of the various causes or even to rank-order them. In several articles on inequality in the US, Tali Kristal has attempted not only to rank-order the causes but to measure their relative strength more precisely (Kristal 2013; Kristal and Cohen 2017). For example, Kristal and Cohen (2017, 187) "find that declining unions and the fall in the real value of the minimum wage explain about half of rising inequality, while computerization explains about one-quarter."

The supply and demand argument underlying the SBTC framework would appear to imply that countries with a large supply of college graduates would have lower tertiary education premia. A comparison of tables B.21 and B.23 shows that this does not hold for the United States. The figures for tertiary education returns are from Weisstanner and Armingeon (2020). They are calculated from LIS data and are the average for two or three country years in the 1990s and 2000s. The United States has the highest average tertiary education premium of the twenty-two countries included in the study. Hanushek et al. (2015) arrive at similar findings in their analysis of PIAAC data (table B.20). They find that the skills premium as measured by the respondents' scores on the PIAAC numeracy test was the highest of any of the twenty-three countries included in the PIAAC study. From table B.20 one can see why: though tables B.22 and B.23 indicate that the human capital stock in the US is excellent, the PIAAC scores in B.20 indicate that it is poor, especially at the bottom.

How does one reconcile the high levels of formal education of the US work force with the poor levels of skills? In our work, we have argued that part of the story is the reliance on private education, particularly at the tertiary level (chapters 4 and 7). High levels of private tertiary spending are associated with high levels of stratification among tertiary degree holders. Autor, Goldin, and Katz (2020, 351) point out that "the largest part of increased wage variance in the twenty-first century comes from rising inequality among college graduates." Prestigious colleges and universities not only arguably impart greater skills; they also carry market value as a credential and make it more likely that the degree holders become embedded in social networks that land them in jobs that carry greater compensation. Kim, Kogut, and Yang's (2016) study shows that the credentials and networks that result from attendance at these colleges and universities are highly consequential for CEO compensation in the USA. For example, they note that "Harvard has a remarkably high number of graduates who become CEOs of the largest U.S. public corporations; 343 CEOs in our sample graduated from Harvard, out of a total of 2,018 CEOs" (p. 310). One might question whether education at Harvard University and Harvard Business School is so superior to that at elite public and private competitors in actual business skills that it merits this level of overrepresentation.

In chapter 7, we argued that the distribution of income in the parental generation was a strong determinant of skills in their offspring generation, and showed that the available evidence supports this argument. There are aspects of the US educational system that contribute to poor skills at the bottom of the skill hierarchy, such as the low levels of prekindergarten enrollment, the socioeconomic segregation of schools, and school stratification created by reliance on local (property) taxes for the funding of education. However, changing these aspects without doing anything about the inequality in the parental generation might not yield great dividends. Chetty et al. (2017) have shown that economic mobility has declined in the US, which they link to rising inequality. They show that "the fraction of children earning more than their parents fell from 92 percent in the 1940 birth cohort to 50 percent in the 1984 birth cohort" (p. 398). Brady (2022) compellingly argues that this study overestimates mobility because it measures intergenerational elasticity improperly. It uses gross earnings, omitting taxes and transfers; it measures childhood income only once instead of averaging over all of childhood; and it measures adult income too early. If properly measured, economic mobility is even lower. What is important for the US case is that childhood income can explain much of Black-White disadvantages in adult income and educational attainment (Brady et al. 2020). Corak (2013, 82) has shown a similar link between economic mobility and inequality cross-nationally. In his study, the United States is the country with the highest inequality and is among the countries (along with the UK and Italy) with the lowest economic mobility.

In the quantitative analysis, we found that immigrant percentage of the population was strongly related to our various measures of inequality.

Immigration did increase significantly in the United States: migrant stock increased from 6 percent of the population in 1960 to 15 percent in 2015. Since the low-skilled are overrepresented among immigrants, this probably contributed to the increase in inequality at the low end of the wage distribution.

Changes in Social Policy

Conventional treatments of US welfare state development begin with the Great Depression and the New Deal and only analyze the early period to explain why nothing developed earlier (Amenta 1998; Skocpol 1992).[4] With the inclusion of education, however, it is clear that one has to go back to the beginning of the nineteenth century, or even to the beginning of the Republic in the late eighteenth century. The first hundred years of the new Republic witnessed the expansion of primary public education to the point where it was close to universal, compulsory, and free, at least in the north and west (Goldin and Katz 2008, chapter 4). The new nation was an agrarian country and thus the structure of landholding was the most important feature shaping the rest of the social structure. There was a sharp division between the large-estate, slave-holding south and the rest of the nation, which was dominated by family farmers. The local communities, with some support from the individual states (not the federal government), funded primary education. The class of family farmers with mid-size farms was sufficiently large to support the schools through local taxes.

These same institutional and social structural features led to the expansion of secondary education in the late nineteenth and early twentieth centuries, with close to universal secondary education achieved by the middle of the twentieth century. Goldin and Katz (2008, 163) point out that this "second great educational transformation would serve to widen the gap between the educational attainment of youths in Europe and America ... [a] gap ... [which] would not again begin to close until well into the latter part of the twentieth century." This expansion of secondary education was followed by a surge in tertiary education after World War II.[5]

By contrast, the United States lagged behind Europe in other areas of social policy (Hicks 1999). The most important reason for this is that the US lagged behind most of Europe in labor organization (Stephens 1979; Hicks 1999). The ranks of the industrial working class were filled by waves of immigrants, which divided the working class, and the manufacturing core—the steel industry, the automobile industry, and the electrical industry, among others—remained unorganized until the Depression.

The Great Depression and the Roosevelt administration were, of course, a turning point for the American welfare state, but few appreciate either the extent of the transformation or how quickly it was accomplished. It was more than the passage of the Social Security Act in 1935, which provided basic pensions, unemployment and disability insurance, and social assistance financed by payroll taxes supplemented by income taxes. A federal minimum wage was established in 1938. Amenta (1998, 7) points out that the "United States became a world leader in public social spending during the Depression and did so on the basis of work and relief, not social insurance." However, the Social Security Act's provisions were permanent achievements while the work and relief schemes were allowed to lapse. Moreover, plans to complement Social Security with provision of comprehensive health care, a perennial election pledge of the Democratic Party, were unsuccessful, and the Johnson administration settled for programs covering only the aged (Medicare) and poor (Medicaid) in 1965 (Maioni 1998). It was not until Obama's Affordable Care Act introduced the individual mandate in 2010 that the United States approached comprehensive health coverage. However, health care delivery remained primarily private and comparatively very expensive.

In addition to Medicare and Medicaid, Johnson's Great Society social programs provided for poverty relief, established Head Start (a preschool program), and greatly increased aid to education at all levels. Medicare was financed by a payroll tax while the other programs were financed by general taxation, primarily progressive income taxes. The minimum wage was increased, and reached its historic peak in real terms in 1968. Public spending on education reached its pinnacle in this period: in 1970, US public spending on education as a percentage of GDP was 7.4 percent, second only to Canada (8.5 percent) and tied with Sweden among OECD countries (Brady, Huber, and Stephens 2020).

Table B.24 and figure A.4 display data on US unemployment benefits. The figures are Scruggs's index of the generosity of unemployment benefits and his data on duration of unemployment benefits (Scruggs and Tafoya 2022). Values on the index would appear to indicate that the US has a fairly generous unemployment benefit system. However, this is due to the heavy weighting of the replacement rate for the first half-year in the index. Following Esping-Andersen (1990), Scruggs's index is an additive index of scores for duration, qualifying conditions, waiting days, coverage, and replacement rate. The replacement rate is only for the first half-year, and it is weighted double. As one can see from the data, the US is very stingy on duration. Normally, unemployment benefits only last twenty-six weeks; they are occasionally extended by Congress to thirty-nine weeks or even longer during recessions. As one can see from table B.25, there are no figures for sick pay benefits because the US has no program providing paid sick days. The United States is the only postindustrial democracy to have no government sick pay program, no child allowance program, and no paid parental leave.

Despite controlling the presidency and both houses of Congress for his first two years in office, Bill Clinton failed to get his signature piece of social legislation, a plan to cover almost all Americans with health insurance, through Congress. In 1997 he did get congressional approval, with some Republican support, of the State Children's Health Insurance Program (SCIP, later renamed CHIP), which covered children in families with household incomes that were modest but too large to qualify for Medicaid. At the time of its creation, SCIP represented the largest expansion of taxpayer-funded health insurance coverage for children in the US since the establishment of Medicaid in 1965.

A social assistance program, Aid to Dependent Children (ADC, later changed to Aid to Families with Dependent Children—AFDC) was included as part of the Social Security Act of 1935. It was originally created for single white women, but this changed during the 1960s as the civil rights movement and the efforts of the National Welfare Rights Organization, whose members were mostly African American women, expanded the scope of welfare entitlements to include black women. Though most AFDC recipients continued to be white, the increase in black female recipients politicized and racialized social assistance programs (called "welfare" in the American parlance). Republican politicians, led by Ronald Reagan, began to exploit the issue: "She has 80 names, 30 addresses, 12 Social Security cards and is collecting veterans' benefits on four non-existing deceased husbands. And she's collecting Social Security on her cards" (Ronald Reagan, January 1976, campaign speech on welfare queens, as reported in the *New York Times*, February 15, 1976).

AFDC benefits, always meager, began to decline in real terms in 1976, perhaps not coincidentally the year of Reagan's "welfare queens" speech. Some centrist Democrats began to get on the anti-welfare bandwagon; in his 1992 presidential campaign, Clinton promised "to end welfare as we know it." The social assistance scheme legislated in 1996 by the Republican Congress and Democratic president, Temporary Aid to Needy Families (TANF), was considerably less generous than its predecessor, AFDC.

This was not initially apparent as the economy was strong in the first years after the reform and few recipients had been affected by the five-year lifetime limit on benefits (two years in some states). More than 13 million people received AFDC benefits in 1995; in 2016, only 3 million received TANF benefits (Semuels 2016). Moreover, the benefits were meager and fell over time (table B.28). In addition, supportive policies to make it possible for single mothers to work, like affordable public daycare and public transit, were inadequate.

More significant for the support of poor families is the negative income tax, the Earned Income Tax Credit (EITC) enacted in 1975, expanded in 1984, and greatly expanded in 1986 and then four more times in new legislation (1990, 1993, and 2001), the last of which passed in 2009 during Obama's first year in office. The EITC offsets Social Security and Medicare payroll taxes and can, if the wage earners' income is low enough, result in an actual cash payment to the low-income wage earner. The level of support is dependent on the earner's income and (beginning with the 1990 legislation) number of children. It is adjusted annually for inflation, so its value does not fall. As one can see from the dates of the legislation, the EITC enjoys bipartisan support; often the laws were passed by a Democratic Congress and signed off by a Republican president.

Figure A.4 shows that benefits in the unemployment insurance system remained stable after the mid-1980s, as did pension and disability benefits. Otherwise, developments in the US welfare state after the Great Society have been positively perverse. Education expenditure declined from its high in 1970 to a low of 5.2 percent in the mid-1990s, where it stabilized. The United States was also a low spender in other human capital spending categories, including ALMP and early childhood education. As noted, Goldin and Katz (2008) argue that the failure to invest in education since the beginning of the last quarter of the twentieth century is the reason SBTC results in growing inequality. One would expect this failure to invest in skills to show up in the various measures of market income inequality (wage dispersion, top 1 percent, market Gini, and market income poverty), as it did in our quantitative analysis.

Faricy (2015; also see Howard 1997 and Hacker 2002) shows that the increases in social spending have come mainly in the form of "tax expenditures"—tax deductions given for social ends such as contributions to private pension plans or private health insurance. The ratio of social tax expenditures to ordinary federal social spending rose from 5 percent in 1975 to 30 percent in 2010 (Faricy 2015, 140). These social tax expenditures accrue overwhelmingly to upper income groups, and thus increase income inequality. From the late 1960s to 2010, the real minimum wage fell by about one-third. Faricy's analysis of time-series data shows that the increases in the social tax expenditure occurred during periods of Republican control of Congress. Conversely, increases in the minimum wage occurred primarily during Democratic administrations.

The first two years of the Obama administration, a period in which both houses of Congress were also controlled by the Democrats, witnessed the first major social policy innovation since Johnson's Great Society in the passage of the Patient Protection and Affordable Care Act (ACA). The ACA expanded coverage by expanding Medicaid and requiring individuals to buy health insurance (the "individual mandate") if they were not otherwise covered (most commonly by employer-provided plans), and provided subsidies to low-income families to help them buy insurance. As a result of the ACA, 88 percent of Americans were covered by health insurance in 2018 (Collins, Bhupal, and Doty 2019).

The Republican Party gained control of the House of Representatives in the 2010 election, and between then and the end of 2016 voted to repeal the ACA more than fifty times, but the bill was never taken up by the Senate and would have been vetoed by Obama had it passed the Senate. The expectation was that the ACA would be repealed when the 2016 election resulted in Republican control of the House, Senate, and White House. The inability of the Republicans to repeal the law indicates that the ACA is proving more resilient than most observers thought.

With regard to the effect of taxes and transfers ("the welfare state") and thus disposable income, it is perhaps surprising to see that redistribution does not change much, beyond fluctuations caused by changes in unemployment (notably the increase in poverty reduction—table A.6) during the Great Recession. The long-term secular upward trend in disposable income inequality is accounted for almost entirely by the long-term secular trend in market income. Given the large tax cuts for upper income groups passed during Republican presidencies, this is rather surprising. One explanation is the passage and expansion of the EITC, the benefits of which go entirely to the bottom quintile of the income distribution. Comparing table A.4, table A.7, and figure A.1, it is apparent that the rise in inequality in the United States is driven to a great extent by the increase in top income earners' share of national income.

It is notable that Social Security, the one cash transfer policy with (near) universal coverage in the United States, has been remarkably stable, despite experiencing the pressures common to mature pay-as-you-go systems and despite dire projections that the program may run out of funds in a couple of decades. Talk about privatization under the George W. Bush administration did not result in legislative proposals. In the debt ceiling negotiations in 2023, the Republicans again exempted Social Security from their demands for deep cuts in social expenditures. This is clearly a result of the broad coverage of the system and the high voter turnout among older generations.

Tax Policy

While the Democrats did support the reduction of the capital gains tax in the late 1970s, the Republican Party has been much more consistent in passing legislation that reduces taxes on higher income groups and corporations. This can be seen clearly in that the Reagan and George W. Bush tax cuts benefited the top income groups. In fact, the evidence shows that benefits of the tax cuts are concentrated on the top 1 percent of income earners. These same groups were favored by the Trump tax cuts of 2017. The top marginal tax rate paid by high income earners fell from 91 percent in the beginning of the 1960s to 70 percent at the start of the Reagan administration. The Reagan tax cuts brought it all of the way down to 28 percent by the end of his two terms. Clinton and Obama increased the top marginal tax rate modestly, while Bush and Trump pushed it back down, but not to the level of the end of Reagan administration.

An analysis of the development of corporate tax rates in our four focal cases shows that corporate tax rates in the United States fell dramatically, though not as much as in Sweden or Germany. The two big cuts occurred in Republican administrations.

As in the other cases (both in this chapter and in the book as a whole), indirect taxes do not change distributive outcomes in the United States much. It is noteworthy that the US relies on indirect taxes less than almost all of the other countries in Warren's (2008, 53) study and shows the smallest increase in the Gini of disposable income once indirect taxes are included, from 34.8 to 35.4. Blasco, Guillaud, and Zemmour (2023, 9) show the same with data for 2012.

Impact of Social Services

Drawing on the two OECD studies of the impact of free or subsidized use of publicly provided social services cited above (Marical et al. 2006;

Verbist, Förster, and Vaalavuo 2012), we can present evidence on how inclusion of such services would change distributive outcomes in the United States and how that would or would not change the US's level of inequality relative to other postindustrial democracies covered in this book. Based on the changes in the levels of spending on public services, we can speculate on how this impact changes through time. Verbist, Förster, and Vaalavuo (2012) show that the US Gini for disposable income in 2007 was 37.2 and that the inclusion of the use of public services lowered it to 30.3, an 18.5 percent reduction in inequality—a bit below the average for our countries (19.8 percent). As the calculations based on their data make clear, this narrowed the gap between the US and the other countries, but the US still had the most unequal distribution of income and in-kind resources of any country. However, the reduction in inequality due to the inclusion of publicly provided services is greater than one might expect given the level of public spending on services as a percentage of household income, which at 13.4 percent places the US in the lower third of all countries in the table.

There are several caveats here with regard to both education spending and health spending, which account for the overwhelming share of public spending in the United States. The OECD studies allocated education spending on the basis of age of children in families. This ignores the tremendous differences in school quality which are surely much greater in the United States than in other countries included in the studies. The studies allocate health expenditure based on the insurance value of the coverage provided. The high cost of health care in the US results in high estimates of the insurance value of Medicaid, CHIP, and other health programs relative to public health programs in other countries.

As mentioned, the two OECD studies are so close together in time that they cannot show any long-term trend. Again, we turn to the long-term trend in the public service spending for some evidence of changes in the impact of publicly provided services on distributive outcomes over time. With regard to education spending, here we are concerned with its impact on immediate consumption, not investment in future skills. As previously noted, US spending on education fell from 7.4 percent of GDP in 1970 to 5.0 percent in 1989, where it stabilized until 2011 before dropping to 4.5 percent in 2018. Public spending on health care rose from 3.6 percent of GDP in 1980 to 8.8 percent in 2018. Most of this increase is due to cost inflation, as the public proportion of total health care spending only rose from 41 percent in 1980 to 50 percent in 2018. Certainly, CHIP and the ACA expansion of Medicaid had equalizing effects, but probably not enough to counteract the declining expenditure on education.

Impact of American Political Institutions

In our quantitative analysis we found some evidence that constitutionally structured veto points affected social rights outcomes; in earlier work we found that veto points had a strong negative effect on social spending (Huber, Ragin, and Stephens 1993; Huber and Stephens 2001). The United States (followed by Switzerland—Immergut 1992) is an extreme case in terms of the number of veto points in the legislative process. Not only does it have actual veto points in that legislation must pass both houses of Congress and successfully cross the president's desk, but it also must surmount additional stumbling blocks in the system, lack of party discipline (as we saw in the case of the abortive Clinton health care reform), and the filibuster in the Senate (as we saw in the case of the Carter labor law reform). The great rural overrepresentation in the Senate is yet another constitutional barrier to progressive legislation contributing to "gridlock" and "drift" (that is, change due to failure to act—Hacker 2005; Hacker and Pierson 2010, 236–37). Finally, the electoral system affords wealthy campaign donors an outsize influence (Witko et al. 2021).

CHAPTER TWELVE

The Cases Compared

Sweden, Germany, and the United States all saw an increase in both market and disposable household income inequality from the pre-2000 period to the 2013–2019 period. Spain saw an increase in market income inequality but essentially stable disposable income inequality if we take the average of the pre-1993 and 1993–1999 periods as a basis for comparison. In Sweden and Germany redistribution declined over this period, whereas in the United States it increased marginally and in Spain more markedly. The ordering of the countries remained totally consistent from 2000 on for redistribution and disposable income inequality, with Sweden showing most redistribution and least inequality, followed by Germany, then Spain, then the United States. Before 2000, Spain was slightly lower than the United States in redistribution, and slightly higher in disposable income inequality.

The trajectory of poverty is somewhat different. Market income poverty went up in Germany, Spain, and the United States, as did disposable income poverty. In Sweden, the crisis in the first half of the 1990s led to a rise in market and disposable income poverty, so that the level in 1993–1999 was higher than in 2013–2019. In Germany, Sweden, and Spain poverty reduction through taxes and transfers declined, but in the United States it actually increased, but not enough to counteract the rise in market income poverty. The ordering in poverty reduction effort is overall the same as for inequality: Sweden with most effort, followed by Germany, then Spain, then the United States. When it comes to disposable income poverty, the ordering of Spain and the United States is reversed in the latest period. Despite the much stronger poverty alleviation effort in Spain, the higher market income poverty resulted in a marginally higher disposable income poverty rate than in the United States.

In broad strokes, one can say that the United States has long had and still has a severe problem at the bottom of the income distribution, with a large share of low-income working people keeping levels of poverty high. Inequality in the US is the highest among the postindustrial democracies because of the combination of the top 1 percent pulling away and the lower half of the income distribution failing to improve their real incomes for some four decades. The American welfare state has long been among the most ungenerous in postindustrial democracies toward working-age people, if not the most ungenerous. Spain's problems have been mainly in the lower half of the income distribution, as income concentration at the top has remained moderate. The country has had to deal with high levels of unemployment and low levels of employment, which have depressed incomes in the lower half of the income distribution and have kept poverty and inequality high. After a period of significant improvement during the boom years, these problems returned after the bust. Spanish governments expanded the welfare state substantially up to 2007, but the safety net of last resort was weakened by the austerity pressures and was not strong enough to counteract the high levels of market income inequality and poverty. In Germany, the main dynamics driving higher inequality and poverty were also at the bottom of the income distribution. Income concentration at the top remained relatively stable at intermediate levels. High levels of unemployment and low levels of employment before 2000 prompted reforms that resulted in the proliferation of low-wage and precarious employment, leaving more people without access to the contributory social safety net, a development reinforced through legislative changes that limited the duration of contributory benefits. In Sweden, the dynamics driving inequality were both at the top and at the bottom of the income distribution. The cuts in unemployment benefits after 2006 resulted in less poverty reduction and an increase in disposable income poverty. Poverty levels in the latest period approximated those during and immediately after the crisis of the 1990s. At the other end, the share of the top 1 percent more than doubled, if capital gains are taken into account. While that is still less than half of the share of the top 1 percent in the United States, and while Sweden has remained among the least unequal of postindustrial democracies, it has been an important change for Sweden.

Top income shares show a steep increase from a relatively high level in the United States, a moderate increase from the same relatively high level in Germany, a steep increase from a very low level to a still comparatively low level in Sweden, and essential stability at a moderate level in Spain (table B.2). Income concentration at the top was of course aggravated by the distribution of wealth through the distribution of capital income. Jäntti, Sierminska, and Van Kerm (2013) show that in Germany, Italy, Luxembourg,

Sweden, and the United States income and wealth are highly, though not perfectly, correlated. Net worth in general is much more unequally distributed than disposable income, but there is variation between countries. Bradbury (2013) finds, for instance, that housing wealth is strongly correlated with income in the United States but weakly correlated in Australia, thus reinforcing income inequality in the former but not in the latter. Gornick, Milanovic, and Johnson (2017, n4) argue that labor income on average accounts for 97 percent of total market income, and in no country of the twenty-four in their study is the labor income share of market income less than 93 percent. But as Nolan and Weisstanner (2019) point out, LIS data underestimate top incomes and thus capital income, so Gornick, Milanovic, and Johnson are correct for their data but not for the real world.

Income concentration in the hands of the top 1 percent clearly contributed greatly to the increase in inequality in the United States. The increase is particularly steep if capital gains are taken into account; with capital gains, the share of the top 1 percent doubled, from 10 percent to 20 percent of total national income, between 1980 and 2010. In Germany, it increased from 10.7 percent to 13.1 percent in the same time period. In Sweden, the share more than doubled, but at 9 percent remained well below the German level and just a little above the Spanish level of 8.7 percent. The difference in the Swedish Gini of disposable income with and without capital gains is 5.2 (24.5 versus 30.7), much larger than the 1.2 difference in the United States and the differences of less than 1 point in six other countries for which we have data. So, if we look at change rather than comparing levels across countries, it becomes clear that the growth of the share of the top 1 percent was an important contributor to rising inequality in Sweden and the United States. The reason the top 1 percent share with capital gains remained higher in Germany than in Spain and Sweden, despite much lower stock market capitalization, has to do with higher overall CEO compensation and greater reliance on stock-based compensation (Croci, Gonenc, and Ozkan 2012).

Labor Markets and Labor Market Institutions

One set of dynamics accounting for increasing market income inequality and poverty is to be found in labor markets and labor market institutions: a combination of rising unemployment and precarious employment (that is, temporary or part-time employment without social benefits and with low pay) and a decline of labor market institutions protecting workers. The other set includes dynamics at the very top: the increasing share of the top 1 percent, particularly if capital gains are counted in, linked to growing capitalization of the stock market and the spread of the shareholder value model of corporate governance. Wage dispersion among full-time employed workers actually remained relatively stable (table B.1). We see a slight increase in the 50-10 ratio after 2000 and in the 90-50 ratio after 2005 in Germany and the United States, but either a slight decline or a very slight increase in Spain and Sweden, respectively, in both ratios. The ordering remains the same for the 90-50 ratio, with Sweden having the lowest ratio, followed by Germany, then Spain, then the United States. The ordering for the 50-10 ratio is different: Sweden and the United States remain the extremes, but Spain and Germany trade places from 2000 on. This suggests that the rise in precarious employment in Germany also depressed wages among full-time employed workers at the 10th percentile. The United States has had a large low-wage sector since at least the 1980s. As discussed below, the quality and distribution of human capital helps to explain differences between countries in market income inequality and poverty.

Digging deeper into the reasons for the problems in the lower half of the income distribution in the United States, Spain, and Germany, we see similar dynamics but with different weights. The low-pay share of employment in 2010 was a quarter in the United States, 19 percent in Germany, and 14 percent in Spain (table B.5). Low levels of industrial employment certainly contributed to that picture in the United States and Spain, with 11.5 percent and 13.6 percent respectively, but less so in Germany (20 percent). Spain had a very high level of unemployment (20 percent), but again less so Germany (7 percent), with the United States at 10 percent. The same ordering applies to levels of employment, with Spain clearly lowest at 59 percent (table B.7). Overall employment levels closely track female employment levels, which were at 52 percent in Spain (table B.9). Whereas women's employment can clearly serve as a buffer against poverty, the question of whether women's employment has an equalizing or dis-equalizing impact on household income distribution is disputed (Gornick and Jäntti 2013a). Harkness (2013), in an analysis of data for seventeen countries in 2004, finds that overall women's employment has an equalizing effect on income distribution. The reason for this may be that the middle three income quintile groups come to resemble the top quintile more than the bottom quintile. In the bottom fifth, the minority of households include two earners, whereas in the other quintiles a majority of households include two earners.

Adding to the low-income problem, much employment in Spain was temporary, accounting for roughly a quarter of the labor force. Finally, Spain had the lowest share of employment in dynamic knowledge-intensive sectors. So, Spain's economy, with large tourism, construction, and agricultural sectors, simply did not produce a sufficient number of stable jobs to absorb those in the labor force, not to mention drawing inactive women into the labor force as second earners who could provide a buffer against poverty in case of the primary income earner's job loss.

Germany's employment levels had remained relatively stable, at 65 percent, from 1980 to 2000. This was lower than in Sweden and the United States (table B.7). The labor market reforms of the early 2000s then created many part-time and precarious jobs, and reforms to promote work/family conciliation drew more women into the labor force, so that employment levels climbed higher than those in the United States (table B.9). This trajectory is mirrored in unemployment levels that rose after unification and by 2005 were higher than those in the other three countries, but after that they fell below those of the other three countries (table B.8). In contrast to Spain, part-time employment in Germany grew more than temporary employment, but much of this newly created employment provided low pay. This explains why increases in employment have not necessarily had a commensurate effect on inequality. Marx (2013) shows that whereas employment rates went up considerably in many European countries from 1995 to 2007, inequality and poverty did not reflect those increases; in fact, in several countries employment growth was accompanied by rising inequality and relative poverty. The principal reasons are that (1) job growth did not sufficiently benefit poor families (many jobless families with complex problems remained jobless; and in some cases jobs were taken by second earners, or as second jobs); (2) pay from the jobs did not necessarily lift people out of poverty; and (3) median equivalent income shifted upward in association with job growth, which lifted the 50 percent of median income threshold for poverty and thus caused an increase in relative poverty.

The United States had lower unemployment and higher employment levels that Spain, but a larger low-wage sector. This has to do with both lower human capital at the bottom and weaker labor market institutions in the United States. The high levels of wage coordination and contract extension in Spain explain the comparatively low 50-10 wage dispersion. However, the high levels of unemployment and temporary employment and the low levels of employment explain the high levels of market income poverty. The United States had by far the lowest employment protection legislation for the entire period, for both temporary and permanent employees (table B.13), and the lowest union density and contract coverage (to be discussed below). The United States also had by far the lowest PIAAC numeracy scores at the 5th percentile among our four countries (table B.20), whereas at the median they were similar to Spanish scores, both clearly below Sweden and Germany.

Despite the increase in the share of the top 1 percent, Sweden remained the least unequal among our four countries. The 50-10 ratio in 2018 was the same as in 1980, and the 90-50 ratio increased marginally over this period. Sweden has long had the highest employment levels, and up to the crisis of the early 1990s also had the lowest unemployment levels. Between 1995 and 2005 the United States had lower unemployment, and from 2010 on Germany did, but Sweden remained in second place or close to it. Part-time employment is at roughly the same level as in Spain, but most part-time work in Sweden carries social benefits proportionate to hours worked. Temporary employment is some 10 percentage points lower than in Spain and somewhat higher than in Germany.

Turning from employment, unemployment, and skill levels to labor market institutions, we see another set of reasons why Sweden has done comparatively well and the United States has done so poorly by the lower half of income earners. Sweden has retained the strongest institutions for the protection of all workers, and the United States has the weakest. Despite a decline from 78 percent in 1980 to 60 percent in 2019, union density remained much higher in Sweden than in the other three countries (table B.17). Contract coverage remained roughly stable at a very high level, as did wage coordination. Contract coverage remained almost as high in Spain, whereas it has declined very significantly in Germany; wage coordination remained high in all three countries. However, as our case studies showed, in both Germany and Spain the proliferation of opt-out clauses has severely watered down the actual impact of contract extension and wage coordination. Greater union density has supported stronger enforcement of contracts and wage coordination in Sweden. In the United States, contract coverage fell to the same low levels as union density, and wage coordination has been at the lowest levels since 1985, so workers have very little institutional leverage to protect their interests. This applies to protection of wages and working conditions at all levels, including the bottom, and to restraints on the share of the top 1 percent, which are essentially nonexistent in the United States. Union strength must be credited with keeping the top 1 percent share, even including capital gains, lower in Sweden than in the other three countries until 2010, when it reached the same level as Spain, despite the fact that stock market capitalization was more than double what it was in Germany, and much higher than in Spain as well (tables B.2 and B.15).

A final factor contributing both to rising market income inequality in all countries and to the perennially last (or first in inequality) place of the United States is the process of deregulation of energy, transportation, and communications sectors. As table B.14 shows, Germany, Spain, and Sweden all had similarly high degrees of regulation in 1980. Starting in 1990 and accelerating between 1995 and 2010, they all radically deregulated these sectors. The United States started out with much lower regulation and then deregulated further, so that by 2015 all countries were at essentially the same level of deregulation, with Germany marginally lower than the other three. As discussed above, the process of deregulation destroyed stable and relatively well-paying public-sector jobs, and created lower-paying and more precarious jobs at the bottom and more opportunities for highly paid executive positions at the top.

Human Capital

We see clear differences in skill distributions between countries. Generally, mean skill levels as measured by literacy and numeracy skills tests administered to the adult population in the IALS (OECD 1997) study were highest in the Nordic countries, a little lower in the Netherlands and Germany, in the middle in the UK and the US, and lowest in Portugal and other countries like Poland and Slovenia. Spain and Italy were not included in that study. In the mean scores on the PIAAC study, some two decades later (OECD 2013) the Nordic countries and the Netherlands remain at the top, but Germany has slipped to the middle and the United States has slipped below the UK, roughly halfway between the UK and Spain. Spain and Italy have the lowest mean scores in that study; Greece and Portugal were not included. It is important to note that over all the differences at the top are smaller than the differences at the bottom. The mean of the adjusted numeracy score for the eighteen countries in the study (no data for Australia, Greece, Luxembourg, and Portugal) at the 5th percentile is 156 and the standard deviation is 32; at the 95th percentile the mean is 345 and the standard deviation is 15. Our findings in chapter 7 suggest that this is a result of differences in the public commitment to investment in education and differences in levels of poverty and inequality in the parents' generation, all of which affect the bottom much more than the top.

When we look at the scores at the bottom, the 5th and the 25th percentile, we see an interesting pattern. In the IALS study, Germany and Sweden (along with the Netherlands) ranked at the top of the dozen participating countries in both literacy and numeracy. The US, UK, Canada, and Australia ranked very low at the 5th percentile. Some two decades later, in the PIAAC study, Germany's and the Netherlands' 5th percentile numeracy scores had fallen well below those of Finland and Sweden. Germany's 25th percentile and mean numeracy score had also fallen clearly below those of the Nordic countries and the Netherlands. Spain and Italy, which had not been part of the IALS study, had the lowest 5th and 25th percentile numeracy scores of any European country, but still slightly above those of the United States.

On the 75th and 95th percentile numeracy scores in the PIAAC study, Finland, Sweden, Norway, Denmark, and the Netherlands rank at the top, and Germany, Belgium, and Canada follow close together. Spain and Italy again rank at the very bottom among the European countries, below the United States at the 75th and 95th percentiles but tied with the United States for the lowest mean. What stands out is that Italy and Spain rank very low on all measures, whereas the United States ranks particularly low at the bottom, with scores comparable to those of Italy and Spain. Finally, it is notable that Germany has lost ground at the bottom as well. Clearly, the low scores of the adult population of Italy and Spain at all levels are a legacy of comparatively late development, a rural structure of large landholdings in key areas, and a strong role for the Catholic church in education, all of which combined to restrict universalization of quality public education. In the United States, the low scores at the bottom reflect a combination of racial segregation and the dependence of education funding on local property taxes, along with lower public spending on education overall.

Given the poor skills at the bottom, returns to skills were by far the highest in the United States. Interestingly, figures for formal schooling show the United States on top, with 93 percent of the population having completed secondary education, compared to only 44 percent in Spain (table B.22). The same is true for tertiary education completion, with 31 percent in the United States, compared to 16 percent and 17 percent in Germany and Spain (table B.23). However, the quality of education varies tremendously in the United States, so returns to tertiary education are the highest among our four countries (table B.21). This has to do with the local financing and control of education in the United States and the heavy reliance on private spending both overall and particularly in tertiary education. As table B.21 shows, the percentage of private spending at all levels in the United States is twice what it is in Germany and Spain, and at the tertiary level it is two and a half times as much as in Spain and more than three times as much as in Germany. This model of financing leaves a large portion of the population behind and creates an elite among those with tertiary education who can use their credentials and connections to gain access to high-paying positions.

In Germany, unlike in the United States (and, to a lesser extent, Spain), the problem is not the quality of human capital at the bottom. The PIAAC scores at the 5th percentile and the median were closer to Sweden than to the United States and Spain, though returns to skills were close to those in Spain (table B.20). Returns to tertiary education, in contrast, were lower than in Spain, despite similarly low levels of tertiary education completion (table B.23). However, secondary education completion increased rapidly in Germany, and the system of vocational education and training provided a significant pool of highly skilled workers without completed tertiary education, which kept the returns to tertiary education in check. Also, Germany has a low reliance on private education spending at all levels, including tertiary education.

Sweden stands out in its human capital base. Its PIAAC adjusted numeracy scores at the 5th percentile and the median were highest among the four countries, and returns to skills were by far the lowest (table B.20). The same is true for returns to tertiary education, even though tertiary education completion is much lower than in the United States and only some 2 percentage points higher than in Germany and Spain (tables B.21 and B.23). Sweden has the lowest private education spending at all levels, including tertiary education, so quality of education is much more even than in the other three countries. These factors account for the relative stability of wage dispersion, but the combination of rising unemployment and declining unemployment benefits contributed to the rise in disposable income poverty.

Social Policy

A comparison of market and disposable income poverty between Sweden and Germany shows that market income poverty has actually been higher in Sweden than in Germany since 2007, whereas disposable income poverty has remained lower. Certainly the stronger poverty reduction efforts are a key reason. Though poverty reduction in Sweden fell below the level of the other Nordic countries from 2007 on, it remained well above the levels of our other three countries. The fall in unemployment benefit generosity contributed to the decline in poverty reduction, but we need to keep in mind that the unions negotiated higher unemployment benefits that are not captured by the Scruggs index, which only considers legislated programs. Also, generosity of sickness benefits remained much higher than in Germany and Spain, and of course in the United States such benefits are lacking altogether. In addition, social assistance benefits in Sweden show a stark decline, which also contributed to the decline of poverty reduction. Nevertheless, these benefits remained the most generous among the three countries (table B.28).

In Germany, the rising levels of market and disposable income inequality have been closely related to rising levels of market and disposable income poverty. As noted, the low-wage sector grew to 19 percent of employment (table B.5), and part-time employment grew to 22 percent (table B.10). The continuing decline of union density and contract coverage were at the heart of these developments. These trends entailed a marked increase in market income poverty, from one of the lowest levels in any postindustrial country to an average level for continental countries, and an even more marked increase in disposable income poverty, from one of the lowest levels to an average level for Anglo-American countries. As tables A.5–A.7 show, the poverty reduction effort fell steeply. Unemployment generosity benefits fell in the wake of the Hartz reforms, and sickness benefits fell as well. Unfortunately, our index of unemployment generosity is only based on the main social insurance-based scheme and does not catch the elimination of the second tier of unemployment assistance by the Hartz reforms. What the elimination of this tier meant was that a much larger share of the unemployed were transferred to social assistance, and social assistance was never very generous. Indeed, it remained essentially stable at a low level (though much higher than in the United States) from 1990 to 2009 (table B.28).

Spain was among the countries with the highest market income poverty levels in the pre-2000 period. During the boom years, market income poverty fell to intermediate levels, but after 2007 it climbed to the second highest level among postindustrial democracies, behind only Ireland. Poverty reduction after 2007 fell compared to the pre-2000 period, and disposable income poverty climbed to the highest level, rivaled only by Greece (tables A.5–A.7). Unemployment and sickness pay generosity actually remained stable, but rising unemployment and the large share of temporary employment meant that fewer people had access to these programs, leading to greater reliance on social assistance. As we discussed in our case study, social assistance in Spain is a patchwork of poorly coordinated means-tested noncontributory benefits and minimum income schemes, and the generosity of these schemes varies greatly among the Autonomous Communities. Our data reflect the situation in Madrid, one of the more generous areas, and they show a significant decline in generosity from the pre- to the post-2000 period. Total spending on the non-aged as a percentage of GDP rose in the first years of the crisis to reach German levels, but then declined under the austerity programs imposed by the conservative government backed by the Troika. So, the welfare state effort was simply insufficient to counter the steep rise in market income poverty.

For the entire period under examination, the United States actually had lower market income poverty and much lower poverty reduction than Spain. Up to 2007, the United States also had the highest disposable income poverty among postindustrial democracies, only to trade places with Greece and Spain after 2007, though with less than 1 percentage point difference. The index of unemployment generosity is somewhat lower than in the other three countries up to 2005, but is higher than Sweden's and remains comparable to those in Germany and Spain from 2010 on. However, the duration of unemployment benefits was only 26 weeks up to the 2007 crisis—half of the duration in Germany, a third of the duration in Sweden, and a quarter of the duration in Spain. During the crisis the duration was extended to 99 weeks, but by 2015 it was down to only 20 weeks. Also important for the low poverty reduction is the total absence of sick pay and the very low value of social assistance. The big drop in the value of social assistance occurred between 1995 and 2000, and thereafter the decline continued to by far the lowest level among our three countries. The social safety net of last resort is simply very weak in the United States. The only reason disposable income poverty in Spain rose slightly above the level in the United States in the post-2007 period is the extremely high level of unemployment and thus of market income inequality in Spain.

Looking at the politics behind the changes in labor markets and the welfare state, we can see a clear pattern in Sweden and Spain, where we did not have coalition governments as in Germany or a centrist and a right-wing party as in the United States. In Sweden, the economic crisis of the early to mid-1990s induced both the bourgeois government of 1991–1994 and the Social Democratic government of 1994–1998 to cut the replacement rate in unemployment insurance, but beginning with the Social Democratic governments elected in 1998 and 2002 and the four-party bourgeois governments (the "Alliance") elected in 2006 and 2010, there are strong partisan differences in unemployment insurance policy. The Social Democrats raised the replacement rate back to 80 percent and raised the ceiling on replacement rates twice. The Alliance governments cut replacement rates and increased qualifying conditions. Above all, they greatly reduced the subsidies to the trade union-run Ghent system and differentiated the contributions by unemployment risk, which hit blue-collar workers the hardest and led to drastic declines in the coverage of the system. As a result, redistribution declined and disposable income poverty rose to close to the OECD average (tables A.6–7).

In Spain it was the PSOE government under González, from 1982 to 1996, that modernized and expanded the welfare state by universalizing health care and education and introducing noncontributory benefits. During the recession of the early 1990s, the González government reformed the unemployment compensation system to reduce replacement rates and lengthen qualifying periods, but at the same time the government improved benefits for outsiders by strengthening noncontributory programs. The PP government under Aznar reintroduced conservative measures into the education system with an early division between academic and vocational tracks and a religious education requirement in all schools. It did not introduce any major innovations in the welfare state, instead benefiting from high growth of the economy from the late 1990s on. Indeed, between 2000 and 2007 market income poverty declined markedly, but poverty reduction also declined, with the result that disposable income poverty actually increased. The PSOE government under Zapatero from 2004 to 2011 then massively expanded early childhood education and care, introduced the universal care system, and expanded parental leave and unemployment benefits before coming under severe austerity pressures in the wake of the financial crisis and cutting back expenditures. The subsequent conservative government under Rajoy intensified cutbacks on pensions, unemployment compensation and assistance, and social services. This meant a severe reduction of national social transfers to regional and local authorities, and thus of the latter's capacity to provide a safety net of last resort. The government also implemented labor market reforms that deliberately weakened labor in 2012 and did not change course once the external pressures abated.

In order to understand the politics in the Spanish case, we must also account for the impact of external pressures. As Scharpf (2021) argues, the policies required by the European Monetary Union during and after the Euro crisis had an asymmetric effect on the northern and southern economies.

Spain was wrongly accused of fiscal irresponsibility. The increase in the public debt was a result of the government taking on the debt of private banks (Blyth 2013). Nevertheless, the policies focused on fiscal retrenchment and on reducing unit labor costs and fostering an export-led recovery. But these policies could only be successful in the northern countries with large export sectors. The export sectors of the southern economies were too small to generate much economic growth, and fiscal austerity and wage depression deepened the recession in the large domestic sectors (Scharpf 2021, 179–80). Since these policies continued, Spain continued to experience low growth, low employment, and high public debt.

Prolonged economic hardship caused the Spanish party system to implode in the 2015 election. Both main parties lost large vote shares to new challenger parties. This made government formation and governing much more difficult. Nevertheless, when the PSOE under Sánchez returned to power in 2018, they immediately set about improving the safety net again, beginning with increases in means-tested child benefits in 2019 and moving on to the introduction of a national minimum income scheme in 2021. Similarly, the PSOE/UP government reversed the 2012 labor market reforms and introduced new measures to protect labor after 2020.

Labor market and social policy legislation in Germany was more negotiated between the two main parties because of the need for consent of the Bundesrat, where the party in opposition was often sufficiently strongly represented to have veto power. Party coalitions were frequent at the level of the Länder, and of course at the national-level Grand Coalitions between the Social Democrats and the Christian Democrats governed from 2005 to 2009 and from 2012 to 2021. The important Hartz reforms were carried out by a Red-Green coalition government, but the government was under intense pressure from the opposition and from employers because of the financial burden resulting from high unemployment levels, and the opposition wanted more far-reaching measures. Moreover, reforms intended to increase employment that actually created more precarious employment had started under the Kohl CDU/CSU/FDP government. We do see clear partisan differences in goals and negotiating positions. Prominently, the introduction of the minimum wage in 2015 came in response to demands from the Social Democrats in negotiations for the Grand Coalition, and this measure was needed to halt the erosion of wages at the bottom. In the area of work/family conciliation, the Social Democrats were clearly leading. In 2003 the Red-Green government reached an accord with the Länder to finance the transition to full-day schools, and in 2004 they passed the Day

Care Expansion Act. The SPD's 2005 election manifesto proposed further expansion of childcare for children under three years old and expanded parental leave. Under the Grand Coalition, the CDU picked up these proposals and a Christian Democratic minister championed them. However, the CDU/CSU/FDP coalition government in 2013 de-emphasized the work/family conciliation aspect again and introduced a childcare allowance for parents taking care of their kids at home. The 2021 election campaign of the SPD included plans for raising the minimum wage and expanding the social safety net, and the increase in the minimum wage to 12 Euros was accepted in the coalition negotiations.

In the United States we continue to observe clear partisan differences in goals and negotiating positions after 1980 as well, though the policy legacies and the entire agenda in labor market and social policy was less redistributive from the start, divided government was a frequent occurrence, and the Democratic Party is internally very heterogeneous and includes some very conservative senators. It was the Republican Reagan administration that unleashed the attack on unions. Between 1980 and 1990, union density dropped from 22.1 to 15.5 percent, compared to a drop from 34.9 to 31.2 percent in Germany, stability in Spain, and a slight upward trend in Sweden. The Reagan administration also implemented major tax cuts: they cut the top marginal tax from 70 percent to 28 percent during their two terms in office. The Democratic Clinton administration proposed a health care reform to universalize coverage, but despite Democratic control of Congress during the first two years, this reform was stymied by opposition from Republicans and from interest groups that prevailed on some Democrats to oppose it as well. It was also Clinton, though, who signed the welfare reform legislation produced by the Republican-controlled Congress that shrank the social safety net. On the other hand, his administration expanded the Earned Income Tax Credit. The Bush tax cuts were the next major step toward concentrating income at the top and restricting funding for social programs to help those at the bottom. The Democratic Obama administration then succeeded in passing the Affordable Care Act, which has ever since been a target of continuous attacks from Republicans. They also expanded the Earned Income Tax Credit. Trump then returned to the Republican master plan—to cut taxes and claim fiscal responsibility to restrain expenditures on social programs. Finally, the Democratic Biden administration proposed the most ambitious reform agenda since Johnson's Great Society, only to be stymied by two conservative Democratic senators in the evenly divided Senate.

CHAPTER THIRTEEN

Conclusion

Our data have shown general trends toward higher inequality and poverty, with very few exceptions, but also persistent important differences in the levels of poverty and inequality between countries. Looking at the big picture, the rank ordering of regime types remains the same, with the Nordic countries the least unequal, followed by the western European and then the Anglo-American countries, and the southern European countries the most unequal in disposable income. The gap between the Nordic and the western continental European countries narrows a bit, whereas the gap between the western continental European and the Anglo-American countries widens. We see essentially the same pattern for disposable household poverty.

However, as we have shown, these general trends followed different patterns, with different combinations of trends at the top and at the bottom of the income distribution. In some countries, specifically the Anglo-American countries, the top 1 percent greatly increased their share of national income. In others, particularly the southern European countries, the low-income groups grew, and in still other countries both things happened. The postindustrial countries in our analyses were exposed to similar transformations in their economies and labor markets, such as skill-biased technological change and globalization, which led to dualization of labor markets with a division between higher-skill winners and lower-skill losers. However, different insertions into the world economy combined with different legacies in human capital shaped the relative size of these groups. Moreover, persistent differences in labor market institutions protected the interests of the losers from SBTC and globalization to different degrees.

As countries were confronted by increasing market income inequality and poverty, they initially tended to respond with established social policies. Particularly in the western continental European countries, early retirement and disability benefit programs expanded greatly, leading to a perceived crisis of inactivity and straining government budgets. To deal with this crisis, activation became the new center of policy efforts, accompanied by gradual retrenchment of the generosity of unemployment compensation, particularly in its length, in some countries. Moreover, the changes in the labor market meant that fewer people qualified for the traditional unemployment schemes and became dependent on income-tested social assistance. In response, social democratic parties and unions in several countries intensified efforts to improve the social safety net for labor market outsiders. Nevertheless, these efforts were not successful in preventing the rise in disposable income poverty.

Our tables A.3 and A.6 show that the 1990s were the decade of strongest average reduction in poverty and inequality in all country categories except for southern Europe. From 2000 on, inequality reduction declined to pre-1993 levels in the Nordic and the western continental European countries and remained roughly stable in the Anglo-American countries. Poverty reduction shows a similar pattern, though it remained higher than in the pre-1993 period in the Nordic and the Anglo-American countries. Southern Europe, as a laggard in welfare state construction, expanded redistribution from the 1990s on but at the same time saw poverty reduction decline due to austerity in the wake of the 2008 financial crisis.

Changes in the Economy and Labor Market

We did find some evidence for the impact of technological change and globalization on inequality in our quantitative analyses, but they were substantively less important than labor market institutions and policy variables. Trade openness had the weakest substantive effect among our significant variables on the 50-10 wage ratio, and technological change (measured with change in total factor productivity) had an effect similar to those of deregulation and wage coordination on the 90-50 ratio, much weaker than union density. Trade openness, financial services sector size, and technological change had the three substantively weakest of the significant effects on the top 1 percent share. Technological change also had the weakest effects on the Ginis of market and disposable household income.

Trade openness was the only technological change and globalization variable with substantively strong effects. Trade openness enhanced inequality reduction. Given that we controlled in this model for generosity of unemployment and sickness compensation and labor market institutions, we interpret the effect of trade openness in part as an indicator of need. Trade openness arguably increases unemployment and puts downward pressure on wages at the bottom of the wage scale, creating greater inequality, so with unemployment compensation held constant, greater trade openness will create more inequality reduction. In our analysis of welfare state generosity in unemployment and sickness compensation, trade openness had the second most important substantive effect (after left government), enhancing generosity. These results lend support to the compensation hypothesis that claims that governments of all stripes have on average tended to counter increased labor market insecurity and wage competition caused by imports with a strengthening of the social safety net. However, in our case studies we saw that governments in Germany, Spain, and Sweden cut unemployment benefits in response to long periods of high unemployment.

Deregulation of the energy, transportation, and communications sectors was the final variable that entailed significant change in the economy and labor markets and had significant and substantively strong effects on inequality. Deregulation of course was a policy decision, but the fact that it happened in all countries, on roughly the same schedule and with roughly the same endpoint, suggests that technological changes were constraining policy choices (figure A.10). Higher levels of regulation had substantively strong restraining effects on the 50-10 and 90-50 ratios, on the top 1 percent share, and on the Ginis for market and for disposable household income. Given how strong and uniform the process of deregulation was across countries, this process is clearly one of the reasons for the trend to increasing inequality. Whereas deregulation of telecommunications was certainly driven by technological constraints, it is not clear that deregulation of utilities and public transportation was equally unavoidable. The experiences with privatization of railroads have been anything but positive.

As one would expect, higher levels of unemployment were substantively important for both market and disposable household inequality and poverty in our analyses. That unemployment will drive up market inequality and poverty is obvious, but that it continues to drive up disposable household income inequality and poverty even when controlling for generosity of unemployment compensation is less self-evident. It suggests that prolonged high levels of unemployment put pressures on welfare states that exceed their redistributive capacity in the form of additional social assistance policies. In our analysis of the pre- and post-2000 periods we saw that unemployment has become a robust and substantively important predictor of disposable household income poverty only since 2000. This suggests that welfare states by and large have fallen short of neutralizing the effects of higher levels of unemployment on poverty and inequality, though welfare state programs remain a crucial weapon.

Finally, levels of employment had the strongest substantive effect on market household income poverty. Higher numbers of households with more members in paid work are the strongest antidote to poverty. Since overall levels of employment are highly correlated with women's employment (r = .88), they respond to policies that draw women into the labor force, prominent among them work/family conciliation policies, which in the case of early childhood education and care also function as investment in human capital.

Labor Market Institutions

In every one of our analyses of inequality, labor market institutions that strengthen the position of labor had not only statistically significant but substantively important inequality-reducing effects. Union density showed substantively strong and statistically robust associations with most of our measures of inequality. It had by far the largest substantive effect on the 90-50 wage ratio, and the second largest (behind employment protection legislation) on the 50-10 ratio. Wage coordination also had important effects on both ratios. Employment protection legislation had a robust and substantively large effect on the 50-10 ratio, suggesting that it can help to prevent the emergence of an underclass of poorly paid workers. For the top 1 percent share, contract coverage had the substantively strongest moderating effect, followed by union density as the third strongest, and wage coordination as strong as stock market capitalization, working in opposite directions. For the Gini of household market income inequality, union participation in minimum wage setting had the third strongest substantive effect. For inequality reduction and for the Gini of disposable household income, union density retained an important direct effect, even with the most important variable—welfare state generosity—in the equations.

Labor market institutions themselves exhibited trends toward weakening, but very important differences persisted—and these differences continue to matter. Union density declined essentially everywhere, but to very different degrees (figure A.8). Mean union density, calculated on the basis of the Visser data, for our twenty-two postindustrial countries dropped from 46 percent in the 1975–1985 period to 31 percent in the post-2010 period. However, Denmark and Sweden dropped from 78 to 69 and 62 percent, respectively, whereas Germany dropped from 35 to 18 percent, Spain from 19 to 17 percent, and the United States from 22 to 11 percent. When we compared the pre-2001 with the post-2000 period, we found that the substantive effect of union density on the Gini of disposable household income declined, but it remained the second most important variable. Similar to union density, contract extension has declined and employment protection has been scaled back, but important differences remain. Bargaining coverage actually declined much less on average than did union density, from 72 percent in 1975–1985 to 63 percent in the post-2010 period. It remained virtually unchanged in Sweden, at 88 percent, and even increased in Spain, from 73 to 81 percent, whereas it dropped in Germany from 85 to 57 percent and in the United States from 24 to 12 percent. As our results show, these differences continued to matter greatly, despite the proliferation of opt-out clauses we found in our case analyses.

Tomaskovic-Devey, Rainey, and Avent-Holt (2020) came to the same conclusion that the weakening of labor market institutions that strengthen the bargaining power of employees is associated with an increase in earnings inequality. They analyzed administrative earnings data from fourteen countries for the period 1993 to 2013 and found that earnings inequality was shifting to between-workplace wage dispersion in twelve of them. Their explanation of this was that firms with market or organizational power (such as superstar firms like Microsoft, Apple, Google, and Amazon) could accumulate national and global income and engage in outsourcing and other forms of externalized production. They considered six labor market institutional protections and showed that the growth of between-workplace inequality was less restrained the weaker these institutional protections became.

In their analysis of increasing inequality in the knowledge economy, Diessner, Durazzi, and Hope (2023) find that the impact of digitalization (measured by ICT capital stock per employee) on inequality was contingent on labor market institutions. Strong labor market institutions (in this case, bargaining coverage) reduced the impact of the growth of ICT on inequality, a finding similar to our own on the moderating effect of labor market institutions on the impact on inequality of globalization and long-term economic transformation.

Distribution of Human Capital

Human capital spending showed a substantively moderate negative effect on the 90-50 ratio and on the Gini of household market income. The effect was substantively even stronger on the Gini of disposable household income; it was the third strongest effect, after welfare state generosity and union density. For the top 1 percent share we used the narrower measure of public spending on tertiary education, and it also had a moderately strong negative effect. These effects taken together indicate that indeed a greater public commitment to investment in human capital at all levels will work against rising inequality.

We found no direct effects of human capital spending on the 50-10 wage ratio and on poverty. These non-findings suggests that the negative effects of human capital spending on inequality work in the middle and the upper half of the income distribution. They appear to support those critics of social investment who argue that it helps those who are better prepared to take advantage of education and training opportunities, rather than the truly disadvantaged. Our findings in chapter 7 offer an additional complementary explanation. We found that the numeric PIAAC scores at the 25th percentile and the mean are more highly correlated to poverty and inequality in the 1980s, roughly a generation before the tests were taken, than to education spending (table 7.2). We further found that high levels of poverty and inequality in the 1980s (the parents' generation) depressed these scores among adults in the twenty-first century, even controlling for human capital spending. We found the same relationship between contemporaneous levels of poverty and inequality in the society and students' 5th percentile and mean math scores on the PISA tests, again controlling for public education spending and total education spending.

These findings square with the many studies that have shown a high intergenerational reproduction of educational attainment and suggest that it is the children of the poor who are disproportionately left out of the benefits of human capital spending. The fact that levels of poverty and inequality in the society are so important for skills at the bottom matters. We have also shown strong relationships between adult skills and the education premium (table 7.5) and between the inequality in adult skills and wage dispersion (table 2.2). In other words, low skills at the bottom are the mechanism for the intergenerational reproduction of poverty and inequality. Without addressing poverty and inequality, investment in education alone will not break this cycle. Nevertheless, of course, investment in human capital is crucial to prepare a larger share of the population for success in the labor markets of knowledge societies.

Immigration presents a problem for human capital at the bottom. Germany's fall in the rankings on the 5th and 25th percentile numeracy scores between the IALS and PIAAC studies arguably reflects the increase in immigration. Though the percentage of foreign-born population was very similar in Sweden and Germany (table B.16), Sweden had from the beginning put great effort into integration of immigrants, providing free language classes. These classes were made mandatory for asylum seekers in October 2021. Comprehensive preschool education contributed further to equalizing the educational playing field for the children of immigrants. Germany until the twenty-first century only provided such integration measures to immigrants of German descent, not to guest workers and their families. Particularly Turkish and Arab immigrants tended to encounter racial discrimination and obstacles to integration (Silver 2010). Accordingly, they tended to interact with others in their communities and to raise their children in these communities until compulsory school age, which put both adults and children at a disadvantage in skills acquisition.

Social Policy

In earlier work on distributive outcomes, we found that welfare state generosity was strongly associated with egalitarian outcomes (Bradley et al. 2003; Moller et al. 2003; Huber and Stephens 2014). In this book we replicated that finding and extended it with better inequality data and better measures of social policy generosity. We saw repeatedly that the most important variable for reduction of poverty and inequality was the generosity of social rights. Our social rights variables—the generosity of unemployment and sick pay benefits and the parental leave replacement rate—were strongly and robustly associated with redistribution, and somewhat less strongly with poverty reduction effected by taxes and transfers. We found similar associations of our social rights variables with disposable income inequality and disposable income poverty.

As noted, the Scruggs unemployment generosity index only captures the replacement rate for the first half-year and weights this replacement rate twice as much as duration and qualifying conditions, so it is an imperfect measure. In fact, if we compare the period from 1975 to 1985 with the post-2010 period, the average of the Scruggs unemployment generosity index for all countries remains essentially unchanged. In our four cases, it falls from an average of 11.8 to 10 in Germany and from 10.3 to 8.1 in Sweden, but increases from 9.6 to 11.4 in Spain and marginally from 10.1 to 10.6 in the United States. However, as Clasen and Clegg (2012) argue, traditional contribution-based unemployment compensation programs have been shrinking in their reach due to changes in employment structure and have been transformed in the course of wider reforms of labor market policy. They identify three major trends operating to different degrees and at different speeds in different countries: (1) benefit homogenization, or a trend toward fewer tiers of unemployment protection; (2) diminishing differences between these tiers in rules and benefits and a tendency for the creation of a single benefit for working-age people; and (3) tighter coupling of passive and active labor market policy through an emphasis on activation. We have certainly seen these trends in our case studies, with the Hartz reforms in Germany, the unemployment compensation reforms in Sweden, and the minimum income schemes tied to activation in Spain. Clearly, such reforms might have the potential to provide a more egalitarian social safety net, but the shrinking coverage of this safety net is having the opposite effect. The trends in disposable income poverty suggest that the reforms have not realized their potential.

In chapter 6, we analyzed the antecedents of generous social policy. We found that partisan government had a strong effect on variations in our social policy indicators. Left government had the largest effect on variations in social policy generosity for the working-age population (measured by the generosity of sick pay and unemployment insurance) of any independent variable, the second largest on parental leave, and the third largest on human capital spending. Moreover, female representation in parliament, which is causally interrelated with left government, had the second largest effect on variations in human capital spending. Christian democratic government had modest effects on all three policy variables.

If we combine our findings on the direct effects of partisan government and its very strong indirect effects (via social policy) on distributive outcomes with the strong effects of labor market institutions, our analysis provides very strong evidence in support of power resources theory. Declining union density is one of the most important reasons, possibly the single most important reason, for rising income inequality across the cases in our quantitative analysis. However, we want to insist that political choices remain the key to challenging inequality, and that it continues to matter who makes these choices. Declines in union density are certainly driven in part by deindustrialization and the disappearance of public-sector jobs in deregulated sectors of the economy, but policies protecting union organization can facilitate unionization of the service sector. Legislation on contract extension and on the minimum wage can compensate to some extent for declining union density in protecting low-wage workers. Moreover, as both our quantitative analyses and our case studies have shown, social policy generosity, public versus private education funding, and family/work conciliation policies have strong effects on inequality, and they are all choices made by governments, not paths dictated by inexorable external pressures. External pressures have reduced the choices open to governments in macroeconomic management and taxation policies, but choices remain, as the marked differences in these policies between countries demonstrate. Our case studies have shown that left-of-center parties have consistently chosen pro-labor and redistributive social policies to a greater extent than have center or right parties.

Impact of Taxation

As we discussed, redistribution happens overwhelmingly on the expenditure side, not through taxation. In Wang and Caminada's (2011) data for the entire population (not just the working-age population) around 2004, the mean for nineteen postindustrial countries shows 15 percent of redistribution effected through taxes, including mandatory payroll taxes, and 85 percent through transfers. The Anglo-Saxon countries on average redistribute less than the continental European and the Nordic countries, but they redistribute a larger share through income and mandatory payroll taxes than the other two sets of countries. We have also discussed Warren's (2008) and Blasco, Guillaud, and Zemmour's (2023) findings on the impact of indirect taxes, which show that these taxes are regressive and thus further reduce redistribution through the tax system. They also show that indirect taxes do not meaningfully alter the differences in the distributive profile of tax systems. The magnitude of taxation matters greatly, however, because it determines the share of resources available for redistribution through transfers and public services. And here we saw a common problem—a decline of corporate taxation from initially very high levels in some countries (see figure B.1), particularly Germany and Sweden, to similarly low levels, arguably as a result of deregulation of capital markets. We see a notable increase in the average index of deregulation of capital markets and a decline in the standard deviation of the measure across twenty-one postindustrial countries in the first half of the 1990s, and a notable drop in the average corporate tax rate in the late 1990s and the first half of the 2000s.

We saw greater differences between countries in the effective top marginal taxes rates. In the 1980–1992 period, Sweden and the United States represented the extremes, with average rates of 76 and 41 percent. Though rates declined in most countries thereafter, large differences remained. In the period from 2000 to 2017 the data have a mean of 45 percent, with a minimum of 33 percent (New Zealand, 2011–2017) and a maximum of 62 percent (Denmark, 2008 and 2009). As a result of the Bush tax cuts, the rate in the United States declined from 45 to 41 percent, to rise again in 2012 to 46 percent. From 2000 to 2017 the rate decreased from 48 to 44 percent in Spain and from 54 to 47 percent in Germany, ending up close to the US rate, but it rose from 55 to 60 percent in Sweden.[1] We have to note, however, that these data are based on tax returns and thus overestimate the actual tax bite on top incomes because of loopholes that allow for tax avoidance and because of illegal tax evasion. We see even greater differences in total government revenue and thus the potential redistributive capacity of the government. The highest level reached in the 2000–2017 period in the United States was 33 percent of GDP, compared to 40 percent in Spain (at the height of the boom), 45 percent in Germany, and 57 percent in Sweden. Clearly, there is economic room for higher taxes and revenue particularly in the United States, but also in Spain and Germany. However, raising taxes is politically very difficult in periods of stagnating wages, because in situations where individuals perceive that their economic situation is in decline, their tolerance for taxation decreases (Jacques and Weisstanner 2022).

Politics of Redistribution

We have demonstrated the pivotal role played by policy, from policies that protect the position of labor to social investment and welfare state generosity, in counteracting the trends toward increasing inequality and poverty driven by technological and demographic changes. Policies, of course, are the product of politics and thus of the outcome of elections that shape the power balance between political parties with different social bases and ideological commitments. Political institutions matter because they influence the balance of power between political parties and the ease with which parties can shape policies. We have shown substantively important effects of government by left parties on welfare state generosity, parental leave, and human capital spending. We also showed substantively weaker positive effects of government by Christian democratic parties on welfare state generosity and parental leave, and a weak negative effect on human capital spending. Constitutional dispersion of power, measured by the number of veto points, had a positive effect on welfare state generosity and a negative effect on parental leave, indicating that dispersion of power made cutbacks of generous programs that had been installed before the 1980s more difficult, while at the same time hindering the establishment of new programs of parental leave. In our analyses of reduction of inequality and poverty we found direct effects of left government even when controlling for our measures of policy that of course only capture a segment of possible redistributive policies. Government by the Left was tied with the level of unemployment for the strongest substantive effect (of course in different directions) on disposable income poverty.

As the literature has amply demonstrated, both social democratic and Christian democratic parties, along with traditional conservative parties, have seen their stable voter bases shrink (Kitschelt and Rehm 2015). Changes in labor markets (specifically the decline of unionization but also increasing mobility between jobs) have weakened solidarity and attachment to traditional labor parties. Immigration has generated a backlash and has been the key issue behind the rise of new anti-immigrant parties. The percentage of voters who switched parties increased from an average of 20.5 percent in 1990 to 24 percent in 2015 in fifteen EU countries (Keman 2020, 441). The share of votes received by established parties declined between 1955–1965 and 2001–2011 by 14 percent in Australia, Canada, and the UK, by 25 percent in the Nordic countries and in in the western continental European countries, and by 52 percent in Italy and Japan. In the same time period, new left-libertarian parties increased their share of the vote by 4, 9, 8, and 3 percent in these respective groups of countries, and new right-authoritarian parties increased theirs by 1.5, 11, 12, and 3 percent (Kitschelt and Rehm 2015, 198). In Spain, the spectacular rise of new parties came after the period analyzed in the Kitschelt and Rehm study. To summarize these figures in a different way, in the Nordic countries the established parties lost 25 percent of the vote; the New Left gained 9 percent and the New Right 11 percent; and the trends were very similar in the continental European countries. New parties—that is, parties formed after 1985—gained an average of 25 percent of the vote in elections after 2015 (Keman 2020, 438).

These changes have increased the need for coalition governments and for larger coalitions as well, which in turn has made policy innovation more difficult. In particular, the pursuit of redistributive policies has been made more difficult by the shifting base of left parties. Kitschelt and Rehm (2022) argue that a realignment process has taken place in the transition to the knowledge economy. People with low income and low education used to be the core support base of the Left, and people with high income and high education used to be the core support base of the Right, whereas people with high education and low incomes, and people with low education and high incomes, were cross-pressured in their party preferences. Increasingly, they argue, the low income/high education group has become the core support base of the Left, and the high income/low education group the core support base of the Right, whereas the low/low and high/high groups have become cross-pressured. People with low education and in blue-collar jobs have become more likely to vote for anti-immigrant parties, whereas people with high education in sociocultural professional occupations have become more likely to vote for left parties, though not necessarily for traditional left labor parties—rather, for left-libertarian or green parties (Abou-Chadi and Hix 2021). However, recent work (Abou-Chadi, Mitteregger, and Mudde 2021) has shown that this does not imply a strong voter movement from the Social Democrats to the far right; rather, most people voting for the far right previously either did not vote or voted for other right parties. There is a debate about the degree to which a new cleavage structure has replaced religion and class (Marks et al. 2021), but there is consensus that politics is multidimensional and that party choices are not governed by distributive issues alone. Rather, the second cultural (or particularism versus universalism) dimension is important as well (Häusermann and Kriesi 2015). Moreover, different subgroups of supporters of redistribution have different preferences for traditional social safety nets over social investment, which in a context of austerity has made it more difficult for left parties to attract broad support for feasible policy packages.

However, the conflict of interests between labor market insiders and outsiders and the choice of unions and traditional left parties to defend the interests of insiders only (Rueda 2007) has been exaggerated. In particular the Spanish Socialist Party introduced and expanded noncontributory social safety nets, partly in response to union pressure (Natili 2019; Guillén, Álvarez and Adão e Silva 2003). In general, the post-2007 economic crisis has created room for new anti-inequality redistributive coalitions. Traditional social democratic parties not only in Spain but also in Germany, France, and the Netherlands have extended their appeal to those in precarious labor market positions (Schwander 2019). Green parties are generally in favor of social investment and work/family conciliation policies, which means they have common ground with more traditional left parties on these issues.

Constraints of European Integration

There is no question that conservative economic policy at the European level contributed to rising inequality in EC/EU countries. After the French U-turn in macroeconomic policy in the early 1980s, Mitterrand promoted monetary integration as a way to wrest control of European macroeconomic policy from the Bundesbank (Marsh 2011). Instead the opposite happened: Germany, the strongest European economy and therefore in a strong position to shape European institutions, had a tradition of central bank independence and a historic preoccupation with price stability. German negotiators insisted on an independent European Central Bank with the charge to keep inflation under control, and on budgetary and economic convergence as a condition of membership in the monetary union (Ross 2011, 324). Thus, German macroeconomic policy, which targeted only inflation and not unemployment or growth, was extended to all European Union countries. The 1992 Maastricht Treaty outlined five criteria for inclusion of a country in the common currency at the end of that decade: a budget deficit of no more than 3 percent, a total debt of no more than 60 percent of GDP, a low inflation target, a limit on long-term interest rates, and a stable exchange rate. These targets were extended with some modification in the Stability and Growth Pact of 1997. This meant that left governments were already constrained in efforts to expand social programs in the lead-up to the Euro. Though serious doubts emerged regarding the figures Greece presented to gain entry, and over time many countries exceeded these ceilings at some point, the ceilings did constitute real constraints. Brady and Lee (2014) showed that from the late 1980s to 2008, adoption of the Euro did have a significant negative effect on government spending in seventeen affluent democracies.

Since there are no growth, unemployment, or employment criteria, EU macroeconomic arrangements hinder the achievement of low unemployment and high employment. The European Economic Strategy (EES), and the Lisbon Strategy that followed, set an employment target of 70 percent of the working-age population. However, this is "soft law"—the Open Method of Coordination has no enforcement mechanisms. In fact, EU macroeconomic policy has hindered the achievement of the EES employment target, and the Commission has on occasion reverted to neoliberal policy prescriptions diametrically opposed to those suggested by the Lisbon Strategy. As Vandenbroucke, Hemerijck, and Palier (2011) note, "The Annual Growth Strategy (AGS), published by the European Commission in February 2011, marks a return to social retrenchment and deregulation, reminiscent of the OECD jobs study of the mid-1990s."

As noted, the Spanish government, in response to bank failures resulting from the Great Recession, bailed out the failing banks and took on their debt, which together with similar developments in the Eurozone periphery resulted in the sovereign debt crisis. After first responding to the Great Recession with countercyclical measures, the Zapatero government came under intense pressure from the EU and imposed austerity measures. We argue that this austerity was counterproductive. It assumed that Spain's problems were a product of fiscal indiscipline. In fact, Spain ran budget surpluses from 2005 through 2007 and its total debt was less than 50 percent of GDP—well below Stability and Growth Pact limits. The problem was a failure of bank regulation at the national and EU level: Spanish banks accumulated a lot of bad debt during the mid-2000s real estate bubble, which put the government in the position of letting the banks fail or adopting their obligations. Ireland followed a similar sequence of budget surpluses and low debt in 2005–2007, real estate bubble and banking collapse, followed by government assumption of bank debt leading to skyrocketing debt and deficits (32 percent of GDP in 2010!).

The Troika (EC, ECB, and IMF) austerity formula assumes that a country can export its way out of an economic crisis. Scharpf (2021) showed that this is not possible for most countries on the European periphery (Ireland excepted). The difference in export success between CMEs and the countries in the European periphery (again, Ireland excepted) is striking. The growth models of these other countries require stimulation of domestic demand (Hall 2018; Baccaro and Pontusson 2016).

To reform European economic governance in a fashion that produces more employment and less unemployment requires institutional change, an increase in fiscal capacities at the European level, and a change in the targets of economic policy. EU leaders pressed the introduction of the Euro despite the fact that they knew the European Union was far from being an optimal currency area: (1) European countries' economies were subject to asymmetric shocks; (2) de facto labor mobility between countries was far too low; and (3) there was no sizable tax and transfer system at the central level to offset the asymmetric shocks and lack of labor mobility (no significant fiscal union). As Börzel and Risse (2018, 88–90) point out, the Eurocrisis did stimulate a series of reforms that facilitated fiscal transfers within the Eurozone, and to a lesser extent throughout the entire EU. The Fiscal Compact, the European Stability Mechanism, Outright Monetary Transactions, the Banking Union, the Macro-Economic Imbalance Mechanism, and European Semester in different ways facilitated fiscal integration without substantially expanding the actual tax and transfer authority of the EU. In addition, the Banking Union reintroduced a measured financial re-regulation designed to prevent some of the abuses that led to the banking collapses that precipitated the Great Recession.

The COVID crisis stimulated another round of EU budgetary reforms that may turn out to be more consequential for the volume of fiscal transfers than the post-Euro crisis round of reforms. The Next Generation EU, adopted by the European Council in July 2020, calls for €807 billion in grants and loans from 2021 to 2026 for recovery from the pandemic (https://commission.europa.eu/strategy-and-policy/recovery-plan-europe_en). Together with the EU's Multiannual Financial Framework, the packages are projected to reach a total outlay of €1,824.3 billion. As Hooghe and Marks (2009) argue in their post-functionalist European integration theory, since the Dutch and French Maastricht referenda of 1992 public opinion has been a constraint on further European integration, particularly fiscal integration that involves transfers between countries. Arguably, welfare state solidarity does not extend to citizens of other countries because, as in the wake of the Eurocrisis, their difficulties are seen as products of their own (or at least their own government's) failings. In the case of the COVID crisis, this was a narrative not easy to defend, which arguably made it easier to justify significant fiscal transfers. For all these EU institutional reforms to have maximum impact on employment, unemployment, and growth and therefore on inequality, a change in targets is also necessary. Basically, low unemployment, high employment, and rapid (green) growth must be given parity with fighting inflation.

The aftermath of the Euro crisis also saw a reinvigoration of the EU social agenda. From 2017 on, a variety of directives were issued, such as the European Pillar of Social Rights, a directive on minimum protection of workers in precarious jobs, and a directive on a decent minimum wage. Discussions on a directive on national minimum income schemes were stalled as of mid-2023. Whereas the extent to which national governments will implement these directives will depend on domestic political power distributions, there is no doubt that the international environment in Europe has become more permissive for bold reforms by left parties that attempt to improve the position of labor and the strength of the social safety net.

Immigration

The extent to which immigration has contributed to higher inequality and poverty, in both direct and indirect ways, remains contested. Immigration accelerated in Europe in the 1990s, with the refugee flows after the end of the Cold War and the eruption of conflict in the Balkans. It continued in the twenty-first century with refugee flows from the Middle East and Africa. Earlier immigration in Europe had mostly been legal, in the form of recruitment of guest workers, and later, family reunification. From the 1990s on, the population of immigrants became more complex, with the addition of refugees who were legally admitted, refugees who were awaiting adjudication of their claims, and irregular migrants.

Treatment of immigrants with regard to access to the labor market and to social services varied widely. As we saw in our case studies, the difference in levels of employment and unemployment between citizens and immigrants was much larger in Germany and Sweden than in Spain and the United States. Language ability—Latin American migrants to Spain and the widespread use of Spanish in the United States—can explain only part of this difference. The other part is greater toleration of the informal economy. In contrast to the United States, the Spanish PSOE government in 2004 passed very generous immigration legislation that, among other provisions, granted regular and irregular migrants full access to health, education, and social services (Pérez 2011).

In Europe, immigrants from different regions have been treated very differently. Citizens of EU member states have gradually acquired rights to residence in any of the member states, though clauses remain that allow expulsion on the grounds of public policy (undue burden on the social safety net), public security, or public health (Ferrera 2012). After five years without expulsion, the immigrant's right to residence becomes permanent, and so does access to social assistance. As Ferrera (2012) notes, however, member states have tried to water down these directives and preserve an ultimate authority over access to their needs-based safety nets. Third-country nationals have been treated very differently: countries have retained the right to decide how many to admit and what benefits they may access. Roemer (2017) found that more generous welfare states among eighteen OECD countries granted immigrants greater access to benefits in the 1980–2010 period, controlling for restrictiveness of overall immigration policy. This suggests that institutional legacies outweighed attempts from the Right to spread welfare chauvinism.

Access to the labor market for immigrants is essential not only for their integration but also for the potential for the Right to politicize the issue of immigration and generate a welfare state backlash. Competition for unskilled jobs can be grounds for anti-immigrant sentiment, but that experience is confined to people seeking unskilled jobs. Seeing immigrants idle around town as a result of their exclusion from the labor market is an experience shared by much larger sections of the population, and it makes people susceptible to the anti-immigrant and anti-welfare state propaganda from the Right alleging that immigrants are just here to live off the taxes of hard-working citizens.

Efforts to fan the flames of welfare chauvinism spread in the 1990s and accelerated with the waves of migration in the twenty-first century. Need-based programs became particularly vulnerable to attacks by the Right on the grounds that these programs promoted "benefit tourism," as in the case of the Austrian minimum income schemes (Natili 2019, 288). The solution implemented by the Danish Right, with the support of the anti-immigrant Danish People's Party, was to introduce different conditions of access to benefits for new entrants and large families, mostly migrants (Natili 2019). Magni (2022) showed pervasive welfare chauvinism in the United States, the United Kingdom, France, and Italy, even extending to immigrants from Western countries.

The extent to which the efforts to spread welfare chauvinism were successful in undermining support for the welfare state more broadly remains disputed. Brady and Finnigan (2013), in a study of 17 affluent democracies between 1996 and 2006, found only very limited support for the argument that immigration undermined public support for social policy. On the contrary, they found some evidence that migration had positive effects on welfare attitudes. Breznau et al. (2022), in a massive meta-analysis of the results of seventy-three independent research teams that were all analyzing the same data for thirty-one countries, found that of the 1,253 models analyzed, 25 percent showed positive effects (immigration did undermine support for government social policy), 17 percent showed negative effects, and a full 58 percent showed no significant effects. The last survey wave analyzed in that study was from 2016, so the data should have captured the effects of the new waves of immigration.

Pressures for immigration in the form of refugee flows and flows of people seeking a better life are unlikely to diminish. If those are to be managed without growing inequality and poverty and without a growing voter base for the anti-immigrant Right, governments need to invest in the institutions that process immigrants in a speedy manner and in services that facilitate their integration into society and the labor market. Access to social services is a crucial component of integration into the society.

Determining the number of immigrants and of asylum seekers—to the extent that the number of asylum seekers can be controlled—is a different and even more difficult question. For the Left, it presents a conflict between values of solidarity and pragmatic considerations of the society's capacity to absorb large number of immigrants. Here it is important to keep in mind that studies show immigrants to be net contributors to the welfare state (https://www.oecd.org/migration). Moreover, in the context of aging societies in Europe, immigrants fill in the younger ranks and important jobs in the labor market, frequently in public and private personal care services.

Speculation and Prescription

Our findings that strength of labor and of left parties and the nature of social policies have had the substantively most important effects on inequality and poverty raise the question of whether unions and left parties could have done more to arrest growing inequality and poverty. Were there policy options not taken? Or did the constraints resulting from technological changes and globalization, including European integration, simply foreclose other options? What role did the rise to dominance of neoliberal economic doctrine in the economics profession and beyond play in shaping policy choices? Of course, there are no conclusive answers to these questions, but they are worth pondering in the hope that the tentative answers might provide some pointers for the future.

To start with technological change, we saw that deregulation of energy, transport, and telecommunications had strong effects on all of our measures of market income inequality, and also on disposable household income inequality. The fact that deregulation happened in all countries at around the same time, regardless of partisan incumbency, and ended up at a similarly low level suggests that technological change left little room for choice. To take just two examples: With the proliferation of cell phones, it became immensely more difficult to maintain a public monopoly on telecommunications. And with the spread of satellite TV, it became close to impossible for public TV channels to maintain a monopoly. However, it is much less clear why public transportation became deregulated and partly privatized. Rail transport lends itself much better to a national monopoly. So, we have to allow for the importance of beliefs in the efficiency of markets in the age of neoliberal hegemony to explain some of these policy choices.

Another major and rather uniform policy change, the drop in corporate taxation, arguably contributed to limits on the state's redistributive capacity by limiting resource availability. Again, capital mobility and competition for investment in jobs between and within states arguably limited the capacity of any one government to keep corporate taxation at levels above those of the competitors. On the other hand, costs—be they labor costs or costs in terms of taxation—are not the only considerations corporations take into account when they decide to invest in a country. Qualifications of the labor force, infrastructure, and market access matter as well. Again, we have to come back to the intellectual hegemony of neoliberalism in the 1980s and 1990s, which also affected the policy choices of center-left parties.

There is little disagreement that the economics profession changed in that neoclassical or neoliberal theories [these are not the same thing] became dominant in academic circles and thus shaped the thinking of graduate students who would go on to serve in the public and private sectors as advisers to governments and corporate executives. The apparent inability of Keynesian economics to provide solutions to the stagflation of the 1970s opened the space for belief in the magic of free markets and adherence to monetarism to spread (Blyth 2013). Three key policy prescriptions were deregulation, independence of central banks, and balanced budgets. Deregulation extended to all types of markets and industries, including capital markets and labor markets. Deregulation of capital markets then became a self-reinforcing process: once the largest economies had done so, others had to follow suit in order to attract investment in their economies.

Liberalization of labor markets was arguably the most contentious measure. Not just the EU, but the OECD (in its Jobs Study of 1994) insisted that the cure for high levels of unemployment was a dismantling of employment protections. Moderate labor market liberalization was accompanied by a shift in emphasis from passive to active labor market policy.[2] Generosity—particularly in duration—of unemployment benefits was reduced, and receipt of benefits was made conditional on active job search and rapid acceptance of whatever jobs were available. That employers and right-wing parties embraced these policy ideas is not surprising. What is surprising is that social democratic governments followed suit to the extent that they did, even in countries that lacked the programs to provide the "flexicurity" to protect people in an environment with widespread unstable and marginal employment.

As just noted, to begin to understand such choices we must keep in mind the training at leading universities of economic experts working for left parties and governments, and their formative experiences. As Blyth (2013) points out, in the 1970s monetarism and public choice theory replaced Keynesianism as the dominant economic theories. What they had in common was a view of state stimulation of the economy to combat unemployment as necessarily a source of inflation and economic instability. Public choice theory saw politicians as narrowly interested in maximizing votes, willing to use public expenditures for that purpose, and thus committed to creating a political business cycle. Therefore, economic policy making had to be insulated as much as possible from political pressures through the creation of independent central banks and through a general retrenchment of state intervention in favor of greater reliance on markets. These dominant economic theories were imparted to graduate students who, among other careers, would go on to advise governments and serve in public office. Real-world experiences, particularly the stagflation of the 1970s and the disastrous French experience with a stimulus program during the first two years of the first Mitterrand government, prepared the ground for the absorption of these new theories by throwing doubt on the continued viability of reliance on demand management and making economists in political leadership positions more receptive to the arguments of market fundamentalists.

Mudge (2018) argues that internationalized and finance-oriented economists working for left parties gained the upper hand in internal party struggles in Sweden, Germany, and the UK, as well as in the Democratic Party of the United States. These advisers and officeholders pushed for what they saw as a modernization of left politics, which involved greater reliance on markets, calls on personal responsibility, and greater flexibility in labor markets—all key elements of "Third Way" policies. Whereas one can certainly trace changes in the economics profession and internal differences of opinion in social democratic parties and governments, it would be a mistake to ignore the real constraints under which these governments operated.

Mudge (2018) and Blyth (2001) argue that a group of market liberal-oriented economists centered around Finance Minister Kjell-Olof Feldt came to dominate the economic policy of the Swedish Social Democratic Party upon its return to government in 1982. In the 1980s, this manifested in massive deregulation. Mudge and Blyth, as well as Lindvall (2010), contend that when the economic crisis hit in 1990, the Social Democrats abandoned the goal of low unemployment as the centerpiece of macroeconomic policy, replacing it with low inflation and budget balance. Indeed, subsequent Social Democratic governments were never able to get unemployment below 5.5 percent, compared to the 1.5 to 3 percent that prevailed between 1960 and 1990.

As we pointed out in chapter 10, in interviews with Lindvall (2010, 112), Allan Larsson, Feldt's successor as finance minister, and Ingvar Carlson, then prime minister, contended that the party had not abandoned full employment as a central goal of its macroeconomic policy. Both of them argued that to combat unemployment it was necessary to combat inflation. A lacuna in the arguments of Mudge and Blyth is their understanding of Swedish macroeconomic policy in the Golden Age. As mentioned in chapter 10, the Rehn-Meidner macroeconomic prescriptions included low inflation and tight fiscal policy, both of which were intended to facilitate wage restraint and thus export competitiveness. So targeting low inflation and budget balance was hardly new. It was just harder to achieve then, given the decontrol of international and domestic credit markets. For the criticism of the market liberal turn of European social democracy to be compelling, the critics need to specify what alterative policies could have been pursued given the prevailing economic rules of the game.

When trying to understand policy choices by left governments, we must consider the national and international contexts in which they assumed power, in addition to understanding the thinking of economic advisers. In the UK, New Labour's Third Way under Tony Blair was a major representative of the new promarket thinking. The Labour government had to operate in an economy and society that had undergone a profound market-oriented reorientation under Thatcher. The Thatcher government had not only privatized key economic sectors and sold off a major share of public housing, but had also deliberately weakened unions, lowered taxes on the wealthy, and scaled back the welfare state. In addition, European integration and global capital markets had advanced, and Labour was acutely aware of the need to maintain investor confidence. Their response was to affirm their belief that markets were a good thing and that a Labour government could manage the market society well and improve its human consequences. In concrete terms, they made a commitment to letting the

Bank of England set interest rates outside the control of the government and to respecting the spending limits set by the Conservatives for the first two years after Labour took power in 1997 (Cronin 2011). Labour did have some notable successes: Its policies did reduce child poverty and its investment in the NHS and education after 2000 represented the largest increases in social spending in British history. In addition, Labour did deliver some moderate labor market re-regulation to the union movement.

However, New Labour made no meaningful attempt to restrain the growth of the top1 percent income shares. At least initially, New Labour ideologically radically disconnected the issues of inequality and poverty, as exemplified by the 1998 statement of Labour Party cabinet minister Peter Mandelson that he was "intensely relaxed about people getting filthy rich as long as they pay their taxes." This quote and the party's policy at the time illustrate the view of the leadership that there was little causal link between the income shares going to the very top income groups and those going to the rest of the population—a notion that our analysis of top income shares in chapter 3 disputes. Our "resource constraint" mechanism argues that top income groups and the rest of the population compete, at least in part, and perhaps in large part, for income shares from the same pool. Years later, at the World Economic Forum in Davos in 2012, Mandelson said "I don't think I would say that now. Why? Because amongst other things we've seen that globalisation has not generated the rising incomes for all." He went on to argue for more government intervention in the economy, including a "modern industrial policy," saying among other things that "We have got to do far more in our country and the government has got to help the private sector to do this, to innovate and specialise in the production of high-value-added goods" (Malik 2012).

In Germany, when the Social Democrats won the 1998 elections and formed a coalition government with the Greens, they were saddled with the financial burden of unification. The previous Christian Democratic/Free Democratic coalition government had already tried to pass legislation to deregulate the labor market and cut benefits. The Social Democrats opposed these cuts, but at the same time the wing around Schröder came to embrace the need for more market-oriented policies and particularly for activation of the unemployed. The widespread use of early retirement to deal with unemployment had swelled the ranks of pension recipients; unemployment was already high and rose even higher by 2005, which let the costs of unemployment compensation escalate. At the same time, revenue of the central and local governments declined due to the recession of the early 2000s and a 2000 reform of corporate taxation. Carlin et al. (2015, 63) call the fiscal situation at the end of 2002 the most severe budgetary crisis faced by local governments since World War II, and the federal government was in similarly dire financial straits. This is the context in which the highly consequential Hartz reforms were passed. Would the situation have been different without the 2000 corporate tax reform? Could the Red/Green government have resisted the pressures from business and the opposition for this tax reform in the context of international competition for investment? And would alternative policy choices have been possible while the opposition controlled the Bundesrat?

Alternative policy options were least available in Spain. The transformation of private debt into public debt and the ensuing sovereign debt crisis forced the PSOE government to accept the harsh austerity prescriptions of the Troika, which not only halted all further progress in social policy but forced cutbacks in existing programs. A theoretical alternative to austerity would have been a stimulus program to restart growth, but the ECB and the IMF demanded the opposite and thus aggravated the recession. As Armingeon and Baccaro (2012) argue, other theoretical options would have involved financial guarantees to reduce the interest that southern European countries had to pay on international bond markets, but such measures were opposed by Germany and other core European countries. So, there were no alternatives to austerity open to individual social democratic governments in the crisis situation, and the financial and political interest constellation in the EU prevented the construction of a collective alternative.

Arguably, policy makers in the United States had the most room for policy choices. The US Federal Reserve Bank has always targeted unemployment and growth as well as inflation. It is widely perceived that inflation has taken priority since the high inflation of the 1970s. Much more important for inequality are the low levels of redistribution and poverty reduction effected by the tax and transfer system (tables A.3 and A.6). The tax cut policies of the Reagan, George W. Bush, and Trump administrations aggravated the situation. The presidents and their congressional allies advocated for these cuts because of their supposed positive effects on economic growth, which in every case failed to materialize. As Krugman (2012) argues, economic growth would have been much more effectively stimulated by using that fiscal room to increase expenditure, every dollar of which would have provided fiscal stimulation. The long-term effects on growth would have been particularly great if these resources were invested in physical infrastructure and human capital, for instance by greatly expanding the woefully inadequate US early childhood education and care system, which would have reduced inequality in the short run (by allowing more parents to work more) and in the long run by improving the skills of those at the bottom.

Like the European Union, the US moved to re-regulate the financial sector after the Great Recession to prevent the abuses that contributed to the depth of the recession. The Dodd-Frank Wall Street Reform and Consumer Protection Act is widely regarded as the premiere legislative achievement of the Obama administration, rivaled only by the Affordable Care Act. In addition to reining in financial sector abuses, it also increased consumer financial protection. It passed by a party-line vote that was enabled by the support of three Republican senators, which avoided a filibuster that would have killed the billed. It was partially repealed by the Trump administration in 2018, primarily by exempting small banks from its provisions. Bank regulation is crucial to prevent bailouts that induce governments to impose austerity policies that in turn aggravate unemployment and thus increase poverty and inequality.

Given the importance of the strength of organized labor in determining variations in inequality and redistribution over time and across countries, a glance at figure A.8 could make one very pessimistic about reversing—or even just halting—the growth of inequality in these knowledge economies. Given that some of the underlying causes of de-unionization—deindustrialization and dualization—are likely to continue, such pessimism seems merited. Two caveats soften the picture painted by the figure. First, other aspects of the institutional strength of labor, contract coverage, wage coordination, and works council powers have not declined nearly as much as union density. Second, the figure still shows remarkable cross-national variation. The high levels of union density in the Nordic countries and Belgium show that it is possible to unionize the difficult-to-organize private service-sector workers. The difference in the trajectory of union membership in Canada and the United States since 1970, once part of a unified union movement at least in industry, indicates the US path was not historically locked in (see figure A.8). Riddell (1993, 143) summarizes his careful comparative study of union density in the United States and Canada as follows: "On the whole these findings support the hypothesis that much of the Canada-U.S. unionization gap can be attributed to inter-country differences in the legal regime pertaining to unions and collective bargaining and to differences in overt management opposition to unions (itself possibly a consequence of differences in collective bargaining laws and their administration)." Recent unionization success in hard-to-organize enterprises like Amazon, Starbucks, and Google Fiber does buck the lock-in story for the US. However, the failure of the Biden administration to pass meaningful labor law reform despite Democratic majorities in the House and Senate, repeating the failure of the Carter administration, underlines the importance of the anti-majoritarian features of American political institutions. In particular, the existence of the filibuster makes passage of ambitious reforms virtually impossible without a supermajority.

The challenge for social policy is to prevent it from replicating the insider/outsider divisions of the labor market. Income protection and access to social services need to be decoupled from stable employment. Countries with tax-financed national health care systems are closer to this goal than are countries with insurance-based health care systems. Other care services, particularly child and elderly care, have largely been put on the same basis. Changing unemployment protection systems to deal with labor market instability is a more difficult undertaking, particularly in countries with generous systems where unions have negotiated benefits additional to the national systems. The Danish "flexicurity" system, which has been identified as a "best practice" to promote employment by the European Union through the Open Method of Coordination, can serve as a model here. Danish policy makers and welfare state scholars view flexicurity as entailing a "golden triangle" with a three-sided mix of (1) flexibility in the labor market (moderate EPL by the standards other CMEs and southern European countries), (2) generous unemployment benefits, and (3) active labor market policy with rights and obligations for the unemployed. Certainly, a key feature of any unemployment protection system has to be retraining and labor market support.

Retraining coupled with financial support during spells of unemployment combines social consumption with social investment. As our findings in chapter 7 have demonstrated, direct anti-poverty and anti-inequality policies, or social consumption, are essential for social investment to have egalitarian effects. Opponents of redistribution have framed social investment as being in competition with social consumption, and this competition as pitting older and lower-skilled against younger and better-skilled groups. Without denying real resource constraints, left parties and governments need to emphasize the common interests of these groups in increasing taxation of high-income groups to fund both effective anti-poverty policies and social investment policies. Communicating the essential mutually supportive relationship between the two is not only good policy, but also good politics. It helps to build political coalitions in support of stronger social protection and social investment and in support of efforts to rein in the income share of top groups.

Clearly, pursuing effective anti-poverty and social investment policies requires resources. This in turn entails the need to articulate the urgent need for tax increases on top earners and on wealth, something that left parties over the past thirty years have mostly shied away from. On the contrary, top income tax rates, along with inheritance taxes and corporate income taxes, have all fallen since 1980 (Emmenegger and Lierse 2022). The Right and business interests have been highly successful in framing tax increases as a danger to investment and economic stability and convincing the public that inheritance taxes would irreparably damage small enterprises and small farms. Emblematic of this success is the ability of the Republicans in the United States to make the label "death tax" stick to inheritance taxes. On the other hand, tax cuts have been framed as lifting all boats, even if the benefits accrue to top income earners only. Yet the question remains why left parties have not been counter-mobilizing more aggressively on the issue of taxing the rich.

Tax competition, or the fear of losing top income earners to countries with lower taxes, may be part of the reason. However, most tennis stars have already moved to Monaco; in other words, those for whom relocating is easy have already done so. An additional reason must be that left politicians believe that campaigning on tax increases is not a winning strategy. To that one might counter that the campaign emphasis should be on the programs tax increases could finance. Fastenrath et al. (2022) provide an interesting additional explanation for the German case. Based on interviews with twenty-five German politicians, mostly but not exclusively from the left, they confirm the importance of negative framing of tax increases by business and their political allies, but they also find that left parties have few tax experts compared to center-right parties. This puts them at a disadvantage in hammering out the intricate details of tax legislation, and it undermines their self-confidence when engaging in debates about taxation. This may or may not be the case for left parties in other countries; even if it is the case, recognition could be the first step toward correction. In other words, deliberate efforts to create tax expertise among their ranks should be a priority for left parties.

Given the key role of labor market institutions and of social policy in shaping both pre- and post-tax and transfer inequality, the fundamental question one must ask is what the chances are for building and sustaining political coalitions supportive of strengthening the position of labor and of expanding inequality-reducing policies. Building such coalitions is particularly difficult in contexts of high inequality, because inequality tends to intensify through a self-reinforcing political process. This process is most visible in the United States (Kelly 2020), where political institutions are highly susceptible to minority vetoes, where the electoral system discourages party discipline, and where campaign donations shape the congressional agenda (Witko et al. 2021). The influence of money on elections and the political agenda is weaker (though not absent) where there is strict legislation on political campaigns and the electoral system encourages party discipline, as in Sweden, Spain, and Germany. As noted, the problem in the latter set of countries is party system fragmentation. A further common problem for all countries is increasing vote volatility and weakened ties between voters and parties.

In the face of these challenges, what should be priorities for parties of the left? To summarize, there are two sets of priorities: (1) policy reforms in financial and labor markets and in social policy, and (2) party-building and campaign regulation. Of central importance is the protection of labor organization and the strengthening of labor participation in decision-making at all levels, from works councils at the enterprise level to coordinated collective bargaining and minimum wage setting at the national level. Governments should also strengthen financial regulation to prevent boom-and-bust cycles that increase unemployment. Superstar firms should be constrained in their ability to extract rents due to monopolistic or oligopolistic positions through anti-trust regulation, which would dampen the increase in between-workplace inequality. In the area of social policy, investment in human capital and equalization of access to quality education at all levels is crucial for a society to function well in the knowledge economy, where old jobs keep disappearing and new jobs with new skill requirements keep emerging. Support for training and retraining of adults in the new economy needs to be complemented by generous unemployment benefits. Also, access to the social safety net, to health care, and to other social services needs to be decoupled from stable employment and financed via taxation to accommodate the changing labor market. Finally, the resources to do all this need to come from a strengthened tax system that is able to capture taxes from high earners and from wealth. In addition to domestic efforts along these lines, international efforts need to be intensified to close tax havens for individuals and corporations.

The second set of priorities begins with investing in party-building at all levels, from local to regional and national, as a means to reach voters directly rather than just through media. Preventing private money from financing political campaigns should be another step. Ideologically left parties should beware of losing the vision of a more solidaristic society and of simply becoming better managers of "capitalism with a human face" than their center-right competitors. Left parties moving too close to the center open the way for radical parties to the left and the right. Moves to the center also tend to downplay programmatic competition in favor of competition on valence issues or personal qualities, where left parties have no inherent advantage. Instead, left parties should confront the problems of inequality and poverty head-on and present bold visions of how to handle them. These visions may fail to pass into legislation, as Biden's "build back better" has failed, but they may pave the way for less ambitious legislation, such as Biden's Inflation Reduction Act, and at the very least they will disseminate the idea that things could be better and that it makes a difference which parties are in office.

Theories of Redistribution, Theories of the State

In chapter 3 we found very strong support for the PRT theory of redistribution. Indeed, five of the seven independent variables in our final equation predicting levels of redistribution were consistent with the hypotheses of PRT and together explained 55 percent of the variation in redistribution. By contrast, the variable suggested by the influential Meltzer and Richard (MR) (1981) theory, the ratio of the mean to median market income, was wrongly signed and the zero-order correlation was (is) actually negative, −.44. MR has been the point of departure for the political science literature on redistribution for almost two decades now.[3] Many of the citations to MR are for the argument that voters below the mean in the income distribution are likely to support redistribution. However, this argument is hardly original; it dates back at least to Karl Marx and was a staple of comparative political sociology by the 1950s (Lipset 1959; Alford 1964). What is distinctive about MR is the hypothesis that inequality and redistribution are positively and strongly related. In truth, the basic premise of the MR thesis is implausible. It asserts that a major feature of social structure, the very system of stratification of society, is self-negating. The usual assumption in sociology, political science, and anthropology is that social structures reproduce themselves.

In its initial elaborations, PRT was presented as a theory of the state, an alternative to pluralism and orthodox Marxism (Korpi 1978 and 1983; Stephens 1979). The theory argued that, in the absence of working-class organization, the orthodox Marxist theory was essentially correct: public policy was formed according to the interests of capital. While the theory did see an important role for active participation by capitalists in the policy-making process, the primary mechanisms by which the rule of capital was secured was through the structural dependence of the state on capital — that is, the dependence of state policy makers on capital's willingness to invest — and through hegemony, ideological domination. As Mann (1973) points out, socialism, or any other ideology that imagines a substantially different way of organizing society, is learned. Everyday consciousness will reproduce itself, and thus is a conservative force. An important part of the organizing task of the working-class movement was to promote a counter-hegemony, an alternative image of how society might be organized. The theory hypothesized that the state would respond to changes in working-class organization, and the main mechanism by which this response was effected was electoral: the working-class movements organized and propagandized for electoral support for social democratic parties, which when they attained office would pass legislation favorable to working-class interests.

The very strong support for PRT, and especially the strong support for the PRT explanation of redistribution, also supports the theory of the state underlying PRT. This theory holds that state policy responds to the balance of power in society, which in turn is shaped by the organization of labor. The weakening of labor counter-hegemony across our cases helps explain variations in income inequality outcomes within and across countries. Since inequality in economic resources has a feedback effect on inequality in political resources, unless counteracted by organization among those with few economic resources, and since such counteracting organization has declined, we can say that almost all the cases in our analysis are less genuinely democratic than they were forty years ago, taking equality of political resources as a yardstick. Our case studies support this view, though institutional barriers to democratic representation in the United States outlined in chapter 11 do make it an extreme case even at the outset. Indeed, the implications of the PRT view for the democratic process in the US are that the United States is not very democratic, that the political process did not work the way pluralists described it. While many comparativists accepted this argument, or at least accepted the legitimacy of the argument in academic discourse, it was treated as heretical in American political science, at least in the sub-field of American politics (e.g., Dahl 1961). Witness how

CONCLUSION

William Domhoff's work was dismissed out of hand by Americanist political scientists. This has changed in the past two decades as prominent Americanists have adopted a more critical view of American democracy, one that is much more compatible with PRT (e.g., see Hacker and Pierson 2010; Kelly 2009 and 2020; Gilens 2012; Faricy 2015; Page, Seawright, and Lacombe 2018; and Witko et al. 2021).

APPENDIX A

Figures and Tables, All Countries

TABLE A.1. **Variable Definitions and Sources**

	Definition	Original data source
Inequality measures		
Wage dispersion 50-10 ratio	Ratio of gross earnings received by a worker at the 50th earnings percentile to that received by a worker at the 10th percentile	OECD*
Wage dispersion 90-50 ratio	Ratio of gross earnings received by a worker at the 90th earnings percentile to that received by a worker at the 50th percentile	OECD*
Top 1% income shares	Income of the top 1% as a percentage of total income	WID*
Market income inequality	Gini of household market income of the working-age population	LIS, SILC, and OECD*
Redistribution	(Market income Gini − disposable income Gini) / market income Gini	LIS, SILC, and OECD*
Disposable income inequality	Gini of disposable household income of the working-age population	LIS, SILC, and OECD*
Market income poverty	Relative household market income poverty rate (%) of the working-age population	LIS, SILC, and OECD*
Disposable income poverty	Relative household disposable income poverty rate (%) of the working-age population, 50% of median	LIS, SILC, and OECD*
Poverty reduction	Reduction in relative poverty rate (%) of the working-age population, as a result of taxes and transfers	LIS, SILC, and OECD*
Skill measures		
Math mean score	Mean score on PISA's mathematical literacy component	PISA
Math 25th percentile score	25th percentile score on PISA's mathematical literacy component	PISA
Numeracy adjusted score	25th percentile and mean numeracy score adjusted for literacy-related non-responses, Study of Adult Skills	OECD PIAAC
Mean literacy score	Mean literacy score in the Study of Adult Skills adjusted for literacy-related non-responses	OECD PIAAC

continues

TABLE A.I. *(continued)*

	Definition	Original data source
Numeracy 95-5 ratio	95th to 5th percentile numeracy score adjusted for literacy-related non-responses, Study of Adult Skills	OECD PIAAC
Education premium	The percentage difference between the median wage of full-time workers with tertiary education and the median wage of individuals without tertiary education (pre-tax)	Weisstanner and Armingeon (2020)
Power resources variables		
Left government	Seats of leftist parties as proportion of the seats of all governing parties, cumulative from 1945 to date of observation	Brady et al. (2020)*
Union density	Net union membership as a percentage of employed wage and salary earners	Visser (2019)*
Wage coordination	Coordination of wage setting, coded 1 (most fragmented) to 5 (most centralized)	Visser (2019)*
Contract coverage	Employees covered by wage bargaining agreements as a percentage of all employees with the right to bargaining	Visser (2019)*
EPL	Employment protection legislation, coded 0 (least strict) to 6 (most strict)	OECD*
Minimum wage setting	Minimum wage setting, government involvement: 0 = no minimum wage, 1 = minimum wage is set by government without fixed rule, 2 = minimum wage set by government or courts, 3 = minimum wage set by negotiation with union involvement	Visser (2019)*
Works council rights	Powers of works councils: ranges from 0 to 3 with 0 indicating no works council and 3 indicating extensive right of works councils	Visser (2019)*
Voter turnout	Votes cast in the most recent election as a % of registered voters	Brady et al. (2020)*
Other political variables		
Secular center and right government	Seats of secular right and center parties as a proportion of the seats of all governing parties, cumulative from 1945 to date of observation	Brady et al. (2020)
Christian democratic government	Seats of Christian and Catholic right and center parties as proportion of the seats of all governing parties, cumulative from 1945 to date of observation	Brady et al. (2020)*
Women in parliament	Percentage of members of the lower house of national parliament who are women	Inter-Parliamentary Union*
Veto points	Additive index of presidentialism, strong bicameralism, federalism, and regular use of referenda	Brady et al. (2020)*
Proportional representation	0 = single-member district, plurality; 1 = mixed; 2 = proportional representation	Brady et al. (2020)*
Long-term economic change		
Industrial employment	Industrial employment as a percentage of total working-age population	OECD†

TABLE A.1. (*continued*)

	Definition	Original data source
Technological change	Ten-year average change in total factor productivity (calculations by the authors)	Penn World Tables†
Product market regulation	Total regulation in energy, transport, and communications on a scale from 0 (least regulation) to 6 (most regulation), simple mean of the seven sectoral indicators	OECD†
Dynamic service employment	Employment in dynamic services as a % of the working-age population	Hope and Martelli (2019)
Policies		
Parental leave benefits	Average replacement rate in parental leave for the first year	Gauthier (2011), updated by authors
Non-aged welfare state generosity	Index of generosity of sickness pay leave and unemployment benefits combining replacement rates, qualifying conditions, and duration	Scruggs and Tafoya (2022)†
Social assistance generosity	Net minimum income benefit replacement rates, average of three family types	Wang and Van Vliet (2016)
Human capital spending	Public spending on education, daycare, and active labor market policies as a % of GDP	OECD†
Public education spending	Public education spending, % GDP	WDI†
Private education spending	Private education spending as a % of total education spending	OECD†
Private tertiary education spending	Private tertiary education spending as a % of total tertiary education spending	OECD†
Top marginal tax rates	Top marginal income tax rates	Roine et al. (2009)
Government revenue	Total government revenue as a % of GDP	OECD†
Globalization		
Third world imports	Manufacturing imports from developing countries as a % of GDP	OECD†
Trade openness	Sum of exports and imports as a % of GDP	Penn World Tables†
Outward FDI	Outward direct investment flows as a % of GDP	IMF†
Immigration	International migrant stock as a % of the population	World Bank†
Capital market openness	An index of capital controls in which high values mean few or no controls on cross-border capital movement	Chinn and Ito (2006, 2021)†
Trade surplus	Trade surplus (deficit) as a % of GDP	Penn World Tables†
Financialization		
Financial sector size	Value added by the financial intermediation sector as % of GDP	EU KLEMS, OECD
Stock market capitalization	Market value of publicly listed stocks as a % of GDP	Roine et al. (2009); Beck, Demirgüç-Kunt, and Levine (2009)†
Needs/social risks		
Unemployment rate	The number of unemployed persons as a % of the civilian labor force	OECD†

continues

TABLE A.1. (*continued*)

	Definition	Original data source
% children in single-mother households	Children living in single-mother households, as a % of total children	LIS and SILC
Employment	Civilian employment as a % of total working-age population	OECD†
Other independent variables		
Economic growth	Per capita GDP growth	Penn World Tables†
Low education	% of the adult population with less than secondary school completion	Barro and Lee (2013)†
Average level of education	Average years of education of the adult population	Barro and Lee (2013)†
Mean to median ratio	Mean to median ratio of household income in the working population, own calculations with LIS and SILC data	LIS and SILC
Skew	Ratio of 90-50 wage ratio to 50-10 wage ratio	OECD†

*Available in Brady, Huber, and Stephens (2020)
†Available in Brady, Huber, and Stephens (2020)

TABLE A.2. **Market Income Inequality by Welfare State Regime and Period**

	Pre-1993	1993–1999	2000–2007	2007–2012	2013–2019
Nordic countries					
Denmark	34.2	36.4	36.3	37.4	38.9
Finland	31.2	38.8	38.7	37.6	38.7
Norway	29.8	33.8	39.0	38.2	39.1
Sweden	35.3	41.7	38.6	39.5	40.7
Mean	32.6	37.7	38.2	38.2	39.4
Western continental Europe					
Austria		39.7	39.5	41.6	41.9
Belgium	37.9	40.2	41.3	41.6	40.9
France	41.7	41.2	40.1	40.7	42.3
Germany	34.4	37.8	41.1	40.7	41.3
Netherlands	38.7	37.8	38.6	37.6	38.9
Switzerland	34.3		30.7	31.5	33.7
Mean	37.4	39.3	38.6	39.0	39.8
Southern Europe					
Greece		39.3	39.3	42.9	43.5
Italy	37.3	41.3	40.0	40.5	43.2
Portugal			44.7	44.4	44.6
Spain	38.0	43.6	37.1	42.0	44.2
Mean	37.7	41.4	40.3	42.5	43.9
Anglo-American countries					
Australia	38.1	41.6	41.0	40.6	40.9
Canada	35.2	39.6	40.5	40.5	39.7
Ireland		45.3	43.3	51.3	48.6
New Zealand	39.4	43.1	42.4	40.3	41.7
UK	35.8	43.5	43.6	44.2	41.7
USA	38.8	43.5	44.1	46.2	46.1
Mean	37.5	42.8	42.5	43.9	43.1

TABLE A.3. **Redistribution by Welfare State Regime and Period**

	Pre-1993	1993–1999	2000–2007	2007–2012	2013–2019
Nordic countries					
Denmark	34.5	42.2	38.1	36.6	34.4
Finland	33.3	40.2	32.2	29.4	30.1
Norway	24.7	29.9	32.3	32.4	30.7
Sweden	34.5	41.7	38.3	34.4	32.1
Mean	31.8	38.5	35.2	33.2	31.8
Western continental Europe					
Austria		31.4	32.5	31.7	30.9
Belgium	40.1	36.1	34.9	34.0	34.8
France	23.9	31.0	28.5	30.1	31.3
Germany	27.8	31.9	32.3	28.3	26.8
Netherlands	34.5	31.7	29.0	29.5	28.3
Switzerland	10.7		9.9	10.8	13.9
Mean	27.4	32.4	27.9	27.4	27.7
Southern Europe					
Greece		12.8	15.4	21.1	21.1
Italy	17.1	15.9	18.7	17.7	20.6
Portugal			18.3	23.3	25.0
Spain	17.3	16.0	14.7	20.7	21.4
Mean	17.2	14.9	16.8	20.7	22.0
Anglo-American countries					
Australia	25.2	26.8	26.2	21.8	23.4
Canada	18.3	24.4	19.9	19.9	19.7
Ireland		26.2	28.4	40.3	37.3
New Zealand	26.8	23.7	22.2	20.7	16.8
UK	21.2	23.8	21.8	26.2	25.5
USA	17.5	17.1	16.0	17.5	19.1
Mean	21.8	23.7	22.4	24.4	23.6

TABLE A.4. **Disposable Income Inequality by Welfare State Regime and Period**

	Pre-1993	1993–1999	2000–2007	2007–2012	2013–2019
Nordic countries					
Denmark	21.7	21.2	22.5	23.7	25.5
Finland	20.8	23.2	26.2	26.5	27.1
Norway	22.4	23.7	26.3	25.8	27.1
Sweden	23.2	24.3	23.8	25.9	27.6
Mean	22.0	23.1	24.7	25.5	26.8
Western continental Europe					
Austria		27.3	26.6	28.4	28.3
Belgium	22.7	25.6	26.9	25.9	26.1
France	31.7	27.9	28.5	29.3	27.1
Germany	24.8	25.7	27.9	29.2	30.3
Netherlands	25.2	25.8	27.4	26.5	27.9
Switzerland	30.6		27.7	28.1	29.0
Mean	27.0	26.5	27.5	27.9	28.1

continues

TABLE A.4. (*continued*)

	Pre-1993	1993–1999	2000–2007	2007–2012	2013–2019
Southern Europe					
Greece	38.9	34.6	33.2	33.8	34.3
Italy	30.9	34.7	32.7	33.3	34.3
Portugal			36.6	34.1	33.4
Spain	31.4	36.6	31.6	33.5	34.7
Mean	33.7	35.3	33.5	33.7	34.2
Anglo-American countries					
Australia	28.5	30.5	30.3	31.1	31.3
Canada	28.7	30.1	32.5	32.5	31.9
Ireland		33.4	30.9	30.6	30.5
New Zealand	28.8	32.9	33.0	31.9	34.7
UK	28.1	33.1	34.1	32.6	31.7
USA	32.0	36.1	37.1	37.5	38.0
Mean	29.2	32.7	33.0	32.7	33.0

TABLE A.5. **Market Income Poverty by Welfare State Regime and Period**

	Pre-1993	1993–1999	2000–2007	2007–2012	2013–2019
Nordic countries					
Denmark	16.0	17.3	16.8	18.3	18.3
Finland	11.0	18.9	16.5	16.8	16.7
Norway	10.0	15.0	17.8	19.0	19.2
Sweden	16.9	24.8	18.2	19.9	20.1
Mean	13.5	19.0	17.3	18.5	18.6
Western continental Europe					
Austria		18.2	18.0	19.6	19.0
Belgium	18.3	21.4	19.4	19.9	20.3
France	18.2	23.9	23.7	25.8	25.7
Germany	12.0	15.2	17.9	17.2	17.4
Netherlands	15.0	16.2	15.4	14.5	16.0
Switzerland	9.0		5.7	6.0	8.3
Mean	14.5	19.0	16.7	17.2	17.8
Southern Europe					
Greece		20.8	16.5	19.0	20.0
Italy	16.4	23.4	19.6	18.4	20.3
Portugal			20.1	17.8	17.9
Spain	19.7	24.0	16.6	22.5	24.7
Mean	18.1	22.7	18.2	19.4	20.7
Anglo-American countries					
Australia	14.9	18.8	19.1	16.5	16.1
Canada	14.9	18.5	17.3	18.0	17.8
Ireland		26.5	22.8	33.1	27.4
New Zealand	17.2	18.7	18.5	15.7	15.2
UK	13.7	19.9	18.7	21.3	19.7
USA	15.1	16.5	16.9	20.9	19.3
Mean	15.2	19.8	18.9	20.9	19.3

TABLE A.6. **Poverty Reduction by Welfare State Regime and Period**

	Pre-1993	1993–1999	2000–2007	2007–2012	2013–2019
Nordic countries					
Denmark	62.3	73.0	65.4	61.5	57.5
Finland	52.6	72.8	64.7	63.1	64.4
Norway	46.0	56.4	63.1	66.5	59.6
Sweden	49.4	62.5	68.5	58.2	54.7
Mean	52.6	66.2	65.4	62.3	59.1
Western continental Europe					
Austria		59.5	58.6	54.9	51.6
Belgium	78.2	66.5	61.9	55.7	55.1
France	49.3	65.2	65.5	72.1	74.0
Germany	53.7	58.3	56.1	48.9	42.2
Netherlands	71.5	59.4	63.3	63.3	51.6
Switzerland	9.1		−4.1	−1.7	16.2
Mean	52.4	61.8	50.2	48.9	48.5
Southern Europe					
Greece		40.4	29.9	22.0	18.2
Italy	44.1	43.2	41.0	31.1	25.8
Portugal			43.4	32.9	30.2
Spain	49.8	41.5	27.0	26.6	32.5
Mean	47.0	41.7	35.3	28.2	26.7
Anglo-American countries					
Australia	40.2	50.4	45.7	38.7	42.7
Canada	11.3	12.1	19.9	19.9	19.7
Ireland		61.3	52.0	72.2	66.8
New Zealand	63.0	59.4	45.3	43.1	36.2
UK	49.0	54.9	52.0	60.1	55.5
USA	16.3	18.4	16.7	29.1	22.7
Mean	36.0	42.8	38.6	43.9	40.6

TABLE A.7. **Disposable Income Poverty by Welfare State Regime and Period**

	Pre-1993	1993–1999	2000–2007	2007–2012	2013–2019
Nordic countries					
Denmark	6.1	4.7	5.8	7.0	7.7
Finland	5.1	5.1	5.8	6.2	5.9
Norway	5.3	6.5	6.5	6.4	7.8
Sweden	8.6	9.3	5.7	8.3	9.1
Mean	6.3	6.4	6.0	7.0	7.6
Western continental Europe					
Austria		7.4	7.4	8.9	9.2
Belgium	3.9	7.1	7.4	8.8	9.1
France	9.2	8.2	8.0	7.1	6.7
Germany	5.6	6.3	7.8	8.8	10.0
Netherlands	4.3	6.6	5.6	5.3	7.7
Switzerland	8.2		5.9	6.1	6.9
Mean	6.2	7.1	7.0	7.5	8.3

continues

TABLE A.7. *(continued)*

	Pre-1993	1993–1999	2000–2007	2007–2012	2013–2019
Southern Europe					
Greece		12.4	11.2	14.8	16.2
Italy	9.1	13.3	11.3	12.7	15.0
Portugal			10.8	11.9	12.5
Spain	9.8	14.0	12.0	14.0	16.6
Mean	9.5	13.2	11.3	13.4	15.1
Anglo-American countries					
Australia	8.9	9.3	10.4	10.1	9.4
Canada	11.3	12.1	19.9	19.9	19.7
Ireland		10.3	10.7	9.2	9.1
New Zealand	6.4	7.6	10.1	8.9	9.7
UK	6.8	8.9	8.9	8.5	8.7
USA	12.6	13.5	14.1	14.7	14.9
Mean	9.2	10.3	12.4	11.9	11.9

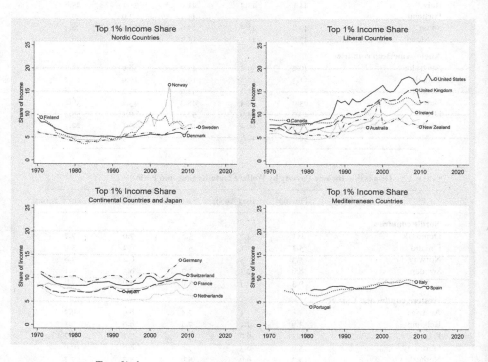

FIGURE A.1. Top 1% shares

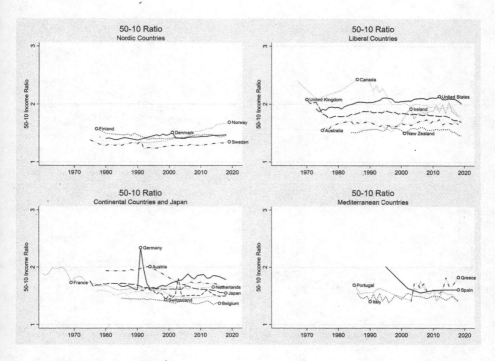

FIGURE A.2. 50-10 wage ratios

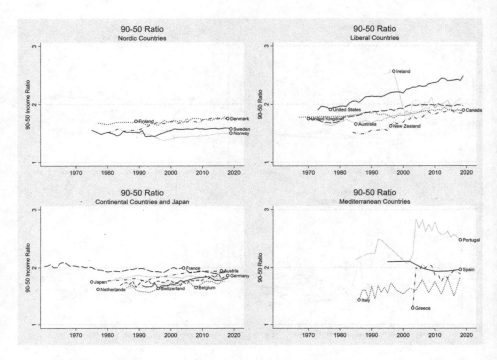

FIGURE A.3. 90-50 wage ratios

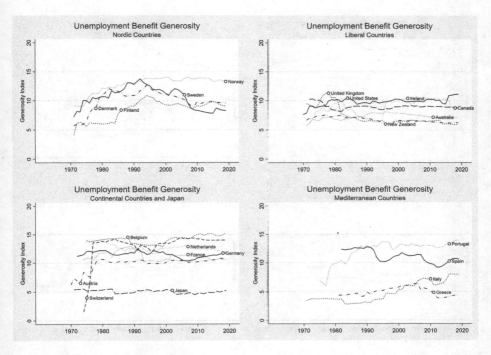

FIGURE A.4. Unemployment benefit generosity

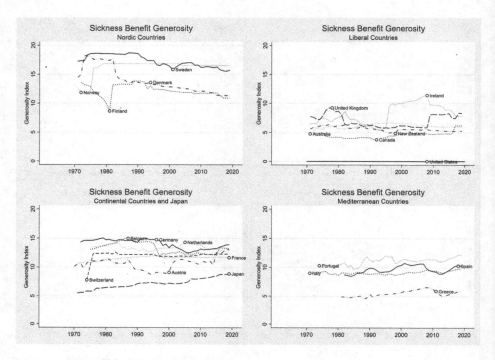

FIGURE A.5. Sickness benefit generosity

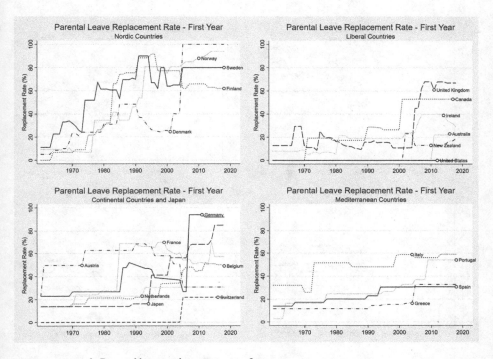

FIGURE A.6. Parental leave replacement rate—first year

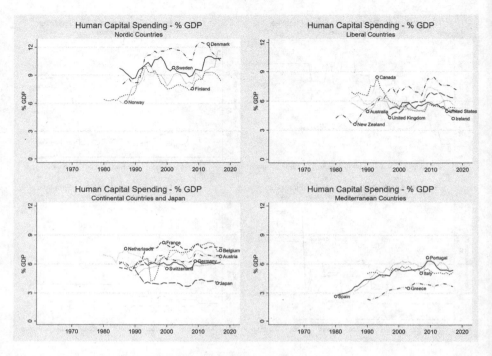

FIGURE A.7. Human capital spending—% GDP

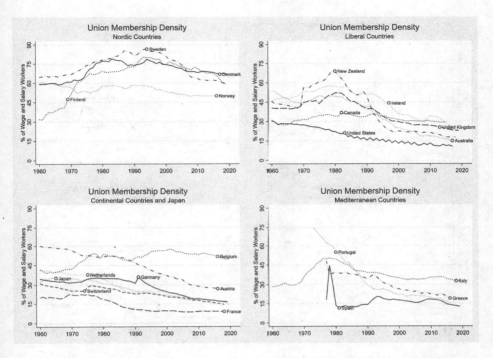

FIGURE A.8. Union density

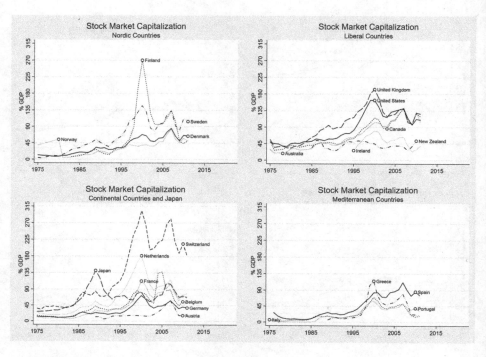

FIGURE A.9. Stock market capitalization — % GDP

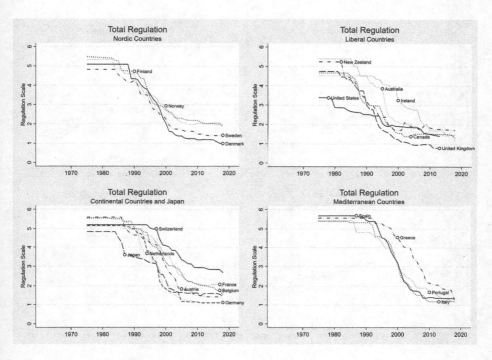

FIGURE A.10. Regulation

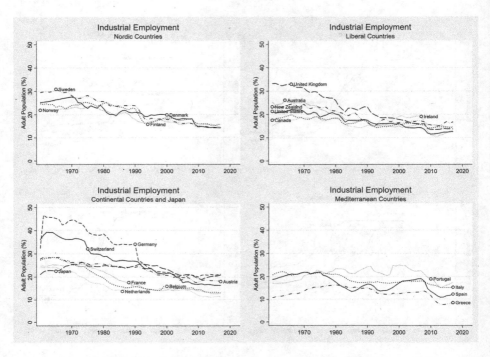

FIGURE A.11. Industrial employment

APPENDIX B
Figures and Tables, Case Studies

TABLE B.1. **Wage Dispersion**

	90-50 ratio				50-10 ratio			
	Germany	Spain*	Sweden	US	Germany	Spain	Sweden	US
1980			1.5	2.0			1.3	1.9
1985	1.7		1.5	2.1	1.7		1.3	2.0
1990	1.7		1.5	2.1	1.6		1.3	2.0
1995	1.7	2.1	1.6	2.2	1.7	2.0	1.4	2.1
2000	1.8	2.1	1.7	2.2	1.7	1.6	1.4	2.0
2005	1.7	2.0	1.6	2.3	1.8	1.6	1.4	2.1
2010	1.8	1.9	1.6	2.4	1.9	1.6	1.4	2.1
2015	1.9	1.9	1.6	2.4	1.8	1.6	1.3	2.1
2018	1.9	2.0	1.6	2.4	1.8	1.6	1.3	2.1

*closest year

TABLE B.2. **Top 1% Income Shares (% of Market Income)**

	Top 1%				Top 1% including capital gains			
	Germany	Spain	Sweden	US	Germany	Spain	Sweden	US
1980	10.6		4.1	10.0	10.7		4.1	10.0
1983	9.8	7.7	4.1	11.6	9.9	7.8	4.5	11.6
1986	10.2	8.2	4.1	15.9	10.5	8.9	4.5	15.9
1989	10.52	8.5	4.5	12.6	11.4	9.0	5.5	14.5
1992	10.43	8.2	5.0	13.5	10.6	8.4	5.8	14.7
1995	8.8	7.9	5.3	13.5	9.2	8.3	6.0	15.2
1998	10.9	8.1	5.9	15.3	11.9	8.8	8.2	19.1
2001	11.1	8.6	6.0	15.4	11.4	9.6	8.6	18.2
2004	10.6	8.7	5.7	16.3	11.1	10.2	7.9	19.8
2007	12.9	9.0	6.9	18.3	14.0	11.2	10.0	23.5
2010		8.1	6.9	17.5	13.1	8.7	9.0	20.0

TABLE B.3. **Top 10% Income Shares (% of Market Income)**

	Top 10%				Top 10% including capital gains			
	Germany	Spain	Sweden	US	Germany	Spain	Sweden	US
1980	31.7		22.7	32.9	31.9		22.8	34.6
1983	30.7	33.3	22.4	33.7	31.4	33.4	22.7	36.4
1986	31.4	34.7	22.4	34.6	32.1	35.2	22.8	40.6
1989	32.7	35.7	22.6	38.5	33.5	36.1	23.6	40.1
1992	32.2	33.9	24.3	39.8	33.5	34.2	25.3	40.8
1995	31.4	33.4	24.9	40.5	31.8	33.8	25.8	42.1
1998	34.7	33.0	25.9	42.1	35.5	33.9	28.3	45.4
2001	35.9	33.4	26.8	42.2	36.2	34.2	28.9	44.8
2004	33.5	33.2	26.3	43.6	36.0	34.6	26.3	46.4
2007	38.6	33.3	27.8	45.7	39.6	35.3	31.7	49.7
2010		32.1	28.3	46.4	39.8	32.6	31.0	48.0

TABLE B.4. **Disposable Income Gini (Working-Age Population)**

	Without capital gains	Including capital gains	N
Canada	32.5	32.9	11
Denmark	23.9	24.3	6
Finland	24.6	25.7	9
France	27.8	28.0	2
Japan	30.8	31.1	3
Norway	26.2	27.0	6
Sweden	24.5	30.7	3
United States	36.0	37.2	21

TABLE B.5. **Low Wage/Low Pay Share**

	Germany	Spain	US
1980			22.0
1985			23.7
1990			23.0
1995	13.6		25.2
2000	15.8		24.7
2005	17.5		24.0
2010	18.9	14.2	25.3
2015	19.4		25.0

TABLE B.6. **Industrial Employment**
(% of Working-Age Population)

	Germany	Spain	Sweden	US
1980	38.5	17.6	25.6	20.2
1985	33.9	13.6	23.8	17.5
1990	34.1	16.8	23.8	17.5
1995	23.4	13.9	18.4	16.1
2000	22.0	17.3	17.9	16.1
2005	19.7	18.7	16.2	14.2
2010	20.0	13.6	14.7	11.5
2015	20.7	11.6	14.2	12.3
2018	21.3	12.8	14.5	12.9

TABLE B.7. **Employment (% of Working-Age Population)**

	Germany	Spain	Sweden	US
1980	65.0	49.9	79.4	66.1
1985	60.6	43.8	79.7	67.8
1990	65.1	49.8	81.5	72.3
1995	64.5	46.0	70.9	71.7
2000	65.4	55.7	72.9	73.3
2005	66.0	63.8	73.5	71.5
2010	70.5	59.1	74.1	67.0
2015	74.9	58.1	78.4	70.2
2018	77.8	62.8	80.3	72.8

TABLE B.8. **Unemployment**

	Germany	Spain	Sweden	US
1980	3.2	10.5	2.0	7.1
1985	7.2	19.7	2.9	7.2
1990	4.7	15.5	1.7	5.6
1995	8.3	20.8	8.8	5.6
2000	8.0	11.9	5.6	4.0
2005	11.3	9.2	7.6	5.1
2010	7.0	19.9	8.6	9.6
2015	4.6	22.1	7.4	5.3
2020	3.8	15.5	8.3	8.1

TABLE B.9. **Female Employment**

	Germany	Spain	Sweden	US
1980	48.7	28.1	72.4	55.1
1985	46,6	25.4	75.9	59.1
1990	56.0	31.4	79.4	64.8
1995	55.2	31.2	69.6	65.7
2000	58.2	40.5	71.0	67.9
2005	60.3	51.3	71.0	66.1
2010	65.9	52.2	70.9	63.0
2015	70.7	53.4	76.0	66.0
2018	73.7	57.3	78.3	68.2

TABLE B.10. **Part-Time Employment**

	Germany	Spain	Sweden
1985	11.0		
1990	13.4	4.6	14.5
1995	14.2	7.0	15.1
2000	17.6	7.5	14.0
2005	21.5	10.8	13.5
2010	21.8	12.2	14.5
2015	22.4	14.5	14.1
2017	22.2	13.8	13.8

TABLE B.11. **Temporary Employment**

	Germany	Spain	Sweden	US
1985	10.0			
1990	10.5	29.8		
1995	10.4	35.0		5.1
2000	12.7	32.2	15.2	
2005	14.2	33.4	15.8	4.2
2010	14.5	24.7	16.4	
2015	13.1	25.1	17.2	
2017	12.9	26.7	16.9	

TABLE B.12. **Employment in Dynamic Knowledge-Intensive Sectors**

	Germany	Spain	Sweden	US
1980	7.0	2.6	5.9	8.5
1985	7.2	2.8	6.5	10.1
1990	8.9	4.1	8.3	12.0
1995	8.1	4.4	7.9	12.5
2000	9.8	5.7	10.2	14.1
2005	10.9	6.7	10.7	13.6
2007	12.0	7.3	11.3	13.9

Source: Hope and Martelli (2019).

TABLE B.13. **Employment Protection Legislation**

	Germany Temporary EPL	Germany Permanent EPL	Spain Temporary EPL	Spain Permanent EPL	Sweden Temporary EPL	Sweden Permanent EPL	US Temporary EPL	US Permanent EPL
1985	5.0	5.0	3.8	3.5	4.1	2.6	0.3	0.1
1990	3.3	2.5	3.8	3.5	4.1	2.6	0.3	0.3
1995	3.1	2.6	3.3	2.4	1.8	2.6	0.3	0.1
2000	2.0	2.6	3.3	2.4	1.4	2.5	0.3	0.1
2005	1.0	2.6	3.3	2.4	1.4	2.4	0.3	0.1
2010	1.0	2.6	3.0	2.4	0.8	2.4	0.3	0.1
2015	1.1	2.6	2.5	2.0	0.8	2.4	0.3	0.1
2019	1.4	2.6	2.5	2.0	0.8	2.4	0.3	0.1

TABLE B.14. **Regulation**

	Germany	Spain	Sweden	US
1980	5.2	5.7	4.8	2.9
1985	5.2	5.7	4.5	2.7
1990	5.0	5.5	4.3	2.5
1995	3.8	4.5	3.1	2.1
2000	1.9	3.2	2.3	1.9
2005	1.2	1.8	1.7	1.9
2010	1.1	1.4	1.5	1.6*
2015	1.1	1.4	1.4	1.4^
2018	1.1	1.4	1.4	

* 2008; ^ 2013

TABLE B.15. **Stock Market Capitalization**

	Germany	Spain	Sweden	US
1975–1982	11.0	12.7	9.2	43.7
2000–2007	51.4	85.8	111.5	136.8

TABLE B.16. **Immigrant Stock (% of Adult Population)**

	Germany	Spain	Sweden	US
1980		1.6	7.5	7.2
1985		1.9	7.8	8.2
1990	7.5	2.1	9.2	9.2
1995	9.1	2.6	10.6	10.7
2000	11.0	4.1	11.3	12.3
2005	12.7	9.4	12.5	13.3
2010	14.4	13.5	14.8	14.3
2015	14.9	12.7	16.8	14.5

TABLE B.17. **Union Density**

	Germany	Spain	Sweden	US
1980	34.9	13.3	78.0	22.1
1985	34.7	12.4	81.3	17.4
1990	31.2	13.7	80.0	15.5
1995	29.2	18.2	83.1	14.3
2000	24.6	17.4	81.0	12.9
2005	21.5	15.9	74.2	12.0
2010	18.9	18.3	63.5	11.4
2015	17.6	15.2	61.7	10.7
2019	16.6	12.5	59.6	10.7

TABLE B.18. **Contract Coverage**

	Germany	Spain	Sweden	US
1980	85	76.0	85	25.7
1985	85	86.0	85	20.5
1990	85	87.0		18.3
1995	80.8	93.0	94	16.7
2000	67.8	92.0	94	14.9
2005	64.9	85.1	94	13.7
2010	59.8	87.2	91	13.1
2015	56.8	86.7	90	11.5
2018	54.0	80.1	88	11.2

TABLE B.19. **Wage Coordination**

	Germany	Spain	Sweden	US
1980	4	4	5	2
1985	4	4	4	1
1990	4	2	3	1
1995	4	2	3	1
2000	4	2	4	1
2005	4	3	4	1
2010	4	3	4	1
2015	4	3	4	1
2019	4	3	4	1

TABLE B.20. **PIAAC Scores**

	Returns to skills[1]	PIAAC adjusted numeracy score 5th percentile	Median
Germany	.235	168	275
Spain	.228	144	250
Sweden	.121	182	284
United States	.279	99	253

[1]Hanushek et al. (2015).

TABLE B.21. **Returns to Tertiary Education**

	Returns to tertiary education*	Private % of total education spending, 2010 Tertiary	All levels
Germany	.414	18	16
Spain	.550	22	16
Sweden	.180	10	3
United States	.620	58	32

*Weisstanner and Armingeon (2020)

TABLE B.22. **Secondary Education Completion**

	Germany	Spain	Sweden	US
1980	17.0	12.8	48.9	77.1
1985	19.8	14.5	53.3	78.5
1990	35.9	16.3	58.8	80.0
1995	48.0	23.1	63.6	82.2
2000	58.5	32.5	70.2	84.1
2005	74.1	41.5	78.1	89.1
2010	81.1	44.3	76.3	93.2

TABLE B.23. **Tertiary Education Completion**

	Germany	Spain	Sweden	US
1980	4.5	4.6	9.4	18.1
1985	5.0	5.1	10.6	22.4
1990	8.5	5.5	12.3	25.1
1995	10.7	8.0	14.0	24.7
2000	12.9	12.4	15.1	26.7
2005	13.5	15.5	17.8	27.9
2010	16.1	17.0	18.6	30.9

TABLE B.24. **Unemployment Insurance Generosity and Duration**

	Generosity index				Duration (weeks)			
	Germany	Spain	Sweden	US	Germany	Spain	Sweden	US
1980	12		10.2	10.4	52	52	60	26
1985	11.3	9.8	10.9	10.5	52	52	60	26
1990	11.7	11.2	12.4	10.0	52	104	60	26
1995	11.4	9.7	12.3	9.9	52	104	60	26
2000	11.3	10.8	11.5	10.6	52	104	60	26
2005	10.5	11.2	11.4	9.9	52	104	60	26
2010	10.8	9.8	8.3	10.2	52	104	60	99
2015	11.4	9.9	7.8	9.5	52	104	60	20
2019	10.7	10.6	8.3	11.1	52	104	60	20

TABLE B.25. **Sickness Pay Generosity**

	Germany	Spain	Sweden	US*
1980	14.8		18.1	0
1985	14.9	7.3	18.0	0
1990	14.4	8.7	18.2	0
1995	14.9	8.3	17.2	0
2000	14.5	9.4	16.4	0
2005	12.7	10.5	17.0	0
2010	13.2	9.3	16.2	0
2015	13.2	9.5	16.3	0
2019	13.9	10.3	15.7	0

* No national legislation.

TABLE B.26. **Parental Leave Benefits**

	Germany	Spain	Sweden	US
1980	26.9	20.2	61.5	0.0
1985	26.9	20.2	53.3	0.0
1990	49.9	23.1	70.0	0.0
1995	45.9	30.8	67.0	0.0
2000	38.0	30.8	64.0	0.0
2005	27.0	31.0	80.0	0.0
2010	94.0	31.0	80.0	0.0
2015	92.0	31.0	80.0	0.0
2017	92.0	31.0	80.0	0.0

TABLE B.27. **Human Capital Spending (% GDP)**

	Germany	Spain	Sweden	US
1985		3.3	9.7	
1990		4.4	8.7	
1995	6.1	4.9	9.9	
2000	5.9	5.5	9.7	5.2
2005	5.9	5.4	9.2	5.2
2010	6.3	6.3	9.5	5.8
2015	6.0	5.4	10.8	5.0
2017	6.2	5.4	10.8	5.1

TABLE B.28. **Social Assistance Adequacy**

	Germany	Spain	Sweden	US
1990	37	51	61	35
1995	38	40	59	32
2000	34	34	44	27
2005	38	35	43	25
2009	37	34	39	23

APPENDIX C
Operationalization of Variables

The variables included in the quantitative analyses in chapters 2–7 are listed in table A.1.

Dependent Variables

Measures of Inequality

Our main source for data on household income inequality, poverty, and redistribution is merged LIS, SILC, and OECD data described below. There are at least two alternative income inequality datasets that contain pooled time-series data for the countries covered in this book, both derived from the Paris School of Economics (PSE) top incomes/income distribution project (Blanchet et al. 2021). There are some differences between Blanchet et al. (2021) and Blanchet, Chancel, and Gethin (2022), but in both cases the researchers make decisions about the classification of social transfers and public provision of welfare state services that make it impossible to actually test the impact of the welfare state on redistribution and thus on disposable income inequality—two of the primary concerns of chapters 3 and 5.

The PSE group developed the original top incomes dataset from tax records, which was arguably an improvement on survey data for the study of top incomes, because surveys underestimate top incomes. In moving to develop overall income distribution data (e.g., Gini index), they added survey evidence for information on incomes below top incomes and made the income distribution figures compatible with national accounts. Following the lead of Blanchet et al. (2021), Blanchet, Chancel, and Gethin (2022) included pensions, unemployment insurance, and disability insurance as market income. The logic appears to be that they view these as deferred wages. This logic would also apply to all contributory social insurance constructed in accordance with Bismarckian principles (Palier 2010) and thus, by fiat, make most transfers in western and northern Europe, as well as US Social Security and unemployment insurance, not redistributive by definition. This clearly flies in the face of the evidence. In the case of in-kind public services other than health (mainly education), the researchers assume that it is distributed according to disposable income, and thus also not redistributive. They distribute health care expenditure as a lump sum to all income units, which is consistent with the assumption that the government is delivering insurance to the population, rather than actual health care to recipients of the services. This is consistent with the practice of other welfare state researchers and is reasonable, except in the US where the inefficiency of the system significantly increases the measured redistribution.

Our approach is to analyze household income, top incomes, and wage dispersion separately. We stick to a traditional definition of the welfare state as all publicly provided transfers and services; therefore we do not count these transfers and services as part of market income. We analyze welfare state redistribution with the survey-based household income data from LIS (Luxembourg Income Study), EU-SILC (European Union Statistics on Income and Living Conditions), and OECD (Organisation for Economic Co-operation and Development). We deal with the distributive effect of indirect taxes and public social services by citing comparative research that analyzes these topics in depth.

Our wage dispersion variables are OECD data on the ratio of earnings of a full-time employee at the 90th percentile to those of a full-time employee at the median, and the ratio of the earnings of a full-time employee at the median to those of a full-time employee at the 10th percentile.

Our top income shares variable is the share of total national income going to the top 1 percent of income units—individuals or households, depending on the tax laws of the country and period. The data come from the World Inequality Database (Alvaredo et al. 2015). They are derived from tax returns and capture pre-tax and transfer income. For reasons explained above, we use these data rather than the combined data that replaced them on the Paris School of Economics income distribution website.

Market household income is defined as all income from labor (wages and salaries as well as self-employment income), capital (financial interest and dividends and real estate income), and private transfers (inter-household transfers and transfers from nonprofit institutions). Although the LIS harmonization process is very thorough, they ultimately rely on microdata collected by countries in sometimes different manners. In some country years, market income is pre-transfer but post-tax (40 observations out of a total of 291), and in others some taxes may be included but others not (12 observations). In order to adjust for this, we examined neighboring observations for the same country and then harmonized the post-tax and mixed tax data to match the pre-tax and transfer observations.

Disposable household income includes market income plus all public transfers and less all direct taxes. Following LIS convention, market income is bottom-coded at zero while disposable income is top- and bottom-coded via the interquartile range as $Q_3 \times (Q_3/Q_1)^3$ and $Q_1/(Q_3/Q_1)^3$, respectively. In the case of both market and disposable income, the standard International Labor Organization (ILO) recommended equivalency scale is used for both LIS and SILC data, in which a household's income is divided by the square root of the number of household members (*Household Income / √# Household Members*).

These variables are calculated using a combination of data from LIS and SILC. Both the LIS and the SILC database include detailed, individual- and household-level data on income, labor market, and demographic characteristics. We used these microdata to create country-year-level variables, and harmonized the two series. We include working-age (18–64) people, with or without children, nested inside households. We drop all households with elderly members, as this would exaggerate market income inequality and redistribution in countries with generous public pension systems.

Finally, we combined the LIS/SILC series with OECD data on disposable and market income inequality. This is helpful because the series without the OECD data is heavily skewed toward years post-2003. The correlation for market income inequality between LIS/SILC and the OECD is .90; for disposable income inequality it is .96. Although the correlation for market income inequality is lower than we would have liked, we have determined that the temporal imbalance caused by omitting the OECD data is more problematic than the lower-than-desired correlation. Because the OECD microdata are not in the public domain (unlike the LIS and SILC data), we were unable to recalculate the inequality figures to achieve a higher correlation with the combined LIS and SILC data. Our procedure for combining the series was to use LIS when it was available, then to add SILC data for the missing LIS data points, and finally to add OECD data when LIS and SILC were not available. We only use OECD data when the others are unavailable because, as noted, we do not have microdata from this source. In order to adjust for any discrepancies between the data sources, we examined neighboring observations for the same country and then harmonized the OECD data (and sometimes the SILC data) to match the LIS data. The combined series has 484 observations for market and disposable income inequality and inequality reduction: 291 from LIS, 111 from SILC, and 82 from the OECD.[1]

Our measure of redistribution is calculated as the Gini of market income inequality minus the Gini of disposable household income inequality divided by the Gini of market income inequality.

Our main poverty variables are market income poverty rates of individual working-age people (ages 18–64), with or without children, nested inside households; and poverty reduction effected by direct taxes and transfers among these households. As in our analysis of inequality, we drop all households with elderly members, as this would exaggerate market poverty rates in countries with generous pension systems. We first create a relative poverty line of 50 percent of median (disposable) household income; then we drop all households with elderly members; then we calculate the percentage of households whose income falls below this threshold, weighted by the number of working-age household members. This provides the percentage of the working-age population whose household income falls below the relative (disposable household income) poverty line.

We use the standard International Labor Organization (ILO) recommended equivalency scale, in which a household's income is divided by the square root of the number of household members. As just noted, we define the working-age market income poverty rate as the percentage of working-age people whose household market incomes fall below 50 percent of the median disposable household income. We use a relative poverty rate centered around disposable household income so that we may study poverty reduction using the same poverty line. Our measure of poverty reduction is calculated as the (working-age) market income poverty rate minus the (working-age) disposable household income poverty rate, divided by the market income poverty rate. We are again using a combination of LIS, SILC, and OECD data.

Skill Measures

Our measure of skills inequality is the numeric test scores on the OECD's Programme for the International Assessment of Adult Competencies (PIAAC)

Survey of Adult Skills, which is an updated version (circa 2010) of the International Adult Literacy Survey (IALS) data Nickell (2004) used (OECD 2013). Like the IALS, the PIAAC researchers administered a Scholastic Aptitude Test (SAT)-like test covering quantitative, literacy, and document-handling skills to a representative sample of the adult population in a large number of OECD member countries. Following Nickell, we measure skill dispersion as the ratio of test scores of adults at the 95th percentile to those of adults at the 5th percentile on the numeracy scale. We also use the numeracy scores at the mean and at the 25th percentile and the literacy scores at the mean.

We measure the distribution of skills among students with results from the Programme for International Student Assessment (PISA), which is run by the Organisation for Economic Co-operation and Development (OECD). The PISA tests are given triennially to fifteen-year-olds across the OECD as well as in several partner countries to evaluate reading, mathematical, and scientific literacy. The scores are then standardized to have an OECD average of 500 with about two-thirds of scores between 400 and 600. We use only the country mean score and 5th percentile score in mathematical literacy for our pooled-cross-sectional analysis, which gives us a measure for the central tendency of skill distribution and a measure of performance for low academic achievers. We use mathematical skills because, as Hanushek et al. (2015) note with regard to PIAAC, they are generally more comparable cross-nationally than literacy skills.

Independent Variables

Power Resources Variables

We measure left incumbency with the share of parliamentary seats of left parties (that is, social democratic, left socialist, communist, and green parties) as a proportion of the seats of all governing parties. We use a cumulative measure from 1946 to the year of observation, as the effects on policies of party control of government build up over the long term (Huber and Stephens 2001). Voter turnout is the percentage of the registered voters who voted.

Wage coordination, union density, contract coverage, union participation in minimum wage setting, and works council rights variables come from Visser's (2019) Database on Institutional Characteristics of Trade Unions, Wage Setting, State Intervention and Social Pacts (ICTWSS). Union density is measured as net union membership as a percentage of wage and salary earners. Wage coordination is measured on a five-point scale with high values indicating high levels of coordination. Contract coverage is the percentage of employees covered by wage-bargaining agreements as a percentage of all employees with the right to bargaining. Union participation in minimum wage setting is measured on a four-point scale that ranges from no minimum wage to minimum wage setting with union involvement. We measure the power of works councils on a four-point scale that ranges from nonexistence of works councils to extensive codetermination rights. Employment protection legislation is measured by an index of overall strictness, ranging from 0 (least strict) to 6 (most strict). This variable is the unweighted average of the sub-indicators of employment protection legislation for regular contracts and temporary contracts.

Other Political Variables

Our additional political variables are Christian democratic government, center-right government, women in parliament, veto points, proportional representation, and voter turnout. Christian democratic government is measured in the same way as left government, as the cumulative proportion of seats held by Christian democratic parties relative to the number of seats held by all governing parties. Similarly, our measure is the cumulative share of parliamentary seats of secular center and right parties as a proportion of the seats of all governing parties. Female percentage of legislative seats is the percentage of seats in the lower house of parliament held by women. Veto points are measured using an additive index (coded 0–6) of presidentialism, strong/weak bicameralism, strong/weak federalism, and regular use of referenda. Proportional representation is coded 0 for single-member district plurality elections, 1 for mixed, and 2 for proportional representation. Voter turnout is the percentage of registered voters who voted.

Long-Term Economic Change

Our variables measuring long-term change in the economy are industrial employment, the ten-year average of total factor productivity change, the OECD regulation measure, employment in dynamic services, and unemployment. Industrial employment is measured as total employees in industry as a percentage of the working-age population. Total factor productivity is measured as the average change of the past nine years plus the year of observation, based on the Penn World Tables. The OECD regulation measure is an index ranging from 0 (least regulation) to 6 (most regulation), calculated as the simple mean of sectoral indicators of regulation in electricity, gas, air transport, rail transport, postal services, and telecommunications. The regulations are coded from the point of view of hindering competition; they include public ownership, barriers to entry, vertical integration, price controls, and market structure (Conway and Nicoletti 2006). Employment in dynamic services as a percentage of the working-age population comes from Hope and Martelli (2019) and includes employment in the three sectors with the highest contribution of value-added growth of ICT capital services. These sectors are post and telecommunications, financial intermediation, and "renting of machinery and equipment and other business activities," which is dominated by business services like legal, technical computer, and advertising. Unemployment is measured as the number of unemployed people as a percentage of the civilian labor force.

Policies

Our welfare state policy variables are social insurance generosity, social assistance, and parental leave benefits. Social insurance generosity is operationalized by an index of sickness and unemployment benefits taken from Scruggs and Tafoya's (2022) Comparative Welfare Entitlements Project (CWEP). The index combines measures of replacement rates for the first six months of benefits, qualifying conditions, and duration; higher values indicate greater generosity. The measure of social assistance generosity combines net basic social assistance, child supplements, refundable tax credits, and other benefits except for housing. It is calculated as a replacement rate of the net average production wage (Wang and van Vliet 2016a).

Parental leave benefits come from Gauthier's (2011) Comparative Family Policy Database and our own coding from country sources and are operationalized as the average replacement rate of parental leave benefits in the first year. For example, if a state provides 100 percent replacement for six months followed by no replacement, the average replacement rate over the year would be 50 percent; similarly, if a state provides 50 percent replacement over the course of the entire year, the average replacement rate over the year would be 50 percent. The measure is taken for the first year alone to discern between long-term, low-replacement leave benefits and short-term, high-replacement leaves; otherwise, a replacement rate of 33 percent over three years would look identical to a leave of 100 percent over one year. This is an important distinction, as there is evidence that long-term, low-replacement leaves can hinder women's reintegration into the labor force and lifetime earnings projections (Morgan and Zippel 2003; Mandel and Semyonov 2005).

Human capital spending includes public spending on education, daycare, and active labor market policies as a percentage of GDP. Private education spending is the share of total education spending that is private, taken from the OECD Education Statistics online database. The OECD series for private education spending begins in 1995, so there are only about 250 observations in our models with private share of education spending and private share of tertiary education spending. Government revenue is measured by total government revenue as a percentage of GDP.

Top marginal tax rates are the actual marginal tax rates of taxpayers with incomes five times the per capita income, approximately the top 1 percent of income earners (Roine, Vlachos, and Waldenström 2009, 979–80). Data from Roine, Vlachos, and Waldenström (2009) were supplemented with data from the OECD Tax Database (Section B1: Personal Income Tax) and the 2014 Economic Freedom Dataset (Gwartney, Lawson, and Hall 2014). Piketty, Saez, and Stantcheva (2014) use statutory tax rates. The correlation between the statutory and effective tax rates is .62, since statutory tax rates "have been binding to quite varying degrees" (Roine, Vlachos, and Waldenström 2009, 979). Conceptually, actual tax rates are more appropriate, but we get very similar results with statutory rates.

Globalization

Our globalization variables are capital market openness, outward direct foreign investment as a percentage of GDP, trade openness, third world imports, immigration, and trade surplus. The measure of capital market openness comes from Chinn and Ito (2006 and 2021) and is an index with low values indicating a lot of controls on cross-border capital movement and high values indicating few or no controls. It is available for 181 countries. For our countries, the index, which by design has a worldwide mean of 0, varies from a low of −1.98 to a high of 2.82 with a mean of 1.49. In other words, the mean of our countries is much higher than the worldwide mean, which indicates that they have much more liberalized capital markets than most of the rest of the world. Outward direct foreign investment comes from the IMF and measures outward direct investment flows as a percentage of GDP. Trade openness comes from the Penn World Tables and is measured as imports plus exports as a percentage of GDP. Third world imports are manufacturing imports from developing countries (as defined by the OECD) as a percentage of GDP. Immigration measures the international migrant stock as a percentage of the population and comes from the World Bank. Trade surplus is calculated as exports minus imports, as a percentage of GDP, from the Penn World Tables.

Financialization

Our two measures of financialization are stock market capitalization and size of the financial sector. Stock market capitalization is measured as the market value of publicly listed stocks as a percentage of GDP. Data from Roine, Vlachos, and Waldenström (2009) were supplemented with data for recent time points from Beck, Demirgüç-Kunt and Levine (2009) and Čihák et al. (2012). Roine, Vlachos, and Waldenström (2009) interpolate the data for 1961–1969 and 1971–1974.

For financial sector size, we took value added from the line "financial intermediation" in the national accounts provided in the EU KLEMS database. For country years not in EU KLEMS, we took data from the OECD STAN database. We divided value added through financial intermediation by GDP taken from the OECD, both in national currency units. There are no data for France and New Zealand.

Social Risks (Needs)

Our measures for social risks are the unemployment rate, the employment rate, and the percentage of children living in single-mother households. Unemployment rates come from the OECD and express the number of unemployed people as a percentage of the civilian labor force. The percentage of children in single-mother households is calculated from a combination of LIS and SILC data, and expresses the number of children living in single-mother households as a percentage of total children. Values for the years with only OECD inequality data were estimated by interpolation. Civilian employment is calculated as the percentage of the total working-age population (15–64) in employment (including the self-employed).

Other Independent Variables

We measure the average level of education as the average years of education attained in the population aged twenty-five and over. The data come from *Barro-Lee Educational Attainment Dataset 1950–2010* (Harvard University, http://www.barrolee.com/). The same data are used to measure the proportion of the population with low education, defined as the proportion of the adult population with less than secondary education. Economic growth is measured by growth of GDP per capita, calculated from the Penn World Tables.

To test the Meltzer-Richard theory of redistribution, we calculated the mean and the median of pre-tax and transfer household income and then divided the mean by the median with the LIS and SILC microdata. We calculated the Lupu-Pontusson skew measure by dividing the 90-50 wage ratio by the 50-10 wage ratio using the OECD wage dispersion data.

APPENDIX D
Statistical Estimations

Pooled time-series data present special challenges for the statistical analyst. Methodologists (e.g., Plümper, Troeger, and Manow 2005, 329; Hicks 1994, 172) identify four problems with OLS estimation posed by the non-independence of observations in pooled time series: errors are (1) serially correlated, (2) cross-sectionally heteroskedastic, (3) often correlated across units due to common shocks, and (4) often autocorrelated and heteroskedastic simultaneously. To deal with these problems, Beck and Katz (1995 and 1996) recommended adding unit and period dummies and a lagged dependent variable to the right-hand side of the equation, calculating panel-corrected standard errors (PCSE), and imposing a common rho for all cross-sections.

Plümper, Troeger, and Manow (2005, 330–34) have countered that including country dummies does more than eliminate omitted variable bias. It also (1) eliminates any variation in the dependent variable that is due to time-invariant factors such as difference in constitutional structures, (2) reduces the coefficients of factors that vary mainly between countries, (3) eliminates any differences in the dependent variable due to differences in the independent variables prior to t_1 in the time series, and (4) "completely absorb(s) differences in the level of the independent variables across the units" (p. 331). We do hypothesize (#1 above) effects of time-invariant factors (veto points), (#3) effects in the levels of our independent variables prior to t_1 on the level of the dependent variable at t_1, and (#4) effects of levels of the independent variables on levels of the dependent variable. In addition, variation in several of our independent variables is primarily cross-sectional (#2).

Our solution is to handle serial correlation by correcting for first-order auto-regressiveness rather than with a lagged dependent variable. Beck and Katz (2004 and 2011) have shown that correcting for first-order autoregressiveness (ar1 corrections) actually does include a lagged dependent variable on the right-hand side of the equation. This statistical setup, PCSE and ar1 corrections, is known as Prais-Winsten estimations. It deals with the problem of serial correlation without (as our results show) suppressing the power of other independent variables (see Huber and Stephens 2000 and 2001).

Prais-Winsten estimations include the value of the dependent variable at t−1 on the right-hand side of the equation. Since our dependent variable series for household income poverty and inequality (chapters 3 and 5) contains gaps, we use Vernby and Lindgren's (2009) dvgreg package, which, following an earlier lead by Iversen and Soskice (2006), develops a method to deal with gaps in the dependent variable. Dvgreg is designed to estimate dynamic panel data models with gaps in the dependent variable but complete or nearly complete data on the independent variables. It generates an estimate of the value of the dependent variable at t−1 for each gap, based on the values of the dependent variable at the previous actual observation and the values of the independent variables. This makes it possible to derive a corrected estimate of ar1. Instead of using panel-corrected standard errors, Vernby and Lindgren deal with heteroskedasticity by using weighted least squares. Vernby and Lindgren (2009, 9) state that "Monte Carlo studies conducted by the authors suggest that the estimates of the coefficients and standard errors are accurate as long as ρ and R^2 are reasonably high, and the gaps are not too long." They illustrate their statistical package with LIS data on redistribution calculated by Bradley et al. (2003). These data have only 61 country-year observations, compared to the 483 country-year observations in our combined LIS, SILC, and OECD series (see chapter 4). In appendix E, we provide robustness tests with alternative estimations. As noted above, fixed effects or country dummies are not appropriate for these data because (1) the theories tested are intended to explain variation between countries as well as within countries (true for all of our dependent variables), and (2) the variation in our wage dispersion data is primarily between countries and not over time. The adjusted R^2 for a regression of the 50-10 wage ratio on a full set of country dummies is .84 while the adjusted R^2 for a regression of the 50-10 ratio on a full set of year dummies is only .01. The adjusted R^2 for a regression of the 90-50 wage ratio on a full set of country dummies is .81 while the adjusted R^2 for a regression of the 90-50 ratio on a full set of year dummies is .00.

There are relatively few gaps in the wage dispersion and top income shares data, so we could have provided Prais-Winsten estimates in those analyses (chapters 2 and 4). However, in the interest of comparability of findings across the dependent variables, we present Vernby-Lindgren dynamic panel estimates in these two chapters as well.

We hypothesize that most of our causes operate over the long term and changes in the dependent variables occur gradually, a case of cumulative causes in Pierson's (2003, 198) typology of causes and effects. Thus, it is appropriate to measure the dependent and independent variables as levels. Moreover, in almost all pooled time-series studies of the determinants of inequality, regardless of whether inequality is measured by wage dispersion, the Gini coefficient of household income, poverty levels, or top income shares, the dependent variable is measured as a level. For this reason, error correction estimation in which the dependent variable is measured as a first difference is not an appropriate technique to model the hypothesized causal processes.

We proceed stepwise in our model-building, testing theoretically meaningful clusters of variables separately and then carrying the statistically significant variables forward to the combined model. We do this to preserve the largest number of observations possible and to show the joint explanatory power of the clusters of variables. Several of our independent variables, such as employment in dynamic services and private share of education spending, are only available for limited periods of time, which causes us to lose observations. This is also why we do not carry private share of education spending forward into the final models, even where it is highly significant.

In order to control for common economic shocks, such as oil price increases or global economic cycles, we include period dummies in the final models. The periods selected are the latter part of the Golden Age of postwar growth (1960–1972), the oil shocks and stagflation of the 1970s (1973–1979), the period of deregulation up to the introduction of the single European market (1980–1992), the global financial crisis (2008–2012), and the post-crisis period (2013–2017). The reference period is 1993–2007, the transition to the knowledge economy.

APPENDIX E
Alternative Statistical Estimators

TABLE E.2. **Alternative Estimators of Wage Dispersion**

	50-10 ratio			90-50 ratio		
	Model 1	Model 2	Model 3	Model 4	Model 5	Model 6
	Dynamic panel model with country dummies	Random effects	Fixed effects	Dynamic panel model with country dummies	Random effects	Fixed effects
Left government	.002	−.001	.002			
Union density	−.001	−.004 ***	−.002	−.004 ***	−.004 ***	−.003 ***
Wage coordination	−.013	−.011	−.014	.019 ^	.019 ^	.021 ^
EPL	−.119 ***	−.133 ***	−.141 ***			
Works council rights				.054	.022	.041
Total factor productivity change				1.253	1.171	1.206
Regulation	.023	.037 ^	.042	−.023 **	−.023 **	−.026 ***
Dynamic service employment	.020 ***	.017 **	.025 ***			
Capital market openness	−.008	−.004	−.007	−.029 ^	−.035 ^	−.038 ^
Outward FDI	−.000	.000	.000			
Trade openness	−.003 ***	−.002 **	−.002 **	−.001 *	−.002 ***	−.002 ***
Immigration	.002	.000	−.002			
Human capital spending	.009	.011	.013	.012 ^	.014 ^	.015 ^
Constant	1.827 ***	1.888 ***	1.761 ***	2.378 ***	2.038 ***	1.957 ***
R² within		.25	.27		.30	.30
R² between		.53	.36		.10	.02
Adjusted R²	0.93 ***	.53 ***	.37 ***	.90 ***	.13 ***	.05 ***
Observations	270	277	277	465	474	474

All models contain period indicators.

* Significant at .05; ** significant at .01; *** significant at .001; ^ significant but contrary to directional hypothesis.

TABLE E.3. **Alternative Estimates for Market Income Gini Index, Redistribution, and Disposable Household Income Gini**

	Market income Gini index			Redistribution			Disposable household income Gini		
	Dynamic panel model with country dummies	Random effects	Fixed effects	Dynamic panel model with country dummies	Random effects	Fixed effects	Dynamic panel model with country dummies	Random effects	Fixed effects
	Model 1	Model 2	Model 3	Model 4	Model 5	Model 6	Model 7	Model 8	Model 9
Union density	-.019	-.000	-.025	.273 ***	.136 ***	.169 ***	-.002	-.052 ***	-.027
Wage coordination	-.229	-.161	-.159						
Minimum wage setting	-.289	-.412	-.461						
Left government				-.091	-.048	-.043	-.357	-.115	-.376
Proportional representation				.054	-1.266	-.792	-.012	.027	-.014
Women in parliament				.077 *	.082 *	.100 **			
Veto points				-3.916 ***	-1.756 ***	-3.818 ***			
Voter turnout				.051	.029	.011	-.068 ***	-.058 ***	-.081 ***
Industrial employment	-.318 **	-.289 **	-.406 ***						
Technological change	-40.884	-21.881 ***	-41.975 *				-3.950	9.844	2.527
Regulation	-.601 **	-.603 ***	-.426 *						
Non-aged welfare state generosity	.047	-.008	.093	.319 *	.401 ***	.354 **	-.147	-.191 ***	-.160
Capital market openness	.404	.538 *	.578 *				-.502 ***	-.346 ***	-.475 ***

continues

TABLE E.3. (*continued*)

	Market income Gini index			Redistribution			Disposable household income Gini		
	Dynamic panel model with country dummies	Random effects	Fixed effects	Dynamic panel model with country dummies	Random effects	Fixed effects	Dynamic panel model with country dummies	Random effects	Fixed effects
	Model 1	Model 2	Model 3	Model 4	Model 5	Model 6	Model 7	Model 8	Model 9
Third world imports	−.182	−.204 ^	−.201 ^						
Immigration				.249 ^	.140	.135	.139 *	−.028	.065
Outward FDI				−.030	−.023	−.022	.007	−.002	−.001
Trade openness				.030	.031	.026	.010	.057 *	.001
Unemployment rate	.298 ***	.294 ***	.261 ***						
% of children in single-mother households	.047	.072 **	.049 *						
Human capital spending	−.357 **	−.376 **	−.358 **				−.439 ***	−.446 ***	−.328 ***
Parental leave benefits				.015	.028 **	.028 **	.003	.000	.003
Constant	49.868 ***	47.169 ***	47.956 ***	22.632 ***	9.217 *	13.003 *	46.609 ***	45.714 ***	48.734 ***
R² within		.62	.63		.12	.13		.48	.50
R² between		.40	.24		.66	.52		.81	.72
Adjusted R²	.86 ***	.48 ***	.39 ***	.85 ***	.55 ***	.45 ***	.92 ***	.79 ***	.70 ***
Observations	308	319	319	441	461	461	361	375	375

All models contain period indicators.
* Significant at .05; ** significant at .01; *** significant at .001; ^ significant but contrary to directional hypothesis.

TABLE E.4. **Alternative Estimators of Top 1% Income Shares**

	Dynamic panel model with country dummies		Random effects		Fixed effects	
	Model 1		Model 2		Model 3	
Secular center and right government	.161	***	.010		.143	***
Union density	−.034	*	−.024	***	−.029	*
Wage coordination	.025		−.377	***	.061	
Contract coverage	−.045	***	−.032	***	−.046	***
Top marginal tax rates	.001		−.011		.006	
Government revenue	.016		.037	^	.013	
Public education spending	.026		−.432	***	.013	
Stock market capitalization	.015	***	.008	***	.014	***
Change in total factor productivity	48.814	***	49.945	***	51.275	***
Regulation	.123		−.504	***	.127	
Trade surplus	.071	**	.005		.061	**
Capital market openness	.075		−.032		.031	
Outward FDI	.020	*	−.011		.019	*
Trade openness	−.006		.000		−.008	
Economic growth	−.001		.000		−.007	
Constant	3.854	*	14.512	***	6.051	***
R^2 within			.63		.71	
R^2 between			.67		.31	
Adjusted R^2	.85	***	.70	***	.47	***
Observations	470		471		471	

All models include period indicators.
* Significant at .05; ** significant at .01; *** significant at .001; ^ significant but contrary to directional hypothesis.

TABLE E.5. **Alternative Estimates for Market Poverty, Poverty Reduction, and Disposable Income Poverty**

	Market poverty			Poverty reduction			Disposable income poverty		
	Dynamic panel model with country dummies Model 1	Random effects Model 2	Fixed effects Model 3	Dynamic panel model with country dummies Model 4	Random effects Model 5	Fixed effects Model 6	Dynamic panel model with country dummies Model 7	Random effects Model 8	Fixed effects Model 9
Union density	.056 <	.028	.039	.096	.070	.022			
Minimum wage setting	−.478 *	−.397	−.364				−.293	−.235	−.330 *
Works council rights	1.449 <	.942 <	1.369 <				−2.161 ***	−1.398 ***	−1.821 ***
Left government				−.109	.009	−.088	−.017	−.028	−.040
Christian democratic government				−.494 <	−.288 <	−.455 <			
Veto points				−6.242 *	−4.386 **	−6.787 **			
Voter turnout				.207 *	.248 **	.212 *			
Industrial employment	−.313 ***	−.308 ***	−.324 ***				−.040 *	−.028 *	−.039 **
Parental leave benefits	−.008	−.004	−.006	−.026	−.010	−.011	.012 <	.010 <	.010 <
Non-aged welfare state generosity	.096	.103	.137 *	.644 *	1.064 ***	.897 **	−.111 *	−.124 **	−.141 **
Capital market openness	.620 **	.593 ***	.607 ***						

TABLE E.5. (*continued*)

	Market poverty			Poverty reduction			Disposable income poverty		
	Dynamic panel model with country dummies	Random effects	Fixed effects	Dynamic panel model with country dummies	Random effects	Fixed effects	Dynamic panel model with country dummies	Random effects	Fixed effects
	Model 1	Model 2	Model 3	Model 4	Model 5	Model 6	Model 7	Model 8	Model 9
Trade openness	-.012	-.013	-.016 ^	.057	.039	.039	-.004	-.007	-.006
Immigration	.426 ***	.391 ***	.395 ***	.062	-.127	-.150	.160 **	.091 *	.162 ***
Unemployment rate							.237 ***	.248 ***	.244 ***
% children in single-mother households	.036	.007	.004						
Employment	-.005	-.028	-.017	-.796 ***	-.862 ***	-.863 ***	.110 ^	.134 ^	.141
Constant	17.329 ***	18.348 ***	16.321 ***	87.413 ***	71.696 ***	88.218 ***	6.568 *	5.145 *	6.045 *
R² within		.63	.63		.22	.23		.41	.41
R² between		.13	.07		.48	.36		.34	.28
Adjusted R²	.85 ***	.29 ***	.21 ***	.83 ***	.47 ***	.37 ***	.83 ***	.41 ***	.37 ***
Observations	440	461	461	436	457	457	456	477	477

All models include period indicators.
* Significant at .05; ** significant at .01; *** significant at .001; ^ significant but contrary to directional hypothesis.

TABLE E.6. **Alternative Estimates of Social Insurance Generosity, Parental Leave Generosity, and Human Capital Spending**

	Social insurance generosity			Parental leave			Human capital spending		
	Dynamic panels with country dummies	Random effects	Fixed effects	Dynamic panels with country dummies	Random effects	Fixed effects	Dynamic panels with country dummies	Random effects	Fixed effects
	Model 1	Model 2	Model 3	Model 4	Model 5	Model 6	Model 7	Model 8	Model 9
Left government	.007	.065 ***	.027	.751 ***	.656 ***	.669 ***	.145 ***	.131 ***	.146 ***
Christian democratic government	.044 ***	.100 ***	.056	−.861 ^	−.859 ^	−1.644 ^	−.004	−.002	−.003
Women in parliament	−1.458 ***	−.197		.031 ***	.086	.125	.023 ***	.024 ***	.022 ***
Veto points	−.329	.147	−.323	−5.817 ***	.260	8.821 ***			
Proportional representation									
Third world imports	−.272 ***	−.361 ***	−.267 ***	.160 ***	−.013	−.104 *	−.107 ***	−.129 ***	−.129 ***
Trade openness	.019 **	.033 ***	.020 **	−.090	−.058	−.040	−.004	−.002	−.002
Outward FDI	−.026	−.007	.028	.374 ***	−.189 *	.175	−.001	−.001	−.001
Immigration				.249	.374 *	.485 *	−.002	−.015	−.014
% children in single-mother households									
Unemployment rate	−.090 **	−.086 ***	−.057 *	−.193 ***	.780 ***	2.950 ^	.627 ^	.437 ^	.534 ^
Military spending (% GDP)				.511 ***	.660 ***	.810 ***			
GDP per capita	.075 ***	.073 ***	.085 ***						
Constant	15.131 ***	14.991 ***	15.633 ***	−.963	5.294 ***	−10.996 ***	3.483 ***	3.690 ***	3.406 ***
R^2 within		.12	.13		.41	.42		.45	.46
R^2 between		.55	.28		.03	.16		.46	.45
Adjusted R^2	.93 ***	.49 ***	0.230 ***	0.743 ***	.12 ***	.01 ***	.892 ***	.46 ***	.44 ***
Observations	846	865	865	933	933	933	600	620	620

All models contain period indicators.
* Significant at .05; ** Significant at .01; *** significant at .001; ^ significant opposite hypothesized direction.

Notes

Chapter One

1. The spike in Norway in 2005 was a result of the pre-announcement of a permanent dividend tax implemented in 2006.

2. See chapter 4 for the construction of the household income combined series. Solt's Standardized World Income Inequality Database (2020) contains data on annual income equality for the period covered in this book, but the microdata are not available for analysis so they are not suitable for our purposes. The database contains data on income inequality on an annual basis.

3. The exceptions are union density (which declines in all countries, the Nordics and Belgium partially excepted) and left government (which varies over time and begins to decline after 2007).

Chapter Three

1. While we believe social rights are highly influential in determining inequality, the current structure of our data limits our ability to adequately measure this effect on market income. The additive benefit measures are helpful in separating take-up from generosity but less so in identifying trade-offs between replacement rates and duration, which we expect to have distinct effects. Therefore, we set a non-directional hypothesis for the non-aged benefit social rights variables.

2. In our 2001 book, which included an analysis of the expansion period of the welfare state (which lasted up to 1985), we found that in the entire dataset left incumbency and union density were so highly correlated (.84) that we could not enter the two variables in the same equation. The correlation between the two variables in the current dataset is .42, so there is no problem having them in the same equation.

Chapter Four

1. Jingjing Huo, our coauthor on earlier versions of this chapter (Huber, Huo, and Stephens 2019), wrote this section.

Chapter Six

1. Our 2001 book, like Esping-Andersen's (1990) book, did not include Greece, Portugal, or Spain, thus the fourth type does not appear there.
2. See Huber and Stephens (2000) for further analysis and discussion of the interrelationship between women's political mobilization and left government.
3. This suggests that the southern regimes might be closer to continental welfare states if the aged and pensions were included in the analysis. In fact, LIS and OECD data show that there remain large differences between the two groups in disposable income and redistribution inequality if the aged are included in the data.

Chapter Seven

1. The data were adjusted by our coauthor Jacob Gunderson (Huber, Gunderson, and Stephens 2020).

Chapter Eight

1. We refer here not to the QCA method but rather to the logic of comparison underlying it, which is a formalization of Mill's comparative method, similar to Skocpol's analytic comparative historical analysis.
2. The figures for the Gini and poverty refer to the working-age population unless otherwise noted.

Chapter Ten

1. Our account of rising inequality in Sweden in the last four decades is largely consistent with the recent conference paper by the Swedish economic historian Erik Bengtsson (2023).
2. Unless otherwise noted, all figures in this paragraph are from Brady, Huber, and Stephens (2020).
3. The government reversed the fee differentiation before leaving office in 2014 when it did not improve employment performance or result in wage restraint, the

expected (by the bourgeois government) effect of the fee differentiation (Kjellberg and Ibsen 2016, 291).

4. The exclusion of 18- to 24-year-olds in order to account for the high proportion of student households in Sweden (see below) only changes this picture marginally: among households aged 25-64, the poverty rate in this most recent period is 8.5 percent in Sweden, compared to an OECD average of 9.7 percent.

5. The high tax rate in 1989 has to be taken with a grain of salt because it ignores the extensive loopholes, opportunities for tax avoidance, and incentives for tax planning that existed in the tax system prior to the 1991 tax reform (Agell, Englund, and Södersten 1996).

Chapter Eleven

1. We refer here to the absolute change, not the percentage change. One can see from table B.2 that top 1 percent income shares including capital gains doubled in the US and more than doubled in Sweden, but the absolute change is greater in the US (10 percent versus 4.9 percent). At this rate of change, Sweden would never catch up to the US. One sees this clearly if one regresses the top 1 percent share on time in each of the two countries. Not only is the intercept much lower in Sweden; the slope is also much lower, .06 versus .18.

2. Fligstein and Shin (2007) date the breakthrough of the shareholder value revolution to the 1980s.

3. Canada continued to permit certification through card check, which is one reason why it has experienced much less de-unionization.

4. In fairness to her, Skocpol (1992) does include an extensive analysis of the development of pensions for Union veterans of the Civil War, which were very generous, if corruptly administered. However, as she makes clear, this pension program was not a stepping stone to later development of pensions in the United States.

5. A significant lacuna in Goldin and Katz's RBET framework is that it does not account for the increase in inequality in the US between the Gilded Age and 1929.

Chapter Thirteen

1. Note that these figures differ slightly from the figures for German top marginal tax rates in chapter 8. The reason is that the figures in this chapter reflect the actual taxes paid by people with an income five times the median (Roine, Vlachos, and Waldenström 2009; OECD Tax Database for the years 2000–2017, accessed February 20, 2019).

2. "Moderate" as compared to throughgoing market liberalization in the case of deregulation of energy, transportation, and communication sectors or compared to labor market liberalization proposed by the OECD Jobs Study.

3. We treat PRT, MR, and other explanations of redistribution at greater length in a companion paper (Huber, Machtei, and Stephens 2022, 2024).

Appendix C

1. LIS added a number of datasets for our countries in the spring of 2023 after we had finished our statistical analysis, which if added to our dataset would bring our total country-years to 559. Adding these observations to the analysis did not make a substantial difference in any of our results, so we opted not to add them. They are included in Huber, Machtei, and Stephens (2024), which extends the analysis of redistribution that appears in chapter 3.

References

Abou-Chadi, Tarik, and Simon Hix. 2021. "Brahmin Left versus Merchant Right? Education, Class, Multiparty Competition, and Redistribution in Western Europe." *British Journal of Sociology* 72: 79–92. DOI: 10.1111/1468-4446.12834.

Abou-Chadi, Tarik, Reto Mitteregger, and Cas Mudde. 2021. *Left Behind by the Working Class: Social Democracy's Electoral Crisis and the Rise of the Radical Right*. Berlin: Friedrich-Ebert-Stiftung.

Abowd, John. 1989. "The Effect of Wage Bargains on the Stock Market Value of the Firm." *American Economic Review* 79 (4): 774–800.

Acemoglu, Daron. 2002. "Technical Change, Inequality, and the Labor Market." *Journal of Economic Literature* 40: 7–72.

Acemoglu, Daron, and David Autor. 2011. "Skills, Tasks, and Technologies: Implications for Employment and Earnings." In *Handbook of Labor Economics*, vol. 4, edited by David Card and Orley Ashenfelter, 1043–1171. Amsterdam: Elsevier.

Acemoglu, Daron, and Andrew Newman. 2002. "The Labor Market and Corporate Structure." *European Economic Review* 46: 1733–56.

Addison, John, and Barry Hirsch. 1989. "Union Effects on Productivity, Profits, and Growth: Has the Long Run Arrived?" *Journal of Labor Economics* 7: 72–105.

Agell, Jones, Peter Englund, and Jan Södersten. 1996. "Tax Reform of the Century—the Swedish Experiment." *National Tax Journal* 49: 643–64.

Aguilar-Hendrickson, Manuel. 2020. "Long-Term Care in Spain: A Reform Failure or the Regulation of a Development Path?" *International Journal of Sociology and Social Policy* 40: 1301–17.

Aguilar-Hendrickson, Manuel, and Ana Arriba González de Durana. 2020. "Out of the Wilderness? The Coming Back of the Debate on Minimum Income in Spain and the Great Recession." *Social Policy and Administration* 54: 556–73.

Alford, Robert. 1964. *Party and Society: The Anglo-American Democracies*. London: John Murray.

Allan, James P., and Lyle Scruggs. 2004. "Political Partisanship and Welfare State Reforms in Advanced Industrial Societies." *American Journal of Political Science* 48: 496–512.

Alm, Susanne, Kenneth Nelson, and Rense Nieuwenhuis. 2020. "The Diminishing Power of One? Welfare State Retrenchment and Rising Poverty of Single-Adult Households in Sweden, 1988–2011." *European Sociological Review* 36: 198–217.

Alper, Kaitlin, Evelyne Huber, and John D. Stephens. 2021. "Poverty and Social Rights Among the Working Age Population in Post-Industrial Democracies." *Social Forces* 99: 1710–44.

Alstadsæter, Annette, and Martin Jacob. 2012. "Income Shifting in Sweden: An Empirical Evaluation of the 3:12 Rules." Stockholm: Ministry of Finance, Regeringskansliet.

Alvaredo, Facundo, Anthony B. Atkinson, Thomas Piketty, and Emmanuel Saez. 2013. "The Top 1 Percent in International and Historical Perspective." *Journal of Economic Perspectives* 27: 3–20.

———. 2015. *The World Top Incomes Data Base*. http://topincomes.gmond.pariss choolofeconomics.eu/. Accessed February 2, 2015.

Alvaredo, Facundo, and Emmanuel Saez. 2010. "Income and Wealth Concentration in Spain in a Historical and Fiscal Perspective." In *Top Incomes in Global Perspective*, edited by Anthony B. Atkinson and Thomas Piketty, 482–559. Oxford: Oxford University Press.

Amenta, Edwin. 1998. *Bold Relief: Institutional Politics and the Origins of Modern American Social Policy*. Princeton, NJ: Princeton University Press.

Armingeon, Klaus, and Lucio Baccaro. 2012. "Political Economy of the Sovereign Debt Crisis: The Limits of Internal Devaluation." *Industrial Law Journal* 41 (3): 254–75.

Armingeon, Klaus, and Giuliano Bonoli. 2007. *The Politics of Post-Industrial Welfare States: Adapting Post-War Social Policies to New Social Risks*. London and New York: Routledge.

Arni, Patrick, Rafael Lalive, and Jan C. van Ours. 2013. "How Effective Are Unemployment Benefit Sanctions? Looking Beyond Unemployment Exit." *Journal of Applied Econometrics* 28: 1153–78.

Arundel, Anthony, Bengt-Åke Lundvall, Edward Lorenz, and Antoine Valeyre. 2007. "How Europe's Economies Learn: A Comparison of Work Organization and Innovate Mode for the EU-15." *Industrial and Corporate Change* 16 (6): 680–93.

Atchison, Amy, and Ian Down. 2009. "Women Cabinet Ministers and Female-Friendly Social Policy." *Poverty & Public Policy* 1: 1–23.

Atkinson, Anthony B. 2005. "Comparing the Distribution of Top Income across Countries." *Journal of the European Economic Association* 3: 393–401.

———. 2007. "The Distribution of Earnings in OECD Countries." *International Labor Review* 146: 41–60. https://doi.org/10.1111/j.1564-913X.2007.00004.x.

———. 2008. *The Changing Distribution of Earnings in OECD Countries*. The Rodolfo Debenedetti Lectures. Oxford and New York: Oxford University Press.

———. 2014. "After Piketty?" *British Journal of Sociology* 65 (4): 619–38.

Atkinson, Anthony B., and Thomas Piketty. 2007. *Top Incomes over the Twentieth*

Century: A Contrast between Continental European and English-Speaking Countries. Oxford: Oxford University Press.

———. 2010. *Top Incomes: A Global Perspective*. Oxford: Oxford University Press.

Atkinson, Anthony B., Thomas Piketty, and Emmanuel Saez. 2011. "Top Incomes in the Long Run of History." *Journal of Economic Literature* 49: 3–71.

Autor, David H. 2014. "Skills, Education, and the Rise of Earnings Inequality among the 'Other 99 Percent.'" *Science* 344: 843–51.

Autor, David H., Claudia Goldin, and Lawrence F. Katz. 2020. "Extending the Race between Education and Technology." *AEA Papers and Proceedings* 2020 (110): 347–51.

Autor, David H., Lawrence F. Katz, and Melissa S. Kearney. 2008. "Trends in U.S. Wage Inequality: Revising the Revisionists." *The Review of Economics and Statistics* 90: 300–323.

Autor, David H., Frank Levy, and Richard J. Murname. 2003. "The Skill Content of Recent Technological Change." *The Quarterly Journal of Economics* 118: 1279–1333.

Baccaro, Lucio, and Martin Höpner. 2022. "The Political-Economic Foundations of Export-Led Growth: An Analysis of the German Case." In (eds.) *Diminishing Returns: The New Politics of Growth and Stagnation*, edited by Lucio Baccaro, Mark Blyth and Jonas Pontusson. Oxford: Oxford University Press.

Baccaro, Lucio, and Chris Howell. 2017. *Trajectories of Neoliberal Transformation: European Industrial Relations Since the 1970s*. Cambridge: Cambridge University Press.

Baccaro, Lucio, and Jonas Pontusson. 2016. "Rethinking Comparative Political Economy: The Growth Model Perspective." *Politics and Society* 44: 175–207.

Bakija, Jon, Adam Cole, and Bradley T. Heim. 2012. "Jobs and Income Growth of Top Earners and the Causes of Changing Income Inequality: Evidence from US Tax Return Data." Unpublished manuscript, August, Williams College, Williamstown, MA. PDF file. https://web.williams.edu/Economics/wp/BakijaCole HeimJobsIncomeGrowthTopEarners.pdf.

Banning, Kevin, and Ted Chiles. 2007. "Tradeoffs in the Labor Union-CEO Compensation Relationship." *Journal of Labor Research* 28 (2): 347–57.

Barro, Robert, and Jong-Wha Lee. 2013. "A New Data Set of Educational Attainment in the World, 1950–2010." *Journal of Development Economics* 104: 184–98.

Bartels, Larry M. 2008. *Unequal Democracy: The Political Economy of the New Gilded Age*. New York: Russell Sage Foundation; and Princeton, NJ: Princeton University Press.

Barth, Erling, and Karl Ove Moene. 2016. "The Equality Multiplier: How Wage Compression and Welfare Empowerment Interact." *Journal of the European Economic Association* 14: 1011–37.

Bartling, Björn, Ernst Fehr, and Klaus M. Schmidt. 2012. "Screening, Competition, and Job Design: Economic Origins of Good Jobs." *American Economic Review* 102 (2): 834–64.

Basu, Pallavi, and Dylan Small. 2020. "Constructing a More Closely Matched Control Group in a Difference-in-Differences Analysis: Its Effect on History Interacting with Group Bias." *Observational Studies* 6: 103–30.

Beck, Nathaniel, and Jonathan N. Katz. 1995. "What to Do (and Not to Do) with Time-Series Cross-Sectional Data." *American Political Science Review* 89: 634–47. https://doi.org/10.2307/2082979.

———. 1996. "Nuisance vs. Substance: Specifying and Estimating Time-Series-Cross-Section Models." *Political Analysis* 6: 1–36.

———. 2004. "Time-Series-Cross-Section Issues: Dynamics." In Annual Meeting of the Society for Political Methodology, Stanford University, July 29–31.

———. 2011. "Modeling Dynamics in Time-Series–Cross-Section Political Economy Data." *Annual Review of Political Science* 14: 331–52. https://doi.org/10.1146/annurev-polisci-071510-103222.

Beck, Thorsten, Asli Demirgüç-Kunt, and Ross Levine. 2009. "Financial Institutions and Markets Across Countries and Over Time: Data and Analysis." *World Bank Policy Research* Working Paper No. 4943. Washington, DC: The World Bank.

Bengtsson, Erik. 2023. "The Longue Durée of Wages and Inequality: Sweden, 1870–2022." Paper delivered at the 29th International Conference of Europeanists, University of Iceland, Reykjavik, June 27–29.

Beramendi, Pablo, Silja Häusermann, Herbert Kitschelt, and Hanspeter Kriesi. 2015. "Introduction: The Politics of Advanced Capitalism." In *The Politics of Advanced Capitalism*, edited by Pablo Beramendi, Silja Häusermann, Herbert Kitschelt, and Hanspeter Kriesi, 1–64. New York: Cambridge University Press.

Berglund, Tomas, and Ingrid Esser. 2014. *Modell i förändring. Landrapport om Sverige*. Partial report 8. Oslo: Fafo/NordMod.

Berglund, Tomas, Kristina Håkansson, and Tommy Isidorsson. 2022. "Occupational Change on the Dualized Swedish Labour Market." *Economic and Industrial Democracy* 43: 918–42.

Blanchard, Olivier, and Dani Rodrik, eds. 2021. *Combating Inequality: Rethinking Government's Role*. Cambridge, MA: MIT Press.

Blanchet, Thomas, Lucas Chancel, Ignacio Flores, and Marc Morgan. 2021. *Distributional National Accounts Guidelines: Methods and Concepts Used in the World Inequality Database*. Paris: Paris School of Economics.

Blanchet, Thomas, Lucas Chancel, and Amory Gethin. 2022. "Why Europe Is More Equal Than the United States?" *American Economic Journal: Applied Economics* 14 (4): 480–518.

Blasco, Julien, Elvire Guillaud, and Michael Zemmour. 2023. "The Inequality Impact of Consumption Taxes: An International Comparison." *Journal of Public Economics* 222 (June): 104897. https://doi.org/10.1016/j.jpubeco.2023.104897.

Block, Richard. 1997. "Rethinking the National Labor Relations Act and Zero-Sum Labor Law: An Industrial Relations Review." *Berkeley Journal of Employment and Labor Law* 18: 30–55.

Blome, Agnes. 2016. "Normative Beliefs, Party Competition, and Work-Family Policy Reforms in German and Italy." *Comparative Politics* 48 (4): 478–96.

Blyth, Mark. 2001. "The Transformation of the Swedish Model: Economic Ideas, Distributional Conflict, and Institutional Change." *World Politics* 54: 1–26.

———. 2013. *Austerity: The History of a Dangerous Idea*. New York: Oxford University Press.

Bonnet, Odran, Pierre-Henri Bono, Guillaume Chapelle, and Etienne Wasmer. 2014. "Does Housing Capital Contribute to Inequality? A Comment on Thomas Piketty's Capital in the 21st Century." *Sciences Po Economics* Discussion Paper No. 2014-07. L'Institut d'études politiques de Paris.

Bonoli, Giuliano, Bea Cantillon, and Wim Van Lancker. 2015. "Social Investment and the Matthew Effect: Limits to a Strategy." In *The Uses of Social Investment*, edited by Anton Hemerijck, 66–76 Oxford: Oxford University Press.

Börzel, Tanja A., and Thomas Risse. 2018. "From the Euro to the Schengen Crises: European Integration Theories, Politicization, and Identity Politics." *Journal of European Public Policy* 25 (1): 83–108.

———. 2018. "Social Dialogue in Germany: Innovation or Erosion?" In *Reducing Inequalities in Europe: How Industrial Relations and Labour Policies Can Close the Gap*, edited by Daniel Vaughan-Whitehead. Cheltenham, UK: Edward Elgar Publishing, and Geneva: International Labour Office.

Boyd-Barrett, Oliver. 1995. "Structural Change and Curriculum Reform in Democratic Spain." In *Education Reform in Democratic Spain*, edited by Oliver Boyd-Barrett and Pamela O'Malley, 6–24. London: Routledge.

Bradbury, Bruce. 2013. "The Fourth Retirement Pillar in Rich Countries." In *Income Inequality: Economic Disparities and the Middle Class in Affluent Countries*, edited by Janet Gornick and Markus Jäntti, 334–61. Stanford, CA: Stanford University Press.

Bradley, David, Evelyne Huber, Stephanie Moller, François Nielsen, and John D. Stephens. 2003. "Distribution and Redistribution in Postindustrial Democracies." *World Politics* 55: 193–228. https://doi.org/10.1353/wp.2003.0009.

Bradley, David H., and John D. Stephens. 2007. "Employment Performance in OECD Countries: A Test of Neoliberal and Institutional Hypotheses." *Comparative Political Studies* 40: 1486–1510.

Brady, David. 2009. *Rich Democracies, Poor People: How Politics Explain Poverty*. Oxford: Oxford University Press.

———. 2019. "Theories of the Causes of Poverty." *Annual Review of Sociology* 45: 155–75.

———. 2022. "Income and Wealth as Salient Gradational Aspects of Stratification." In *Social Stratification*, edited by D. Grusky. 5th edition. New York: Routledge.

Brady, David, Regina S. Baker, and Ryan Finnigan. 2013. "When Unionization Disappears: State Level Unionization and Working Poverty in the United States." *American Sociological Review* 78: 872–896.

Brady, David, and Thomas Biegert. 2017. "The Rise of Precarious Employment in Germany." *Research in the Sociology of Work* 31: 245–71.

Brady, David, Agnes Blome, and Hanna Kleider. 2016. "How Politics and Institutions Shape Poverty and Inequality." In *The Oxford Handbook of the Social Science of Poverty*, edited by David Brady and Linda M. Burton, 117–40. New York: Oxford University Press.

Brady, David, and Ryan Finnigan. 2013. "Does Immigration Undermine Public Support for Social Policy?" *American Sociological Review* 79 (1): 17–42.

Brady, David, Ryan Finnigan, Ulrich Kohler, and Joscha Legewie. 2020. "The Inheritance of Race Revisited: Childhood Wealth and Income, and Black-White Disadvantages in Adult Life Chances." *Sociological Science* 7: 599–627.

Brady, David, Evelyne Huber, and John D. Stephens. 2020. "Comparative Welfare States Data Set." University of North Carolina and WZB Berlin Social Science Center. https://huberandstephens.web.unc.edu/common-works/data/.

Brady, David, and Hang Young Lee. 2014. "The Rise and Fall of Government Spending in Affluent Democracies, 1971–2008." *Journal of European Social Policy* 24 (1): 56–79.

Brady, David, and Kevin T. Leicht. 2008. "Party to Inequality: Right Party Power and Income Inequality in Affluent Western Democracies." *Research in Social Stratification and Mobility* 26: 77–106.

Branco, Rui, Juan Miró, and Marcello Natili. 2023. "Back from the Cold? Progressive Politics and Social Policy Paradigms in Southern Europe after the Great Recession." Paper prepared for the Meetings of the Council for European Studies, Reykjavik, Iceland, June 27–29.

Branco, Rui, Oscar Molina, Paulo Marques, and Madalena Ferreira. 2023. "Solidarity Against the Market? A Study of Leftist Labour Market Reforms in Portugal and Spain Ten Years After the Great Financial Crisis." Paper prepared for the Meetings of the Council for European Studies, Reykjavik, Iceland, June 27–29.

Bratton, Kathleen A., and Leonard P. Ray. 2002. "Descriptive Representation, Policy Outcomes, and Municipal Day-Care Coverage in Norway." *American Journal of Political Science* 46: 428–37.

Breznau, Nate, Eike Mark Rinke, Alexander Wuttke, and Tomasz Zoltak. 2022. "Observing Many Researchers Using the Same Data and Hypothesis Reveals a Hidden Universe of Uncertainty." *Proceedings of the National Academy of Sciences PNAS* 119 (44). https://www.pnas.org/doi/epdf/10.1073/pnas.2203150119.

Brülle, Jan. 2016. "Demographic Trends and the Changing Ability of Households to Buffer Poverty Risks in Germany." *European Sociological Review* 32: 766–78.

Bundesministerium für Familie, Senioren, Frauen und Jugend. 2021. Accessed January 15, 2022. www.bmfsfj.de/bmfsfj/themen/familie/familienleistungen/elterngeld/elterngeld-73752.

Burgess, Katrina. 2004. *Parties and Unions in the New Global Economy*. Pittsburgh, PA: University of Pittsburgh Press.

Bürgisser, Reto. 2022. "The Partisan Politics of Family and Labor Market Policy Reforms in Southern Europe." In *The World Politics of Social Investment, Volume II*, edited by Julian Garritzmann, Silja Häusermann, and Bruno Palier. PAGES. New York: Oxford University Press.

Busemeyer, Marius R. 2015. *Skills and Inequality: Partisan Politics and the Political Economy of Education Reforms in Western Welfare States*. Cambridge and New York: Cambridge University Press.

Busemeyer, Marius, Julian Garritzmann, and Erik Neimanns. 2020. *A Loud But Noisy Signal: Public Opinion and Education Reform in Western Europe*. Cambridge and New York: Cambridge University Press.

Cameron, David. 1978. "The Expansion of the Public Economy." *American Political Science Review* 72: 1243–61.

Campillo, Inés, and Jorge Sola. 2020. "Power Resources Theory: A Critical Reassessment." *Revista Española de Investigaciones Sociológicas* 170: 19–34.

Carlin, Wendy, Anke Hassel, Andrew Martin, and David Soskice. 2015. "The Transformation of the German Social Model." In *European Social Models from Crisis to Crisis*, edited by Jon Erik Dølvik and Andrew Martin, 49–104. Oxford: Oxford University Press.

Castles, Francis G., ed. 1982. *The Impact of Parties*. Beverly Hills, CA: Sage Publications.

Chaqués-Bonafont, Laura, Anna M. Palau, and Frank R. Baumgartner. 2015. *Agenda Dynamics in Spain*. Houndmills, UK: Palgrave Macmillan.

Chetty, Raj, David Grusky, Maximilian Hell, Nathaniel Hendren, Robert Manduca, and Jimmy Narang. 2017. "The Fading American Dream: Trends in Absolute Income Mobility Since 1940." *Science* 356: 398–406.

Chiles, Ted, and James Stewart. 1993. "Union Rent Appropriation and Ex Post Analysis." *Journal of Labor Research* 14: 317–33.

Chinn, Menzie D., and Hiro Ito. 2006. "What Matters for Financial Development? Capital Controls, Institutions, and Interactions." *Journal of Development Economics* 81: 163–92.

———. 2021. "The Chinn-Ito Financial Openness Index." Last accessed October 4, 2022. https://web.pdx.edu/~ito/Chinn-Ito_website.htm.

Chuliá, Elisa. 2011. "Consolidation and Reluctant Reform of the Pension System." In *The Spanish Welfare State in European Context*, edited by Ana Marta Guillén and Margarita León, 285–303. Burlington, VT: Ashgate.

Chwalisz, Claudia, and Patrick Diamond, eds. 2015. *The Predistribution Agenda: Tackling Inequality and Supporting Sustainable Growth*. New York: I. B. Tauris.

Čihák, Martin, Asli Demirgüç-Kunt, Erik Feyen, and Ross Levine. 2012. "Benchmarking Financial Development Around the World." World Bank Policy Research Working Paper No. 6175. Washington, DC: World Bank.

Cingano, F. 2014. "Trends in Income Inequality and Its Impact on Economic Growth." OECD Social, Employment and Migration Working Papers no. 163. Paris: OECD Publishing. http://dx.doi.org/10.1787/5jxrjncwxv6j-en.

Cioffi, John W., and Kenneth A. Dubin. 2016. "Commandeering Crisis: Partisan Labor Repression in Spain under the Guise of Economic Reform." *Politics & Society* 44: 423–53.

Clark, Kim. 1984. "Unionization and Firm Performance: The Impact on Profits, Growth, and Productivity." *American Economic Review* 74 (5): 893–919.

Clasen, Jochen, and Daniel Clegg. 2012. "Adapting Labour Market Policy to a Transformed Employment Structure: The Politics of 'Triple Integration.'" In *The Politics of the New Welfare State*, edited by Giuliano Bonoli and David Natali, 135–57. Oxford: Oxford University Press.

Clauwaert, Stefan, and Isabelle Schömann. 2012. "The Crisis and National Labour Law Reforms: A Mapping Exercise." Working Paper 2012.04, European Trade Union Institute. Brussels.

Collins, Sara R., Herman K. Bhupal, and Michelle M. Doty. 2019. "Health Insurance Coverage Eight Years After the ACA." *The Commonwealth Fund*, February 7. https://doi.org/10.26099/penv-q932.

Conway, Paul, and Giuseppe Nicoletti. 2006. "Product Market Regulation in the Non-Manufacturing Sectors of OECD Countries: Measurement and Highlights." OECD Economics Department Working Papers no. 530. Paris: OECD Publishing. https://www.oecd.org/eco/working_papers.

Corak, Myles. 2013. "Income inequality, Equality of Opportunity, and Intergenerational Mobility." *Journal of Economic Perspectives* 27: 79–102.

Croci, Ettore, Halit Gonenc, and Neslihan Ozkan. 2012. "CEO Compensation, Family Control, and Institutional Investors in Continental Europe." *Journal of Banking and Finance* 36: 3318–35.

Cronin, James. 2011. "Embracing Markets, Bonding with America, Trying to Do Good: The Ironies of New Labour." In *What's Left of the Left: Democrats and Social Democrats in Challenging Times*, edited by James Cronin, George Ross, and James Shoch, 116–40. Durham, NC: Duke University Press.

Dahl, Robert. 1961. *Who Governs? Democracy and Power in an American City*. New Haven, CT: Yale University Press.

Davis, Gerald F. 2009. *Managed by the Markets: How Finance Reshaped America*. Oxford and New York: Oxford University Press.

DeAngelo, Harry, and Linda DeAngelo. 1991. "Union Negotiations and Corporate Policy: A Study of Labor Concessions in the Domestic Steel Industry during the 1980s." *Journal of Financial Economics* 30: 3–43.

Decoster, André, Jason Loughrey, Cathal O'Donoghue, and Dirk Verwerft. 2010. "How Regressive Are Indirect Taxes? A Microsimulation Analysis for Five European Countries." *Journal of Policy Analysis and Management* 29: 326–50.

Dell, Fabien. 2007. "Top Incomes in Germany Throughout the Twentieth Century: 1891–1998." In *Top Incomes over 20th Century*, edited by Anthony B. Atkinson and Thomas Piketty, 365–425. Oxford: Oxford University Press.

Del Pino, Eloísa. 2013. "The Spanish Welfare State from Zapatero to Rajoy: Recalibration to Retrenchment." In *Politics and Society in Contemporary Spain: From Zapatero to Rajoy*, edited by Bonnie N. Field and Alfonso Botti, 197–216. New York: Palgrave Macmillan.

Diessner, Sebastian, Niccolo Durazzi, and David Hope. 2023. "Embedding Skill Bias: Technology, Institutions, and the Skill Bias in Wages and Benefits." Paper presented at the 29th International Conference of Europeanists, University of Iceland, Reykjavik, Iceland, June 27–29.

DiNardo, John, Kevin Hallock, and Jörn-Steffen Pischke. 2000. "Unions and the Labor Market for Managers." IZA Discussion Paper No. 150. *Forschungsinstitut zur Zukunft der Arbeit GmbH*. https://www.iza.org/publications/dp/150/unions-and-the-labor-market-for-managers.

DiPrete, Thomas A. 2002. "Life Course Risks, Mobility Regimes, and Mobility Consequences: A Comparison of Sweden, Germany, and the United States." *American Journal of Sociology* 108: 267–309.

DiPrete, Thomas A., and Patricia A. McManus. 2000. "Family Change, Employment Transitions, and the Welfare State: Household Income Dynamics in the United States and Germany." *American Sociological Review* 65: 343–70.

Dølvik, Jon E., and Andrew Martin. 2015. "From Crisis to Crisis: European Social Models and Labour Markets Outcomes in the Era of Monetary Integration." In *European Social Models from Crisis to Crisis*, edited by Jon Erik Dølvik and Andrew Martin, 325–85. Oxford: Oxford University Press.

Dünhaupt, Petra. 2014. "An Empirical Assessment of the Contribution of Financialization and Corporate Governance to the Rise in Income Inequality." Working Paper No. 41, Institute for International Political Economy, Berlin.

Dustmann, Christian, Bernd Fitzenberger, Uta Schönberg, and Alexandra Spitz-Oener. 2014. "From Sick Man of Europe to Economic Superstar: Germany's Resurgent Economy." *Journal of Economic Perspectives* 28: 167–88.

Eichhorst, Werner, and Paul Marx. 2012. "Whatever Works: Dualization and the Service Economy in Bismarckian Welfare States." In *The Age of Dualization*, edited by Patrick Emmenegger, Silja Häusermann, Bruno Palier, and Martin Seeleib-Kaiser, 73–99. Oxford and New York: Oxford University Press.

Emmenegger, Patrick, Silja Häusermann, Bruno Palier, and Martin Seeleib-Kaiser, eds. 2012. *The Age of Dualization: The Changing Face of Inequality in Deindustrialized Societies*. New York: Oxford University Press.

Emmenegger, Patrick, and H. Lierse. 2022. "The Politics of Taxing the Rich: Declining Tax Rates in Times of Rising Inequality." *Journal of European Public Policy* 29 (5): 647–51.

Enns, Peter, Nathan J. Kelly, Jana Morgan, Thomas Volscho, and Christopher Witko. 2014. "Conditional Status Quo Bias and Top Income Shares: How U.S. Political Institutions Have Benefited the Rich." *Journal of Politics* 76: 289–303.

Ertimur, Yonca, Fabrizio Ferri, and Volkan Muslu. 2011. "Shareholder Activism and CEO Pay." *Review of Financial Studies* 24 (2): 535–92.

Esping-Andersen, Gøsta. 1985. *Politics Against Markets*. Princeton, NJ: Princeton University Press.
——. 1990. *The Three Worlds of Welfare Capitalism*. Princeton, NJ: Princeton University Press.
——. 2003. "A Child-Centered Social Investment Strategy." In *Why We Need a New Welfare State*, edited by Gøsta Esping-Anderson, Duncan Gallie, Anton Hemerijck, and John Myles, 26–57. Oxford: Oxford University Press.
Estevez-Abe, Margarita, Torben Iversen, and David Soskice. 2001. "Social Protection and the Formation of Skills: A Reinterpretation of the Welfare State." In *Varieties of Capitalism: The Institutional Foundations of Comparative Advantage*, edited by Peter Hall and David Soskice, 145–83. Oxford: Oxford University Press.
Etchemendy, Sebastián. 2011. *Models of Economic Liberalization*. New York: Cambridge University Press.
Fallick, Bruce, and Kevin Hassett. 1999. "Investment and Union Certification." *Journal of Labor Economics* 17 (3): 570–82.
Färber, Gisela, and Dominique Köppen. 2020. "The Integration of Refugees in Germany: Intergovernmental Aspects of Public Sector Costs and Benefits." *International Journal of Public Administration* 43: 102–14.
Farber, Henry S., and Robert G. Valletta. 2015. "Do Extended Unemployment Benefits Lengthen Unemployment Spells? Evidence from Recent Cycles in the US Labor Market." *Journal of Human Resources* 50: 873–909.
Faricy, Christopher G. 2015. *Welfare for the Wealthy: Parties, Social Spending, and Inequality in the United States*. Cambridge: Cambridge University Press.
Fastenrath, Florian, Paul Marx, Achim Truger, and Helena Vitt. 2022. "Why Is It So Difficult to Tax the Rich? Evidence from German Policymakers." *Journal of European Public Policy* 29 (5): 767–86. https://doi.org/10.1080/13501763.2021.1992484.
Fauver, Larry, and Michael E. Fuerst. 2006. "Does Good Corporate Governance Include Employee Representation? Evidence from German Corporate Boards." *Journal of Financial Economics* 82: 673–702.
Fehr, Ernst, Holger Herz, and Tom Wilkening. 2013. "The Lure of Authority: Motivation and Incentive Effects of Power." *American Economic Review* 103 (4): 1325–59.
Feldstein, Martin. 1995. "The Effect of Marginal Tax Rates on Taxable Income: A Panel Study of the 1986 Tax Reform Act." *Journal of Political Economy* 103: 551–72.
Ferrarini, Tommy, Kenneth Nelson, Joakim Palme, and Ola Sjöberg. 2012. *Sveriges socialförsäkringar i jämförande perspektiv: En institutionell analys av sjuk-, arbetsskade- och arbetslöshetsförsäkringarna i 18 OECD-länder 1930 till 2010*. Stockholm: SOU S-20.
Ferrera, Maurizio. 1996. "The 'Southern Model' of Welfare in Social Europe." *Journal of European Social Policy* 6: 17–37.

———. 2012. "The New Spatial Politics of Welfare in the EU." In *The Politics of the New Welfare State*, edited by Giuliano Bonoli and David Natali, 256–83. Oxford: Oxford University Press.

Fervers, Lukas. 2019. "Economic Miracle, Political Disaster? Political Consequences of Hartz IV." *Journal of European Social Policy* 29: 411–27.

Flaherty, Eoin. 2015. "Top Incomes Under Finance-Driven Capitalism, 1990–2010: Power Resources and Regulatory Orders." *Socio-Economic Review* 13: 417–47.

Fligstein, Neil, and Taekjin Shin. 2007. "Shareholder Value and the Transformation of the US Economy: 1984–2000." *Sociological Forum* 22: 399–424.

Flora, Peter, and Arnold J. Heidenheimer, eds. 1981. *The Development of Welfare States in Europe and America*. London: Routledge.

Frydman, Carola, and Raven Saks. 2010. "Executive Compensation: A New View from a Long-Term Perspective, 1936–2005." *Review of Financial Studies* 23: 2099–2138.

Gallego, Raquel, and Joan Subirats. 2011. "Regional Welfare Regimes and Multilevel Governance." In *The Spanish Welfare State in European Context*, edited by Ana Marta Guillén and Margarita León, 97–117. Burlington, VT: Ashgate.

Gangl, Markus. 2004. "Welfare States and the Scar Effects of Unemployment: A Comparative Analysis of the United States and West Germany." *American Journal of Sociology* 109: 1319–64.

Garicano, Luis. 2000. "Hierarchies and the Organization of Knowledge in Production." *Journal of Political Economy* 108: 874–904.

Garicano, Luis, and Esteban Rossi-Hansberg. 2006. "Organization and Inequality in a Knowledge Economy." *Quarterly Journal of Economics* 121: 1383–1435.

Garrett, Geoffrey. 1998. *Partisan Politics in the Global Economy*. New York: Cambridge University Press.

Garritzmann, Julian, Silja Häusermann, and Bruno Palier, eds. 2022. *The World Politics of Social Investment, Volumes I & II*. New York: Oxford University Press.

Gauthier, Anne H. 2011. "Comparative Family Policy Database, Version 3" [computer file]. Retrieved from: www.demogr.pmg.de. Netherlands Interdisciplinary Demographic Institute and Max Planck Institute for Demographic Research (distributors).

Gerhard, Bosch. 2015. "The Bumpy Road to a National Minimum Wage in Germany." Unpublished manuscript. https://nationalminimumwage.co.za/wp-content/uploads/2015/09/1018-The-bumpy-road-to-a-National-Minimum-Wage.pdf.

Gilens, Martin. 2012. *Affluence and Influence*. Princeton, NJ: Princeton University Press.

Gingrich, Jane, and Ben Ansell. 2015. "The Dynamics of Social Investment: Human Capital, Activation, and Care." In *The Politics of Advanced Capitalism*, edited by Pablo Beramendi, Silja Häusermann, Herbert Kitschelt, and Hanspeter Kriesi, 282–304. New York: Cambridge University Press.

Gingrich, Jane, and Silja Häusermann. 2015. "The Decline of the Working-Class Vote, the Reconfiguration of the Welfare Support Coalition and Consequences for the Welfare State." *Journal of European Social Policy* 25: 50–75. https://doi.org/10.1177/0958928714556970.

Godechot, Olivier. 2016. "Financialization Is Marketization! A Study of the Respective Impacts of Various Dimensions of Financialization on the Increase in Global Inequality." *Sociological Science* 3: 495–519. https://doi.org/10.15195/v3.a22.

Goldin, Claudia, and Lawrence F. Katz. 2001. "Decreasing (and Then Increasing) Inequality in America: A Tale of Two Half-Centuries." In *The Causes and Consequences of Increasing Inequality*, edited by Finis Welch, 37–82. Chicago: University of Chicago Press.

———. 2008. *The Race between Education and Technology*. Cambridge, MA: The Belknap Press of Harvard University Press.

Gomez, Rafael, and Konstantinos Tzioumis. 2011. "What Do Unions Do to Executive Compensation?" Centre for Economic Performance Discussion Paper no. 720. London School of Economics and Political Science.

Goos, Maarten, and Alan Manning. 2007. "Lousy and Lovely Jobs: The Rising Polarization of Work in Britain." *Review of Economics and Statistics* 89: 118–33.

Goos, Maarten, Alan Manning, and Anna Salomon. 2009. "Job Polarization in Europe." *American Economic Review: Papers & Proceedings* 99: 58–63.

Gordon, Joshua C. 2019. "The Perils of Vanguardism: Explaining Radical Cuts to Unemployment Insurance in Sweden." *Socio-Economic Review* 17: 947–68.

Gornick, Janet, and Markus Jäntti. 2013a. "Introduction." In *Income Inequality: Economic Disparities and the Middle Class in Affluent Countries*, edited by Janet Gornick and Markus Jäntti, 1–47. Stanford, CA: Stanford University Press.

———, eds. 2013b. *Income Inequality: Economic Disparities and the Middle Class in Affluent Countries*. Stanford, CA: Stanford University Press.

Gornick, Janet, Branko Milanovic, and Nathaniel Johnson. 2017. "In Search of the Roots of American Inequality Exceptionalism: An Analysis Based on Luxembourg Income Study (LIS) Data." LIS Working Papers Series No. 692. Luxembourg: Luxembourg Income Study.

Gornick, Janet, and Timothy Smeeding. 2018. "Redistributional Policy in Rich Countries: Institutions and Impacts in Nonelderly Households." *Annual Review of Sociology* 44: 441–68.

Gottschalk, Peter, and Timothy M. Smeeding. 1997. "Cross-National Comparisons of Earnings and Income Inequality." *Journal of Economic Literature* 35: 633–87.

Guillén, Ana. 2010. "Defrosting the Spanish Welfare State: The Weight of Conservative Opponents." In *A Long Goodbye to Bismarck? The Politics of Welfare Reform in Continental Europe*, edited by Bruno Palier, 183–206. Amsterdam: Amsterdam University Press.

Guillén, Ana, Santiago Álvarez, and Pedro Adão e Silva. 2003. "Redesigning the Spanish and Portuguese Welfare States: The Impact of Accession into the European Union." In *Spain and Portugal in the European Union*, edited by Sebastian Royo and Paul Christopher Manuel, 231–68. Portland, OR: Frank Cass.

Guillén, Ana, and Margareta León, eds. 2011. *The Spanish Welfare State in European Context*. Burlington, VT: Ashgate.

Guillén, Ana, and Emmanuele Pavolini. 2015. "Welfare States under Strain in Southern Europe: Overview of the Special Issue." *European Journal of Social Security* 17: 147–57.

Gwartney, James, Robert Lawson, and Joshua Hall. 2014. *Economic Freedom of the World: 2014 Annual Report*. Vancouver, BC: Fraser Institute.

Hacker, Jacob S. 2002. *The Divided Welfare State: The Battle of Public and Private Social Benefits*. New York: Cambridge University Press.

———. 2005. "Policy Drift: The Hidden Politics of US Welfare State Retrenchment." In *Beyond Continuity: Institutional Change in Advanced Political Economies*, edited by Wolfgang Streeck and Kathleen Ann Thelen, 40–82. New York: Oxford University Press.

Hacker, Jacob S., and Paul Pierson. 2010. *Winner-Take-All Politics: How Washington Made the Rich Richer—and Turned Its Back on the Middle Class*. New York: Simon and Schuster.

Hager, Sandy Brian. 2021. "Varieties of Top Incomes?" *Socio-Economic Review* 14 (4): 1175–98.

Hall, Brian, and Jeffrey Liebman. 1998. "Are CEOs Really Paid Like Bureaucrats?" *Quarterly Journal of Economics* 113: 653–91.

Hall, Peter A. 2003. "Aligning Ontology and Methodology in Comparative Research." In *Comparative Historical Analysis: New Approaches and Methods*, edited by James Mahoney and Dietrich Rueschemeyer, 373–406. New York: Cambridge University Press.

———. 2018. "Varieties of Capitalism in Light of the Euro Crisis." *Journal of European Public Policy* 25 (1): 7–30.

———. 2021. "How Growth Strategies Evolve in the Developed Democracies." In *Growth and Welfare in Advanced Capitalist Economies*, edited by Anke Hassel and Bruno Palier, 57–97. Oxford: Oxford University Press.

Hall, Peter, and Daniel W. Gingerich. 2009. "Varieties of Capitalism and Institutional Complementarities in the Political Economy: An Empirical Analysis." *British Journal of Political Science* 39: 449–82.

Hall, Peter, and David Soskice. 2001. "An Introduction to Varieties of Capitalism." In *Varieties of Capitalism: The Institutional Foundation of Comparative Advantage*, edited by Peter Hall and David Soskice. New York: Oxford University Press.

Hammar, Olle, Paula Roth, and Daniel Waldenström. 2021. "Top of the Global Distribution: Income Inequality in a Nordic Welfare State." In *The Mystery of Inequality, Economic Studies*, edited by Olle Hammar, 149–75. Uppsala: Uppsala University.

Hanushek, Eric A., Guido Schwerdt, Simon Wiederhold, and Ludger Woessmann. 2013. "Returns to Skills Around the World: Evidence from PIAAC." NBER Working Paper 19762. Cambridge, MA: National Bureau of Economic Research.

———. 2015. "Returns to Skills Around the World: Evidence from PIAAC." *European Economic Review* 73: 103–30.

Harkness, Susan. 2013. "Women's Employment and Household Income Inequality." In *Income Inequality: Economic Disparities and the Middle Class in Affluent Countries*, edited by Janet Gornick and Markus Jännti, 207–33. Stanford, CA: Stanford University Press.

Häusermann, Silja. 2010. *The Politics of Welfare State Reform in Continental Europe: Modernization in Hard Times*. Cambridge and New York: Cambridge University Press.

———. 2018. "The Multidimensional Politics of Social Investment in Conservative Welfare Regimes: Family Policy Reform between Social Transfers and Social Investment." *Journal of European Public Policy* 25: 862–77.

Häusermann, Silja, and Hanspeter Kriesi. 2015. "What Do Voters Want? Dimensions and Configurations in Individual-Level Preferences and Party Choice." In *The Politics of Advanced Capitalism*, edited by Pablo Beramendi, Silja Häusermann, Herbert Kitschelt, and Hanspeter Kriesi, 202–30. New York: Cambridge University Press.

Heclo, Hugh. 1974. *Modern Social Politics in Britain and Sweden*. New Haven, CT: Yale University Press.

Hedström, Peter. 2008. "Studying Mechanisms to Strengthen Causal Inferences in Quantitative Research." In *The Oxford Handbook of Political Methodology*, edited by Janet M. Box-Steffensmeier, Henry E. Brady and David Collier, 319–35. Oxford: Oxford University Press.

Hemerijck, Anton. 2017. *The Uses of Social Investment*. Oxford: Oxford University Press.

Henrekson, Magnus, and Mikael Stenkula. 2015. "Swedish Taxation since 1862: An Overview." IFN Working Paper no. 1052. Stockholm: Research Institute of Industrial Economics.

Hernández, Adrián, Fidel Picos, and Sara Riscado. 2022. "Moving Towards Fairer Regional Minimum Income Schemes in Spain." *Journal of European Social Policy* 32 (4): 452–66.

Hernes, Helga Maria. 1987. *Welfare State and Women Power: Essays in State Feminism*. Oslo: Norwegian University Press.

Hicks, Alexander. 1994. "Introduction to Pooling." In *The Comparative Political Economy of the Welfare State*, edited by Thomas Janoski and Alexander M. Hicks, 169–88. Cambridge and New York: Cambridge University Press.

———. 1999. *Social Democracy and Welfare Capitalism*. Ithaca, NY: Cornell University Press.

Hicks, Alexander, and Duane Swank. 1992. "Politics, Institutions, and Welfare

Spending in Industrialized Democracies, 1960–1982." *American Political Science Review* 86: 658–74.

Hill, Dana Carol Davis, and Lean M. Tigges. 1995. "Gendering the Welfare State: A Cross-National Study of Women's Public Pension Quality." *Gender and Society* 9: 99–119.

Hilmar, Till, and Patrick Sachweh. 2022. "'Poison to the Economy': (Un-)Taxing the Wealthy in the German Federal Parliament from 1996 to 2016." *Social Justice Research* 35: 462–89. https://doi.org/10.1007/s11211-021-00383-y.

Hobson, Barbara, and Marika Lindholm. 1997. "Collective Identities, Women's Power Resources, and the Construction of Citizenship Rights in Welfare States." *Theory and Society* 26: 475–508.

Hooghe, Liesbet, and Gary Marks. 2009. "A Postfunctionalist Theory of European Integration: From Permissive Consensus to Constraining Dissensus." *British Journal of Political Science* 29 (1): 1–23.

Hooghe, Liesbet, Gary Marks, and Carol Wilson. 2002. "Does Left/Right Structure Party Positions on European Integration?" *Comparative Political Studies* 35 (8): 965–89.

Hope, David, and Angelo Martelli. 2019. "The Transition to the Knowledge Economy, Labor Market Institutions, and Income Inequality in Advanced Democracies." *World Politics* 71: 236–88.

Howard, Christopher. 1997. *The Hidden Welfare State: Tax Expenditures and Social Policy in the United States*. Princeton, NJ: Princeton University Press.

Huber, Evelyne, Jacob Gunderson, and John D. Stephens. 2018. "Private Education and Inequality in the Knowledge Economy." Paper presented at the East Asian Social Policy Research Network Annual Conference, Bristol, UK, July 5–6.

———. 2020. "Private Education and Inequality in the Knowledge Economy." *Policy and Society* 39: 171–88.

Huber, Evelyne, Jingjing Huo, and John D. Stephens. 2015. "Power, Markets, and Top Income Shares." Working Paper no. 404, Kellogg Institute for International Studies, University of Notre Dame.

———. 2019. "Power, Policy, and Top Income Shares." *Socio-Economic Review* 17 (2): 231–53. https://doi.org/10.1093/ser/mwx027.

Huber, Evelyne, Itay Machtei, and John D. Stephens. 2022. "Testing Theories of Redistribution: Structure of Inequality, Electoral Institutions, and Partisan Politics." Paper presented at the Meetings of the American Political Science Association, Montreal, Canada, September 15–18.

Huber, Evelyne, Bilyana Petrova, and John D. Stephens. 2022. "Financialization, Labor Market Institutions, and Inequality." *Review of International Political Economy* 29 (2): 425–52.

Huber, Evelyne, Charles Ragin, and John D. Stephens. 1993. "Social Democracy, Christian Democracy, Constitutional Structure and the Welfare State." *American Journal of Sociology* 99: 711–49.

Huber, Evelyne, and John D. Stephens. 1998. "Internationalization and the Social Democratic Model." *Comparative Political Studies* 31: 353–97.

———. 2000. "Partisan Governance, Women's Employment, and the Social Democratic Service State." *American Sociological Review* 65: 323–42.

———. 2001. *Development and Crisis of the Welfare State: Parties and Policies in Global Markets*. Chicago: University of Chicago Press.

———. 2012. *Democracy and the Left: Social Policy and Inequality in Latin America*. Chicago: University of Chicago Press.

———. 2014. "Income Inequality and Redistribution in Postindustrial Democracies: Demographic, Economic, and Political Determinants." *Socio-Economic Review* 12: 245–67.

Hufkens, Tine, Francesco Figari, Dieter Vandelannoote, and Gerlinde Verbist. 2020. "Investing in Subsidized Childcare to Reduce Poverty." *Journal of European Social Policy* 30: 306–19.

Huo, Jingjing, Moira Nelson, and John D. Stephens. 2008. "Decommodification and Activation in Social Democratic Policy: Resolving the Paradox." *Journal of European Social Policy* 18: 5–20.

Immergut, Ellen M. 1992. "The Rules of the Game: The Logic of Health Policy-Making in France, Switzerland, and Sweden." In *Structuring Politics: Historical Institutionalism in Comparative Analysis*, edited by Sven Steinmo, Kathleen Thelen, and Frank Longstreth, 57–89. Cambridge: Cambridge University Press.

Immervoll, Herwig, Horacio Levy, Christine Lietz, Daniela Mantovani, Cathal O'Donoghue, Holly Sutherland, and Gerlinde Verbist. 2006. "Household Incomes and Redistribution in the European Union: Quantifying the Equalizing Properties of Taxes and Benefits." In *The Distributional Effects of Government Spending and Taxation*, edited by Dimitri B. Papadimitriou, 135–65. New York: Palgrave Macmillan.

Iversen, Torben. 1999. *Contested Economic Institutions: The Politics of Macroeconomics and Wage Bargaining in Advanced Democracies*. New York: Cambridge University Press.

Iversen, Torben, and David Soskice. 2006. "Electoral Institutions and the Politics of Coalitions: Why Some Democracies Redistribute More Than Others." *American Political Science Review* 100: 165–81.

Iversen, Torben, and John D. Stephens. 2008. "Partisan Politics, the Welfare State, and Three Worlds of Human Capital Formation." *Comparative Political Studies* 41 (4-5): 600–637.

Jackson, Gregory, and Arndt Sorge. 2012. "The Trajectory of Institutional Change in Germany 1979–2009." *Journal of European Public Policy* 19: 1146–67.

Jacques, Olivier, and David Weisstanner. 2022. "The Micro-foundations of Permanent Austerity: Income Stagnation and the Decline of Taxability in Advanced Democracies." Luxembourg Income Study (LIS) Working Paper Series no. 839. Luxembourg: Luxembourg Income Study.

Jahn, Detlef. 2018. "Distribution Regimes and Redistribution Effects during

Retrenchment and Crisis: A Cui Bono Analysis of Unemployment Replacement Rates of Various Income Categories in 31 Welfare States." *Journal of European Social Policy* 28: 433–51.

Jämlikhetskommissionen. 2020. "En Gemensam Angelägenhet." *SOU* 2020 (46).

Jäntti, Markus, Eva Sierminska, and Philippe Van Kerm. 2013. "The Joint Distribution of Income and Wealth." In *Income Inequality: Economic Disparities and the Middle Class in Affluent Countries*, edited by Janet Gorncik and Markus Jännti, 312–33. Stanford, CA: Stanford University Press.

Jaumotte, Florence, and Carolina Osorio Buitron. 2015. "Inequality and Labor Market Institutions." IMF Staff Discussion Note 15/14, July, International Monetary Fund. https://www.imf.org/external/pubs/ft/sdn/2015/sdn1514.pdf.

Jencks, Christopher. 1972. *Inequality: A Reassessment of the Effect of Family and Schooling in America*. New York: Basic Books.

Jensen, Michael C., and Kevin J. Murphy. 1990. "Performance Pay and Top-Management Incentives." *Journal of Political Economy* 98: 225–64.

Jenson, Jane. 2009. "Lost in Translation: The Social Investment Perspective and Gender Equality." *Social Politics* 16: 446–83.

———. 2012. "Redesigning Citizenship Regimes after Neoliberalism: Moving Towards Social Investment." In *Towards a Social Investment Welfare State? Ideas, Policies and Challenges*, edited by Nathalie Morel, Bruno Palier, and Joakim Palme, 61–90. Bristol, UK: The Policy Press.

Jenson, Jane, and Rianne Mahon. 1993. "Representing Solidarity: Class, Gender, and the Crisis in Social-Democratic Sweden." *New Left Review* 201: 76–100.

Jessen, Robin. 2016. "Why Has Income Inequality in Germany Increased from 2002 to 2011? A Behavioral Microsimulation Decomposition." German Socio-Economic Panel Papers no. 879, Berlin. http://www.diw.de/soeppapers.

Joskow, Paul, Nancy Rose, and Andrea Shepard. 1993. "Regulatory Constraints on CEO Compensation." *Brookings Papers on Economic Activity: Microeconomics* 1: 1–58.

Joskow, Paul, Nancy Rose, and Catherine Wolfram. 1996. "Political Constraints on CEO Compensation: Evidence from the Electric Utility Industry." *RAND Journal of Economics* 27: 165–82.

Kalleberg, Arne. 2011. *Good Jobs, Bad Jobs: The Rise of Polarized and Precarious Employment Systems in the United States, 1970s to 2000s*. New York: Russell Sage Foundation.

Kangas, Olli. 1991. *The Politics of Social Rights*. Stockholm: Swedish Institute for Social Research.

Kaplan, Steven, and Joshua Rauh. 2013. "It's the Market: The Broad-Based Rise in the Return to Top Talent." *Journal of Economic Perspectives* 27: 35–56.

Karcher, Sebastian, and David A. Steinberg. 2013. "Assessing the Causes of Capital Account Liberalization: How Measurement Matters." *International Studies Quarterly* 57: 128–37.

Katz, Harry, Rosemary Batt, and Jeffrey Keefe. 2003. "The Revitalization of the CWA: Integrating Collective Bargaining, Political Action, and Organizing." *Industrial and Labor Relations Review* 56 (4): 573–90.

Katzenstein, Peter. 1985. *Small States in World Markets: Industrial Policy in Europe*. Ithaca, NY: Cornell University Press.

———. 1987. *Politics and Policy in West Germany: The Growth of a Semisovereign State*. Philadelphia, PA: Temple University Press.

Kelly, Nathan J. 2005. "Political Choice, Public Policy and Distributional Outcomes." *American Journal of Political Science* 49 (4): 865–80.

———. 2009. *The Politics of Income Inequality in the United States*. New York: Cambridge University Press.

———. 2019. *America's Inequality Trap*. Chicago: University of Chicago Press.

Keman, Hans. 2020. "Indirect Democracy in Europe: The Challenge of New Political Parties." In *The European Social Model under Pressure: Liber Amicorum in Honour of Klaus Armingeon*, edited by Romana Careja, Patrick Emmenegger, and Nathalie Giger, 425–45. Wiesbaden: Springer Fachmedien Wiesbaden.

Kenworthy, Lane. 2010. "Business Political Capacity and the Top-Heavy Rise in Income Inequality: How Large an Impact?" *Politics & Society* 38: 255–65.

———. 2011. *Progress for the Poor*. Oxford: Oxford University Press.

Kenworthy, Lane, and Jonas Pontusson. 2005. "Rising Inequality and the Politics of Redistribution in Affluent Countries." *Perspectives on Politics* 3: 449–71.

Kilpi-Jakonen, Elina, Daniela Vono de Vilhena, and Hans-Peter Blossfeld. 2015. "Adult Learning and Social Inequalities: Processes of Equalisation or Cumulative Disadvantage?" *International Review of Education* 61: 529–46. https://doi.org/10.1007/s11159-015-9498-5.

Kim, Jerry W., Bruce Kogut, and Jae-Suk Yang. 2015. "Executive Compensation, Fat Cats, and Best Athletes." *American Sociological Review* 80: 299–328.

Kirchner, Stefan, and Sven Hauff. 2019. "How National Employment Systems Relate to Employee Involvement: A Decomposition Analysis of Germany, the UK, and Sweden." *Socio-Economic Review* 17: 627–50.

Kitschelt, Herbert. 1994. *The Transformation of European Social Democracy*. Cambridge: Cambridge University Press.

Kitschelt, Herbert, Peter Lange, Gary Marks, and John D. Stephens. 1999. *Continuity and Change in Contemporary Capitalism*. Cambridge: Cambridge University Press.

Kitschelt, Herbert, and Philipp Rehm. 2014. "Occupations as a Site of Political Preference Formation." *Comparative Political Studies* 47: 1670–1706.

———. 2015. "Party Alignments: Change and Continuity." In *The Politics of Advanced Capitalism*, edited by Pablo Beramendi, Silja Häusermann, Herbert Kitschelt, and Hanspeter Kriesi, 179–201. New York: Cambridge University Press.

---. 2022. "Polarity Reversal: The Socioeconomic Reconfiguration of Partisan Support in Knowledge Societies." *Politics & Society* 0 (0). https://doi.org/10.1177/00323292221100220.

Kjellberg, Anders. 2011. "The Decline in Swedish Union Density since 2007." *Nordic Journal of Working Life Studies* 1: 63–97.

Kjellberg, Anders, and Christian Lyhne Ibsen. 2016. "Attacks on Union Organizing: Reversible and Irreversible Changes to the Ghent-Systems in Sweden and Denmark." In *Den Danske Modelset udefra comparative perspektiver på dansk arbejdsmarkedsregulering: Et festskrift til professor emeritus Jesper Due og professor emeritus Jørgen Steen Madsen*, edited by T. P. Larsen and A. Ilsøe, 279–302. Copenhagen: Jurist- og Økonomforbundets Forlag.

Koeniger, Winfried, Marco Leonardi, and Luca Nunziata. 2007. "Labor Market Institutions and Wage Inequality." *ILR review* 60: 340–56.

Korpi, Walter. 1978. *The Working Class in Welfare Capitalism*. London: Routledge and Kegan Paul.

---. 1983. *The Democratic Class Struggle*. London and Boston: Routledge and Kegan Paul.

---. 1989. "Power, Politics, and State Autonomy in the Development of Social Citizenship: Social Rights during Sickness in Eighteen OECD Countries since 1930." *American Sociological Review* 54: 309–29.

Krippner, Greta R. 2005. "The Financialization of the American Economy." *Socio-Economic Review* 3: 173–208. https://doi.org/10.1093/SER/mwi008.

---. 2011. *Capitalizing on Crisis: The Political Origins of the Rise of Finance*. Cambridge: Harvard University Press.

Kristal, Tali. 2013. "The Capitalist Machine: Computerization, Workers' Power, and the Decline in Labor's Share with U.S. Industries." *American Sociological Review* 78: 361–89.

Kristal, Tali, and Yinon Cohen. 2017. "The Causes of Rising Wage Inequality: The Race between Institutions and Technology." *Socio-Economic Review* 15: 187–212.

Kristensen, Peer Hull, and Kari Lilja, eds. 2011. *Nordic Capitalisms and Globalization: New Forms of Economic Organization and Welfare Institutions*. Oxford: Oxford University Press.

Krugman, Paul. 2012. *End This Depression Now!* New York: Norton.

Kuivalainen, Susan, and Kenneth Nelson. 2010. "The Nordic Welfare Model in a European Perspective." Stockholm: Institute for Future Studies.

Landsorganisationen i Sverige (LO). 2014. *Makteliten en klass för sig*. Stockholm.

Laparra, Miguel. 2011. "Immigration and Social Policy in Spain: A New Model of Migration in Europe." In *The Spanish Welfare State in European Context*, edited by Ana Marta Guillén and Margarita León, 209–35. Burlington, VT: Ashgate.

Lazonick, William. 2014. "Profits without Prosperity." *Harvard Business Review* 92: 46–55.

Leibfried, Stephan. 1993. "Towards a European Welfare State? On Integrating Poverty Regimes into the European Community." In *New Perspectives on the Welfare State in Europe*, edited by Catherine Jones, 128–51. London: Routledge.

León, Margarita, Emmanuele Pavolini, and Ana M. Guillén. 2015. "Welfare Rescaling in Italy and Spain." *European Journal of Social Security* 17: 182–202.

Lewis, Jane. 1994. "Gender, the Family, and Women's Agency in the Building of 'Welfare States': The British Case." *Social History* 19: 37–55.

Lieberman, Evan S. 2005. "Nested Analysis as a Mixed-Method Strategy for Comparative Research." *American Political Science Review* 99 (3): 435–52.

Lindellee, Jayeon. 2018. *Beyond Retrenchment: Multi-Pillarization of Unemployment Benefits Provision in Sweden*. Lund: Lund University.

Lindvall, Johannes. 2010. *Mass Unemployment and the State*. Oxford: Oxford University Press.

Lipset, S. M. 1959. *Political Man: The Social Bases of Politics*. Garden City, NY: Doubleday.

Little, Thomas H., Dana Dunn, and Rebecca E. Deen. 2001. "A View from the Top." *Women & Politics* 22: 29–50.

Loftis, Matt W., and Peter B. Mortensen. 2017. "A New Approach to the Study of Partisan Effects on Social Policy." *Journal of European Public Policy* 24: 890–911.

Lohmann, Henning. 2009. "Welfare States, Labour Market Institutions and the Working Poor: A Comparative Analysis of 20 European Countries." *European Sociological Review* 25: 489–504.

Lundvall, Bengt-Åke, and Edward Lorenz. 2011. "Social Investment in the Globalising Learning Economy: A European Perspective." In *Towards a Social Investment Welfare State? Ideas, Policies and Challenges*, edited by Nathalie Morel, Bruno Palier, and Joakim Palme, 235–60. Bristol, UK: The Policy Press.

Lupu, Noam, and Jonas Pontusson. 2011. "The Structure of Inequality and the Politics of Redistribution." *American Political Science Review* 105: 316–36.

Magni, Gabriele. 2021. "Economic Inequality, Immigrants, and Selective Solidarity: From Perceived Lack of Opportunity to In-group Favoritism." *British Journal of Political Science* 51: 1357–80.

———. 2022. "Boundaries of Solidarity: Immigrants, Economic Contributions, and Welfare Attitudes." *American Journal of Political Science*. https://doi.org/10.1111/ajps.12707.

Mahoney, James, and P. Larkin Terrie. 2008. "Comparative-historical Analysis in Contemporary Political Science." In *The Oxford Handbook of Political Methodology*, edited by Janet M. Box-Steffensmeier, Henry E. Brady, and David Collier, 737–55. Oxford: Oxford University Press.

Maioni, Antonia. 1998. *Parting at the Crossroads: The Development of Health Insurance in Canada and the United States*. Princeton, NJ: Princeton University Press.

Malik, Shiv. 2012. "Peter Mandelson Gets Nervous about People Getting 'Filthy Rich.'" *The Guardian*, January 26.

Mandel, Hadas, and Moshe Semyonov. 2005. "Family Policies, Wage Structures, and Gender Gaps: Sources of Earnings Inequality in 20 Countries." *American Sociological Review* 70: 949–67.

Mankiw, N. Gregory. 2013. "Defending the One Percent." *Journal of Economic Perspectives* 27: 21–34.

Mann, Michael. 1973. *Consciousness and Action among the Western Working Class*. London: Macmillan.

Marical, F., M. Mira d'Ercole, M. Vaalavuo, and G. Verbist. 2006. "Publicly-Provided Services and the Distribution of Resources." OECD Social, Employment and Migration Working Paper no. 45. Paris: OECD Publications.

Marks, Gary, David Attewell, Jan Rovny, and Liesbet Hooghe. 2021. "Cleavage Theory." In *The Palgrave Handbook of EU Crisis*, edited by Marianne Riddervold, Jarle Trondal, and Akasemi Newsome, 173–93. London: Palgrave Studies in European Union Politics. https://doi.org/10.1007/978-3-030-51791-5_9.

Marsh, D. 2011. *The Euro: The Battle for the New Global Currency*. New Haven, CT: Yale University Press.

Marx, Ive. 2013. "Why Direct Income Redistribution Matters if We Are Really Concerned with Reducing Poverty." Intereconomics: Forum. ZBW—Leibniz Information Centre for Economics. Print version in possession of the author.

Marx, Paul, and Peter Starke. 2017. "Dualization as Destiny? The Political Economy of the German Minimum Wage Reform." *Politics & Society* 45: 559–84.

Mayer, Gerald. 2004. *Union Membership Trends in the United States*. Washington, DC: Congressional Research Service.

Meidner, Rudolf, and Berndt Öhman. 1972. *Fifteen Years of Wage-Policy*. Stockholm: Swedish Trade Union Confederation.

Meltzer, Allan H., and Scott F. Richard. 1981. "A Rational Theory of the Size of Government." *Journal of Political Economy* 89: 914–27.

Meyer, Brett. 2016. "Learning to Love the Government: Trade Unions and Late Adoption of the Minimum Wage." *World Politics* 68: 538–75.

Misra, Joya, Stephanie Moller, and Michelle J. Budig. 2007. "Work—Family Policies and Poverty for Partnered and Single Women in Europe and North America." *Gender & Society* 21: 804–27.

Mocan, H. Naci. 1999. "Structural Unemployment, Cyclical Unemployment, and Income Inequality." *Review of Economics and Statistics* 81: 122–34.

Molina, Óscar, and Alejandro Godino. 2013. "Economic Reforms and the Labor Market: Zapatero's Endless Period in the Wilderness." In *Politics and Society in Contemporary Spain: From Zapatero to Rajoy*, edited by Bonnie N. Field and Alfonso Botti, 101–21. New York: Palgrave Macmillan.

Moller, Stephanie, Evelyne Huber, John D. Stephens, David Bradley, and François Nielsen. 2003. "Determinants of Relative Poverty in Advanced Capitalist Democracies." *American Sociological Review* 68: 22.

Mooi-Reci, Irma, and Jacobo Muñoz-Comet. 2016. "The Great Recession and the Immigrant-Native Gap in Job Loss in the Spanish Labour Market." *European Sociological Review* 32: 730–51.

Moreira, Amílcar, Ángel Alonso Domínguez, Cátia Antunes, Maria Karamessini, Michele Raitano, and Miguel Glatzer. 2015. "Austerity-driven Labor Market Reforms in Southern Europe: Eroding the Security of Labor Market Insiders." *European Journal of Social Security* 17: 202–25.

Morel, Nathalie, Bruno Palier, and Joakim Palme, eds. 2013. *What Future for Social Investment?* Bristol, UK: Policy Press.

Morgan, Kimberly J. 2013. "Path Shifting of the Welfare State: Electoral Competition and the Expansion of Work-Family Policies in Western Europe." *World Politics* 65: 73.

Morgan, Kimberly J., and Kathrin Zippel. 2003. "Paid to Care: The Origins and Effects of Care Leave Policies in Western Europe." *Social Politics: International Studies in Gender, State & Society* 10: 49–85.

Morris, Martina, and Bruce Western. 1999. "Inequality in Earnings at the Close of the Twentieth Century." *Annual Review of Sociology* 25: 623–57.

Mudge, Stephanie. 2018. *Leftism Reinvented: Western Parties from Socialism to Neoliberalism*. Cambridge, MA: Harvard University Press.

Muñoz de Bustillo Llorente, Rafael, and Fernando Pinto Hernández. 2018. "Against the Wind: Industrial Relations in Spain during the Great Recession and Its Aftermath." *Economia & Lavoro* 52: 87–104.

Myles, John. 1984. *Old Age and the Welfare State*. Boston: Little, Brown.

Naldini, Manuela. 2003. *The Family in the Mediterranean Welfare State*. London and Portland, OR: Frank Cass.

Nam, Yunmin. 2020. "Do Welfare Benefits Compensate for Globalization among Affluent Democracies?" *Journal of European Social Policy* 30: 158–75.

Natili, Marcello. 2019. *The Politics of Minimum Income: Explaining Path Departure and Policy Reversal in the Age of Austerity*. Cham, Switzerland: Palgrave Macmillan.

Nelson, Kenneth. 2012. "Counteracting Material Deprivation: The Role of Social Assistance in Europe." *Journal of European Social Policy* 22: 148–63.

Nelson, Moira, and John D. Stephens. 2011. "Do Social Investment Policies Produce More and Better Jobs?" In *What Future for Social Investment?* edited by Nathalie Morel, Bruno Palier, and Joakim Palme, 205–34. Bristol, UK: Policy Press.

———. 2013. "The Service Transition and Women's Employment." In *The Political Economy of the Service Transition*, edited by Anne Wren, 147–70. Oxford: Oxford University Press.

Nickell, Stephen. 2004. "Poverty and Worklessness In Britain*." *The Economic Journal* 114: C1–25. https://doi.org/10.1111/j.0013-0133.2003.00193.x.

Nolan, Brian. 2017. "Social Investment: The Think Line between Evidence-Based Research and Political Advocacy." In *The Uses of Social Investment*, edited by

Anton Hemerijck, 43–50. Oxford: Oxford University Press.

Nolan, Brian, Max Roser, and Stefan Thewissen. 2016. "Stagnating Median Incomes Despite Economic Growth: Explaining the Divergence in 27 OECD Countries." *Vox EU*, August 27. http://voxeu.org/article/economic-growth-stagnating-median-incomes-new-analysis.

Nolan, Brian, and David Weisstanner. 2019. "Has the Middle Secured Its Share of Growth or Been Squeezed?" INET Oxford Working Paper no. 2019-09, INET, Department of Social Policy and Intervention, and Nuffield College, University of Oxford.

O'Conner, Julia S., Ann S. Orloff, and Sheila Shaver. 1999. *States, Markets, Families: Gender, Liberalism and Social Policy in Australia, Canada, Great Britain and the United States*. Cambridge: Cambridge University Press.

OECD. 1994a. *OECD Economic Survey: Sweden 1994*. Paris: Organisation for Economic Co-operation and Development.

———. 1994b. *The OECD Jobs Study: Facts, Analysis, Strategies*. Paris: Organisation for Economic Co-operation and Development.

———. 1997. *Literacy in the Information Age*. Paris: Organisation for Economic Co-operation and Development.

———. 2000. *Education at a Glance: OECD Indicators*. Paris: Organisation for Economic Co-operation and Development.

———. 2008a. *Education at a Glance: OECD Indicators*. Paris: Organisation for Economic Co-operation and Development.

———. 2008b. *Growing Unequal? Income Distribution and Poverty in OECD Countries*. Paris: Organisation for Economic Co-operation and Development.

———. 2011. *Education at a Glance: OECD Indicators*. Paris: Organisation for Economic Co-operation and Development.

———. 2013. *OECD Skills Outlook 2013: First Results from the Survey of Adult Skills*. Paris: Organisation for Economic Co-operation and Development.

———. 2020. *International Migration Outlook 2020*. Paris: Organisation for Economic Co-operation and Development.

———. 2021. *Does Inequality Matter? How People Perceive Economic Disparities and Social Mobility*. Paris: Organisation for Economic Co-operation and Development. https://doi.org/10.1787/3023ed40-en.

Oesch, Daniel. 2013. *Occupational Change in Europe: How Technology and Education Transform the Job Structure*. Oxford: Oxford University Press.

Olson, Mancur. 1965. *The Logic of Collective Action*. Cambridge, MA: Harvard University Press.

Orloff, Ann Shola. 1993. *The Politics of Pensions: A Comparative Analysis of Britain, Canada, and the United States, 1880–1940*. Madison: University of Wisconsin Press.

———. 2010. "Gender." In *The Oxford Handbook of the Welfare State*, edited by Francis G. Castles, Stephan Leibfried, Jane Lewis, Herbert Obinger, and Christopher Pierson, 252–64. New York: Oxford University Press.

Österman, Marcus. 2017. "Tracking Detracking Reforms: Political Explanations of Institutional Tracking in Education." Working paper, Department of Government, Uppsala University.

Page, Benjamin I., Jason Seawright, and Mathew J. Lacombe. 2018. *Billionaires and Stealth Politics*. Chicago: University of Chicago Press.

Palier, Bruno. 2010. *A Long Goodbye to Bismarck? The Politics of Welfare Reform in Continental Europe*. Amsterdam: Amsterdam University Press.

Palme, Joakim. 1990. *Pension Rights in Welfare Capitalism*. Stockholm: Swedish Institute for Social Research.

Pampel, Fred, and John Williamson. 1988. "Welfare Spending in Advanced Industrial Democracies, 1950–1980." *American Journal of Sociology* 50: 1424–56.

———. 1989. *Age, Class, Politics, and the Welfare State*. New York: Cambridge University Press.

Paulus, Alari, Holly Sutherland, and Panos Tsakloglou. 2009. "The Distributional Impact of In Kind Public Benefits in European Countries." Discussion Paper no. 4581. Bonn: Institute for the Study of Labor.

Payne-Patterson, Jasmine, and Adewale A. Maye. 2023. "A History of the Federal Minimum Wage." Working Economics (blog), August 31. Economic Policy Institute, Washington, DC.

Pedulla, David S., and Sarah Thébaud. 2015. "Can We Finish the Revolution? Gender, Work-Family Ideals, and Institutional Constraint." *American Sociological Review* 80: 116–39.

Pérez, Sofia. 2011. "Immigration and the European Left." In *What's Left of the Left: Democrats and Social Democrats in Challenging Times*, edited by James Cronin, George Ross, and James Shoch, 265–89. Durham, NC: Duke University Press.

Pérez, Sofia, and Martin Rhodes. 2015. "The Evolution and the Crises of the Social Models in Italy and Spain." In *European Social Models from Crisis to Crisis*, edited by Jon Erik Dølvik and Andrew Martin, 177–213. Oxford: Oxford University Press.

Perotti, Enrico, and Ernst-Ludwig von Thadden. 2006. "The Political Economy of Corporate Control and Labor Rents." *Journal of Political Economy* 114 (1): 145–75.

Philippon, Thomas, and Ariell Reshef. 2012. "Wages and Human Capital in the US Finance Industry: 1909–2006." *Quarterly Journal of Economics* 127 (4): 1551–1609.

Pierson, Paul. 1994. *Dismantling the Welfare State? Reagan, Thatcher and the Politics of Retrenchment*. New York: Cambridge University Press.

———. 2001. *The New Politics of the Welfare State*. Oxford and New York: Oxford University Press.

———. 2003. "Big, Slow-Moving, and . . . Invisible: Macrosocial Processes in the Study of Comparative Politics." In *Comparative Historical Analysis in the Social Sciences*, edited by James Mahoney and Dietrich Rueschemeyer, 177–207. Cambridge: Cambridge University Press.

REFERENCES

Piketty, Thomas. 2001. *Les Hauts Revenus en France au 20e Siècle: Inégalités et Redistribution, 1901–1998*. Paris: B. Grasset.

———. 2003. "Inequality in France, 1901–1998." *Journal of Political Economy* 111: 1004–42.

———. 2014. *Capital in the Twenty-First Century*. Cambridge: The Belknap Press of Harvard University Press.

Piketty, Thomas, and Emmanuel Saez. 2007. "How Progressive Is the U.S. Federal Tax System? A Historical and International Perspective." *Journal of Economic Perspectives* 21: 3–24.

Piketty, Thomas, Emmanuel Saez, and Stefanie Stantcheva. 2014. "Optimal Taxation of Top Labor Incomes: A Tale of Three Elasticities." *American Economic Journal: Economic Policy* 6: 230–71.

Piketty, Thomas, and Gabriel Zucman. 2014. "Capital Is Back: Wealth-Income Ratios in Rich Countries 1700–2010." *Quarterly Journal of Economics* 129: 1255–310.

Plümper, Thomas, Vera E. Troeger, and Philip Manow. 2005. "Panel Data Analysis in Comparative Politics: Linking Method to Theory." *European Journal of Political Research* 44: 327–54.

Pontusson, Jonas. 1992. *The Limits of Social Democracy: Investment Politics in Sweden*. Ithaca, NY: Cornell University Press.

Pontusson, Jonas, David Rueda, and Christopher R. Way. 2002. "Comparative Political Economy of Wage Distribution: The Role of Partisanship and Labour Market Institutions." *British Journal of Political Science* 32: 281–308. https://doi.org/10.1017/S000712340200011X.

Ragin, Charles. 1987. *The Comparative Method: Moving beyond Qualitative and Quantitative Strategies*. Berkeley: University of California Press.

Ragnitz, Joachim. 2009. "Ostduetschland heute: Viel erreicht, viel zu tun." *Ifo Schnelldienst* 62 (18): 3–13.

Rasmussen, Magnus Bergli, and Jonas Pontusson. 2018. "Working-Class Strength by Institutional Design? Unionization, Partisan Politics, and Unemployment Insurance Systems, 1870–2010." *Comparative Political Studies* 51: 793–828.

Riddell, Craig W. 1993. "Unionization in Canada and the United States: A Tale of Two Countries." In *Small Differences That Matter: Labor Markets and Income Maintenance in Canada and the United States*, edited by David Card and Richard B. Freeman, 109–48. Chicago: University of Chicago Press.

Rodríguez Sumaza, Carmen, María de las Mercedes Prieto Alaiz, Juan María Prieto Lobato, and Jesús García-Araque. 2020. "Heterogeneidad Territorial de las Políticas Públicas de Protección Social: El Caso de las Rentas Mínimas de Inserción en España." *Revista de Ciencia Política* 40: 675–97.

Roemer, Friederike. 2017. "Generous to All or 'Insiders Only'? The Relationship between Welfare State Generosity and Immigrant Welfare Rights." *Journal of European Social Policy* 27 (2): 173–96.

Roine, Jesper, Jonas Vlachos, and Daniel Waldenström. 2009. "The Long-Run Determinants of Inequality: What Can We Learn from Top Income Data?" *Journal of Public Economics* 93: 974–88.

Ross, George. 2011. "European Center-Lefts and the Mazes of European Integration." In *What's Left of the Left: Democrats and Social Democrats in Challenging Times*, edited by James Cronin, George Ross, and James Shoch, 319–42. Durham, NC: Duke University Press.

Rothstein, Bo. 1992. "Labor Market Institutions and Working-Class Strength." In *Structuring Politics: Historical Institutionalism in Comparative Analysis*, edited by Sven Steinmo, Kathleen Thelan, and Frank Longstreth. Cambridge: Cambridge University Press.

Royo, Sebastián. 2000. *From Social Democracy to Neoliberalism: The Consequences of Party Hegemony in Spain, 1982–1996*. New York: St. Martin's Press.

Ruback, Richard, and Martin Zimmermann. 1984. "Unionization and Profitability: Evidence from the Capital Market." *Journal of Political Economy* 92 (6): 1134–57.

Rueda, David. 2007. *Social Democracy Inside Out: Partisanship and Labor Market Policy in Advanced Industrialized Democracies*. Oxford: Oxford University Press on Demand.

Rueda, David, and Jonas Pontusson. 2000. "Wage Inequality and Varieties of Capitalism." *World Politics* 52: 350–83. https://doi.org/10.1017/S0043887100016579.

Rueschemeyer, Dietrich, Evelyne Huber Stephens, and John D. Stephens. 1992. *Capitalist Development and Democracy*. Chicago: University of Chicago Press, 1992.

Saez, Emmanuel, and Michael R. Veall. 2007. "The Evolution of High Incomes in Canada, 1920–2000." In *Top Incomes over the Twentieth Century*, edited by Anthony B. Atkinson and Thomas Piketty, 226–308. Oxford: Oxford University Press.

Scharpf, Fritz. 1997. "Balancing Sustainability and Security in Social Policy." In *Family, Market, and Community: Equity and Efficiency in Social Policy*, 211–22. Social Policy Studies no. 21. Paris: Organisation for Economic Co-operation and Development.

———. 2021. "Forced Structural Convergence in the Eurozone." In *Growth and Welfare in Advanced Capitalist Economics*, edited by Anke Hassel and Bruno Palier, 161–200. Oxford: Oxford University Press.

Scheve, Kenneth, and David Stasavage. 2009. "Institutions, Partisanship, and Inequality in the Long Run." *World Politics* 61 (2): 215–53.

Schwander, Hanna. 2019. "Are Social Democratic Parties Insider Parties? Electoral Strategies of Social Democratic Parties in Western Europe in the Age of Dualization." *Comparative European Politics* 17: 714–37.

Schwartz, B., and Björn Gustafsson. 1991. "Income Redistribution Effects of Tax Reforms in Sweden." *Journal of Policy Modeling* 13: 551–70.

Scruggs, Lyle, and James P. Allan. 2006. "The Material Consequences of Welfare States: Benefit Generosity and Absolute Poverty in 16 OECD Countries." *Comparative Political Studies* 39: 880–904.

———. 2008. "Social Stratification and Welfare Regimes for the Twenty-First Century: Revisiting the Three Worlds of Welfare Capitalism." *World Politics* 60: 642–64.

Scruggs, Lyle A., and Gabriela Ramalho Tafoya. 2022. "Fifty Years of Welfare State Generosity." *Social Policy and Administration* 56: 791–807.

Seeleib-Kaiser, Martin. 2016. "The End of the Conservative German Welfare State Model." *Social Policy and Administration* 50: 219–40.

Semuels, Alana. 2016. "The End of Welfare as We Know It." *The Atlantic*, April 1.

Silver, Hilary. 2020. "The Social Integration of Germany Since Unification." *German Politics and Society* 94: 166–88.

Skocpol, Theda. 1988. "The Limits of the New Deal System and the Roots of Contemporary Welfare Dilemmas." In *The Politics of Social Policy in the United States*, edited by Margaret Weir, Ann Shola Orloff, and Theda Skocpol, 293–312. Princeton, NJ: Princeton University Press.

———. 1992. *Protecting Mothers and Soldiers*. Cambridge: Harvard University Press.

Skocpol, Theda, ed. 1984. *Vision and Method in Historical Sociology*. Cambridge and New York: Cambridge University Press.

Skocpol, Theda, and Margaret Somers. 1980. "The Uses of Comparative History in Macrosocial Inquiry." *Comparative Studies in Society and History* 22 (2): 174–97.

Solt, Frederick. 2020. "Measuring Income Inequality Across Countries and Over Time: The Standardized World Income Inequality Database." *Social Science Quarterly* 101: 1183–99.

Sorge, Arndt, and Wolfgang Streeck. 2018. "Diversified Quality Production Revisited: Its Contribution to German Socio-economic Performance over Time." *Socio-Economic Review* 16: 587–612.

Soskice, David. 2014. "Capital in the Twenty-First Century: A Critique." *British Journal of Sociology* 65: 650–66.

Stephens, John D. 1979. *The Transition from Capitalism to Socialism*. London: Macmillan Education UK. https://doi.org/10.1007/978-1-349-16171-3.

Stephens, John D., Evelyne Huber, and Leonard Ray. 1999. "The Welfare State in Hard Times." In *Continuity and Change in Contemporary Capitalism*, edited by Herbert Kitschelt, Peter Lange, Gary Marks, and John D. Stephens, 164–93. New York: Cambridge University Press.

Stetson, Dorothy M., and Amy Mazur. 1995. *Comparative State Feminism*. Thousand Oaks, CA: Sage Publishing.

Streeck, Wolfgang. 2007. "Endgame? The Fiscal Crisis of the German State." MPIfG Discussion Paper 07 (7). Cologne: Max Planck Institute for the Study of Societies.

Swank, Duane. 2002. *Global Capital, Political Institutions, and Policy Change in Developed Welfare States*. Cambridge: Cambridge University Press.

Tarrow, Sidney. 2010. "Bridging the Quantitative-Qualitative Divide." In *Rethinking Social Inquiry: Diverse Tools, Shared Standards*, 2nd ed., edited by Henry E. Brady and David Colliers, 101–10. Lanham, MD: Rowman and Littlefield.

Thelen, Kathleen. 2014. *Varieties of Liberalization and the New Politics of Social Solidarity*. Cambridge and New York: Cambridge University Press.

———. 2021. "Transition to the Knowledge Economy in Germany, Sweden, and the Netherlands." *Comparative Politics* 51: 295–315.

Thelen, Kathleen, and Marius R. Busemeyer. 2011. "Institutional Change in German Vocational Training: From Collectivism toward Segmentalism." In *The Political Economy of Collective Skill Formation*, edited by Marius R. Busemeyer and Christine Trampusch. Oxford and New York: Oxford University Press.

Thévenon, Olivier, and Anne Solaz. 2013. "Labour Markets Effects of Parental Leave Policies in OECD Countries." OECD Social, Employment and Migration Working Papers no. 141. Paris: Organisation for Economic Cooperation and Development.

Tinbergen, Jan. 1974. "Substitution of Graduate by Other Labour." *Kyklos* 27: 217–26.

Tomaskovic-Devey, Donald, Anthony Rainey, and Dustin Avent-Holt. 2020. "Rising Between-Workplace Inequalities in High-Income Countries." *Proceedings of the National Academy of Sciences* 117 (17). https://doi.org/10.1073/pnas.1918249117.

Towers, Brian. 1989. "Running the Gauntlet: British Trade Unions under Thatcher, 1979–1988." *Industrial and Labor Relations Review* 42: 168–88.

Trampusch, Christine. 2009. *Der erschöpfte Sozialstaat. Transformation eines Politikfeldes*. Frankfurt a.M.: Campus.

———. 2020. "The Politics of Shifting Burdens: German Fiscal Welfare Corporatism." In *The European Social Model under Pressure: Liber Amicorum in Honour of Klaus Armingeon*, edited by Romana Careja, Patrick Emmenegger, and Nathalie Giger, 159–76. Wiesbaden: Springer Fachmedien Wiesbaden.

Vandenbroucke, Frank, Anton Hemerijck, and Bruno Palier. 2011. "The EU Needs a Social Investment Pact." *Observatoire social européen*, Opinion paper number 5, May.

VanHeuvelen, Tom. 2023. "The Right to Work and American Inequality." *American Sociological Review* 88 (5): 810–43.

Van Kersbergen, Kees. 1995. *Social Capitalism: A Study of Christian Democracy and the Welfare State*. London: Routledge.

Van Lancker, Wim, Joris Ghysels, and Bea Cantillon. 2015. "The Impact of Child Benefits on Single Mother Poverty: Exploring the Role of Targeting in 15 European Countries." *International Journal of Social Welfare* 24: 210–22.

Vartianen, Johana. 2011. "Nordic Collective Agreements—A Continuous Institution in a Changing Economic Environment." *Comparative Social Research* 28: 331–64.

REFERENCES

Verba, Sidney, Norman H. Nie, and Jae-on Kim. 1978. *Participation and Political Equality: A Seven-Nation Comparison.* Cambridge: Cambridge University Press.

Verbist, Gerlinde, Michael Förster, and Maria Vaalavuo. 2012. "The Impact of Publicly Provided Services on the Distribution of Resources: Review of New Results and Methods." OECD Social, Employment and Migration Working Papers no. 130. Paris: Organisation for Economic Co-operation and Development.

Vernby, Kåre, and Karl-Oskar Lindgren. 2009. "Estimating Dynamic Panel Models When There Are Gaps in the Dependent Variable." Department of Government Studies in Political Economy and Welfare Working Paper Series 1, Uppsala University.

Visser, Jelle. 2013. "ICTWSS: Database on Institutional Characteristics of Trade Unions, Wage Setting, State Intervention and Social Pacts in 34 countries between 1960 and 2012." Amsterdam: University of Amsterdam.

———. 2019. "ICTWSS Database." Version 6. Amsterdam Institute for Advanced labour Studies (AIAS), University of Amsterdam. https://www.ictwss.org/downloads.

Volscho, Thomas, and Nathan J. Kelly. 2012. "The Rise of the Super-Rich: Power Resources, Taxes, Financial Markets, and the Dynamics of the Top 1 Percent, 1949 to 2008." *American Sociological Review* 77: 679–99.

Wallerstein, Michael. 1999. "Wage-Setting Institutions and Pay Inequality in Advanced Industrial Societies." *American Journal of Political Science* 43: 649. https://doi.org/10.2307/2991830.

Wang, Chen, and Koen Caminada. 2011. "Disentangling Income Inequality and the Redistributive Effect of Social Transfers and Taxes in 36 LIS Countries." LIS Working Papers Series No. 567, Luxembourg Income Study.

Wang, Jinxian, and Olaf van Vliet. 2016a. "Social Assistance and Minimum Income Benefits: Benefit Levels, Replacement Rates and Policies across 26 OECD Countries, 1990–2009." *European Journal of Social Security* 18: 333–55.

———. 2016b. "Social Assistance and Minimum Income Levels and Replacement Rates Dataset." Leiden University. https://www.universiteitl-eiden.nl/en/law/institute-for-tax-law-andeconomics/economics/data-sets/the-social-assistance-and-minimum-income-levels-andreplacement-rates-dataset.

Wängnerud, Lena. 2000. "Testing the Politics of Presence: Women's Representation in the Swedish Riksdag." *Scandinavian Political Studies* 23: 67–91.

Warren, Neil. 2008. "A Review of Studies on the Distributional Impact of Consumption Taxes in OECD Countries." OECD Social, Employment and Migration Working Papers No. 64. Paris: Organisation for Economic Co-operation and Development.

Weir, Margret, Ann Shola Orloff, and Theda Skocpol. 1988. "Introduction: Understanding American Social Politics." In *The Politics of Social Policy in the United States*, edited by Margaret Weir, Ann Shola Orloff, and Theda Skocpol, 1–37. Princeton, NJ: Princeton University Press.

Weisstanner, David, and Klaus Armingeon. 2020. "How Redistributive Policies Reduce Market Inequality: Education Premiums in 22 OECD Countries." *Socio-Economic Review* 18: 839–56.

Welsh, Helga A. 2010. "Higher Education in Germany." *German Politics and Society* 28: 53–70.

Western, Bruce, and Jake Rosenfeld. 2011. "Unions, Norms, and the Rise in US Wage Inequality." *American Sociological Review* 76: 513–37. https://doi.org/10.1177/0003122411414817.

Wilensky, Harold. 1975. *The Welfare State and Equality*. Berkeley and Los Angeles: University of California Press.

———. 1981. "Leftism, Catholicism, and Democratic Corporatism." In *The Development of Welfare States in Europe and America*, edited by Peter Flora and Arnold J. Heidenheimer, 314–78. London: Routledge.

Witko, Cristopher, Jana Morgan, Nathan J. Kelly, and Peter K. Enns. 2021. *Hijacking the Agenda: Economic Power and Political Influence*. New York: Russell Sage Foundation.

Woo, Jaejoon, Elva Bova, Tidiane Kinda, and Y. Sophia Zhang. 2016. "Distributional Consequences of Fiscal Adjustments: What Do the Data Say?" *IMF Economic Review* 65 (2): 273–307.

Wood, Adrian. 1994. *North-South Trade, Employment, and Inequality: Changing Fortunes in a Skill-Driven World*. IDS Development Studies Series. Oxford and New York: Clarendon Press and Oxford University Press.

Wu, Nan. 2022. "Immigrants Punch Above Their Weight as Taxpayers." *Immigration Impact* (blog), American Immigration Council, April 14. https://immigrationimpact.com/2022/04/14/immigrants-as-taxpayers-2022/.

Index

Abowd, John, 82
active labor market policies (ALMP), 194
Acuerdo Económico y Social ('AES), 176–77
Acuerdo Nacional sobre el Empleo, 176
Affordable Care Act (ACA), 215, 223, 226, 229, 243, 267
Agrarian Party, 205–6
Aguilar-Hendrickson, Manuel, 189
Aid to Families with Dependent Children (AFDC), 224–25
Alliance, the, 208, 240–41
Arriba González de Durana, Ana, 189
austerity, 23, 168–70, 178–80, 183, 188–89, 202, 231, 240, 242, 255, 257, 266
Autonomous Communities (ACs), 172, 182, 184, 186–89, 240
Autor, David H., 51, 220–21
Aznar, José María, 183, 187, 241

Banking Union, 258
Biden, Joe, 243, 268, 271
Blair, Tony, 264
Blasco, Julien, 166, 191, 211–12, 252
Blome, Agnes, 159–60
blue-collar workers, 30, 33–34, 44–45, 154, 195, 202, 241. *See also* white-collar workers
Blyth, Mark, 263–64
Bonnet, Odran, 75
Bradbury, Bruce, 232
Bradley, David, 46–47
Brady, David, 2, 94, 128, 221, 256, 260
Breznau, Nate, 128, 260
Busemeyer, Marius R., 31–32, 43

Bush, George H. W., 85
Bush, George W., 215, 243, 253, 266
Business Roundtable, 219

campaign finance, 1, 270–71
capital gains, 198–99
Capital in the Twenty-First Century (Piketty), 72
Capitalist Development and Democracy (Rueschemeyer, Stephens, and Stephens), 13
capital market openness, 31–39, 47–48, 57–61, 64, 80, 87–98, 100–109, 120–21, 123–24
Carlin, Wendy, 266
Carlsson, Ingvar, 204, 264
Carter, Jimmy, 219, 268
Catholicism, 115, 183, 187
Chetty, Raj, 221
childcare, 8–9, 56, 97, 116, 129, 131, 159, 162, 175, 183, 186, 188–89, 242–43
Christian democratic parties, 9, 12, 16, 55, 64–65, 96–109, 116–26, 251, 253–54
Christian Democratic Union (CDU), 22, 144, 153, 155, 160, 242–43
Christian Social Union (CSU), 22, 242–43
civil rights movement, 224
civil society organizations, 54–55
Clark, Kim, 82
Clinton, Bill, 10, 24, 224, 243
collective bargaining, 7, 33–34, 44, 79–80, 83–85, 95, 146, 150–51, 155, 178, 180
Communist Workers' Commissions (CCOO), 176–77, 186

Comparative Family Policy Database, 116
comparative historical analysis, 17, 19, 143
Comparative Welfare Entitlements Project, 51, 116
compensation hypothesis, 41, 105, 118, 246
contract coverage, 23, 33–37, 39, 48–49, 60, 74–80, 89–90, 101, 152, 169–78, 213, 219, 235, 247, 267
contract extension, 151, 234–35, 248, 251
coordinated market economies (CMEs), 15, 73–74, 196
Corak, Myles, 221
COVID-19, 258

Danish People's Party, 260
Danish Right, 260
daycare. *See* childcare
Day Care Expansion Act, 242–43
deindustrialization, 6–7, 20, 22, 59–62, 90, 95, 219
Democratic Party, 24, 215, 219, 223–26, 243
deregulation, 2, 6–7, 30, 42–47, 62, 69–74, 85–95, 100, 144, 150, 153, 176, 194–217, 236, 246, 252, 261–65. *See also* regulation
derogation clauses, 151
digitalization, 248
disability benefits, 225, 245
discretionary learning employment, 197
Dodd-Frank Wall Street Reform and Consumer Protection Act, 267
Domhoff, William, 273
dualized labor markets, 7, 146, 155–56, 186, 216, 244, 267
Dustmann, Christian, 149
dynamic knowledge sectors, 30, 73, 91, 234
dynamic service sectors, 36–38, 60, 62, 66, 101, 124

early childhood education, 9–10, 206, 214, 223, 225, 241, 247, 250, 267
early childhood education and care (ECEC), 159
Earned Income Tax Credit (EITC), 225–26, 243
education premium, 31, 43, 51, 79, 132–39, 158–59, 198, 214, 220
employment protection legislation (EPL), 7, 33, 40, 42, 49, 60, 101, 213, 219–20, 234–35, 247. *See also* labor legislation
Enns, Peter, 76

Ertimur, Yonca, 81
Esping-Andersen, Gøsta, 14, 113, 115–16, 207, 223–24
European Central Bank (ECB), 13, 168–69, 178–79, 205, 256–57, 266
European Commission, 10, 13, 184, 257
European Economic Strategy (EES), 256–57
European Monetary Union, 241–42
European Pillar of Social Rights, 258
European Semester, 258
European Stability Mechanism, 258
European Union (EU), 10, 169–70, 172, 256–59, 262
European Working Conditions Survey, 149, 197
Eurozone, 178–79, 257–58
expenditure-to-GDP ratio, 51

factory councils, 176
Faricy, Christopher G., 225
Federal Labor Authority (FLA), 153
Feldt, Kjell-Olof, 263–64
feminism, 115
Ferrarini, Tommy, 207
Ferrera, Maurizio, 14, 259
financialization, 6, 76, 87–88, 90–91, 213–14, 263. *See also* high income earners
Fiscal Compact, 258
"flexicurity," 268
Forbes's Executive Compensation Surveys, 80–81
Ford, Gerald, 84–85
formal comparative analysis, 143
Franco, Francisco, 21, 170–71, 176, 182, 184
Free Democratic Party (FDP), 22, 242–43

Gauthier, Anne H., 116
gender, 50, 53, 55–56, 114, 175, 178, 188, 206
General Confederation of Workers (UGT), 176–77, 186
Ghent system, 208, 241
Glass-Steagall Act, 217
globalization: consequences of, 7; and Germany, 146; and high earners, 73–76; and inequality, 3, 5–6, 44, 65, 71, 245; and knowledge economy, 30; and labor markets, 1–2, 7, 20–21, 24, 47, 244; and poverty, 94–96, 100, 105; and redistribution, 57–58; statistical analyses of, 38–43; tables, 59; and unemployment, 7, 205

González, Felipe, 170, 182, 241
Great Depression, 222–23
Great Recession, 226, 257–58, 267
Great Society, 215, 223, 225, 243
Growing Unequal? (OECD report), 131
Guillaud, Elvire, 166, 191, 211–12, 252

Hall, Peter A., 15, 18, 77, 196
Hanushek, Eric A., 137, 197, 220
Harkness, Susan, 233
Hartz reforms, 10, 144, 147, 153–55, 161, 165, 239, 242, 251, 266
Hemerijck, Anton, 257
Hernes, Helga Maria, 115
high income earners: and CEO compensation, 7, 80–85, 91, 216–17, 221, 232; and collective bargaining, 80, 84; and education, 32, 79, 130; and Germany, 145, 148, 165, 231–32; and inequality, 233; and interest rates, 85–86; and politics, 76–79, 84–85, 90, 265; rise of, 72–76; and Spain, 22, 170–71, 174, 231–32; statistical analyses of, 3–4, 35–36, 86–91; and stock markets, 198; and Sweden, 174, 194, 198–99, 212, 231–32, 235–36; and United States, 24, 146, 171, 174, 214, 216–18, 226, 231–32, 235, 243. *See also* financialization
household income: analyses of, 3, 19, 58–70; and education, 50–51; and the elderly, 58–59; and inequality, 8, 46, 49, 53, 166–67, 192, 217, 228, 230; and single parents, 49–50, 54, 61, 64, 96, 100–101; stagnation, 1; and Sweden, 201
human capital spending, 25, 31–34, 37–40, 43–45, 50, 59–63, 66–71, 75, 86, 96, 101–2, 109–11, 116–26, 129–40, 214, 248–49. *See also* public education spending
Huo, Jingjing, 73

Immergut, Ellen M., 57
immigration, 7, 31, 37–38, 57–71, 101–11, 120–28, 154–57, 181–82, 205, 221–23, 249–61
import substitution industrialization (ISI) model, 170, 172
indignados, 179
industrial employment, 66, 69, 87–88, 100–101, 109, 145, 157, 170–72, 194–95, 203–4, 214–16, 233
inequality (background on), 4–5
Inflation Reduction Act, 271

interest rates, 85–86, 178, 201–2, 205, 265
International Adult Literacy Survey (IALS), 31, 157–58, 194, 236–37, 249–50
International Monetary Fund (IMF), 13, 168–69, 178, 257, 266
Iversen, Torben, 57, 97, 118

Jämlikhetskommissionen, 199
Jenson, Jane, 206
job search theory, 52
Johnson, Lyndon B., 215, 223, 243
Joskow, Paul, 81
journalism, 81

Kangas, Olli, 114–15
Katzenstein, Peter, 41, 58, 118, 121–22
Kelly, Nathan J., 84, 215
Keynesian economics, 262–63
Kitschelt, Herbert, 3, 254–55
Kjellberg, Anders, 209
Kohl, Helmut, 163, 242
Korpi, Walter, 114–15, 199
Krippner, Greta R., 76, 217
Kristal, Tali, 76, 220
Krugman, Paul, 266–67

labor legislation, 2, 33, 36–38, 85. *See also* employment protection legislation (EPL)
Larsson, Allan, 204, 264
left parties, 3, 33–37, 44, 49, 55–57, 60, 63–66, 70, 93, 96–97, 101–9, 116–26, 251–56, 261–64, 269–71. *See also* Communist Workers' Commissions (CCOO); Partido Socialista Obrero Español (PSOE); right parties; Social Democratic Party (SPD)
Leibfried, Stephan, 14
liberal market economies (LMEs), 15–16, 73–74, 76–79
Lieberman, Evan S., 17
Lindvall, Johannes, 204, 264
Lisbon Agenda, 10, 256–57
LO, 199–200, 202, 205, 209
Logic of Collective Action, The (Olson), 218
logic of industrialism, 115, 119
low-skill labor, 1–3, 6, 29–31, 42–43, 47, 95–96, 173, 182, 205, 216, 222. *See also* blue-collar workers; skilled labor; white-collar workers
Luxembourg Income Study (LIS), 5, 47, 198–99

Maastricht Treaty, 256
Macro-Economic Imbalance Mechanism, 258
Magni, Gabriele, 260
Mandelson, Peter, 265
Mankiw, N. Gregory, 74–75
Mann, Michael, 272
Marical, F., 166, 192, 212
Marx, Ive, 155, 234
Marx, Karl, 271–72
Medicaid, 223–24, 226, 228–29
Medicare, 223, 225
Meltzer and Richard (MR), 56, 271
Merkel, Angela, 153, 164–65
military spending, 119–21, 123–24
minimum income, 11, 52, 186–90, 209, 240, 242, 251, 258, 260
Minimum Insertion Income, 52
minimum wage, 3, 33, 49, 59–70, 85, 95, 100–106, 110, 144, 152–55, 177, 181, 219–26, 242–43, 251
Mitterrand, François, 256, 263
Mudge, Stephanie, 196, 263–64
Multiannual Financial Framework, 258
Myles, John, 113

National Labor Relations Act (NLRA), 85
National Labor Relations Board, 82
National Mediation Office, 202
National Welfare Rights Organization, 224
New Deal, 222
New Labour, 10, 264–65
Next Generation EU, 258
Nickell, Stephen, 31, 43
Nordic Capitalisms and Globalization (Kristensen and Lilja), 196
Nordic model, 9–10, 75, 116, 130

Obama, Barack, 215, 223, 225–26, 243, 267
Occupy Wall Street, 72
Oesch, Daniel, 2, 147
Olson, Mancur, 218
Open Method of Coordination, 256, 268
organizational constraint, 83, 90
Organisation for Economic Co-operation and Development (OECD), 1, 5, 31, 47, 131–34, 150, 179, 194, 196, 204, 208–11, 227–28, 260, 262
Outright Monetary Transactions, 258

Palier, Bruno, 257
Palme, Joakim, 114–15
parental leave, 9, 53–70, 95–109, 116–28, 160–61, 186–88, 206, 224, 241, 254
Partido Popular (PP), 23, 169, 177, 179, 181, 183–84, 191, 241
Partido Socialista Obrero Español (PSOE), 23, 169–71, 176–91, 241–42, 259, 266
partisan incumbency hypothesis, 77
part-time employment, 7, 22, 144, 148–49, 153–54, 160, 175, 177, 232–35, 239
pension systems, 5, 8, 20, 162–64, 171, 177, 179, 185–90, 210, 225
Petrova, Bilyana, 90–91
Piketty, Thomas, 72, 75–76, 78, 217
Podemos, 169, 190
politics. *See* campaign finance; deregulation; labor legislation; left parties; right parties; *and specific political parties and politicians*
Pontusson, Jonas, 208
poverty: behavioral, 94; and children, 1, 32, 132, 134–37, 140, 203, 237, 249, 265; disposable income, 5, 23–24, 94–95, 98–99, 106–8, 110–11, 133, 144, 193, 209, 213, 230, 238, 241, 246–47, 251; and family, 29, 50, 54; and Germany, 21–22, 143–47, 155–57, 161–62, 230–31, 233, 238–39; and inequality, 93, 249; and left governments, 33, 261; market income, 5, 14, 19–20, 94–98, 100, 102, 105, 109–11, 169, 203, 225, 230, 232–34, 238–39, 241, 247; and politics, 21, 55, 93–94, 96–97, 109, 209; reasons for, 2; and single mothers, 8, 162, 203; and Spain, 22, 168, 170–71, 175, 181, 188–90, 230–31, 233–34, 239–40; statistical analyses of, 93–94, 96–112, 245; structural, 94; and Sweden, 23, 193, 203, 205, 210, 230–31, 238–39; and theory, 17–18; trends, 244; and unemployment rate, 69, 239; and United States, 23–24, 213, 230–31, 233, 266; and welfare states, 3, 58
power resources theory (PRT), 3, 5, 12–13, 32–40, 56, 72–80, 89–96, 114–15, 122, 251, 271–73
Prais-Winsten estimations, 35
pre-distribution agenda, 9, 14, 130
private education spending, 30–31, 38, 43, 50, 78–79, 87–88, 129–30, 137–40, 182–84, 214, 220, 238, 252

INDEX

private-sector employment, 2, 7, 42, 150, 176, 202, 217
process tracing, 143
Programme for International Student Assessment (PISA), 32, 132–37, 185, 249
Programme for the International Assessment of Adult Competencies (PIAAC), 35–37, 43, 129, 132–37, 157–58, 184–85, 197, 220, 235–38, 249–50
proportional representation (PR) electoral systems, 57, 64–65, 104, 117–18, 120–24, 127
public choice theory, 263
public education spending, 3, 31–32, 43, 50–51, 74–75, 78, 86–89, 116–17, 129–40, 182–84, 192, 222–29, 252. *See also* human capital spending
public pensions, 93
public-sector employment, 7, 30, 42, 44, 150, 176, 179–80, 201, 204, 217, 236
public social services, 212
public transfers, 5–6, 29, 46, 51, 54, 58, 70, 96, 98. *See also* taxes

race, 221, 224, 237
Race between Education and Technology, The (Goldin and Katz), 216
Ragin, Charles, 143
Rajoy, Mariano, 169–70, 179, 183–84
Rasmussen, Magnus Bergli, 208
ratchet effect, 13
Reagan, Ronald, 77, 85, 90, 195, 215, 219, 224, 243, 266
redistribution, 10–14, 46–48, 53–71, 97–98, 127, 144–47, 168–71, 206–7, 213–15, 230, 241, 252–56
regulation, 37–42, 45, 51, 60, 62–63, 66–69, 80–82, 89–90, 101, 246, 270. *See also* deregulation
Rehn-Meidner model, 199–201, 204, 264
relocation, 30–31
replacement rates, 51–53, 116, 125, 160–61, 163, 177, 179, 185–88, 206–10, 223–24, 241
Republican Party, 24, 214, 224, 226, 243, 267, 269
resource constraint, 82–83, 85, 90
retrenchment, 13, 115, 208, 242, 245, 263
Riddell, Craig W., 267–68

right parties, 35, 44, 55, 57, 76–77, 84–86, 93, 116, 240, 254–56, 260–61. *See also* left parties; Partido Popular (PP); Republican Party
"right to work" (RTW) laws, 218
Roemer, Friederike, 260
Roosevelt, Franklin D., 215, 223

SACO, 195, 197, 202, 209
Sánchez, Pedro, 242
Scharpf, Fritz, 241
Schröder, Gerhard, 152–53, 265
Scruggs, Lyle, 51, 115–16, 120, 207–8, 223, 239, 250
secondary education, 96, 99, 112, 116, 155, 157, 174, 184, 192, 206, 214, 222, 237
service jobs. *See* dynamic service sectors; low-skill labor
skill-biased technological change (SBTC), 5–8, 30–31, 47, 75, 78, 88, 91, 95, 100, 194, 197, 215–16, 220, 225, 244. *See also* technological change
skilled labor, 1–2, 29–31, 42, 47, 51, 173, 216. *See also* low-skill labor
Skocpol, Theda, 143
social assistance generosity, 3, 29, 48–65, 71, 95, 100–110, 153, 161–62, 209, 224–25, 239–40, 262–63
social consumption, 19, 51, 129, 132, 140, 268
social democratic parties, 11–12, 16, 55, 193, 254–55
Social Democratic Party (SPD), 22, 144, 153–55, 193, 201–2, 204–8, 210–12, 240–42, 255, 263–65
Social Democratic Workers Party (SAP), 23
social insurance generosity, 3, 48, 51–54, 58–71, 95, 98, 103, 106–8, 116–28, 153
social integration, 181, 250, 259–61
Social Investment Package for Growth and Social Cohesion, 10
social investment policies, 9–11, 51, 130–32, 139–40, 249, 268–69
social rights, 6, 20–21, 51–54, 57, 59, 65, 70–71, 94–95, 100–105, 113–14, 125–27, 250
social risks, 49, 51, 54–55, 59, 62, 65, 67, 70, 94–96, 102–5, 118, 130–31, 157
Social Security, 79, 170–72, 177, 188, 225–27
Social Security Act, 215, 223–24
social transfers, 34
solidaristic wage policy, 199–200, 206

Soskice, David, 4, 57, 73, 75, 97, 118
southern regime, 14, 127
Spanish Socialist Party, 255
Stability and Growth Pact, 256
state-centric welfare, 115, 118
State Children's Health Insurance Program (SCIP), 224, 228–29
Statistics on Income and Living Conditions (SILC), 5, 47, 94, 99
Sweden Democrats, 205
Swedish Employers Federation (SAF), 199–200
Swedish Institute for Social Research, 113–14

Tafoya, Gabriela Ramalho, 51
Taft-Hartley Act, 214–15, 218
Tarrow, Sidney, 17
taxes: and competition, 269; and Germany, 147, 152–53, 163–66, 252–53, 265–66; and globalization, 2, 57; and health care, 268; and household income, 46, 54; and marginal rates, 74, 76, 78–79, 84, 87–89, 148, 191, 211, 252–53; and market income, 29; and poverty, 6, 96, 98, 269; and redistribution, 252, 262, 265; and social investment, 131; and Spain, 174, 183, 190–92, 253; and Sweden, 192, 207, 210–12, 252–53; and trends, 4–5; and unemployment, 70; and United States, 215, 221, 223–26, 237, 243, 253, 267, 270. *See also* public transfers
TCO, 195, 197, 202, 209
technological change: and Germany, 146–47, 149, 173; and high earners, 74–75, 77; and inequality, 3, 5–6, 60, 63, 66–68, 70–71, 245, 261–62; and labor markets, 1–2, 7, 20–21, 30, 44; and Nordic model, 75; and regulation, 42; and Spain, 173, 175; and Sweden, 175, 196; and United States, 215–16. *See also* skill-biased technological change (SBTC)
Temporary Aid to Needy Families (TANF), 224–25
temporary contracts, 7, 177–80, 186, 204, 234–35
tertiary education, 31–32, 78–80, 87–88, 112, 116, 130–48, 157–59, 197–98, 206, 212–22, 237–38
Thatcher, Margaret, 77, 85, 90, 195, 264

Thelen, Kathleen, 2, 203, 218
third world imports, 2, 7, 30–31, 34, 37, 47–48, 57–61, 64, 95, 97, 101, 104, 117, 120
Three Worlds of Welfare Capitalism, The (Esping-Andersen), 14, 16
Tinbergen, Jan, 216
Toledo Pact, 186
total factor productivity change, 38–40, 42
trade openness, 30–31, 34, 37–44, 57–71, 75, 95, 100–108, 111, 118, 120–28, 245–46
triangulation, 16–17
Trump, Donald, 215, 243, 266–67
tuition, 159, 184, 210, 212

unemployment: and collective bargaining, 44; and Europe, 257–58; and Germany, 22, 143–49, 152–55, 162–63, 231, 234, 242, 246, 265; and immigrants, 157, 259; and inequality, 20, 62, 232–33, 246; and labor market integration, 9; and poverty, 2, 96, 100–101, 247, 250–51; rate, 37, 61–64, 66–71, 101–10, 120–22, 125; and Spain, 22–23, 168, 170–73, 175, 177–79, 182, 187–90, 231, 239–42, 246; structural, 49; and Sweden, 23, 193–94, 200, 202–5, 207–10, 231, 235, 246; theories of, 52; and trade openness, 58; and unemployment insurance generosity, 119; and United States, 214, 216, 223–26, 234
unions: density of, 21–23, 73, 84, 89–90, 95–96, 100–101, 104, 247–48, 251, 267; and disposable income inequality, 63, 66–69; and executive pay, 72, 76, 79–83; and Germany, 144–46, 149–55, 163–64, 247; and inequality, 5, 7; and legislation, 19; and market income inequality, 49, 59–60; opposition to, 85; and poverty reduction, 68–69, 96, 245, 255, 261; protecting, 270; and redistribution, 63–65, 70; and Spain, 169, 176–77, 179–80, 186–88, 247; and Sweden, 193–95, 199–200, 202–3, 208–10, 218–19, 235–36, 241, 247; and theory, 3, 12, 32–34, 74, 77; and United States, 213–16, 218–20, 235, 243, 248, 267–68; and wages, 20, 35–45, 70, 91–92, 102, 110–11. *See also* minimum wage; works council rights
universal health care, 171, 223–24, 241
US Federal Reserve Bank, 266

Vandenbroucke, Frank, 257
VanHeuvelen, Tom, 218
Van Kersbergen, Kees, 115
van Vliet, Olaf, 51–52, 161, 188, 209
Varieties of Capitalism (VoC), 15, 91, 196
Vartianen, Johana, 200–203
veto-points framework, 57, 64–65, 97, 103–5, 117–18, 120–24, 126, 229, 254, 270
vocational education, 155–58, 184
voting, 11–12, 21, 55, 63–71, 97, 103–6, 109, 117–24, 214, 254–55, 270–71

wage coordination, 33–42, 49, 59–60, 74, 79, 89–90, 101, 145, 194, 200–203, 213–14, 234–35, 247, 267
wage dispersion: discussion of, 3, 29; and disposable income inequality, 66; and full-time workers, 233; and Germany, 145, 148, 233; and globalization, 31, 38, 44–45; and household market income inequality, 46, 48–49, 53, 59–61; and human capital spending, 32, 43, 129–30, 140, 205; and low-wage work, 8; and market income poverty, 99–101; and politics, 73; and skills dispersion, 35–36; and Spain, 174–75, 233; and structural change, 41–42; and Sweden, 193–94, 197, 200–201, 203, 233; and technological change, 30; and theory, 34; and unemployment, 49; and unions, 20, 33–34, 37–42, 70, 91, 137; and United States, 214, 218–22, 225, 233
wage inflation, 202

wage negotiations, 52
Wagner, Adolph, 119
Wagner's Law, 119
Wallerstein, Michael, 34
Wang, Jinxian, 51–52, 161, 164, 188, 209, 252
Warren, Neil, 165, 211, 252
welfare state (discussion of), 2–4, 9–15, 19–25, 46–57, 69–71, 113–19, 126–31, 144–47, 156–57, 169–71, 193–95, 205–7, 214–15, 222–26, 231, 240–41, 246–50, 253–54, 260–61, 268. *See also* childcare; early childhood education and care (ECEC); minimum income; parental leave; pension systems; social assistance generosity; social insurance generosity; social investment policies; social rights
white-collar workers, 6, 30, 33–34, 44–45, 195, 197, 202–3, 209. *See also* blue-collar workers
Wilensky, Harold, 115
Witko, Cristopher, 215
women, 8–12, 53–56, 64–65, 97, 104–31, 148–68, 175, 188, 194–95, 216, 233–34, 247
work-life reconciliation strategies, 53
works council rights, 33, 38–39, 60, 77, 90–111, 144, 151–52, 213, 219, 267. *See also* unions
World Inequality Database, 86

Zapatero, José Luis Rodríguez, 169, 178–79, 183, 257
Zemmour, Michael, 166, 191, 211–12, 252